ENCYCLOPEDIAS OF THE HUMAN EXPERIENCE

David Levinson, Series Editor

ETHNIC RELATIONS

A CROSS-CULTURAL ENCYCLOPEDIA

David Levinson

ABC-CLIO
Santa Barbara, California
Denver, Colorado
Oxford, England

Library of Congress Cataloging-in-Publication Data

Levinson, David, 1947–
    Ethnic relations : a cross-cultural encyclopedia / David Levinson
       p.   cm. — (Encyclopedias of the human experience)
    Includes bibliographical references (p.   ) and index.
    1. Ethnic relations—Cross-cultural studies—Encyclopedias.
    I. Title. II. Series.
GN496.L48 1994   305.8—dc20   94-40253

ISBN 0-87436-735-2 (alk. paper)

01 00 99 98 97 96 95 94   10 9 8 7 6 5 4 3 2 1 (hc)

ABC-CLIO, Inc.
130 Cremona Drive, P.O. Box 1911
Santa Barbara, California 93116-1911

This book is printed on acid-free paper ∞.
Manufactured in the United States of America

CONTENTS

CONTENTS

PREFACE

Ethnic relations is a topic of much concern in the world today, and because ethnic conflict is now considered to be the major form of violent conflict around the world, some argue that ethnic relations is the most important issue faced by the world community. Ethnic relations today are important not just because of these highly visible and troubling ethnic conflicts, but also because there are a number of relatively new forms of ethnic relations that need to be sorted out by the members of cultural groups in contact with one another.

Through labor migration and the spread of refugees in the last 25 years, some nations such as England, France, and Germany, which were relatively homogeneous culturally, are now home to large populations of people who look different, speak different languages, and bring with them different cultural traditions than the traditional population. Thus, some culturally homogeneous nations around the world are becoming multicultural with major implications for the internal structure and dynamics of those societies.

In other nations, past colonization stripped many groups—usually the indigenous peoples—of their land, rights, and traditional cultures; in the twentieth century, they live as second- or third-class citizens in their homelands. Around the world, these groups are asserting their rights, causing a major shift in the nature of relations between state governments, other citizens, and the indigenous communities within their borders. In still other nations, ethnic minorities are asserting their rights and demanding equal treatment under the law; in the extreme, ethnic minorities in a number of nations are seeking independence as autonomous nation-states or provinces in order to preserve their culture. Finally, the end of colonialism in Africa and elsewhere in the twentieth century alongside other factors has led to competition for economic and political power among indigenous ethnic groups in many nations and the difficult task of creating a single nation-state from a mix of different cultural groups.

Thus, patterns of ethnic relations around the world are varied today and different from those in the past when it was more common for one group within a nation or one nation to dominate others simply through the use of force. This variety is mainly a post–World War II development and is due to a mix of factors including the end of colonialism; the more rapid spread of a world economy; a rapid increase in the number of migrants, refugees, tourists, and others, creating more extensive and intensive contact among peoples from different cultures; and a growing concern with human rights in the world community, as reflected in the work of the United Nations and other organizations.

Among the alphabetically arranged entries in this volume, I provide two major categories of information relevant to ethnic relations. The first is definitions and cross-cultural information about general topics in ethnic relations such as assimilation, conflict, genocide, and tourism. Also included are definitions and cross-cultural information about processes and structures that underlie or are major components of ethnic relations, such as irredentism, ethnocentrism, stereotyping, and race.

The second category of information is in the form of descriptive profiles of 38 ethnic conflicts around the world. The purpose of these profiles is fourfold: (1) to provide examples of the five major forms of ethnic conflict around the world—separatist, internal rivalry, conquest, survival, and irredentist; (2) to provide real-life examples of many of the concepts discussed in the volume, for example, refugees, ethnonationalism, human rights, indigenous rights, genocide, and ethnocide; (3) to provide descriptive summaries of the ethnic groups involved in conflicts today; and (4) to describe the history, issues, causes, consequences, and current status of major ethnic conflicts around the world as of early 1994. Space limitations mean that not every ethnic conflict around the world can be profiled here. Some important ones not profiled are those involving ethnic political rivalries in Kenya, political rivalries in South Africa, and the independence movement in New Caledonia. Other conflicts such as that in Afghanistan, which are not clearly or mainly ethnic, are also not included. The 38 conflicts covered here are, however, representative of conflicts around the world in general. Information in the profiles comes from a variety of sources. In addition to those listed at the end of each profile, key information sources include the *Encyclopedia of World Cultures,* the *Information Please Almanac* for 1994, and the *Refugee Report.* Current events information is taken from newspaper and television news reports, with the two most important of these sources being the *New York Times* and "The McNeil-Lehrer News Hour" on PBS.

In the back of this volume readers will find an annotated directory of organizations whose programs have an impact on ethnic relations on a global scale. An end-of-book subject index

provides an additional point of access to information in the entries.

As in other volumes in this series, the dual emphasis is on both similarity and variation across cultures around the world. Thus, the definitional and conceptual entries provide examples drawn from many different cultures to describe variation across cultures. Similarly, the profiles of conflict situations are of 38 different conflicts, but as a group they serve as contemporary examples of many basic and global features of ethnic conflict and ethnic relations.

Ethnic relations is a relatively new topic of study and an exceedingly complex one. It draws the attention of anthropologists, geographers, sociologists, political scientists, historians, humanists, economists, biologists, journalists, government officials, and others. Each of these professions brings with it a different perspective to the study and our understanding of ethnic relations. The perspective in this volume is primarily within the anthropological framework; however, information from other perspectives is included as well. Especially when the perspectives differ widely, I have tried to bring in information representing the alternative viewpoints. Among basic issues as yet unresolved by students of ethnic relations are the definitions of such basic concepts as ethnicity and ethnic group, the delineation of clear markers of ethnic group identity, and the basic mechanism of ethnic identity and solidarity. Issues such as these remain unresolved because the study of ethnic relations is relatively new; the multidisciplinary perspective, while broadening our understanding of ethnic relations, also brings with it more complexity and alternative viewpoints; and the global nature of ethnic relations makes it necessary for us to consider variation as well as similarities across cultures.

For persons born and raised in the United States, much about ethnic relations in other parts of the world may seem new and strange. This is because in many ways beliefs about and the structure and dynamics of ethnic relations in the United States are different from those elsewhere, for at least three reasons. The first is that in the United States there has long been a belief in ethnic assimilation—that is, life will be better for all and the United States will be a more powerful nation if each group gives up much of its own identity for a shared identity as Americans. While this model has some truth in the case of Americans of European ancestry, so far it does not accurately describe the experience of many Americans of African, Latin American, or Asian ancestry. Still, though, it is a powerful belief shared by many Americans and one that differs from that of many other peoples around the world, who take the opposite view that their nation or culture will be better off if it is ethnically homogeneous. A second major reason is that the United States, with the exception of its several million native American Indian peoples, is a nation of immigrants or descendants of immigrants. Thus, ties to the ethnic homeland and native language that are so much a part of eth-

nic relations and especially of ethnic conflict elsewhere are less important for Americans. A third major reason is that despite far more rapid communication and transportation, the United States has always been and to a large extent still is isolated from other nations and ethnic groups around the world and lacks a history of such conflict. For these and other reasons, concepts such as consociational democracy, irredentism, and ethnic conflict over homelands are largely foreign to the experience of most Americans. At the same time, of course, some aspects of ethnic relations are quite familiar, such as race and racism, genocide, and ethnic conflict over scarce societal resources such as employment or educational opportunities. But our understanding of these familiar issues can benefit by considering how they are defined and experienced in other cultures.

In closing, I would like to thank Diane Wyckoff for her assistance in preparing the profiles of ethnic conflicts and Patricia Andreucci for her library and general research assistance.

ETHNIC RELATIONS
A CROSS-CULTURAL ENCYCLOPEDIA

declared itself a sovereign state. Most Georgians belong to the Georgian Orthodox Church.

The autonomous region of Abkhazia is located within the Republic of Georgia, covering 3,300 square miles between the Black Sea and the Caucasus mountain range. Abkhazia is bordered by Russia on the north, and by the Georgian provinces of Svanetia and Mingrelia on the south. As of 1989 the population of Abkhazians (or *Apswa*, their self-designation) was estimated at 102,938. Abkhazians constitute about 2 percent of the population of Georgia. Although the majority of Abkhazians reside within their own autonomous region, they constitute a minority (about 18 percent) of the population in their own land. Other groups in Abkhazia include Georgians, Russians, Mingrelians, Armenians, Ukrainians, and Greeks. About a third of Abkhazians live in towns or cities, with the majority of rural Abkhazians living in the northern sector of the republic. Although Georgian is the official language, the Abkhaz language is widely used among Abkhazians, and belongs to the northwest Caucasian family. In the 1940s and 1950s, as part of an attempt to Georgianize the Abkhazians, the Abkhaz language was banned in public domains. Nearly 80 percent of Abkhazians are also fluent in Russian. Approximately 50 percent of Abkhazians are Orthodox Christian, and the other half are Sunni Muslim. In the past, Abkhazians had close ties to other peoples in the Caucasus, such as the Circassians; these ties were weakened during the Soviet period when communication among different groups was channeled through the central government in Moscow.

It is generally believed that the Abkhazians are the indigenous people of the territory that they currently inhabit. There is archaeological evidence of their presence as far back as 4000 B.C. In the eighth century, the Abkhazian tribes came together to form one ethnic entity distinct from others in the region by language and customs, but in the tenth century Abkhazia lost its

ABKHAZIANS AND GEORGIANS

The Republic of Georgia encompasses 26,911 square miles and is bordered by the Black Sea on the west, Turkey and Armenia on the south, and Azerbaijan on the southeast. It is separated from Russia on the northeast by the main range of the Caucasus Mountains. Georgia was annexed by Russia in 1801 and entered the USSR in 1922, becoming a constituent republic in 1936. In 1993 Georgia's population was estimated at 5.5 million, 70 percent of which was ethnically Georgian. The remainder of the population is composed of small percentages of other ethnic groups, the largest being Armenians at 7 percent and Russians at 6 percent. The official language is Georgian, and in 1989, 33 percent of the people considered Georgian their native language. In the former Soviet Union, Russian was a mandatory school subject, and approximately 33 percent of Georgians, mainly those living in cities, speak the language fluently. On 9 April 1991, following the collapse of communism and a 99-percent-in-favor vote on a referendum for Georgian independence, Georgia

*Man in Sukhumi left homeless from Georgian–
Abkhazian hostilities.*

with leaders in Georgia began a Georgianization program. Through forced relocations, deportations, and executions the Abkhazian population was reduced to 17.1 percent of the population of Abkhazia. In addition, efforts were made to destroy Abkhazian culture by rewriting its history to describe Abkhazians as recent arrivals to the region, closing Abkhazian schools, and banning Abkhazian publications in the Georgian language. Even today, many Georgians view Abkhazians as a guest people in Georgia and some even deny that Abkhazians are a distinct ethnic group.

The current violent separatist conflict between Abkhazians and Georgians is a repeat of this old pattern of Abkhazian quests for independence and Georgian repression. In the late 1980s, taking advantage of the *glasnost* and decentralization movements sweeping Russia, Abkhazia requested a return to its status as an independent republic, similar to that which they enjoyed from 1921 to 1931. In 1991 their plans left open the possibility of association with the Russian Federation. Upon Georgia's independence from the USSR, a new attempt at so-called Georgianization of Abkhazia began. Abkhazia resisted, declared its sovereignty, and united with other ethnic minorities in the Caucasus region of Georgia and Russia. In August 1992 Georgia moved troops into Abkhazia, destroying Abkhazian cultural institutions in the capital city of Sukhum. The Abkhazians resisted, and in August 1993, in response to armed Abkhazian resistance, Georgian head of state Eduard Shevardnadze declared martial law in the region, effectively putting himself in direct control and banning all political protests. The effect of martial law was minimal and fighting continued through 1993, resulting in the loss of more than 2,000 lives. In the later months of 1993, Abkhazians won some significant battles as they acquired control over the main route that connects Sukhum, the capital of Abkhazia, to the rest of Georgia. The situation is further compli-

independence and was integrated into the united Georgian state. In the seventeenth century they separated from the unstable Georgian polity and became an independent polity, and under the influence of the Ottoman Empire many Abkhazians converted to Islam. Abkhazians fought for independence from tsarist Russia during the first half of the nineteenth century, but were defeated in the 1870s. The subsequent exodus of nearly half the Abkhazian population to surrounding regions, mainly in Russia, resulted in the current situation where Abkhazians are a minority in their homeland. Abkhazia enjoyed a decade (1921–1931) of independence under the former Soviet Union, but in 1931 Joseph Stalin (himself a Georgian) declared Abkhazia a republic within Georgia, and along

cated by allegations that Russia has been supporting Abkhazia both economically and militarily. There are claims that Russian troops have fought alongside Abkhazians, and that Russian mercenaries have aided the Abkhazians. Georgia feels betrayed by Russia, which it believes covets Abkhazia for itself. Russia has officially denied these allegations.

Many Georgians outside of Abkhazia believe not only that the region should not be allowed to secede for political reasons, but that in fact Abkhazians are not ethnically different from Georgians and therefore have no need for a separate state. Abkhazians see themselves as facing another situation in which their survival as a people is threatened by the Georgians, and believe that they have the opportunity to protect their future by establishing their own independent state.

Benet, Sula. (1974) *Abkhasians—The Long-Living People of the Caucasus.*

Hewitt, B. George, and Elisa Watson. (1994) "Abkhazians." In *Encyclopedia of World Cultures. Volume 6, Russia/Eurasia and China,* edited by Paul Friedrich and Norma Diamond, 5–10.

Lang, David M. (1966) *The Georgians.*

Suny, Ronald G. (1988) *The Making of the Georgian Nation.*

ALBANIANS AND SERBS

Serbs were the largest of the ethnic groups that formed the former Yugoslavia. In 1990 there were an estimated 8.5 million Serbs in Yugoslavia; the overwhelming majority are now found in Serbia and Bosnia-Herzegovina. Serbia is located in the Balkans, and is bounded by Hungary to the north, Romania and Bulgaria to the east, Albania and Macedonia to the south, and the former Yugoslav republics of Bosnia-Herzegovina and Croatia on the west. During the era of the Yugoslavian nation, the borders of Serbia expanded greatly because of the conflict with the Croats and the Bosnian Muslims. Whether these borders become permanent is dependent on the outcome of ongoing hostilities with the Bosnians. Serbia also encompasses the formerly autonomous province of Kosovo-Metohija, the home of about 2 million Albanians, with the Serbs a minority in the province (10–15 percent of the population). Serbs speak a dialect of Serbo-Croatian, which they write in a Serbian variation of Cyrillic script.

Serbs moved into the region now known as Serbia about A.D. 500–600 and had established a Serbian polity by the ninth century. In the fourteenth century the region was conquered by the Ottoman Empire and many Serbs fled west to the Alps. After a series of revolts, Ottoman control ended, and in 1830 Turkey recognized Serbia as an autonomous unit, although still a possession of the Ottoman Empire. In 1882 it became an autonomous state, and in 1918 Serbia was joined with Croatia and Slovenia as a condition of the Treaty of Versailles; after World War II, Yugoslavia was created. Serbia was a largely rural, agricultural region, but since World War II, the population has become mainly urban, and wage-earning has become a major source of income for most families. Most Serbs are adherents of Serbian Orthodoxy.

As noted above, about 2 million Albanians live in the Kosovo Province in southwestern Serbia, which borders Albania. Another 3.5 million Albanians live in Albania. Albanians trace their ancestry to the Illyrians, who arrived from the east in what is now Albania in at least 1000 B.C. Slavic speakers, presumably including ancestors of modern-day Serbs, began entering the region from the north and east by the sixth century, and the Illyrians fled from what is now the Kosovo region. After rule by various empires, Albania became an independent republic in 1918. Under Ottoman rule most Albanians converted to Islam, and perhaps as many as 70 percent are nominally Muslim, although from 1967 to 1990 Albania was officially an atheist nation.

The conflict between the Serbs and Albanians in Kosovo Province is an irredentist one with both claiming ownership of the province. The Serbian claim rests on the claim of first settlement, the symbolism of the region as the site of the Serbian defeat by the Ottoman Empire in 1389, which solidified the Serbs as an ethnic group, and current Serbian political control of the province. The Albanian claim also rests on claim of first settlement, as well as on the demographic reality that they constitute about 90 percent of the population in the province and are the fastest growing ethnic group in Europe. The nation of Albania, while morally supporting the Kosovo Albanians, is not a source of material support due to its own weak economic and military stature in the region. While the dispute over the Kosovo region goes back centuries, the current conflict began in 1989 when Albanians vigorously sought greater self-determination for the region. These wishes were rebuffed by the ruling Serbs and in 1990, in response to continued demands, the Serbian government declared a state of emergency in the Kosovo Province, ended autonomy, and instituted direct rule from the Serbian capital of Belgrade. As part of direct rule, Albanians have been dismissed from their jobs, hospitals and health clinics shut down, schools closed, newspapers banned, and restrictions placed on rights to political assembly. The Albanians have responded by calling on international opinion and creating their own institutions—schools and health clinics staffed by Albanians dismissed by the Serbs—and in 1993 they independently elected their own Parliament. So far, the confrontation has been largely nonviolent, although at least two dozen Albanians have been killed by border guards along the Albania-Kosovo border, and by 1993 the Serbs had an army of 100,000 near the Serbian border, creating fear among the Albanians that the Serbs might be planning a Bosnian-style ethnic cleaning campaign. At this point, the Albanians are without military options and are counting on their sizable majority population in the region to be a deterrent to Serbian aggression. Calls by the Albanian government for outside intervention have not led to any international mobilization and Serbia has made it difficult for outside observers to assess the situation.

Halpern, Joel M., and Barbara Kerewsky-Halpern. (1986) *A Serbian Village in Historical Perspective.*

Hasluck, Margaret. (1954) *The Unwritten Law in Albania.*

Simic, Andrei. (1973) *The Peasant Urbanites.*

ANTI-SEMITISM Anti-Semitism is the hatred of, discrimination against, and persecution of Jews simply because they are Jews. The term was first used by the German political writer and anti-Semite Wilhelm Marr in 1879 in his pamphlet "The Victory of Judaism over Germanism." In fact, the label *Semite* is a misnomer as there is no such thing as a Semitic people or race. Rather, *Semitic* refers to a group of related languages that includes Hebrew, Arabic, Aramaic, and Assyrian. *Anti-Semitism*, however, refers specifically to hatred of Jews, and not to speakers of other Semitic languages.

Anti-Semitism can take a number of distinct forms, including economic, religious, racial, political, and social. Economic

Caretaker at synagogue in Los Angeles wipes off swastika, December 1938.

anti-Semitism is reflected in government policies or social practices that deny Jews certain economic opportunities available to non-Jews. These can include restrictions on enrollment in educational institutions; outright banning of Jews; quota systems; denial of access to certain professions; social pressures to take up professions considered inferior, such as moneylending in the past; and special taxes levied on Jewish landowners, such as those that were common in Europe up to the late 1800s. Religious anti-Semitism is hatred of Jews because they are of a different religion; in the past this meant non-Christian, and recently some experts suggest that Islamic anti-Semitism may be religious in part as well. Much of the history of anti-Semitism revolves around the persecution of Jews because of a theological difference with Christianity and the belief that Jews were responsible for the death of Jesus Christ. Racial anti-Semitism appeared in Europe in the late 1800s after Jews were effectively emancipated in many nations, and was based on the notion that Jews were a distinct "race" who were strangers and outsiders in every nation where they lived. Additionally, because Jews were perceived as a distinct race, Jewishness was viewed as an inherent trait that was passed on through birth; one could not become a non-Jew. Political anti-Semitism is the use of or stirring up of hatred or resentment of Jews by political parties or leaders as a means of gaining or retaining political power. Political anti-Semitism is a form of scapegoating—the blaming of Jews for various societal problems. Social anti-Semitism is the exclusion of Jews from all or some of the social institutions of society. In medieval Europe, for example, Jews were residentially excluded—required to live in Jewish quarters called *ghettos,* or on Jewish streets in villages. In the twentieth century in the United States, informal housing patterns effectively confined Jews to certain neighborhoods and excluded them from various social organizations.

While there was some prejudice against Jews prior to the Christian era, anti-Semitism as it has existed throughout the centuries is mostly a product of Christianity. The basis of Christian anti-Semitism contains three related beliefs: (1) that Jews killed Christ and bear a collective responsibility for that act, (2) that Jews are evil and do the work of the Devil, and (3) that Jews are beyond redemption. After A.D. 321, when Christianity became the religion of Imperial Rome, these beliefs led to restrictions on Jews, although they were never fully enacted as the empire fell into a period of decline. The decline of the Roman Empire was followed by a short period of general acceptance of Jews in Europe by theologians, some of whom argued for the protection of Jews.

However, the Middle Ages saw Christian anti-Semitic beliefs about Jews transformed into practice throughout Europe. Anti-Semitism throughout the Middle Ages was frequent and common, taking the form of expulsions from cities and nations, wholesale massacres, forced suicides, attempts to force mass conversions, bans on membership in craft guilds and universities, and the required wearing of distinctive clothing such as hats or a cloth marker on outer garments. Writings and art of this period were filled with stereotypical portrayals of Jews, often depicted as in league with the Devil. Two surviving developments from the Middle Ages, particularly among rural peoples in Europe, are the blood libel and Passion Plays. The blood libel claims that Jews ritually kill Christian children and use their blood in the preparation of unleavened bread eaten during the Passover holiday. Passion Plays openly depict Jews as the murderers of Christ and the enemy of Christianity; they were and remain a popular form of entertainment.

During the reformation, the fate of Jews depended on the dominant Christian religion in the nation or region. Catholicism and the Lutheran branch of Protestantism were strongly anti-Semitic, while the Calvinist branch of Protestantism was less so. In Catholic nations, the ghetto emerged in the sixteenth century as a mechanism for isolating Jews from the rest of society. During the Enlightenment, beginning in the early eighteenth century, Jewish isolation began to lessen, and various theologians and philosophers argued for the treatment of Jews on equal terms with Christians.

In the nineteenth century, the racist version of anti-Semitism emerged in what is now Germany and Austria, with Jews considered genetically different and inferior, and classified as outsiders. This racial anti-Semitism became a feature of German daily life. In Russia, Jews were confined to a region known as the "Pale of Settlement" and were the object of frequent riots, looting, killings, expulsions, and government-organized or backed pogroms. In Russia, and later in Austria, Germany, and elsewhere in Europe, racial anti-Semitism was merged with political anti-Semitism as political leaders used Jews as scapegoats to explain political and economic problems and to direct attention away from government failures. Racial/political anti-Semitism culminated in the rise of the Nazis in Germany and the subsequent genocidal killing of some 5 to 6 million Jews between 1941 and 1945 in what is called the *Holocaust*. During this same period, anti-Semitism was also reflected in the refusal of some nations, such as the United States and Canada, to accept any significant number of Jewish refugees fleeing Nazi persecution.

A survey of 60 nations in 1991 indicated that anti-Semitism is still common around the world. In fact, the survey indicates that anti-Semitism reached its highest point since World War II in 1991, and that Europe remains the most common arena for anti-Semitism. One element of the revival of anti-Semitism is revisionist history that downplays or altogether denies the Holocaust. Although countered by mainstream historians, this literature enjoys a wide reading around the world. In formerly Communist nations of Eastern Europe, such as Poland, Hungary, and Romania, political anti-Semitism has reappeared as a component of the xenophobia and nationalism that has emerged with efforts to establish capitalist economies and democratic governments. In Poland, for example, some political leaders and political parties are openly anti-Semitic, blaming various economic ills on Jewish influence and control. In fact, there are less than 5,000 Jews in Poland, with virtually no political power, suggesting a phenomenon called *anti-Semitism without Jews*—Jews are to blame even if they are not an actual physical presence. In Germany, where the small Jewish population of about 35,000 is strongly assimilated, anti-Semitism has reemerged as part of the neo-Nazi xenophobia, but is unsupported by the state. In the former USSR, anti-Semitism has also reemerged alongside nationalism in nations such as the Ukraine and Russia, but official policies designed to protect minority rights and the freedom of Jews to emigrate has lessened its impact. A relatively new form of anti-Semitism is the Islamicization of anti-Semitism in Arab and Muslim nations as part of the ongoing Arab-Israeli and Israeli-Palestinian conflict and the spread of Islamic fundamentalism. That anti-Semitism is increasing in Egypt, the one Arab nation with peaceful relations with Israel, is a sign to some that peace in the Middle East may not bring with it an end to anti-Semitism nor an end to Israeli animosity toward Arabs.

See also GENOCIDE; GHETTO; MIDDLEMAN MINORITIES; RACE AND RACISM; SCAPEGOAT; STEREOTYPES; XENOPHOBIA.

Anti-Semitism World Report. (1992).

Curtis, Michael, ed. (1986) *Antisemitism in the Contemporary World.*

Gutman, Israel, ed. (1990) *The Encyclopedia of the Holocaust.* 4 vols.

Lipstadt, Deborah. (1993) *Denying the Holocaust: The Growing Assault on Truth and Memory.*

Wistrich, Robert S. (1991) *Antisemitism: The Longest Hatred.*

Wyman, David S. (1984) *The Abandonment of the Jews: America and the Holocaust 1941–1945.*

APARTHEID

Apartheid is a form of ethnic stratification particular to the nation of South Africa, the major features of which are the segregation of whites and nonwhites, and beliefs in the biological purity of all races, as well as white biological and cultural supremacy. The ideal was complete separation of whites and nonwhites; however, this was never completely the reality because interaction that benefited whites was permitted (although severely circumscribed). The system served as a mechanism by which the white numerical minority (about 17 percent of the population) maintained political control and exploited the African majority (about 70 percent of the population) as a source of labor. Apartheid is now ending in South Africa, as Africans are becoming full participants in the political system and as the numerous laws enacted under apartheid are being repealed.

In its fully developed form, apartheid came into being following the 1948 national election. However, separation of whites and nonwhites and exploitation of the latter by the former had been a major feature of South African society since the arrival of Dutch settlers in the 1650s. At first, when European settlement was mainly on the coast, small slave colonies were established. Later, in the 1700s and 1800s, Dutch settlers, called *Boers* and now referred to as *Afrikaners,* established all-white regions in the interior. In 1902 the British deposed the Dutch, established South Africa as a British colony, and banned Africans from political participation. During these centuries of European expansion and domination, the basic elements of apartheid were put in place, including separation of whites and nonwhites (black Africans, mixed-ancestry Coloureds, and Asians), the exploitation of African labor, and the confinement of Africans to native reserves that occupied only 13 percent of the land.

With the election of the Afrikaner-backed National party in 1948, the apartheid system became the official government policy with various laws based on the separation of whites and nonwhites, and white dominance, being enacted to ensure compliance with the policy. The basic features of apartheid have been labeled by sociologist Pierre van den Berghe as *microsegregation, mesosegregation,* and *macrosegregation.*

Microsegregation refers to policies and practices designed to eliminate or limit interaction between whites and nonwhites and include:

1. Classifying all newborn citizens as black, white, Asian, or mixed ancestry

2. Segregating public spaces such as parks and beaches, public facilities, and services such as hospitals and public transportation

3. Prohibiting Africans from entering white areas except to perform work, usually of a menial nature

4. Establishing separate schools for whites and Africans

5. Outlawing African opposition parties and jailing and torturing political opponents

6. Disenfranchising Africans in national elections

7. Preventing Africans from serving in the military

8. Paying whites and white retirees more than Africans

9. Requiring Africans to carry identification books to be shown to white authorities on demand

10. Outlawing sexual relations and marriage between Africans and whites

Mesosegregation refers to the policy of separate development started in the 1950s, the primary manifestation of which was the establishment of racially homogeneous residential areas. *Macrosegregation* is an extension of mesosegregation, as it was the actual placement of Africans in racially segregated homelands. The key elements of meso- and macro-segregation were the establishment of African homelands and the assignment and/or transfer of Africans to those homelands. Some of the homelands were classified as independent nations (Transkei, Bophuthatswana, and Venda), and their residents and those assigned to live there were no longer considered citizens of South Africa. Unfortunately, since other nations did not recognize these homelands as independent nations, their residents then became nationless. Additional measures called for the administrative linking of urban African neighborhoods with homelands, restrictions on relocation from one homeland to another, and a crackdown on "illegal" Africans in white zones.

Beginning in the late 1970s, and then accelerating from the late 1980s into the 1990s, was a weakening and finally an end of the apartheid system with the adoption of a new national constitution in December 1993 that made blacks and whites equal as a matter of government policy. Initially, this weakening took the form

Park in central Johannesburg, South Africa, 1965. Benches are "for whites only."

A   11

of the rescinding of some of the harshest elements of the homelands policy and administrative inaction in implementing some provisions. In the late 1980s and early 1990s, various laws, such as those requiring racial classification of newborns and detention of political prisoners, were abolished. The April 1994 national election produced a transition in political power to Africans led by Nelson Mandela. A combination of internal factors and sanctions applied by the world community and individual nations ultimately led to the end of apartheid. Internal factors include political resistance by the African National Congress, an expanding economy that required more African laborers in white urban areas, and the psychological impact of South Africa's exclusion from the world community. Outside action that likely pressured the South African government to alter its policies included the United Nations–imposed arms embargo, trade restrictions, and the refusal of foreign banks to loan the South African government and South African institutions money for capital investment.

As in other nations, the end of colonial domination (in South Africa in the form of apartheid) has created conflict among groups over political power. The African National Congress, with a large but not exclusively !Xhosa constituency, has been the dominant African political party, and took power following the April election. The Zulu, who dominate the Inkatha Freedom party, are eager to maintain political control in the Natal, their homeland, as well as to assure themselves a place in the national government. For their part, a minority of Afrikaners are demanding an independent province for themselves, which they call *volkstaadt,* or people's state. Both groups were deeply divided over whether they should participate in the April elections, but despite some preelection violence, the election was marked by a high voter turnout followed by a peaceful transition of power.

See also CASTE; COLONIALISM; MINORITY RIGHTS; RACE AND RACISM.

Kalley, Jacqueline A. (1989) *South Africa under Apartheid.*

Lambley, Peter. (1980) *The Psychology of Apartheid.*

Marquard, Leo. (1962) *The Peoples and Policies of South Africa.*

Smith, David M. (1983) *Living under Apartheid.*

van den Berghe, Pierre L. (1978) *Race and Racism: A Comparative Perspective.* 2d ed.

———. (1981) *The Ethnic Phenomenon.*

ARMENIANS AND AZERBAIJANI TURKS

The Republic of Armenia is located in the southwestern region of the former Soviet Union, south of Georgia, north of Iran, east of Turkey, and west of the Republic of Azerbaijan. In total, Armenia encompasses 11,306 square miles. Its population in 1993 was estimated at 3.6 million, 93.5 percent of which were ethnic Armenians, the others being mainly Kurds, Russians, and Ukrainians. Prior to the recent conflict with the Azerbaijani Turks, perhaps 6 percent of the population of Armenia was Azerbaijani. Armenia is called *Hayasdan* by its inhabitants, who refer to themselves as *Hay.* Armenians are Christian, having converted to Christianity as early as A.D. 300. Most Armenians belong to the Armenian Apostolic Church centered in the Republic.

Sixty percent of Armenians reside in Yerevan, the capital city. What is now Armenia proper was formerly called Eastern Armenia, with Western Armenia located in eastern Turkey. To escape the Turkish genocide of 1915, which led to at least 1.5 million Armenian deaths, many Armenians fled from the western region to the eastern region or elsewhere, creating an international Armenia diaspora. In the late nineteenth century the tsarist government in Russia tried to forceably convert the Armenians to the Russian Orthodox Church. Armenia became part of the USSR in 1922 and became an independent state when the Soviet Union collapsed in 1991.

The Republic of Azerbaijan is 33,400 square miles, bordered by Russia and Georgia on the north, Iran on the south, Armenia on the west, and the Caspian Sea on the east. In 1993 its population was estimated to be 7.3 million, with 83 percent being Azerbaijani Turks and the remainder being Russian and Armenian. The republic forms the northern sector of Azerbaijani territory, with the east and west Azerbaijani provinces in Iran forming the southern sector. Azerbaijanis are adherents of Islam; about 75 percent are Shi'ite, and 25 percent are Sunni. The official language is Azerbaijani, a dialect of Turkish, although the Soviet government considered it a separate language. Azerbaijani culture, which has been repressed both in the former Soviet Union and Iran, is a synthesis of elements from pre-Islamic Turkish, Iranian, and Islamic cultures.

Azerbaijan joined the Soviet Union in 1922 and became an independent state when the USSR disbanded in 1991. Azerbaijan and Armenia both suffered under the Russification programs of the Soviet era, and both are now members of the Commonwealth of Independent States created from the former Soviet republics. Nationalism is strong in both nations and contributes to the reluctance of either party to settle the current conflict peacefully.

Armenian-Azerbaijani relations have always been difficult. Where the Christian and Muslim worlds meet, the region has been the locale for violent conflict for centuries, and as a result has been ruled by various empires including the Iranian, Persian, Roman, Ottoman, Mongol, and Russian.

The current conflict between the Armenians and the Azerbaijani Turks dates to the 1920s and is irredentist, involving conflicting claims on the enclave of Nagorno-Karabakh, located within the Republic of Azerbaijan, but afforded a distinct status by the Soviet government in 1923. Nagorno-Karabakh is inhabited mainly by Armenians, who see it as part of their ancestral homeland—a claim contested by the Azerbaijani Turks. Its population is approximately 170,000.

In the past five years since the fighting has intensified, more than 3,000 people have been killed and hundreds of thousands have been displaced. In 1988 the Armenian majority in Nagorno-Karabakh demanded autonomy, promoting demonstrations of support in Armenia countered by anti-Armenian riots in Azerbaijan. In Nagorno-Karabakh, the Azerbaijani militia attempted to expel Armenians from the region. In response, Armenia began a military offensive in which they opened a "corridor of life" from Armenia to the enclave, allowing refugees easier access to Armenia. Already trying to cope with poverty and homelessness, Armenia was struck by an earthquake in 1988 that left 500,000 people homeless. This created further problems for the Armenian government and lessened their willingness to accept large numbers of Armenians from Nagorno-Karabakh. Still, tens of thousands of refugees have settled in Armenia. In 1992 the Azerbaijani blocked gas pipelines to Armenia, making winters unbearable without heat.

Officially, Armenia has not entered into the war, although popular opinion clearly is supportive of the Armenians in Nagorno-Karabakh. For Armenia to recognize the enclave formally would be the equivalent of declaring war on Azerbaijan, which Armenia apparently prefers to avoid due to international repercussions. For example, Azerbaijan's historically close relationship with Turkey poses a large threat to Armenian autonomy. Despite such possibilities, for the most part Armenia has had its way in the war, and after five years, nearly 3,000 deaths, and the dislocation of hundreds of thousands of noncombatants, Armenia has gained control of almost the whole Nagorno-Karabakh territory, as well as another area inside Azerbaijan and a land corridor to Armenia. In part, Armenian success has been the result of political unrest in Azerbaijan that has left the republic essentially leaderless at times.

Attempts at peace plans negotiated by the United States, Russia, and Turkey have been unsuccessful, and Armenia has rendered Azerbaijan virtually incapable of real resistance. Nearly 1 million people in Azerbaijan have been displaced. The road to a peace settlement will be long and difficult, a continual danger being the involvement of Turkey, Iran, and Russia, all of whom have reportedly increased their military presence at their borders with Azerbaijan.

See also IRREDENTISM.

Altstadt, Audrey L. (1992) *The Azerbaijani Turks: Power and Identity under Russian Rule.*

Matossian, Mark K. (1962) *The Impact of Soviet Policies in Armenia.*

Suny, Ronald G. (1983) *Armenia in the Twentieth Century.*

ASSAMESE IN INDIA

The name *Assamese* refers to two categories of people. First, it refers to the residents of the state of Assam in northeast India, a population that includes the indigenous Assamese, indigenous tribal peoples, and immigrants from Bangladesh (mainly Muslim Bengalis), Hindus from elsewhere in India, and refugees from Myanmar (Burma). Second, it refers to the indigenous Assamese, descendants of the original inhabitants of the region. Although population figures are unreliable, it is likely that the indigenous Assamese are now a numerical minority in Assam, a development not unrelated to the Assamese ethnic separatist movement that took a violent turn from 1987 to 1991. The state of Assam is connected to the rest of India by a narrow corridor through Himalayan states and Bangladesh, and is bordered by the nations of Bangladesh, Myanmar, Bhutan, and China. Geographically, politically, and culturally, the Assamese and Assam State have always been somewhat isolated from mainstream Indian society. In 1981 the population of Assam was estimated at over 21 million, with less than half of the population speaking Assamese. Assam (then called Asam or Aham) was originally ruled by Shan peoples from Myanmar, and modern-day Assamese culture reflects influences from Southeast Asia. The modern boundaries of Assam were established during the 1880s during the period of British colonial rule that also saw the arrival of peoples from other regions who came as migrant laborers to work on the tea plantations.

The region's economy is undeveloped despite abundant natural resources. Nearly 25 percent of India's crude oil comes from Assam, as well as most of its tea and jute. Assam is inhabited by a variety of ethnic groups, with the Assamese proper, Bengalis, and Indian Hindus the most prominent. The Assamese religion is a form of Hinduism. The Bengali community is composed primarily of those who settled in Assam seeking refuge from the poverty of their Bangladesh homeland.

The ongoing effort by the Assamese to protect their cultural and political integrity and maintain their traditional homeland began in the early 1980s when Assamese students led a campaign to persuade the Indian government in New Delhi to halt the flow of immigrants from Bangladesh, who were blamed by the Assamese for the region's economic problems. The campaign officially ended in 1985 when an agreement was reached with then–prime minister Rajiv Gandhi and local elections put a new state government into office. Shortly after, a major ethnic separatist movement emerged, under the name the United Liberation Front of Assam (ULFA), whose expressed goal was to establish a socialist nation in Assam. At first, the ULFA enjoyed much popular support by using claims that India was neglecting the region, and from 1987 to 1990 ran an independent, officially unrecognized government. Between 1987 and 1990 the ULFA collected the equivalent of several hundred million dollars from Assamese plantation owners and other businesses, claiming that these companies had been exploiting the natural resources without reinvesting their profits in the region. Some tea plantations ceased operation rather than accede to what they saw as terrorist demands by the ULFA. Over these few years, the ULFA became increasingly violent, and popular support turned to fear and suspicion as the population witnessed the execution of police and government officials. Much of the money collected by the ULFA was used to purchase weapons from international arms dealers, particularly in Myanmar and Singapore. Financial resources were also used to support military training and establish contacts with other militant ethnic groups in neighboring nations. Much of the military training took place in Myanmar, and although the Myanmar government did not openly support the ULFA, it is likely that it was aware of the group's mission and activities.

In response to the terrorism and money collecting (which some called extortion), the Indian government banned the ULFA in 1990, deposed the state government, and sent in an Indian army contingent to restore order. In 1991 the ULFA kidnapped six officials and oil executives, who were released six months later. In January 1992 negotiations between Prime Minister Narashima Rao and the moderate faction of the ULFA produced an accord that gave the

Assamese more political autonomy, major Indian investment in Assam, and constitutional protection for the small Assamese communities. However, with a continuing weak economy, minority status for the indigenous Assamese, and other ethnic unrest in the region, Assam remains a region with potential for future ethnic conflict.

Cantlie, Audrey. (1984) *The Assamese.*

ASSIMILATION

Assimilation is the process through which an ethnic group loses its distinct cultural and ethnic identity and is absorbed by another group. The assimilation process can take three forms. First, it can be a process through which immigrant groups conform to and ultimately become part of the dominant cultural group in their new homeland. In the United States, this process is called Anglo conformity in reference to the assimilation of European ethnic groups to the dominant Anglo-Saxon culture of the United States. For the assimilating group, assimilation progresses through a series of stages. The first stage is cultural assimilation, or acculturation, during which the ethnic group changes its values and norms to conform to the values and norms of the dominant cultural group. This involves learning and using the language of the dominant group, becoming a citizen of the nation, altering traditional beliefs about the nature of the world, and changing religious practices to conform to dominant religious practices. For some groups, where assimilation is blocked by the dominant culture, the process ends at acculturation—for example, African-Americans in the United States and Cape Coloureds in South Africa. In other groups, cultural assimilation is followed by structural assimilation in which

Maori women and children, New Zealand. Children are often the first to adopt customs of other cultures.

members of the ethnic group begin to participate in relationships with institutions and members of the host society. These include the use of professional services; friendships with people from mainstream society or other ethnic groups; membership in political parties, labor unions, civic organizations, and other voluntary associations; and residence in ethnically mixed neighborhoods. Structural assimilation is then followed by a series of other types of assimilation including identificational (one's self-identity becomes based on being a member of the host society), marital (intermarriage with members of other ethnic or religious groups), behavioral and attitudinal (the degree of discrimination the group actually encounters, or believes that it does), and civic (participation in host-society political issues, such as agreement with the majority on key issues, and interest in issues of importance to the general population).

This general pattern of assimilation that takes place over two or three generations is typical of the experience of many European ethnic groups in the United States, although all groups have also retained some aspects of their traditional culture, as reflected in food preferences, eating patterns, the importance and patterning of family relationships, religious practices, and use of the native language in private or the retention of certain native terms.

The assimilation of Italian-Americans in a Chicago suburb from the 1890s through the 1940s is an example of this form of assimilation. Single Italian laborers began settling in the community in the 1890s. At first they were a small, isolated group who lived next door to one another in an area covering only a few blocks. By 1911 they had established a local society, built their own church, and retained the services of a priest. Their isolation from the outside community at this time was also encouraged by the negative stereotyping of the neighboring English and German communities who saw the Italians as dirty, violent, and unwilling to learn English. In 1917 the situation began to change rapidly as Italians supported the war effort through the purchase of war bonds, and Italians who served in the U.S. military returned from World War I; in 1919 an Italian was elected alderman, and he stressed the importance of becoming an American and the value of hard work in order to succeed. His efforts were supported by the American Legion, which ran an Americanization program in the community. In 1923 the assimilation process began gathering momentum as Italians moved to other neighborhoods in the town, began giving their children American first names, and married Catholic non-Italians. Additionally, employment opportunities for men expanded, and more were employed in the skilled trades and sales than previously. Contact with the dominant culture further eroded the traditional culture as baseball and bowling replaced *bocci* as the favorite sports, and stage shows replaced more traditional forms of entertainment. Following World War II, children began attending college, and the Italian community became politically influential by electing members to local government positions.

The second type of assimilation process is known as the "melting pot," and suggests that all ethnic groups contribute something of their traditional culture, resulting in a new, distinct culture. The melting pot process involves four stages: (1) contact between groups, (2) competition, (3) accommodation, and (4) assimilation. While at one time the United States was often described as a melting pot, it is now clear that the Anglo-conformity model is a more accurate representation of the U.S. situation regarding the assimilation of European immigrants. It is also the case that in some ways the United States is a triple melting pot, with immigrant groups forming Protestant, Catholic, and Jewish overarching ethnic collectives. Modern Canadian culture is sometimes described as the product of a melting pot process involving European immigrant groups that has produced a new Canadian national consciousness different from the founding French and British cultures. Canada is also an officially multicultural and bilingual nation.

The third assimilation process results in a situation of partial assimilation where the minority group adopts many aspects of the dominant culture while at the same time retaining many of its own customs and beliefs. The Chinese in Thailand, who constitute about 10 percent of the population and work as farmers, store owners, and businessmen, are an example of this assimilation pattern. The Chinese speak both Chinese (among themselves and at home) and Thai (in public and business). Many Chinese children attend Thai schools, but many parents choose to send their children to Chinese bilingual schools and, if they can afford the cost, send older children to schools in Taiwan. Chinese businessmen belong to the Chinese associations, but they also belong to the Thai counterparts, and have helped to forge alliances between Thai and Chinese associations. Many Chinese and Thai are Buddhists, but the former are Mahayana Buddhists and the latter Theravada Buddhists. Additionally, some Chinese continue traditional ancestor worship, and most celebrate Chinese holidays such as the New Year. Finally, intermarriage is somewhat limited between the two groups and kinship practices differ, with the Chinese emphasizing relations through the father's line and the Thai through the mother's line. Thus, while the Chinese are an integral part of the Thai economy, they remain separate in many ways from the Thai community and maintain many traditional Chinese beliefs and customs.

Another form of assimilation is *forced assimilation* or *ethnocide*, in which the dominant group seeks to eradicate the minority culture or cultures and totally integrate the group into mainstream culture. Forced assimilation has been common in some regions of settlement colonization such as the United States, where government policies at various times have been directed at totally assimilating American Indians. Forced assimilation was also the policy in the former Soviet Union where non-Russian ethnic groups were "Russified"—forced to use the Russian language in place of their native tongue, participate in the Russian-dominated government and economy, accept the official Soviet version of history, and give up their traditional religion. These practices have mostly ended with the collapse of the Soviet Union and there is now a large-scale effort by dozens of ethnic minorities in the former Soviet Union to re-create their traditional cultures.

From a worldwide perspective, assimilation in any form is relatively unusual in most nations, where the pattern has been either one of excluding minorities from mainstream society or limiting participation to the level of acculturation. Those countries where assimilation has been common are the United States, Canada, Australia, Brazil, Argentina, and Israel. But even in these countries, some groups have not been assimilated—in the United States and Canada, American Indians and African-Americans; in Israel, Arabs, Beta Israel (Falasha), and others;

in Brazil, the indigenous Indians; in Argentina, Jews; in Australia, aboriginal peoples; and in New Zealand, the indigenous Maori. In general, it seems that assimilation is more likely to occur when the groups are physically similar (different skin colors being a major bar to assimilation in many nations throughout history); culturally similar, especially if they speak the same or related languages; the new group is small; the new group is lower in status than the host group; the new group is dispersed throughout the host nation; and the group wishing to assimilate is an immigrant rather than an indigenous group.

While many nations resist assimilating groups that are culturally or physically different, there are also ethnic groups that themselves choose to resist assimilation. In the United States and Canada, these include the immigrant Amish, Hutterites, Mennonites, Old Believers, Hasidic Jews, and Doukhobors. They have managed to remain separate and avoid assimilation by living in their own homogeneous communities, retaining the use of their native language (although many individuals are bilingual), requiring endogamous marriage, strictly adhering to their traditional religion, and engaging in economic enterprises that are mainly self-sufficient or do not require intensive interaction by all members of the group with other American and Canadian communities.

See also ETHNOCIDE; SYNCRETIC CULTURES.

Bun, Chan Kwok. (1993) "Rethinking Assimilation and Ethnicity: The Chinese in Thailand." *International Migration Review* 27: 140–168.

Burnet, Jean R., and Howard Palmer. (1989) *Coming Canadians: An Introduction to a History of Canada's Peoples.*

Gordon, Milton. (1964) *Assimilation in American Life: The Role of Race, Religion, and National Origins.*

Jebsen, Harry, Jr. (1976) "Assimilation in a Working Class Suburb: The Italians of Blue Island, Illinois." In *The Urban Experience of Italian-Americans,* edited by Pat Gallo, 64–84.

O'Leary, Timothy J., and David Levinson, eds. (1990) *Encyclopedia of World Cultures. Volume 1, North America.*

Olson, James S. (1979) *The Ethnic Dimension in American History.*

Thernstrom, Stephan, ed. (1980) *Harvard Encyclopedia of American Ethnic Groups.*

Thompson, Richard H. (1989) *Theories of Ethnicity: A Critical Appraisal.*

van den Berghe, Pierre L. (1981) *The Ethnic Phenomenon.*

AUTONYM

An autonym (also called an *autodenomination* or *self-name*) is an ethnic group's name for itself. Although it would seem that every ethnic group would be called by the name it prefers for itself, this is not always the case, especially for many small, non-Western cultures. One common result of contact between European colonial nations and indigenous peoples was the renaming of the latter by the former. This renaming took place for a number of reasons. In some cases, the group's name for itself is the same as the word for *people* or *the people* in its language. For example, the Navajo (a large American Indian nation, numbering about 200,000) autonym is *Dine,* meaning "the people." Similarly, the Kapauku people of Papua New Guinea call themselves *Me,* also meaning "the people" in their language. Often, the group's name for itself was not used by outsiders; they instead gave the group a different name, which then became the most often used name for the group. Outsiders sometimes ignored the people's own name for themselves because the two uses of the same word confused other outsiders (mainly the white colonizers, traders, or missionaries who had first outside contact with the group), or because the outsiders cared little about what the people called themselves. New names assigned by outsiders were often based on some local environmental factor or some unique feature of the group. Thus, the Navajo are called such because they were agriculturalists; the word probably derives from a neighboring American Indian group's word for "cultivated field," indicating the importance that the Navajo placed on agriculture. Similarily, the Pawnee, an American Indian nation of the plains, called themselves *Chahiksichahiks,* meaning "men of men." The name Pawnee is a corruption of *pariki,* meaning horn and referring to the traditional men's hairstyle with the scalplock stiffened and curved like a horn. Ignoring native names and imposing their own on indigenous peoples was another manifestation of the ethnocentrism and racism that characterized European colonization. Not uncommonly, the indigenous people regarded some of these names as derogatory and did not use them to identify themselves.

Today, many of these names are seen as inappropriate because they were imposed by outsiders, and as many of the indigenous peoples around the world seek political and cultural self-determination, they are reviving the use of their autonyms. This is especially true in groups that view the names imposed by outsiders as derogatory or stereotypical. So, for example, the Ajie-speaking people of New Caledonia now call themselves *Kanak* as part of their struggle for political independence. Similarly, in North America, the Tipai-Ipai nation of southern California prefers to be called *Kumeyaay,* its traditional name for itself, while the Nootka of Vancouver Island now prefer Westcoast People.

This trend toward the reintroduction of autonyms is not confined to Western peoples. Upon the breakup of the Soviet Union in 1991, the Belorussians renamed their republic *Belarus.* Similarly, the Slav-Macedonians of what was southern Yugoslavia are seeking nation status under the name Macedonia, a movement resisted by Greece, which believes that the name more correctly belongs to the northwestern region of Greece.

The situation with regard to ethnic group names has now become exceedingly complex, and some groups are known by multiple names. For example, Vietnamese hill people are still called *Montagnards* (French for "mountaineers") by Westerners, *Muong* by the ethnic Vietnamese, and they call themselves *Mol,* meaning "man." Similarly, Cambodians are called *Cambodians* or *Khmer* by outsiders, and call themselves *Khmae.* In Colombia, where skin color, ethnicity, and social class became interconnected through colonialism, the recent development of black consciousness and political movements has led to a complex naming system for Afro-Colombians. The label *Afro-Colombians* is actually a generic one, and is rarely used by the people themselves. *Negro,* meaning "black," is used by some Afro-Colombians, but is considered insulting by others. *Moreno,* meaning brown, and *gente de color* are also used as self-names by some. People on the Pacific coast often use *libres,* meaning "free people," while *costeño,* meaning "coastal dweller," is understood as a general reference to Afro-Colombians, as many live on the coast.

The widespread practice of ethnic groups renaming themselves is an important demonstration of self-determination for these groups and their individual members as it symbolizes the end of colonial dominance and, not surprisingly, often accompanies efforts to achieve political, legal, social, and economic autonomy. In North America, numerous indigenous nations and minority groups are now opting for their own names, or choosing names more consistent with their history and cultural traditions: Dine (formerly Navajo or Navaho), African-Americans (formerly Colored, Negroes, blacks), Latinos (formerly Hispanics), Inuit (formerly Polar Eskimo), Westcoast People (formerly Nootka), Tohono O'Odham (formerly Pima), Quechuan (formerly Yuma), and Teton or Lakota (formerly and incorrectly Sioux), among others.

Levinson, David, ed. (1991–1994) *Encyclopedia of World Cultures.* 10 vols.

Wade, Peter. (1993) *Blackness and Race Mixture: The Dynamics of Racial Identity in Colombia.*

As of 1993 there were about 5.5 million people worldwide who considered themselves adherents of the Baha'i faith, although no official membership had been published. The largest populations of Baha'i were found in India and Malaysia, each with nearly 1 million followers. The population estimates for Iran vary from 150,000 to 300,000, making the Baha'i community a small religious minority in Muslim Iran, with a total population of 62.8 million.

Iran is a Shi'ite Muslim nation, the only nation whose official religion is that particular branch of Islam. Iran was predominantly Sunni Islam until the sixteenth century, when the conversion to Shi'ite began. A major difference between Shi'ite and Sunni is in determining qualifications for the succession of the prophet Muhammed. Shi'ites maintain that hereditary succession is the only acceptable means for the spiritual leader.

The Baha'i faith has its origins in one of the many sects within the Shi'ite Muslim religion and, through a number of changes in the belief and doctrine of the religion, has emerged as a relatively "new" world religion. The Baha'i faith is directly preceded in its developmental line by the Babis, an extremely militant group who were prepared to die in order to convert the whole world to their faith. As a result, Babis were subject to mass repression in the mid-eighteenth century, finally resulting in the execution of their spiritual leader, the Bab. The Baha'i faith began in the quest for his successor and the change in the new leader's methods and beliefs. Baha'ulla and his successors in turn transformed militant Babism into Bahaism, a quiet, peaceful, and faithful sect who have never collectively advocated violence of any sort. In the last century, Bahaism has become well established throughout the world as its own religion, as it has moved away from traditions that bound it to other religions with which it was associated. It has, of course, remained influenced by several major world religions by virtue of its history and location of origin, and has been generally characterized by peaceful expansion and harmonious relations with adherents of other religions, with the exception of the small population in Iran.

Among the major tenets of modern Bahaism are: (1) the belief that all religions are derived from the same ultimate beliefs and that all are equally valid; (2) the holy personages and prophets of all religions are manifestations or messengers of the same deities; (3) the requirement of a communal gathering every nineteenth day; and (4) egalitarianism in the form of ignoring wealth distinctions and stressing equality between the sexes participating in the Baha'i religion.

Baha'is in Iran have been persecuted for as long as they have existed as a group, and indeed prior to that, when the religion had not yet evolved from Babism. In fact, many of the current popular attitudes toward Baha'is stem in part from the fact that Iranians have taken little notice of the transformation from Babism to Bahaism. Memories of militant Babist tactics have carried over to the present day and form the basis of stereotypes that are not based on current reality. The larger problem is that Bahaism is not recognized by Iranian Shi'ite Muslims as a religion, and therefore Baha'is are not classified as a religious minority. Instead, they are second-rate citizens, not equal, and in danger of persecution although the Iranian constitution currently offers protection for religious minorities. Baha'is are not Muslims, although they do believe in Muhammed as well as many other prophets before him. They also, however, believe in prophets who came after him, and herein lies a basic conflict with Islam. If Baha'is did not follow some Islamic beliefs and believed in an entirely different set of prophets, Baha'i might be considered a religion by Muslim and Iranian law. But since they acknowledge Muhammed as an important prophet, but reject the notion that he was the last, Bahaism is seen not as a separate religion but rather as heresy. There are only five pillars of Islam; the most important is to proclaim faith in Allah and belief in Muhammed as his only (last) prophet. Acknowledgment of his existence is required and any (perceived) rejection of his importance is unacceptable. For this reason, the extreme persecution of the Baha'is has not drawn sympathy from the majority of Iranians. Regardless of the fact that participation in partisan politics is not permitted within the religion and is in fact grounds for expulsion, Baha'is have been accused of numerous alliances within unpopular regimes. Baha'is around the world have pledged loyalty to the government in power in Iran, and have always stood by that pledge, regardless of whether or not they believed in the current system.

The persecution of the Baha'i community in Iran has been intense. Reports of torture of Babis date to the mid-eighteenth century, just prior to the emergence of Bahaism. For well over a century, Baha'is have been socially, economically, and physically persecuted by society as well as the government, to an extent seldom seen in

any other nation in recent times. That any Baha'i settlements remain in Iran is a testimony to their enduring faith and sense of community. At times Baha'is have been the victims of random violence carried out by Iranian citizens but instigated directly and publicly by the government. They have been forbidden to publish their literature or to worship openly. Their schools have been closed and ceremonies such as marriage have not been recognized by the government. In the early 1980s, many spiritual leaders were executed or imprisoned for belonging to the Baha'i faith, with official explanations given as fabricated criminal offenses. Throughout the Baha'i community, countless people have been victims of mob lynching, stoning, and deaths involving torture. No prosecution of anyone involved in the death of a Baha'i has been reported.

The Baha'i community has also been the victim of economic persecution by the state as well as by individual citizens. Destruction and seizure of personal and commercial property from Baha'is resulted in losses equivalent to tens of millions of dollars (from a population of, at most, 300,000) by the early 1980s. All property belonging to Baha'is collectively has been officially confiscated by the government, and dismissal from employment for being a Baha'i is common.

Rather than halt persecution of Baha'is in reaction to international public opinion, the Iranian government has chosen to deny or defend its actions. Because of limited contact with the Western world for over a decade, the current status of the Baha'i community is unclear, although there is no doubt that they are still a persecuted minority, given the authoritarian, fundamentalist nature of recent Iranian governments. In December 1993 in Iran, three Baha'is were sentenced to death for "holding feasts, owning books, and being 'unprivileged infidels at war with the Muslim nation.'" In the same month, the United Nations General Assembly voted to censure Iran for human rights violations because of Iranian repression of the Baha'i religion and culture.

Cooper, Roger. (1982) *The Baha'is of Iran.*

Esslemont, J. E. (1980) *Baha'u'llah and the New Era.* First published 1923.

BASQUES IN SPAIN AND FRANCE

The Basque country covers 20,747 square kilometers in the border region of Spain and France. The large majority of the Basque population, which totaled nearly 3 million in 1975, lives on the Spanish side, with only about 10 percent of the population in France. There are seven distinct regions in Basque country: Four are in Spain (Bizkaia, Gipuzkoa, Nafarroa, and Araba) and three in France (Lapurdi, Behe-Nafarroa, and Zuberoa). The Basques refer to Basque country as *Euskal-Herria* or *Euskadi* (meaning "country of the Basques") and the ongoing ethnic separatist movement seeks to make the region an autonomous Basque nation. About 30 percent of Basques speak the Basque language fluently, with the majority speaking either Spanish or French as their primary language. The Basque language is a language isolate, and is unrelated to any other language. Basque language-education programs have been effective in increasing the number of Basque speakers. Almost all Basques are Roman Catholics.

The origin of the Basques is unknown, although they were a recognizable population in the region before the Middle Ages. Their history has been one of successful resistance to incursions and rule by various external powers, including the Romans, Gauls, Moors, French, Castilles in Spain, and various other European kingdoms. Following the French revolution, autonomy in the French region was weakened by centralized rule from Paris, and in the nineteenth and twentieth centuries internal wars in Spain weakened Basque political autonomy. Basque control of their homeland was also threatened in the nineteenth century by the arrival of many people from elsewhere in Spain to work in the developing industries of the region. Also, Basque culture was harshly repressed under the Franco regime until the rise of democracy in Spain in 1975. To this day, Basques and non-Basques in the region maintain social distance between themselves.

At present, the economy in the region is based on a combination of industry (now predominant), agriculture, tourism, and fishing on the coast. With steel plants, major shipbuilding facilities, and various tourism opportunities, the Basque region is one of the most prosperous in Spain. Agriculture is predominant in the southern reaches of the Basque region, where wheat, olives, and grapes are particularly important crops.

The history of outside efforts to conquer the region, and the arrival of Spanish workers by the turn of the twentieth century, led to a Basque nationalist movement that has grown substantially over the course of the century. In reaction to the political repression under Franco in Spain, the ETA *(Euskadi to Azkatasuna,* or "Basque Homeland and Liberty") organization was founded, becoming the principal vehicle for resistance and ethnic separatism in the region, and developing a worldwide reputation as a violent terrorist group willing to kill civilians in order to achieve its goals. While civilians are among the more than 700 who have died in the ethnic conflict of the last three decades, most attacks have been aimed at the police, army, and *Guardia Civil.* The latter is a Spanish paramilitary civil guard whose presence in the Basque region is deeply resented, and whose visibility is a source of tension and violence. The ETA's primary political support comes from the Herri Batasuna political party.

With the arrival of democracy in Spain, the Basques became more involved in national affairs and more interested in protecting their interests peacefully. In early 1989 the ETA agreed to a cease-fire and peace talks with the Spanish government, talks that ended when each side accused the other of reneging on previously agreed-to promises. Violence then resumed, with the ETA claiming responsibility for bombing a rail line. The Basque community moved toward greater internal political cohesion in 1992 as the Basque National party, the dominant party in the Basque region, and the Herri Batasuna party began talks to operate for a common goal. Also in 1992, Spanish concern over possible Basque terrorism increased due to the World's Fair scheduled for Seville and the Summer Olympics scheduled for Barcelona. Crackdowns on Basques in France, long thought to be a shelter for ETA leaders, resulted in a number of arrests. The conflict took on a wider international scope when alleged ETA members in Uruguay were arrested and faced deportation.

While some terrorist activity has been attributed to the ETA in France, the attacks have been designed mainly to capture the attention of the Spanish government. It has long been believed by Spanish authorities that the ETA regards the French Basque region as a safe haven, out of the reach of troops stationed along the border. In 1987, France and Spain signed an antiterrorism agreement that has served to increase the number of arrests of members of the ETA, such as those in France noted above. At the present time, there are indications that a more moderate view dominates the Basque community, while both the Spanish and French governments remain inflexible as regards the issue of Basque autonomy.

Douglass, William A. (1975) *Echalar and Murelaga: Opportunity and Rural Exodus in Two Spanish Basque Villages.*

Heiberg, Marianne. (1989) *The Making of the Basque Nation.*

Ott, Sandra. (1981) *The Circle of Mountains: A Basque Shepherding Community.*

Wieviorka, Michel. (1993) *The Making of Terrorism.* Translated by David G. White.

Zulaika, Joseba. (1988) *Basque Violence: Metaphor and Sacrament.*

BOAT PEOPLE

A term used since 1978 for refugees from Southeast Asia, primarily Vietnam, *boat people* refers to emigrants who fled by boat (and land) to seek asylum in other nations, mainly the British Territory of Hong Kong, but also in Thailand, Malaysia, Indonesia, and the Philippines.

The large-scale emigration from Vietnam following the Vietnam War began with some 200,000 people leaving between 1975 and 1977, with many settling in the United States. This initial wave of Vietnamese was composed of individuals linked to the United States and the defeated South Vietnamese government, and therefore tended to be better educated, have more wealth, and were more likely to be Christian than the Vietnamese who fled in later years. Their adjustment to the nations in which they settled, such as the United States, Canada, Norway, New Zealand, France, and Australia, tended to be smoother than those who left in subsequent years.

The exodus of the boat people began in 1978 when about 85,000 people, mostly from rural areas, left Vietnam to seek refuge in Indonesia, Thailand, Malaysia, the Philippines, and Hong Kong, from where they hoped to immigrate to other nations. Many of those who fled Vietnam did so in unseaworthy crafts, and even those that were seaworthy were subject to attack by pirates, a presence on these seas for centuries. Between 1978 and 1993, about 800,000 people were re-settled in nations of second asylum where they expected to stay permanently. Up until 1988, most of these refugees eventually moved on to nations of settlement, with the United States admitting the majority, and significant numbers of Vietnamese also settling in Canada, Australia, France, Germany, Britain, and Norway. It is estimated that only half of those who left ultimately reached their destinations in the Southeast Asian refugee camps; about 90,000 people remain unsettled, approximately 45,000 of them in Hong Kong detention centers.

The boat people population actually is composed of two distinct ethnic groups—the Vietnamese and the Chinese who resided in Vietnam. In 1978 hostilities broke out between Vietnam and China; the Vietnamese government encouraged the Chinese to leave, but charged them a large exit fee, which forced many to become boat people. About 280,000 fled to southern China and are now permanently settled there. Others fled to refugee centers in Hong Kong and elsewhere, and ultimately settled in Western nations, as did the ethnically Vietnamese boat people. As elsewhere in their diaspora, many of the Chinese had been shopkeepers and small-business owners in Vietnam, and had assimilated in varying degrees into Vietnamese society.

For the ethnic Vietnamese who fled after 1978, a variety of factors was responsible for the continued large flow of refugees into the 1990s. Among these were dislocations and economic hardships caused by the Vietnam War, economic sanctions placed on Vietnam by the United States and other nations after the war, the difficulties for rural peoples in the South in adjusting to Communist rule, and the lure of expecting a better life in the West.

Following the Chinese departures in 1979, the number of boat people seeking refuge annually ranged from 20,000 to 75,000 through 1986.

Boatload of Vietnamese refugees off the shore of Hong Kong, 1989.

More significantly, during this period the number leaving the refugee camps for resettlement (mostly in Western nations) was higher each year than the number of new arrivals. Thus, while the flow of boat people continued, their total number in refugee centers declined. In 1987, however, the situation reversed, a pattern that escalated in 1988 with the number of new arrivals (45,000) nearly double that of those departing for resettlement. From 1988 on, the majority of asylum-seekers came from what had been North Vietnam prior to unification in 1975; before 1988, asylum-seekers came mainly from the former South Vietnam.

Beginning in 1988 the boat people became an international issue, with questions raised about the accuracy of their classification as political refugees, the quality of care in refugee centers, the role of Vietnam in encouraging them to leave, and the role and responsibility of the international community and the United Nations, which had been managing the process and the refugee centers. Driving this questioning was "compassion fatigue" in both the asylum and settlement nations, meaning that they were running out of patience, time, and resources to deal with the increasing refugee flow, especially since many suspected that those from North Vietnam were not political refugees but economic refugees fleeing poverty, and as such were not entitled to asylum and resettlement. In reaction, Hong Kong began efforts in 1988 to determine refugee status, and in 1989 the international community adopted the Comprehensive Plan of Action (CPA) to end the boat people problem. The CPA is designed to classify asylum-seekers as either political or nonpolitical refugees, to encourage the return of nonpolitical refugees to Vietnam, and to deter nonofficial departures from Vietnam.

The CPA program, which used monetary payments to induce nonpolitical refugees to return to Vietnam (this aspect of the program was dropped in 1991 because of abuses), and still uses denial of access to Western nations for resettlement, has been effective. Some 36,000 individuals voluntarily repatriated to Vietnam by 1993, and only 12 asylum-seekers arrived in Hong Kong in 1993. Various aspects of the program have been questioned by human rights and refugee advocates. First, it is exceedingly difficult to determine whether or not a person is a political refugee, making it easy for officials wishing to return asylum-seekers to classify them as nonrefugees. Second, the living conditions in most, if not all, refugee centers have been routinely described as horrendous and inhumane, leading some to believe that such conditions may be evidence of a policy of "humane deterrence" meant to encourage refugees to return home. Third, in 1989 and again in 1991 following a repatriation agreement between Britain and Vietnam, Hong Kong actively engaged in involuntary repatriation, a practice that puts political refugees at risk of persecution, imprisonment, or death on return to their homeland. Fourth, despite reassurances from the U.N., which monitors and manages the program, some advocates question the quality of life afforded returnees in Vietnam. For the international community, the goal remains the same—an end to the boat people problem—meaning the placement of all 90,000 boat people still in refugee centers (half in Hong Kong) and an end of the flow of refugees from Vietnam, which seems to have occurred in 1993. In February 1994 the Vietnam exodus was declared officially over by the U.N., and Vietnamese refugees in the future will not be granted special status but will be treated like other refugees seeking asylum in the country where they arrive. As for refugees settled in Western nations, their experience has been mixed, although it seems that over time the quality of their lives has improved.

Del Mundo, Fernando. (1993) "Vietnamese Returnees Find New Hope in the Future." *Refugees* 92: 34–36.

Donnelly, Nancy D. (1992) "The Impossible Situation of Vietnamese in Hong Kong's Detention Centers." In *Selected Papers on Refugee Issues*, edited by Pamela A. DeVoe, 120–132.

Gold, Stephen J. (1992) *Refugee Communities*.

Grimes, Seamus. (1993) "Residential Segregation in Australian Cities: A Literature Review." *International Migration Review* 27: 103–120.

Hauff, Edvard, and Per Vaglum. (1993) "Integration of Vietnamese Refugees into the Norwegian Labor Market: The Impact of War Trauma." *International Migration Review* 27: 388–405.

Knudsen, John Chr. (1992) "'To Destroy You Is No Loss.'" In *Selected Papers on Refugee Issues,* edited by Pamela A. DeVoe, 133–144.

BODO IN INDIA The Bodo are a tribal people located in the Cachar district of the northeastern Indian state of Assam and also in Nagaland State. Assam is bordered on three sides by China, Myanmar, and Bangladesh, and is connected to the rest of India by a narrow land corridor. The state of Assam, though named for what was once the dominant ethnic group—the Assamese—is now home to a mix of ethnic groups and the scene of considerable ethnic conflict. The Bodo are predominantly Hindu cultivators of rice who account for approximately 10 to 15 percent of the state's 23 million people. The area most heavily populated by the Bodo is north of the Brahmaputra River, although they still only account for, at most, 40 percent of the population in northern Assam. The whole state is rich in oil, tea, timber, and jute, but it is the northern tea-growing regions of Tezpur, Darrang, Goalpara, and Kokrajhar that have suffered from the violent destruction of bridges, railroads, roads, schools, stores, and homes in another of India's many indigenous rights conflicts.

The Bodo began their campaign for an independent state within India in 1988, citing economic and social neglect by the state government and the nontribal Assamese. Their desire for a separate homeland has manifested itself in the form of a guerrilla war led by young militants drawn largely from the All Bodo Students Union. Indian paramilitary groups have been dispatched to the region in an effort to contain the violence and destruction. The Bodo rebellion has concentrated its efforts on controlling the region's supplies and halting the transportation of tea, the major export of the state of Assam. Bodo extremists have called for total shutdowns of all economic activity to protest neglect by the government in response to their demands. Those who have not complied with these demands have been harassed and even killed as a result.

It is unlikely that state and central government will meet these demands from such a small population, especially to discourage numerous other tribes of the region and elsewhere in India from seeking separate states as well.

Danda, Dipali G., and Sanchita Ghatak. (1985) *The Semsa and Their Habitat.* Anthropological Survey of India, Memoir No. 64. Calcutta.

BOSNIANS-CROATS-SERBS The ongoing war in the former Yugoslavia began in 1991 with Croatia and Slovenia declaring independence from Yugoslavia, and continues into 1994. Fighting among the Serbs, Bosnian Muslims, and Croats has resulted in over 100,000 deaths and has created over 1.7 million refugees. The conflict has also added the term *ethnic cleansing* to the lexicon of ethnic relations.

The modern nation of Yugoslavia began in 1918 as the Kingdom of Serbs, Croats, and Slovenes, with the name changed to Yugoslavia in 1929. Following devastation in World War II, the Federal People's Republic of Yugoslavia was formed as a Communist nation under the rule of Marshall Tito in 1945. The World War II experience, in which many Bosnians and Croats supported the Germans while the Serbs resisted and suffered Nazi atrocities, is one factor underlying the current conflict among these groups.

Communist Yugoslavia was composed of the six states of Slovenia, Croatia, Serbia, Montenegro, Bosnia-Herzegovina, and Macedonia. Following Tito's death in 1980, various steps were taken to preserve the multiethnic nation, including a presidency that rotated among the various ethnic groups and street signs in both the Latin (for Croats) and Cyrillic (for Serbs) versions of Serbo-Croatian. Still, conflict between the Croats and Serbs continued, and in 1991 both Croatia and Slovenia declared themselves independent republics, followed by Bosnia-Herzegovina and Macedonia. The post-1991 version of Yugoslavia is composed of only the republics of Serbia and Montenegro, and is not recognized as the nation of Yugoslavia by the entire international community.

Serbs were the largest of the ethnic groups that formed the former Yugoslavia. In 1990 there were an estimated 8.5 million Serbs in Yugoslavia; the overwhelming majority are now found in Serbia and Bosnia-Herzegovina. Serbia is located in the Balkans and is bounded by Hungary to the north, Romania and Bulgaria on the east, Albania and Macedonia on the south, and the former Yugoslav republics of Bosnia-Herzegovina and Croatia on the west. Due to the conflict between the Croats and the Bosnian Muslims, the borders of Serbia have been expanded greatly from what they were during the days of the Yugoslavian nation. Whether these borders become permanent is dependent on the outcome of ongoing hostilities with the Bosnians. Serbia also encompasses the formerly

Serbians fleeing the Republic of Krajina following Croatian attack, February 1993.

autonomous provinces of Kosovo-Metohija, the home of about 2 million Albanians, with the Serbs a minority in the province (10–15 percent of the population), and Vojvodina, with a large though minority population of Hungarians.

Slavic peoples began entering the Balkan region between the fifth and seventh centuries. They encountered the Illyrians, already settled on the plains, whom they displaced into the highlands. The Illyrians were subsequently referred to as Vlachs, and eventually reemerged as a distinct though separate group within Slavic society. From the ninth century, the Slavs were subject to outside pressures from the Germans, Hungarians, Austrians, and the Byzantine Empire, all of which influenced migration and settlement patterns throughout the region. Beginning as early as the thirteenth century, the region came under Ottoman influence, which eventually caused many Slavs to flee into the highlands and east, and others, such as large numbers of Albanians and Bosnians near the coast, to convert from Christianity to Islam. The conversion of Bosnians to Islam is another factor in the current conflict between the Serbs and Bosnians. The Serbs, who fought against the Ottoman Empire and were forced to flee, see the Bosnians as collaborators who benefited economically and politically by converting to Islam. The decay of the Ottoman Empire, beginning by 1800, allowed the Slavs to migrate back into the lowlands and reestablish settlements there.

Serbs moved into the region now known as Serbia about A.D. 500–600 and had established a Serbian polity by the ninth century. In the fourteenth century the region was conquered by the Ottoman Empire, and many Serbs fled west to the Alps. After a series of revolts, Ottoman control ended, and in 1830 Turkey recognized Serbia as an autonomous unit. In 1882 it became an autonomous state; in 1918 it was joined with Croatia and Slovenia, and after World War II incorporated into Yugoslavia. Serbia was a largely rural, agricultural region, but since World War II the population has become mainly urban, and wage-earning has become a major source of income for most families. Serbs speak a dialect of Serbo-Croatian, which they write in the Serbian Cyrillic script. Most Serbs are Eastern Orthodox Christian.

In the former Yugoslavia, Croats (also called Croatians) numbered about 4.5 million, with about 3.5 million in Croatia. The others, who lived in Bosnia-Herzegovina, Serbia, and Slovenia, have now fled those regions due to the ongoing war. The Croats live mainly in rural areas, although in southern Croatia the majority live in cities. The Croats emerged as a distinct ethnic group in the seventh century, and after centuries of self-rule became linked with Hungary in the twelfth century. They were then under Austrian (Hapsburg) and Ottoman rule, and a part of the Austro-Hungary Empire. After World War I, they joined with Serbia and Slovenia to form the predecessor of the modern Yugoslavia, and following World War II became one of Yugoslavia's six states. In 1991 Croatia became an independent nation. Croatians are mainly Roman Catholic.

Bosnians, or Bosnian Muslims, numbered about 1.8 million in the Bosnia-Herzegovina state of the former Yugoslavia. They constituted 44 percent of the state's population, with Serbs accounting for 31 percent and Croats 17 percent. The current population of the republic and the ethnic distribution are unknown, but the figures are now far different from those of 1990. Bosnian Muslims live primarily in the cities, where they hold many professional and government positions. Although called "Turks" by some Serbs, Bosnian Muslims are ethnically Serbs. They converted to Islam under Ottoman rule beginning in the fifteenth century. Many of those who converted were Bogomils, considered a heretical sect outside both Catholicism and Orthodox Christianity. Under Ottoman rule, Bosnian Muslims were freed from paying the taxes extracted from the Slavic peasants; they often lived in or near fortified towns and were established as a merchant class. Bosnian religious practice was not repressed under Communist rule, and Islam most closely resembles that practiced in Turkey. It is less rigorous than Islam practiced in the Middle East, with perhaps one-third of Muslims marrying non-Muslims. Bosnians also eschew Islamic fundamentalism and claim that an independent Bosnia would be a secular state with religious freedom guaranteed for all. As with the Serbs and Croats, Bosnians speak a variant of Serbo-Croatian.

The distinction among the Serbs, Croats, and Bosnians is based on a combination of kinship, language, and religion. Bosnians reckon descent bilaterally (through the lines of both mother and father) and generally count back only about three generations. For Serbs, descent is more important; they emphasize the father's line and count as far back as nine generations. Croats are somewhere in between these two extremes. All three ethnic groups speak Serbo-Croatian, although dialect differences mark the home region of speakers. Finally, religion is the most visible marker of ethnic identity, as the three groups are adherents of different religions, and the symbols of those religions, such as churches or mosques, mark the ethnic makeup of different rural communities or urban neighborhoods. During the war, religious buildings have been a frequent target for the opposing groups.

The war in Croatia began in 1991 following the 25 June decision by Croatia to secede from Yugoslavia and become an independent nation. Preferring that Yugoslavia remain a nation composed of its six states and concerned about the welfare of 600,000 Serbs residing in Croatia, Serbia responded by invading. The battle was waged by the Serb-dominated Yugoslav army and local Serb militia against the Croatian state army, with the latter badly overmatched, at least initially. Outside observers suggested that, despite evidence of Croat attempts

to ethnically cleanse regions of Serbs, the Serbs were mainly interested in creating a "Greater Serbia" crafted from Serbia proper and regions of other republics with large Serb populations. By the end of the year the Croats had halted the Serb advance and had begun to reclaim some lost territory. In January 1992 both sides agreed to a cease-fire and pledged to allow a United Nations peacekeeping force to patrol the regions of greatest conflict. In March a U.N. force of 1,500 entered the region to patrol mainly Serb-held areas called U.N. Protected Areas, and while hostilities largely ceased, ethnic cleansing by both sides continued by means of the forced expulsion of entire communities. In January 1994 Serbia and Croatia entered into agreements that for all practical purposes established Croatia as a separate nation and called for the establishment of formal relations between the two nations. The agreement also created hope that the protracted conflict between Croats and Serb nationalists in western Croatia might soon end, as Serb support for the nationalists was clearly weakening.

All told, the Serb-Croat war produced more than 10,000 deaths, left over 13,000 people unaccounted for, and drove nearly 700,000 Croats from their homes. About half are now refugees in other former Yugoslav republics and European nations including Germany, Hungary, and Switzerland, while the remainder are internally displaced in Croatia. Peace between Croatia and Serbia will likely lead to the return of many refugees and the permanent resettlement of internally displaced peoples, mainly Croats in Croatia.

The ongoing war in Bosnia-Herzegovina began in 1992 as a Serbian reaction to a Bosnian desire for independence. The exact motivation for the attack by the Bosnian Serb forces and the Serb-dominated Yugoslav National Army is not clear. Some view the assault as motivated by a Serbian desire to be the majority ethnic group in the region. Others see it as a Serbian land-grab against a weaker neighbor, and still others see it as a Serbian effort to prevent the establishment of an Islamic state in the Balkans. Old animosities between the groups also play a role in the conflict, and perhaps are a factor in the extreme nature of the violence and the number of civilian victims. The Bosnia war began with a Serbian invasion of eastern and northern Bosnia, and the killing and driving out of Bosnian Muslims and Croats. The Serbs used a combination of artillery attacks on civilians, torture, massacres, mass rapes, forced detention, expulsions, burnings, and looting in a campaign of ethnic cleansing designed to leave the regions inhabited only by Serbs. In some places Serbs were the dominant population; in others, a minority. For their part, the Croats attacked western Bosnia in an effort to drive out Serbs and Bosnians and to create a purely Croat zone in Bosnia. As of January 1994, with the war continuing, over 100,000 people have been killed; over 60,000 are missing; 1.1 million fled the region and are now refugees, mainly in the other former Yugoslav republics; and 740,000 are displaced within Bosnia. What was Bosnia-Herzegovina is now divided among the Serbs, Croats, and Bosnians. The Serbs control two-thirds of the region. The Croats control a small north-south strip along the southwestern border with the region of Croatia on the Adriatic Sea. Bosnia controls a strip running through the center of the region from west to east and then north, to the northwest corner bordering Croatia and Serbia, as well as enclaves in Serb-controlled eastern Bosnia. A number of cities in Bosnia-held territories such as Tuzia, Sarajevo, Gorazde, Zepa, and Srebrenica are designated as safe areas by the U.N. As of January 1994 a better organized Bosnian army was making inroads against Serb-held towns and cities, and by mid-year, signs of a Bosnian-Croatian alliance were emerging.

Efforts by the international community to end the fighting, despite charges against all three groups of a general lack of concern for the rights and lives of civilians, have been limited and ineffectual. For the most part, the European community and the U.N. have attempted to provide humanitarian aid through convoys, airlifts, and refugee-assistance programs; have tried to limit the dispersal of refugees to other areas of the former Yugoslavia; and have threatened various sanctions as well as the use of ground troops and air strikes. Peacemaking efforts were hindered by disagreements about strategy and tactics among European nations and the United States. Negotiations backed by the U.N. and European Community have accomplished little, and numerous cease-fires have been openly violated by the Serbs. Economic sanctions imposed by the U.N. on Serbia and Montenegro, the banning of flights over Bosnia, an arms embargo, and efforts to inspect detention camps have done little to deter the Serbs.

The Serbs see themselves as the victims of a Western anti-Serbian campaign, and defend their actions on the grounds that they were compelled to act to save 1.5 million Serbs stranded in the newly independent nations of Slovenia, Croatia, and Bosnia-Herzegovina. As regards Croatia, there is evidence that efforts were made to remove Serbs from the region. Serbs are also perplexed by their belief that other nations seem to have forgotten that they resisted the Nazis, and suffered for their actions, while the Croats aided the Nazis. Most observers now expect that any resolution will be on Serbian terms and will result in the partition of Bosnia into Serb, Croat, and Bosnian Muslim zones. So far, the Bosnians have resisted Serbian and Croatian offers of peace based on a partitioned Bosnia and the European Community's desire for a similar result. In January 1994, as part of a peace agreement between Serbia and Croatia, the leaders of the Serb and Croat regions of Bosnia also entered into an agreement that called for the establishment of diplomatic relations between the two de facto regions. This development is expected to put more pressure on the Bosnian Muslims to accept a partitioned Bosnia.

Balkan War Report. (1992–) Bulletin of the Institute for War & Peace Reporting.

Erlich, Vera S. (1966) *Family in Transition.*

Halpern, Joel M., and Barbara Kerewsky-Halpern. (1986) *A Serbian Village in Historical Perspective.*

Hammel, Eugene A. (1993) "Demography and the Origins of the Yugoslav Civil War." *Anthropology Today* 9: 4–9.

Lockwood, William G. (1975) *European Moslems: Economy and Ethnicity in Western Bosnia.*

Magas, Branka. (1993) *The Destruction of Yugoslavia: Tracking Yugoslavia's Break-Up 1980–1992.*

Sekelj, Laslo. (1993) *Yugoslavia: The Process of Disintegration.* Translated from Serbo-Croatian by Vera Vukelic.

U.S. Committee for Refugees. (1993) *World Refugee Survey.*

were various categories of merchants, farmers, and craftsmen; lower still were the castelike blacksmiths, potters, and tanners; and at the bottom were the freed slaves, considered beneath or outside the hierarchy. Castelike groups such as the Beta Israel (blacksmiths) and Cushites (tanners) lived in separate communities, were restricted to only economic relations with the Amhara, and were allowed to marry only within their social category. Similarly, the Shluh in Morocco had three social classes and three castes: (1) aristocracy, (2) religious classes such as descendants of Muhammed, (3) commoners, (4) mixed-ancestry peoples who were mainly blacksmiths and artisans, (5) Jews, and (6) slaves. The last three categories fit the definition of caste groups. Experts are not in complete agreement as to the appropriateness of the use of the caste concept in this way as a label for distinct groups as opposed to a caste system, and, in fact, caste groups are really outcaste groups and therefore outside the system, not part of it. That is, they are considered to be impure and are outside the hierarchical social structure of the societies in which they are found. Still, the notion of caste group tends to distinguish groups who live almost completely outside society from other minority groups whose exclusion is less extreme.

CASTE Caste refers to two different but related forms of human social organization. First, it pertains to the rigid hierarchical system of social organization of South Asia. Second, it means a particular type of social group in a multiethnic society.

Caste Groups

Groups classified as caste groups, such as African-Americans in the United States, Gypsies and Jews in Europe and elsewhere, and Burakumin (formerly called *eta*) in Japan, are so defined because membership in the group is determined by birth and is for life, marriage is restricted to other members of the group, the groups have a clear rank within the society's hierarchy, and the group is stigmatized—considered morally inferior, ritually impure, or genetically inferior—and therefore discriminated against.

For example, traditional Amhara society in Ethiopia was hierarchically organized into a number of strata. At the top were the emperor, wealthy landowners, and the clergy; below them

Caste in South Asia

The term *caste* is from the Portuguese *casta*, and was used by Portuguese explorers in reference to the system of social organization—now commonly known as the caste system—they found upon their arrival in India in the fifteenth century. Although the caste system in South Asia is well described and its dynamics generally understood, it is often difficult for outsiders to fully comprehend the nature, dynamics, and pervasiveness of the caste system among Hindus in South Asia. Part of the difficulty is that, in terms of daily life, the term *caste* actually refers to three different indigenous concepts generally used by the people of Hindu India and South Asia.

First, it refers to the several-thousand-year-old overarching *varna* system, in which all individuals and groups in Hindu society are classified into four ranked categories:

Brahman The highest caste category or *varna* and the highest caste group in any locale. The Brahmans were traditionally priests and served in that role for their village, or more commonly for specific families within the village. Brahmans are also teachers, government workers, and landowners. In recent times, many Brahmans have moved to the cities and entered professions while continuing to control land as absentee landowners. The Brahmans' high status derives from their ritual purity, as evidenced by most being vegetarians, their ability to read Sanskrit, and their knowledge of Hindu ritual. There are hundreds of Brahman castes in South Asia and Southeast Asia.

Kshatriya The second highest caste category, located mainly in northern India; many of the castes within this *varna* claim descent from warrior castes of the past. Kshatriyas eat meat (but not beef), and were traditionally defenders of the caste system and the supremacy of the Brahmans. Today, they are primarily landowners and professionals.

Vaisya The third-ranked caste category, composed of a large number of castes, many traditionally engaged in trading, farming, and moneylending in northern India, where they are a key element in the village economies of the region.

Sudra The lowest of the four caste categories, composed of hundreds of castes throughout India. Traditionally they are small-scale farmers, although in the cities they may be found in all occupations. Those originally classified as Sudras several thousand years ago may have been aboriginal peoples of darker skin color than the Indo-Aryan settlers who formed the three higher *varna*.

A fifth caste (actually an outcaste) category, although not considered as such in the original *varna* system, is the Untouchables (also known as *Panchamas, Pariahs, Harijans, Adi-Dravida,* and since 1949 as the Scheduled Castes). Untouchables are those castes who rank below the Sudra *varna*. Both the number of Untouchable castes and former Untouchables (this category and discriminatory practices directed at its members are now illegal in India) is unknown, although they may number some 200 million individuals in South Asia.

While the caste system in general, and the *varna* categorization in particular, is associated with Hindu India, the social organization of non-Hindu groups in South Asia such as Muslims, Jains, and Jews is also characterized by an overarching caste structure. For example, while Islam has no caste structure and such a structure is absent in Islamic groups outside South Asia, in Pakistan's Islamic society there are four castelike categories. At the top are groups that trace their ancestry to the Middle East—the Sayyid, Shaikh, Mughal, and Pathan. Second in rank are the Muslim Rajputs; third is a collection of occupational castes; and fourth, the sweepers, roughly the equivalent of Hindu Untouchables.

The second indigenous use of the term caste is in reference to *jati. Jati* are hereditary occupational castes or clusters of castes who traditionally performed specific tasks within the village or region. There are several thousand *jati* in India, and many are still so identified, although they no longer perform the traditional occupation. Each *jati*, of course, is classified in one of the five *varna*. Traditionally, at the village level, and to some extent at the regional level, the *jatis* were linked through the *jajmani* system. In the *jajmani* system, occupational castes or families within castes provided services for other castes or families. Traditionally, the caste was paid through reciprocal service or with food, although more recently, financial payments have become the norm. For example, in one northern Indian village there are 12 castes and outcastes. The Khati (carpenter) caste repairs agricultural tools for the Brahman (priest), Baniya (trader), Nai (barber), and Jat (farmer) castes, and receives services from seven other castes. In addition to this structured economic relationship, the *jajmani* system also contains many social rules that reinforce the hierarchical nature of the caste system by restricting contact between higher and lower ranked castes. The strict rules of endogamous marriage and caste membership for life through birth ensure the vitality of the system. The *jajmani* system has persisted for hundreds of years, or even longer in many villages; in some villages it is the primary mechanism of social and economic cohesion. Some observers see the *jajmani* system as an efficient and effective form of local social and economic organization; others find it an oppressive form of organization that benefits the higher castes and exploits the lower ones, especially the Untouchables.

The third indigenous use of the term caste is in reference to *gotra*, kinship groups within a *jati* who marry members of other *gotra* within the same *jati* and who may live in the same village or region and own property jointly.

Basis of the Caste System
The Hindu caste system is intimately tied to the Hindu beliefs of *karma* and *dharma*. An individual's caste position is determined by his or her karma (behavior in a previous life). An individual's future caste position is determined by his or her dharma (behavior in the current life). Thus, acting as prescribed by caste status is the only way an individual can achieve a higher caste rank in the next life. Relations among castes and individuals are governed by the notions of ritual purity, pollution, and obligatory service.

The caste hierarchy is based on the degree of purity exhibited by each *varna* and is maintained by rules that prohibit contact by lower (less pure) castes that would pollute the higher caste. In addition, higher castes do not engage in work that is considered to be polluting to that caste, such as leather-working. As suggested by the *jajmani* system at the village level, the obligations involved in giving and receiving services are a key component of the caste system and serve to make it an economic as well as a social system.

At a more concrete level, the survival of the caste system has rested on five basic practices:

1. Marriage within the caste
2. Eating and drinking only with members of the same or equal castes
3. Membership for life in the caste of one's birth
4. Occupational specialization, with each caste engaged in only one occupation
5. Hierarchical arrangement on the basis of the concepts of pollution and purity

While membership in a caste is for an individual's entire life, meaning that no individual can enter a higher caste, castes themselves can move into a higher *varna* category. For example, a caste could take on a ritually purer occupation. A second and more common way is to emulate the behavior of a higher caste—by using Sanskrit in prayer, retaining Brahman priests, adopting a vegetarian diet, and other purer ritual behaviors. This process, widespread throughout India, is known as *Sanskritization*.

Changes in the Caste System
Over its several-thousand-year history, the caste system in South Asia has undergone a number of changes. The bases of the different *varna* classifications changed at various times; the rules governing the behavior of the *varna* also changed and underwent reinterpretation by religious

Untouchables in India traditionally performed ritually polluting tasks such as shoe-making and repair.

leaders and scholars. The number and types of *jati* have also varied as occupations became more or less important, and as new ones appeared and old ones disappeared. Under British rule, certain *varna* such as the Brahmans enjoyed special status because their history of literacy and scholarship made them ideal choices for employment in government service. Additionally, the British empowered some lower ranking *jati* in some regions by allowing them to vote, which in turn created caste associations who could act as voting blocs.

Both before and following independence in 1948, there has been increased concern about the fate of the Untouchables in the caste system. The Indian Constitution of 1949 banned discrimination against Untouchables and led to the development of various affirmative-action

programs to benefit the Untouchables, now officially called Scheduled Castes, and other poor and disadvantaged groups such as the Scheduled Tribes. Official lists of these groups defined them and made their members eligible for special aid and education programs.

Today, the majority of Indians still live in rural villages. Although outcastes are protected by law, at the local level they are still mostly landless field laborers who are considered to be ritually polluted and therefore banned from using public wells or entering Hindu temples. In these rural communities the now dominant castes are often mid-level castes who increased their wealth and political power through government land reforms, agricultural support, and economic and political opportunities created by the migration of high-caste landowners to the cities. At the same time, in some locales Scheduled Castes with many members have emerged as powerful voting blocs who can effectively challenge the landowners in elections, a source of conflict and violence in some communities. The Sudra castes also see the Scheduled Castes as a threat to their interests because of the advantages that accrue to the latter from affirmative-action programs, and are now demanding equal treatment for themselves.

See also ANTI-SEMITISM; APARTHEID; MIXED-ANCESTRY PEOPLES; RACE AND RACISM.

Berreman, Gerald D. (1979) *Caste and Other Inequities: Essays on Inequality.*

Brass, Paul R. (1983) *Caste, Faction and Party in Indian Politics: Faction and Party.* Volume 1.

———. (1985) *Caste, Faction and Party in Indian Politics: Election Studies.* Volume 2.

de Reuck, Anthony, and Julie Knight, eds. (1967) *Caste and Race.*

De Vos, George, and Hiroshi Wagatsuma, eds. (1966) *Japan's Invisible Race.*

Dumont, Louis. (1970) *Homo Hierarchicus.*

Hockings, Paul, ed. (1992) *The Encyclopedia of World Cultures, Volume 3, South Asia.* (See articles on Brahman; Castes, Hindu; Kshatriya; Muslim; Sudra; Untouchables; Vaisya; Appendix).

Kolenda, Pauline. (1978) *Caste in Contemporary India: Beyond Organic Solidarity.*

Lagacé, Robert O., ed. (1977) *Sixty Cultures.*

Lewis, Oscar. (1965) *Village Life in Northern India.*

Mandelbaum, David G. (1970) *Society in India.* 2 vols.

Myrdal, Gunnar. (1944) *An American Dilemma.*

van den Berghe, Pierre L. (1981) *The Ethnic Phenomenon.*

CATALANS IN SPAIN

In 1993 the population of Spain was estimated at 39.1 million. Of that number, approximately 28 percent are Catalan, with Catalans also forming about 1 percent of the population of France. As are Spaniards generally, Catalans are almost all Roman Catholics. Although Catalans are known in the popular press as residents of the Spanish region of Catalonia, the area known as *Paisos Catalans* (Catalan countries) is actually much larger and includes three regions in Spain, eight provinces, one French department, and the independent state of Andorra. It covers 69,032 square kilometers bordering northeastern Spain and southeastern France.

Contemporary Catalans can trace their presence in the region to at least A.D. 700. Catalonia became an independent kingdom in the eighth century and united with Aragon in the twelfth century to form the Aragon-Catalon Empire, which remained a major power in the western Mediterranean region into the fifteenth century. In 1469 the marriage of Ferdinand and Isabella united Aragon-Catalonia with the western regions of Castile and Leon, forming the core of the modern Spanish nation. Economic and political power then shifted to the western provinces; those in the east, such as Catalonia, fought to maintain their cultural and political autonomy. Revolts in the seventeenth and eighteenth centuries were suppressed by the centralized government. At the same time, many of the regions of Spain that had previously been independent political entities, such as Catalonia, retained some political autonomy—at least until the late eighteenth and nineteenth centuries, when Spain's separate administrative structures were divided into centrally controlled provinces. Catalonia was partitioned into the provinces of Barcelona, Gerona, Lerida, and Tarragona, and each province reported primarily to Madrid rather than to one another, weakening regional ties. Despite this political breakup, the national identity of Catalans has survived in large part because of their efforts to preserve Catalan language and culture.

Economically, Catalonia has been one of the leading regions in Spain since the eighteenth century. Not only was Catalonia one of the first regions to industrialize, it remains a leading contributor to Spain's economy. Although the social classes in Catalan society may have differed on certain local issues, they usually coalesced in their belief that the central government was not giving back to Catalonia nearly as much as it was receiving. Indeed, the central government seemed to concentrate on more backward areas of Spain. As a result, political parties in Catalonia tended to concentrate more of their efforts on local concerns rather than national issues. Madrid began to view these parties and local political organizations as a threat to central control, rather than as a mechanism for dealing with local issues for which the central government had neither time nor interest. Catalans have a tradition of relying on local political organizations and authorities rather than the central government, and they tend to accomplish more in this manner than other regions of Spain who lack strong, local organization.

Despite such organizational success, Catalans were overlooked when it came to positions in central government institutions. This lack of satisfactory representation in Madrid led to increased frustration with the central government. Positions in central public institutions tended to be filled by people from the less developed areas of Spain. Since Catalonia was of such economic importance to Spain, any real or perceived threat of straying from the central government resulted in increased central control to discourage separatist movements. Only when Dictatorship was revoked and the Republic was declared in 1931 was Catalonia's autonomous government, "Generalidad," given substantial recognition from Madrid. However, this only lasted until the end of the civil war and the beginning of Franco's dictatorial regime. Having received autonomy from the Republic, Catalonia naturally took that side in the civil war.

Catalonia suffered under Franco's rule. All autonomous political institutions were abolished and any opposition groups were outlawed. Leaders of all local political organizations were executed or exiled, and replaced by pro-Franco supporters. Throughout Franco's entire regime, only a few conservative Catalan politicians held significant political posts. Perhaps more damaging was Franco's official policy of cultural repression. The region's language, folklore, and political traditions were attacked relentlessly. The Catalan language was outlawed anywhere outside the home, including in church. This policy was enforced most strictly in schools, where teaching the language was not permitted. The study of Catalan culture and history was banned in universities, and even local folk music was not allowed. Immigration to the Catalan region also increased dramatically until less than half the

working class was originally from Catalonia. Certainly, the ominous presence of Franco's paramilitary Guardia Civil added to the air of oppression and fear. Catalonian boycotts and strikes in the 1950s were not taken lightly by the Guardia Civil, and harsh police activity tended to follow relatively peaceful demonstrations by Catalans. Opposition was not tolerated.

Substantial relief from such oppression was not achieved until Franco's death in 1975, at which point Juan Carlos was sworn in as king and presided over the dissolution of Franco's institutions in a relatively smooth transition to liberal democracy. Pressure from Catalonia, as well as the Basque region, for major structural change heightened the already potentially explosive situation.

Unlike the Basque region, pro-regional sentiment in Catalonia had never shown itself in a widespread movement for complete independence. Since the late 1970s, Catalonia's 17 autonomous states have again been recognized by the central government, and local institutions have attempted to rebuild Catalonia's national identity. Catalan is again the main language of schools and government. Today, the situation in Catalonia has improved dramatically since the years of Franco's dictatorship. But Catalans still remember that their frustrations only intensified under Franco; they did not originate with him. While Catalonia has never called for independence, they seek greater political autonomy in which the region's own history, identity, and institutions would be recognized within the Spanish state. One major means of cultural autonomy is the teaching and use of the Catalan language rather than Spanish. The population is about evenly split between Catalan and Spanish speakers, with some being bilingual. At the Summer Olympics, Catalans asked that Catalan be treated as an official language along with Spanish and English. In some towns and cities, instruction is being offered in Catalan rather than Spanish. This policy is resisted by those who believe that Spanish will better serve their children in a nation and world where Spanish is a far more widely spoken language.

Hansen, Edward. (1977) *Rural Catalonia under the Franco Regime: The Fate of Rural Culture since the Spanish Civil War.*

McDonogh, Gary. (1986) *Good Families of Barcelona: A Social History of Power in the Colonial Era.*

Medhurst, Kenneth. (1982) *The Basques and Catalans.*

Woolard, Kathryn. (1989) *Double Talk: Bilingualism and the Politics of Ethnicity in Catalonia.*

CATHOLICS AND PROTESTANTS IN NORTHERN IRELAND

The last remaining section of Ireland that is under British rule, Northern Ireland comprises six of the nine counties of Ulster: Antrim, Armagh, Down, Fermanagh, Londonderry, and Tyrone. In 1993 the census population totaled 1.57 million for the 5,463-square-mile area. The majority of the population occupies the eastern portion of the province; the western half remains largely undeveloped. The populace is divided into two major religious groups: Roman Catholics (34.9 percent) and Protestants (58.2 percent), the overwhelming majority of which are Presbyterian. Cross-cutting religious affiliation are ties to Ireland or Britain, with the majority of Catholics seeing themselves as Irish and the majority of Protestants seeing themselves as British. In addition to religion and national allegiance, the groups are also divided economically. The Catholics perceive themselves as a discriminated-against minority as regards equal opportunity in employment and housing. The conflict is also characterized by considerable ethnocentrism and stereotyping, with a long history of the English defining the Irish as socially inferior. The ongoing conflict over Northern Irish independence from Britain and linkage with Ireland involves a mix of issues including the last vestiges of British colonialism; irredentist desires by the Northern Irish Catholics, the Irish in Ireland, and overseas Irish communities; issues of minority rights; and social-class conflict. To some extent, Northern Ireland is divided along religious lines, with Protestants and Catholics tending to associate primarily with others of their own religion. However, this bifurcation of Northern Irish society is more extreme in urban than rural settlements.

In 1920 the British Parliament passed the Government of Ireland Act, which legislated partition of Ireland, forming what is now known as the Republic of Ireland and leaving Northern Ireland as a province under British rule. This reflected centuries of British control and civil unrest in a geographically united Ireland. During the seventeenth and eighteenth centuries, compensation was given to British soldiers in the form of large plots of Irish land. By the nineteenth century, 80 percent of the land in a predominantly Catholic Ireland was controlled by the Protestant British elite (known as the *Ascendancy*), who accounted for less than 10 percent of the population. The British government later concentrated its colonization efforts in Ulster, the northeastern province, in an attempt to dismantle the strongly Catholic Gaelic culture. This effort succeeded only in Ulster, and was due to the large number of Protestant Scots who emigrated to the area. The resulting hostility has had negative effects for all involved. For example, during the course of industrialization in Ulster, it would perhaps have been beneficial to the Protestant working class to support the reforms demanded by the Catholic population of Ireland.

The working classes of both religious affiliations suffered much the same problems as a result of British rule. But the religious fervor of the era prevented most Protestants from becoming sympathetic to the Catholic demands for change, and kept them loyal to the British government. As a result, working-class Protestants were little inclined to fight for economic reforms that in fact would have served their own interests. Several minimal concessions to the Catholic demand for Home Rule served only to escalate tensions between Catholics and Protestants, prompting the appearance of such militant groups as the Ulster Volunteer Force and the Irish Republican Army (IRA). By the early twentieth century, after continuous failure on the part of the British government to implement any effective reforms, and in reaction to the growing threat of civil war, a compromise was reached in the form of the Government of Ireland Act, which established the Republic of Ireland and kept British sovereignty over the six counties of Ulster.

Although Northern Ireland was intended to be a safely Protestant state, the large minority of Catholics included in the geographic area ensured that religious and class conflict would remain a presence. From its beginning, Northern Ireland has been plagued with violence. Vigilante groups, essentially formed in the prepartition days, developed into organized military and political forces with support within Ireland and among segments of Irish communities overseas, especially in the United States. Responding to the growing violence and to numerous requests by the Unionists in Northern Ireland, in September 1920 the British government organized the Ulster Special Constabulary. One branch of the Constabulary, eventually known as the B Specials, became particularly accomplished in organizing murderous attacks on Catholic communities. These acts of terrorism, along with continued sectarian rivalry, succeeded not only in keeping Protestants loyal to the Ulster government but in further stirring up

Catholics, who were rapidly becoming essentially powerless. To ensure this continued Protestant loyalty, the British fostered the rivalry and instituted policies favoring the Protestant population, further separating the religious factions of the working class. As a result, violence increased on both sides. More than 700 northerners were killed, and more than 25,000 Catholics fled the country.

During the 1960s and 1970s, while the world witnessed the civil rights movement in the United States, a similar movement emerged in Northern Ireland. Partially enabled by a series of reforms implemented to appease the Catholic community, these reforms allowed greater upward socioeconomic mobility for Catholics, particularly in the area of education, and resulted in the growing presence of a Catholic middle class. However, mass demonstrations by the Catholic community prompted the formation of Protestant vigilante groups, who viewed these actions as serious threats. Bombing campaigns by both the Ulster Volunteer Force and the IRA became more frequent. The violence escalated even more after the British government sent troops to Belfast and Londonderry to control it.

After 50 years of civil strife, the British government, with William Whitelaw at the helm as secretary of state for Northern Ireland, resumed direct control over Northern Ireland in 1972, not short of occupation of major cities by the British army. Working closely with Brian Faulkner, former prime minister of Northern Ireland under Unionist rule, they gained support for power sharing with the (moderate) Catholics, and were thus able to win promises from both the British government and the Republic of Ireland of cooperation with northern authorities. The Republic of Ireland further agreed to step up measures against the IRA, who had turned their terrorism focus outside Northern Ireland since the 1950s. In 1974 a coalition government was formed and called the Northern Executive. Although this coalition was composed of members of both the Protestant and Catholic communities, the number of groups opposed to this coalition far outweighed those who supported it, and the anti–power-sharing groups eventually brought about the demise of the coalition government. At that point, all proposed options for a new government with any political viability whatsoever were absolutely opposed by the Catholic community. The formation of the Ulster Defense Association (UDA), recruited mainly from the Protestant working class, meant the strong possibility of civil war in the province. The UDA was unequivocally opposed to any form of Catholic support, from Provisional IRA to moderates. The three major military groups present in the province have clashed on several occasions in different combinations. British army/IRA, UDA/British army, and the ever-present IRA/UDA conflicts have kept the region at a standstill and allowed very minimal progress. At this point, both the Catholics and the Protestants would prefer that the British army withdraw, but both groups have convinced the British government that a withdrawal of military troops will ensure civil war in Northern Ireland. British popular opinion has turned to disgust and a readiness to be rid of the problem. British civilians have been victims of IRA terrorism on too many occasions to sympathize with their plight any longer. Any action by one group seems only to trigger an emotional response by another and, at this point, no groups or coalition of groups have succeeded in implementing a successful solution to the problem. The 1990s have seen an increase in IRA terrorism directed at civilian targets in Northern Ireland and Britain, including bombings in the cities of London and Manchester. The late 1993 development of direct talks between the British government and Sinn Fein (the political wing of the IRA), and private discussions with the IRA itself, have created some hope for a peaceful resolution. Out of these talks came a joint declaration that all parties who renounce violence are welcome to participate in future negotiations, that Northern Ireland will remain part of Britain so long as its citizens wish it to, and that Ireland might revise its constitution to weaken its claim to Northern Ireland. At the same time, violence by both the IRA and Protestant extremists continues.

Darby, John, ed. (1985) *Northern Ireland: The Background to the Conflict.*

Harris, Rosemary. (1972) *Prejudice and Tolerance in Ulster: A Study of Neighbours and "Strangers" in a Border Community.*

Lebow, Richard N. (1976) "Vigilantism in Northern Ireland." In *Vigilante Politics,* edited by H. Jon Rosenbaum and Peter C. Sederberg, 234–258.

Moxon-Browne, Edward. (1983) *Nation, Class, and Creed in Northern Ireland.*

CHAKMA IN BANGLADESH

The People's Republic of Bangladesh is located in South Asia on the north bend of the Bay of Bengal. The nation encompasses 55,813 square miles and is bordered by India on the east, north, and west, and by Myanmar (formerly Burma) on the southeast. In 1993 the estimated population was 114 million with a remarkably homogenous ethnic constitution of 98 percent Bengali, the overwhelming majority of whom are Muslim. The remaining 2 percent is composed of Bihari and tribal peoples, including the Chakma, or *Changma,* as they call themselves. The ongoing conflict between the Chakma and the Bangladesh government concerns Chakma efforts to regain indigenous rights lost during

British colonialism and which further eroded after independence.

The Muslim conquest of the Bengal region of South Asia began in the late twelfth and early thirteenth centuries, following nearly a millennium of successive Buddhist and Hindu rule. During this gradual Muslim invasion, much of the local population converted to Islam. Muslim rule held until the mid-eighteenth century, when Britain gained control of the area that is now Bangladesh, India, and Pakistan. British rule was most favorably accepted by the Hindu population, who responded to the Westernization of the region more readily than did the Muslims. When the independence movement began to develop in the late nineteenth century, the goal of the Hindus was a free, secular state. Muslims advocated a separate Islamic state (Pakistan), which was established in 1947. The Bengal region then found itself a part of two separate nation-states. In India, the western portion of Bengal became the Indian state of West Bengal, and the eastern portion became East Pakistan, separated by some 1,000 miles of India from Pakistan proper. In 1971 civil war broke out in East and West Pakistan (Bengalis versus non-Bengalis), which resulted in Indian intervention and the establishment of the nation of Bangladesh (or "Bengali Homeland") in 1974.

The Chakma are a tribal group who inhabit the Chittagong Hills of southeastern Bangladesh. Some Chakma also live in India (the Chittagong Hills region extends into the Indian northeast). The Chakma are of Southeast Asian origin and the Buddhist faith, and comprise the majority of the tribal population in the Chittagong region, with a 1981 population of 212,000. It is believed the Chakma immigrated to what is now Bangladesh from Burma (now called Myanmar) around the sixteenth century. At that time the area was under Muslim control; the British had not yet arrived. The Chakma entered into a trade agreement with the Muslim leaders and were allowed to live in the Chittagong Hills. After the British gained control of the area in the late eighteenth century, there was periodic fighting between the Chakma and the British until 1787, when Chakma *raja* (leader) Janbrix Khan signed a peace treaty with the British government that maintained peaceful relations until the end of British rule, and the hilly region maintained an officially designated tribal status. This tribal status was revoked in 1964, and in the years since there has been an influx of Bengali Bangladeshis who are overwhelmingly Muslim. As a result, the Chakma (and other tribes) no longer represent the majority in this region; the Chakma now make up only 30 percent of the population. The indigenous language is extinct and the Chakma now speak a dialect of Bangla, the language of the Bengali majority.

In the late 1960s and early 1970s, the Chakma (and the other regional tribes) began to demand greater autonomy and an end to the Muslim influx. In 1972, after a rejection of these demands and only a year after the emergence of Bangladesh as a new nation, the tribal groups formed an organization called the *Shanti Bahini* (meaning "Peace Force"), which has since essentially evolved into a guerrilla army. The Shanti Bahini is not a separatist group; they do not want independence from Bangladesh. Rather, they seek protection of the region's demographic character (end of Muslim settlers), free elections, greater economic and political powers, and the formation of an autonomous state within Bangladesh. The political wing of the Shanti Bahini is the *Jana Sanghata Samiti* (or "People's Struggle Organization").

Since the emergence of Bangladesh, the influx of Muslim settlers to the previously tribal region, and the establishment of the Shanti Bahini, the Chakma have been subjected to a bitter military campaign by the Bangladesh government, which has sent nearly 51,000 refugee tribespeople into India since 1986, mainly into the Indian state of Tripura. In recent years the central government and the Chakma have attempted to negotiate a solution, and in 1993 India and Bangladesh agreed to a plan for the return of the refugees, and Bangladesh agreed to halt the flow of nontribal peoples into the region.

Bessaigner, Pierre. (1958) *Tribesmen of the Chittagong Hill Tracts.*

Chakravarty, S. R., and V. Narain, eds. (1986) *Bangladesh: History and Culture.*

Chaudhuri, Buddhadeb. (1991) "Ethnic Conflict in the Chittagong Hill Tracts of Bangladesh." In *Economic Dimensions of Ethnic Conflict,* edited by S. W. R. de A. Samarasighe and Reed Coughlan.

CHECHEN-INGUSH IN RUSSIA

Chechen-Ingushetia is a predominantly Muslim enclave within the northern Caucasus region of Russia. Chechenia and Ingushetia were separate administrative territories until 1934, when they were joined by the Soviet government into the Chechen-Ingush Autonomous Republic. The traditional Chechen-Ingush territory is located northwest of Georgia, reaching from approximately 42 to 44 degrees north latitude and about 45 to 46 degrees east longitude. In 1989 the combined population was estimated at 1,194,317, composed of 237,438 Ingush and 956,879 Chechen. This figure includes communities formed in Jordan, Turkey, and Syria in the mid-nineteenth century by Chechen and some Ingush who fled there following wars with the Russians in the Caucasus. The Chechen and Ingush languages are distinct from one another, although in those areas where the groups cohabited, both languages are spoken. Traditionally written in Arabic, the script was changed to Latin and then Cyrillic during the Soviet period. Because of Russian dominance, most Ingush are fluent in Russian, as are some Chechen.

Regular contact between the Russians and Chechen-Ingush began in the 1600s when Cossacks invaded the region, and relations have been difficult ever since. The invasion of the Caucasus led to Russian domination and drove some Chechen and Ingush south to Turkey, Jordan, and Syria. During the eighteenth and nineteenth centuries, the Chechen and Ingush converted from their traditional animistic religion to Islam, a move that was most likely politically motivated. It is believed that the groups made the conversion in order to align themselves with the Caucasian resistance to the Russians. Today Islam is the religion of the overwhelming majority of the population and has become a key element in their ethnic identity. Following the Russian Revolution, Chechen-Ingush culture flourished for about two decades before it was repressed under Joseph Stalin. In 1944 Stalin forcefully deported the Chechen-Ingush to Siberia. Although the official reason was that the Chechen-Ingush collaborated with the Nazis, it was more an attempt at cleansing the area of Muslims in case of an invasion by Turkey, a Muslim nation. The group was not allowed to return to their region until 1956 in what was officially labeled "rehabilitation." In their absence, their republic had officially ceased to exist. Present-day tensions between the Ingush and the Ossetes stem from this period in which territory previously controlled by the Ingush came under Ossetian control.

Conflict with the Russians, however, remains a greater threat to Chechen-Ingush cultural and political autonomy. In reaction to the breakup of the Soviet Union and the establishment of an independent Russian nation to be composed of former administrative regions, in 1991 the Chechen-Ingush mounted an

43

independence movement led by General Djokhar Dudayev, who was elected president in October of that year with nearly 85 percent of the vote. In November the Chechen-Ingush Autonomous Republic declared its independence and secession from Russia. Russian president Boris Yeltsin imposed emergency rule on the region in an attempt to suppress another in a series of separatist conflicts facing the former Soviet Union and threatening economic and political stability. The emergency-rule decree included the dispatch of nearly 600 troops to the region and a confiscation of firearms. At this time, the status of the Chechen-Ingush region as an independent republic remains unresolved.

Nichols, Johanna. (1994) "Chechen-Ingush." In *Encyclopedia of World Cultures. Volume 6, Russia/Eurasia and China,* edited by Paul Friedrich and Norma Diamond, 71–76.

COLONIALISM

Colonialism is a form of ethnic, political, and economic relations in which people from one society dominate members of another society (or societies) that is geographically distant and whose members are physically, culturally, and linguistically different. This form of colonialism is called *exploitation colonialism,* and differs from *settlement colonization,* in which a distant people displaces another people or peoples and settles their territory, as occurred in the European conquest of North America, Australia, and New Zealand. Since the sixteenth century, nearly all regions of the world have been at some point under European colonial domination. The only large regions not subject to such domination are Russia, China, Thailand, Iran, and Afghanistan. The major European colonial powers were Britain, France, Germany, Belgium, the Netherlands, Spain, and Portugal. Denmark and Italy were minor colonists, while Japan colonized Korea and islands south of the Japanese archipelago. With the exception of Hong Kong, which will return from British to Chinese control in 1997, all colonial territories are now either independent or semi-independent nations. However, in some places exploitation colonialism has been replaced by newer forms of colonialism such as internal colonialism, neocolonialism, and Third World colonialism.

Internal colonialism is a form of majority group–minority group relations in which the minority group is treated much the same as a colonized group under exploitation colonialism. Thus, internally colonized groups perform a disproportionately high share of low-paid, unskilled labor, are subject to control by the majority, are viewed and treated ethnocentrically in accord with dominant culture values, and are the victims of a racist ideology. For example, in the United States, African-Americans and Mexican-Americans have been described as internally colonized because they have been coerced, through physical force or economic control by the white majority, to live in a foreign society, their participation in American society is restricted, and their traditional cultures are considered inferior by the majority white population. Internal colonialism also refers to the incorporation of culturally different regions into a nation, such as Brittany into France.

Neocolonialism refers to the political and economic relations between developed and developing nations (mostly former colonies) in the world, where the former are able to benefit, at least in part, from previous colonization gained from their superior power and wealth. Among the common features of neocolonialism are an emphasis on the production of raw materials for export in formerly colonized nations, large trade imbalances between developed and developing nations, tourism as a major source of income in developing nations, political control by a Western-educated elite, and a high rate of immigration to industrialized nations.

Third World Colonialism

Third World colonialism is a postcolonial phenomenon in which formerly colonized regions that have become independent nations colonize indigenous, minority peoples within their boundaries as part of economic development, territorial expansion, and the building of a nationalistic sentiment. Bangladesh's efforts to exploit the resources in the territories of internal tribal peoples and Indonesia's efforts to acquire territory and integrate numerous indigenous peoples into Indonesian society are two recent examples.

Indonesia is an island nation (over 13,000 islands) covering some 735,268 square miles of land and water, with a population of 187 million in 1993. Under Dutch rule from 1697 to 1942, it became an independent nation in 1949. Culturally, politically, and economically, the nation is controlled by the Javanese, Madurese, and Balinese, three related island cultures who comprise about 63 percent of the national population. There are altogether over 300 cultural groups in Indonesia. Despite this diversity, there is commonality across Indonesian cultures—about 87 percent of the people are Muslim, the irrigation of rice is the primary traditional subsistence activity of most groups, and nearly all speak Austronesian languages. As part of its nation-building program, the Javanese-dominated Indonesian government has engaged in a number of Third World colonial activities, most of which are little different from earlier European colonialism. These include the taking of territories by military force (such as East Timor and Irian Jaya), the establishment of the Javanese-based Bahasa Indonesian as the national language, and the resettlement of Javanese on other islands, particularly those distant from

African immigrants camped on a street in suburban Paris to protest the scarcity of decent low-income housing, 1992.

Java and the capital city of Jakarta. Indonesian colonialism has been most aggressive in Irian Jaya and East Timor. Irian Jaya is the western region of the island of New Guinea, and the dozens of indigenous peoples there are culturally unrelated to the peoples of Indonesia. In 1969 Indonesia simply made a province of what is now Irian Jaya, an action reinforced by military invasion and occupation, forced relocation of indigenous peoples, and indoctrination into Indonesian culture. Timor, an island in eastern Indonesia, has been occupied by the Indonesians since 1975, and the campaign to incorporate the island and its people into Indonesia has led to massive population relocation and to the killing of several hundred thousand indigenous Atoni.

Exploitation Colonialism

The two key elements of exploitation colonialism were the technological superiority of the European colonists over the native peoples in the New World, Africa, Southeast Asia, and the Pacific, and the use of a racist ideology to justify the genocide and ethnocide typical of both settlement and exploitation colonialism. Some colonial powers such as Germany and Britain viewed non-European peoples as nonhuman, and thus not entitled to the same treatment afforded Europeans. Other colonial powers such as Spain, Portugal, and France were less racist, although they still viewed non-Europeans as inferior forms of humanity who would benefit from colonial domination. Exploitation colonialism was confined mainly to tropical or subtropical climatic regions, primarily because such regions were not hospitable locales for settlement colonization. Rather, because of heat, humidity, and diseases, tropical regions took a high toll on European settlers. The landscape was rarely suitable for European-style agriculture, and many tropical regions were heavily populated by native societies—for example, West Africa—that could offer stiff resistance to European attempts to take land and resources.

Exploitation colonialism was primarily an economic arrangement in which the colonizers used native labor to extract raw materials from the colony. The raw materials were transported to the home country for consumption or for the production of goods, some of which were then sold back to indigenous peoples in the same colonies. Although there were variations from colonizer to colonizer and region to region (detailed below), there were four key elements to successful exploitation colonialism. First, the resident European population was small, and was involved mainly in administering the territory and managing the native labor force. Second, European control was often established through the use of military force and the construction of a transportation system that facilitated the flow of raw materials from the interior to ports for shipment to Europe. Third, colonial economic enterprises such as coffee, tea, and banana plantations and mining operations were completely reliant on local labor to exploit local resources. Fourth, local labor was managed through "indirect rule"—that is, European administrators used local ethnic-group leaders as their agents. Local leaders were often rewarded financially for their efforts and kept in power by the Europeans, who played on existing ethnic rivalries. Laborers were made dependent on European wages once they were drawn into the money economy as consumers of European-produced goods.

Colonialism and Ethnic Relations

Colonialism had a number of immediate and long-term effects on ethnic relations in what is now defined as the Third World. First, under the colonial systems there was a nearly absolute separation of Europeans from native peoples, with the former constituting the upper class and the latter a class of workers. Second, colonial use of existing ethnic rivalries and ethnic managers tended to make some groups dominant over others, which often led to ethnic conflict such as that involving the Hutu and Tutsi in Burundi and Rwanda, and the Sousse and other groups in Guinea. Third, the artificial national boundaries created by the colonial powers in Africa ignored already existing tribal boundaries and has led to ethnic tensions in many multiethnic African nations such as Kenya and Nigeria, hampering both political and economic stability. Fourth, in Latin America there was considerable interbreeding between European colonists and indigenous peoples and Africans (slaves), producing a whole new social category of mixed-ancestry peoples, and a new social order in which relative skin color became a major influence on social status, a pattern that is only now beginning to weaken as both the indigenous peoples and African-Americans emphasize their ethnicity rather than skin color. Fifth, missionary activities, which almost always accompanied colonization, led to the large-scale conversion of many peoples to Christianity, the demise of many indigenous religions, and the development of new, syncretic religions based on a merging of traditional religions and Christianity.

The following three case studies focus on three different colonial powers—Britain, France, and Spain—in three different places—India, West Africa, and Mexico—and highlight some of the major effects on native cultures of colonial domination strategies such as division and conquest, indirect rule, the use of ancient ethnic rivalries, and forced population migrations, as well as the continued effects of those practices.

British Colonialism in Northeast India

Prior to the imposition of British rule, the principal inhabitants of the region of northeast India called *Jhankhand* were dozens of tribal groups, today called Scheduled Tribes. Among the major groups are the Santals (comprised of a dozen or more named subgroups), Oraons, Mundas, and Hos. Traditionally, they were all forest peoples, subsisting through the exploitation of the environment, primarily by plow agriculture and slash-and-burn farming practices, but also by hunting, gathering, and fishing. The forest not only provided food, shelter, and raw materials but also occupied a central place in their worldview and religion. Another key defining concept for these tribal peoples was *diku*, meaning a nontribal outsider whose culture stood in opposition to the central themes of their own tribal culture. Each group was governed by village leaders and religious leaders although, before the arrival of the British, a form of feudalism had already developed, with regional leaders called *rajas* owning much of the land, renting land to poorer individuals who farmed it, and collecting taxes from the inhabitants of their territory.

The British colonial goals were (1) to place regional *maharajah* under their control, thereby giving the British control of the region, and (2) to pacify the region so that trade could flow safely across northern India to and from the Bay of Bengal. British methods included physical force, such as executions and village burning; the creation of a British administrative structure, with responsibilities for oversight of the indigenous population resting with the British officials; and isolation of the "tribals" on the equivalent of reservations while the remainder of the land was controlled and exploited by the British. The effects on the indigenous peoples were far-reaching: They were deprived of the right to control and use much of their land, and famine forced many to migrate to Assam for work on tea plantations. There also were forced migrations to cities, displacement of the majority population by nontribal migrant workers, and urban growth that turned some tribal communities into internal colonies. Following Indian independence, efforts were made to reverse the effects of colonialism on the tribal peoples across India. These included their designation as Scheduled Tribes, special positive discrimination programs such as preference in hiring and guaranteed legislative representation, and inclusion in the regional political-party leadership. However, the tribals remain a numerical and sociological minority in their homeland, and today some are involved in sometimes violent conflict in order to regain their indigenous rights and control over a share of the region's resources.

French in West Africa

The nation now called Guinea was a colony of France from 1898 to 1958. Before French rule, this area went through over a century of indigenous rule. From 1770 to 1830 the region was ruled by the Islamic Almany Empire of Futa Djallow, who used Islam and military power to unify separate hill kingdoms into a centralized cultural and political whole. From 1870 to 1898, the region was ruled by the Mandinka Empire, who used military force rather than Islam as the unifying power before they were defeated by the French. The first task for the French was to establish control, which they accomplished by ignoring the Islamic hierarchy and instead using clan leaders as their local representatives. Their use of clan leaders had the added advantage of reigniting old clan rivalries and boundary disputes, thereby rendering any kind of coordinated opposition to French rule virtually impossible. In addition, the French established a small elite of ethnic Soussou teachers, administrators, and technicians in the city of Conakry, a group that was pushed toward French citizenship following World War II. Economically, the French were mainly interested in the coffee and banana crops, and they built railways and towns inland to support these activities. Following independence in 1958, a major task facing the Guinea government was to establish ethnic cooperation; that is, to reverse the French-encouraged pattern of ethnic rivalry and separatism. To do so, the government mandated ethnic representation in the national assembly and attempted to balance the economic contributions made by different groups to the national economy. However, economic stability was never achieved and ethnic equality did not last, with the Soussou remaining in many of the key government and economic positions while other groups suffered the effects of economic crises such as unemployment.

Spanish in Latin America

Prior to the arrival of the Spanish in 1519, Mexico and Guatemala were the home of American Indian nations who subsisted primarily as farmers. While there were wealth distinctions within these nations, the acquisition of wealth was important only as a source of social status. The Spanish, on the contrary, were interested in exploiting the land and people for raw materials that could be converted into goods for sale. Within the first century of colonization, the Spanish established gold and silver mines; farms growing wheat, sugar cane, cacao,

and indigo, as well as processing centers; and cattle, pork, and sheep ranches. All of these enterprises were managed by Spaniards, with the Indians providing the labor. When there were not enough Indians, slaves from Africa and Asia were imported to fill the gap. Initially, Indian labor was obtained under the *encomienda* system, in which Spanish settlers had the right to tribute and work from Indians in certain villages. This system was replaced by a regulated labor system in which Spanish royalty controlled the temporary allocation of Indian laborers to Spanish settlers. By 1650 about 80 percent of the Indian population had died, primarily because of European-introduced diseases, but also from military campaigns and famine. In order to further exploit the remaining Indian labor, the *hacienda* system evolved, with Spanish colonists owning estates and the Indians living in small, exclusively Indian communities. The Indians worked for the Spaniards, and as they became economically and psychologically dependent on them, they developed into a rural peasantry, an entirely new socioeconomic category in the New World. Despite the economic distance between the Spanish and Indians, there was considerable interbreeding, producing a new social category of individuals of mixed ancestry called *mestizos*. Unlike the Indian peasants, *mestizos* were individualists interested in personal power and wealth, rapidly becoming political and economic middlemen in the Spanish system. Many were later prominently involved in the Mexican and Guatemalan revolutions, land reform movements that ended the hacienda system and formed the new generation of political leaders.

See also ETHNOCENTRISM; RACE AND RACISM; REVITALIZATION MOVEMENTS; SLAVERY; SYNCRETIC CULTURES.

Balandier, Georges. (1970) *The Sociology of Black Africa.*

Blauner, Robert. (1972) *Racial Oppression in America.*

Boahen, A. Adu. (1987) *African Perspectives on Colonialism.*

Corbridge, Stuart. (1987) "Ousting Singbonga: The Struggle for India's Jharkhand." In *Colonialism and Development in the Contemporary World,* edited by Chris Dixon and Michael Heffernan, 153–182.

Dirks, Nicholas B., ed. (1992) *Colonialism and Culture.*

Hechter, Michael. (1975) *Internal Colonialism: The Celtic Fringe in British National Development, 1536–1966.*

Hurtsfield, Jennifer. (1978) "'Internal' Colonialism: White, Black and Chicano Self-Conceptions." In *Ethnic and Racial Studies* 1: 60–79.

Nietschmann, Bernard. (1988) "Third World Colonial Expansion: Indonesia, Disguised Invasion of Indigenous Nations." In *Tribal Peoples and Development Issues: A Global Overview,* edited by John H. Bodley, 191–207.

Slowe, Peter M. (1991) "Colonialism and the African Nation: The Case of Guinea." In *Colonialism and Development in the Contemporary World,* edited by Chris Dixon and Michael Heffernan, 106–120.

van den Berghe, Pierre L. (1981) *The Ethnic Phenomenon.*

Wolf, Eric. (1959) *Sons of the Shaking Earth.*

CONSOCIATIONAL DEMOCRACY

A consociational democracy is a form of national organization that is thought to be tied to peaceful ethnic relations in multiethnic nations. The consociational democracy was first described by political scientist Arend Lijphart. Originally applied to the Netherlands, it has subsequently been used to account for peaceful relations among ethnic groups in Switzerland, Austria, Belgium, and Lebanon, and has been suggested as a solution to ethnic conflict in Canada, Northern Ireland, and emerging Third World democracies.

At its core, a consociational democracy is a nation where ethnic relations are peaceful because of cooperation at the national level among the elites representing each ethnic group. Ethnic elites cooperate with one another when their mutual interests, such as political power and wealth, are more likely to be met through ethnic cooperation than through ethnic competition. The four primary features of consociational democracies are (Lijphart 1977): (1) "government by a grand coalition" of representatives of the ethnic groups in the nation; (2) "the mutual veto or concurrent majority rule"; (3) proportional representation on government bodies and in government employment and in the distribution of government funds; and (4) "a high degree of autonomy for each segment to run its own internal affairs."

In addition, characteristics of nations with a consociational form of government include a clear separation among the ethnic groups, a balance of power among the groups, an external threat shared by all groups, a moderate level of nationalism, relatively little economic and political pressure on the national system, and small size. Additionally, it seems clear that consociational deomcracy does not occur in multiethnic societies where ethnic variation is based on physical differences such as skin color.

The consociational democracy is more a prescription for peaceful ethnic relations in societies where a long history of contact has not led to assimilation than it is a description of the actual state of ethnic relations in any nation. With the exception of Switzerland, there is probably no nation in the world that is currently a consociational democracy. Switzerland's situation is also unique because of its physical isolation from other nations, and the absence of resources that would have made it desirable as a target for conquest. It seems that if consociational democracy were to be an alternative to other forms of ethnic relations in multiethnic nations, it would work best where the ethnic groups are already integrated through mixed living patterns, intermarriage, a shared role and benefits from societal institutions, and perhaps a common religion, such as in Belgium.

See also PLURALISM.

Barry, Brian. (1975) "Review Article: Political Accommodation and Consociational Democracy." *British Journal of Political Science* 5: 477–505.

Brass, Paul R. (1991) *Ethnicity and Nationalism.*

Lijphart, Arend. (1977) *Democracy in Plural Societies.*

van den Berghe, Pierre L. (1981) *The Ethnic Phenomenon.*

COPTS IN EGYPT

The Coptic Church is the oldest church of Egypt, dating back to the first half of the first century A.D. This ancient religion is essentially a breakaway sect of Christianity, distinguished in 451 when the patriarch Dioscorus I was forced to defend his version of Christianity before a council led by the eastern emperor Marcion. In fact, the breakaway sect is actually the original, orthodox version of the church that eventually condemned it. Dioscorus believed in the orthodox interpretation of the coexistence of the divinity and humanity of Christ, and rejected the more modern catechetical school of Alexandria, which was much more of an arena for free religious thinking and scholastic endeavor. What is now distinguished as the Coptic Church are descendants of those followers who believed that this was basically heresy and clung to the original, orthodox roots of the religion and their beliefs about the nature and person of Christ. Dioscorus was condemned by the council and exiled. From this division of the Christian faith, two forms of Christianity emerged. One accepted the rulings of the council and became the mainstream form of Christianity; the other followed the condemned school of thought—this was the Coptic Church.

Copts are the most direct link to the Pharaonic history of Egypt; the name Copt is a derivative of the Greek word meaning "Egyptian." The theological dispute that prompted the Copt split with Rome preempted a period of persecution of the Copts by the Byzantine emperors in an effort to rid Christendom of any separatism. Copts, or Egyptians, were subjected to violence, humiliation, and extreme taxation. Not until the Arab invasion of Egypt was there an effective barrier between the Christians of the East and the West. While many Copts eventually converted to Islam after the Arab invasion of the seventh century, many more remained loyal to the Coptic Church and lived in relative harmony with their Muslim neighbors.

In recent decades, Copts in Egypt, who number 10 million and make up the proportionately largest religious minority in the Middle East, have come under attack by Muslim fundamentalists who seek to make Egypt an Islamic nation. The recent persecution of Coptic Christians is part of a larger fundamentalist initiative that emerged in the late 1970s. The aim of these fundamentalists is to destabilize the country with the use of violence. There are many fundamentalist organizations, most of which not only condone but advocate the taking of power by the use of force. They see this as more than a political agenda; they view it as a religious duty.

Attacks on Christians by Muslim fundamentalists range from public verbal and physical harassment and abuse to massacres such as a May 1992 incident in which Muslims gunned down 13 Christian peasants while they were farming their land. Bombings and the burning of Christian homes and businesses are no longer rare occurrences in Egypt. On a less violent scale, Coptic Christians are the victims of discrimination by the Egyptian government, which has all but removed Copts from positions of power and responsibility in government and the business community. While Copts once enjoyed political and economic prominence in Egypt, Parliamentary representation of Copts in 1993 is less than 1 percent, compared to as much as 10 percent in the 1940s. Although the current administration of President Mubarak, who has been in office since 1981, is relatively liberal and secular, it is drawing increased criticism from Copt leaders, who maintain that discrimination is all too common and that efforts to contain fundamentalist violence are both too little and too late.

The Coptic response to its own persecution has been peaceful and passive. More than half a million have left the country in the last decade, and those who remain follow a policy of nonaction. They remain firm in their profound spirituality, which they say has carried them through the past nearly 2,000 years. The official stand of the church is to reject social and political activism and other confrontational approaches, and instead to be patient. In line with this approach, there is little evidence that any extremist Coptic organizations have emerged in the past few decades.

Masri, Iris Habib el. (1978) *The Story of the Copts.*

Wakin, Edward. (1963) *A Lonely Minority: The Modern History of Egypt's Copts; The Challenge of Survival for Four Million Christians.*

CULTURAL RELATIVISM

The concept of cultural relativism is used in the study of other cultures as both a guiding principle and as a general ethical principle governing the cross-cultural perspective. The concept came into general use in anthropology in the 1930s when it was generally viewed as a dictum that the customs and beliefs of one culture cannot be compared to nor judged on the basis of the customs and beliefs of other cultures. This relativistic view of cultures was partly a reaction to the implicit or explicit racist and ethnocentric social evolutionary thinking of the late 1880s, in which cultures of the world were rated on "civilization" scales based on the assumption that Western culture was superior and non-Western cultures inferior. The relativistic perspective was also based on the widespread belief among social scientists that culture is adaptive and functional, and therefore all beliefs and customs of a particular culture exist because they are of some benefit to that culture.

Today, while some social scientists continue to employ this extreme relativistic view of cultures, others use the concept in a less rigid sense to mean that every culture should be studied and understood in the context of its possibly unique possibilities and limitations, while at the same time leaving open the possibility that some beliefs and practices may be harmful and less adaptive than beliefs and customs found in other cultures. For example, a belief that illness and death is caused by witchcraft may be less adaptive than a belief in the germ theory of disease causation that allows many diseases to be cured or prevented. This application of the concept of cultural relativism allows those who study or work with people from other cultures to question and reject cultural practices such as racial discrimination and child-beating, which are harmful to the victims, while at the same time avoiding ethnocentric judgments of the culture itself.

An alternative to the relativistic view is the univeralist view of cultures. In this view, because of underlying biological and cultural factors, the basic features of all cultures are seen as essentially the same; they differ only in the details having to do with actual behaviors, beliefs, or customs that are manifestations of those basic features. Additionally, some of these features are seen as elementary, and therefore as the basis of other features of culture. For example, the incest taboo that prohibits sexual relations between certain categories of relatives is found in all societies, and it is elementary in the sense that it structures other relations, such as who may marry whom.

There is actually no one universalist position. Absolute universals are features, such as marriage, that appear in all cultures. Near-universals are features, such as romantic love, that appear in nearly all cultures (88 percent of cultures, in one survey). Statistical universals are features that appear in a greater number of cultures than would be expected by chance alone. For example, words that mean "little person" are used in many cultures to refer to the pupil of the eye, evidently because one sees his or her own reflection in another's eye.

Cultural universals result from a number of processes including: (1) diffusion, or the spread of cultural features from one culture to another through either peaceful contact or conquest; (2) common human experience; for example, all people in all cultures react to certain commonalities such as the weather; and (3) biological evolution, which has created inherited predispositions in the human central nervous system that lead to some like behaviors in all people.

If one accepts the universalist view (in any form) it is then logically possible to take it one step further and compare cultures, or even rate them on scales indicating the relative quality of life in the culture. Anthropologist Raoul Naroll, for one, attempted to rate the nations of the world in terms of the physical and mental health of their citizens and the degree of brotherhood, progress, and peace, among other attributes, displayed by the nation. He concluded that Norway was an exemplary society and one that could be held up as the standard for other societies. Similary, the United Nations compiles and publishes a Human Development Index that measures the happiness of the citizens of the countries of the world based on three factors—life expectancy, education, and individual purchasing power. The results of the 1993 Index place the following ten countries at the top of the list: Japan, Canada, Norway, Switzerland, Sweden, the United States, Australia, France, the Netherlands, and Britain. At the bottom of the list are poor, developing nations in Africa such as Somalia, Gambia, Mali, and Afghanistan. The index also shows that within nations there are often wide discrepancies in the quality of life between different groups and regions. For example, in all nations the quality of life is higher for men than for women, and in the United States, the quality of life is much higher for whites than for other ethnic groups.

See also ETHNOCENTRISM.

Benedict, Ruth. (1934) *Patterns of Culture.*

Berry, John W., et al.(1992) *Cross-Cultural Psychology: Research and Applications.*

Brown, Donald E. (1991) *Human Universals.*

Edgerton, Robert B. (1992) *Sick Societies: Challenging the Myth of Primitive Harmony.*

Hanson, F. Allan. (1975) *Meaning in Culture.*

Naroll, Raoul. (1983) *The Moral Order: An Introduction to the Human Situation.*

United Nations. (1993) *Human Development Report.*

CYPRIOTS

The island of Cyprus is an independent republic located in the eastern Mediterranean Sea 64 kilometers south of Turkey and 96 kilometers west of Syria. In 1991 the population was estimated to be 708,000. The capital is Nicosia, with a population of 166,000. The island encompasses 3,572 square miles, and is 141 miles long and 59 miles wide at its widest point. The population is comprised of two major ethnic groups—Greeks and Turks—as well as small populations of Armenians and Maronite Christians.

For more than 3,000 years the large majority of the population has been Greek; in 1991, 78 percent were estimated to be Greek in both language and culture. Greek Cypriots are generally members of the Orthodox Church of Cyprus, which is essentially a spinoff of the Eastern Orthodox Church. It was officially formed when the then-Christian Cypriots were subject to the Byzantine Empire in the second and third centuries. The church was granted autocephalous status in A.D. 488. Although archaeological records trace settlement on Cyprus to before 6000 B.C., it is believed that the first Greek immigrants began to arrive around 1200 B.C., and by 700 B.C., Greeks comprised a major portion of the population.

Cyprus has been ruled by several empires, from the Assyrians to the Persians to direct Greek rule in 323 B.C. Control of the island bounced back and forth among different rulers and was subject to frequent crusades until 1571, with the Turkish invasion. Ottoman rule of Cyprus lasted for approximately 300 years, during which time Muslim Turks established themselves as a strong and sizable minority on the island. Although Turkey maintained sovereignty over the island, unsatisfactory local rule and the fear of Russian penetration of the Ottoman Empire led to the establishment of a British administration with promises of rapid deployment of troops in the event of an attack by Russia. When Turkey entered World War I, the island, which was fighting on the opposite side, was immediately annexed by Britain. Cyprus became a British colony in 1925.

During the period of shifting control and Britain's 60-year hold over the island, two distinct and contradictory political agendas emerged within the Greek and Turkish communities on the island, and have since then played a key role in the ongoing ethnic conflict. *Enosis,* or the desired state of union with Greece, came just short of a battle cry for the Greek population. On the other side was *Takism,* or separation of Turks by Turks from the rest of Cyprus into an autonomous, independent nation. In typical British colonial fashion, a series of ineffective reforms and generally unacceptable political conditions led to frustration for both the Greeks and Turks, with the years between 1931 and 1959 plagued by violence on both sides, including bombings and demonstrations. In 1931 Greek members of the Legislative Council walked out of the Government House as angry crowds calling for *enosis* set it ablaze. This and other such demonstrations of the desire by Greek Cypriots to unite with Greece mobilized Turkish sentiment toward the British despite the fact that as a group they fared no better under British rule. British government, in essence, became another wedge between the Greeks and the Turks, driving them farther apart and sending them to opposite sides of the political spectrum rather than allowing them to cohabitate in a relatively peaceful manner. As agitation for *enosis* continued to increase, it culminated in both Greek and Turkish revolts.

Finally, in a three-way effort by the Greek Cypriots, Turkish Cypriots, and the British, and with the intervention of the United Nations, Cyprus was granted independent republic status by virtue of a constitution that allowed for participation by both Cypriot groups in the legislative, judicial, and executive branches of government. In theory, this represented compromise by all parties, but in practice it may have been too much of a compromise for each, and violence continued in spite of the island's new status as an independent republic. Fearing that the conflict might lead to a full-scale war between Greece and Turkey over control of the island, the U.N. sent a peacekeeping force to Cyprus in 1964 in an effort to contain the situation. A decade later, in reaction to the attempted assassination of the Cypriot president by Greece, Turkish forces seized the northern part of the island and established a Turkish state in that region. However, this independent status has never been formally recognized by any nation other than Turkey.

The current situation in Cyprus has not improved a great deal. Although there is less violence accompanying the Greek/Turkish conflict, this is mainly because the two groups live apart from one another as much as possible, and are basically separated by a guarded border. The northern third of Cyprus remains Turkish—the so-called Turkish Republic of Northern Cyprus continues to be recognized only by Turkey, and U.N. officials estimate that 30,000 Turkish troops are stationed along the unofficial border separating the two regions. The presence of these troops provides Greece with a constant reminder of the Turkish invasion of Cyprus in 1974—an invasion that Greeks feel went unpunished. Although the presence of U.N. forces has managed to keep peace in Cyprus, the two Cypriot communities have continued to grow apart in ways that cannot be controlled by laws or troops. Atrocities committed by both sides against the other are not easily forgotten, and those families displaced by the regional division are unlikely to forgive those who forced them to leave their homes. In fact, approximately 180,000 Greek Cypriots were either forced to leave or fled the northern portion of the island, and nearly 60,000 Turkish Cypriots were forced north. The United States and the other members of the U.N. Security Council have tried to lead Turks and Greeks toward a compromise that would reunify the island into a single state with autonomous Greek and Turkish regions. The U.N. has stated that it cannot maintain peacekeeping forces on the island indefinitely, although they have already been a presence for nearly 30 years.

Ertekun, N. M. (1984) *The Cyprus Dispute and the Birth of the Turkish Republic of Northern Cyprus.*

Kyle, Keith. (1984) *Cyprus.*

Loizos, Peter. (1981) *The Heart Grown Bitter: A Chronicle of Cypriot War Refugees.*

Szulc, Tad. (1993) "Cyprus: A Time of Reckoning." *National Geographic* 184: 104–130.

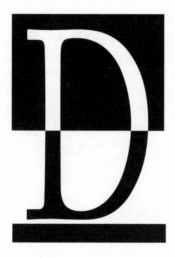

ously, to that homeland in one way or another, and their ethnocommunal consciousness and solidarity are importantly defined by the existence of such a relationship.

This definition covers a very broad range of communities; however, until recently the label *diaspora* has commonly been reserved for ethnic groups with a sizable percentage of their population living outside their homeland for at least several generations but who maintain some ties, even if only symbolic, to the homeland. From this perspective, four major diasporas are the Jewish, Indian, Chinese, and African. A description of each provides some insight into the commonalities that make each a diaspora and also illuminates the cross-cultural variation in diasporas.

DIASPORA

The mass movement of a people or some significant percentage of a population from its homeland to another territory or territories is a common feature of human history. A *diaspora* is a particular form of community formed by a mass movement and resettlement characterized by the following (Safran 1991, 83):

(1) they, or their ancestors, have been dispersed from a specific original "center" to two or more "peripheral," or foreign, regions; (2) they retain a collective memory, vision, or myth about their original homeland—its physical location, history, and achievements; (3) they believe that they are not—and perhaps cannot be—fully accepted by their host society and therefore feel partly alienated and insulated from it; (4) they regard their ancestral homeland as their true, ideal home and as such the place to which they or their descendants would (or should) eventually return—when conditions are appropriate; (5) they believe that they should, collectively, be committed to the maintenance or restoration of their original homeland and to its safety and prosperity; and (6) they continue to relate, personally or vicari-

Jewish Diaspora

The Jewish diaspora, which has lasted for 2,600 years, is considered the oldest, and at one time the term *diaspora* referred specifically to the Jewish one. For 2,000 years the diaspora existed without a Jewish state, and for 1,500 years the Jewish community existed only as a diaspora. The homeland was reestablished with the state of Israel in 1948, although, in a development not found in other diaspora-homeland relations (except for the establishment of Liberia by African-Americans), Israel was organized on principles taken from diaspora communities. One of the most important was the recognition of and allowance for two distinct diaspora religious traditions—Sephardic and Ashkenazic. The Jewish diaspora has existed as such for so long for a number of reasons. The most important is simply the absence of a physical homeland to return to. Others include the classification of Jews as outsiders by many host societies, bans on intermarriage with non-Jews, occupational specialization, a distinct religion, a distinct yearly and weekly calendar and daily schedule, and the central role played by the synagogue as an institution of community cohesion for diaspora communities. The Jewish diaspora differs from others also in that it has not been fixed in a particular place. Rather, the Jewish diaspora has been migratory, with communities relocating, sometimes voluntarily but more often because of expulsion. In the post–World War II world, the major diaspora center is in North America. The major diaspora of Europe disappeared with the deaths of 5–6 million Jews in World War II. The modern diaspora is characterized by relative freedom to practice Judaism openly, the right to settle in Israel, and support for Israel and Judaism through local, regional, national, and international networks or educational, social, political, community, and philanthropic organizations.

African Diaspora

The African diaspora is often equated with the Jewish one, as both were formed through forced expulsion from the homeland and also because both groups have long histories of suffering as victims of persecution in their diasporas. The African diaspora is mainly the product of slavery, first by Islamic nations, and later, on a much larger scale, by European colonial nations exporting slaves to the New World. The major African diaspora centers are Canada, the United States, the Caribbean islands, Middle America, and northern South America, particularly Brazil, Suriname, Colombia, and Venezuela. The United States and Brazil today have two of the four largest African-ancestry populations in the world, and in both nations they are the largest ethnic group.

The large diaspora in Britain is a product of secondary migration from former British possessions in the Caribbean. Here, as with most diasporas, there is considerable internal variation within diasporas. Thus, in the United States, in addition to variation based on social class and place of residence, there is also internal differentiation on the basis of religion and culture, with

a notable distinction between those whose ancestors were slaves in the United States and those whose ancestors were slaves in the Caribbean, such as Jamaicans, but who later migrated to the United States. Although the African diaspora in the New World dates to the early sixteenth century, physical and emotional ties to the African homeland are mainly a twentieth-century development. Because of a loss of links to the homeland cultures (at the time of enslavement the modern nations of Africa did not yet exist), the African homeland ties are to the African continent or, more specifically, to sub-Saharan Africa.

Diaspora ties to the homeland take a variety of forms. These include missionary activities to convert Africans to Christianity, back-to-Africa efforts, educational initiatives, special interest in political developments in Africa by the African-American community, support for African national independence movements, and the support of organizations that support African cultural, political, and educational activities. Recently there has also been the purposeful incorporation of African cultural elements into New World black culture. In the Caribbean and South America, this has taken the form of a more visible and political practice of syncretic religions, such as Voudun in Haiti, that are based on a mix of African and Catholic elements. In North America, links to the African homeland are now visible through the wearing of African dress, ornamentation, and hairstyles; giving children African names; conversion to Islam; the development of syncretic lifestyle ceremonies combining African and American rituals, and the Kwanzaa first fruits festival in the winter. However, as with the Jewish diaspora in North America, there has been no large-scale movement to return to the homeland.

Indian Diaspora

The Indian diaspora is composed of more than 11 million people who were, or whose ancestors

Chinese New Year's celebration in San Francisco. Performance of traditional rituals in diaspora communities helps maintain cultural links to the homeland.

were, from India now residing in 136 different nations. Nations outside of India with the largest Indian populations in 1980 were Nepal (3.8 million), Sri Lanka (1.3 million), Malaysia (1.2 million), Mauritius (625,000), Great Britain (500,000), Guyana (425,000), Trinidad and Tobago (421,000), the United States (365,000), and Fiji (300,000). The Indian diaspora is probably the most widespread of all and, with sizable populations in some nations, the most extensive in human history. It is also one of the oldest, dating to ancient times when people from north India migrated north and east into central Asia, Southeast Asia, and west to East Africa. During the British colonial period beginning in the 1800s, migration increased dramatically as the British exported Indians to other colonies in Africa, the West Indies, and Fiji, where they

worked as plantation workers, indentured servants, and low-level clerks and administrators in the colonial governments. More recently, and especially since the 1950s, Indian migration has been by choice, often involving highly educated Indians seeking employment or additional education in the Western world, particularly in the United States, Canada, Australia, and the Middle East. In the modern period, there has also been considerable secondary migration from nations in Africa, Fiji, and elsewhere to the Western world. While all migrants in the Indian diaspora are from the nation of India, some ethnic or regional groups such as the Sikhs, Gujaratis, and Punjabis make up a disproportionate percentage of the diaspora community.

Today, the Indian diaspora has six types of communities, based on their status within the host nation. In Sri Lanka, Fiji, and formerly in South Africa under apartheid, Indians are second-class citizens who coexist alongside a dominant group—whites in South Africa and Sinhalese in Sri Lanka. In Fiji, indigenous Fijians seized political control in 1987, and although Indo-Fijians are legally full citizens in social, political, and religious contexts, they have become second-class citizens. In Sri Lanka, however, one Indian community—the Tamils of Sri Lanka—are in open rebellion and seek political autonomy. In Trinidad-Tobago the Indians are independent and enjoy full rights, although colonial structures and sentiments remain strong. In Malaysia and East Africa the Indians are an auxiliary minority whose welfare depends on conformity to majority policies. In Myanmar (formerly Burma) and previously in central African nations such as Uganda, Indians are at considerable risk and face expulsion as scapegoats in times of political or economic unrest. In the United States, Canada, and Great Britain, Indians seek permanent residence and expect to assimilate. Finally, in the Middle East, Indians, like all other foreigners, are guest workers essentially without rights and without any expectation of permanent residence.

Although there is variation over time and from place to place, Indians maintain extensive ties with India, or more particularly with the homeland region or community. Indians in East Africa continue to see India as their ultimate place of residence and many return there upon retirement. For Indian merchants, India is a major supplier of goods, often through kinship networks. India is also a major source of spouses, with some Indians returning home to find spouses to take with them to the diaspora home. Contact with India is also maintained through Indian entertainers and religious leaders who travel to overseas communities as well as Indian movies shown privately and publicly overseas. Finally, diaspora Indians pour vast sums of money into the Indian economy through investments, purchases, and remittances, which in 1980 alone totaled some $4.46 billion.

Chinese Diaspora

The Chinese diaspora, commonly referred to as the Overseas Chinese, is composed of major Chinese urban populations in Southeast Asia and North America, and smaller populations elsewhere, including the Caribbean and Europe. Unlike the Jewish and African diasporas, which resulted from expulsion, and the Indian, which is partially voluntary and partially forced, the Chinese diaspora is mainly voluntary, both in Southeast Asia and North America. The diaspora began in the fourteenth century in Southeast Asia when the Chinese were drawn to major ports. After 1842 the Chinese were employed as laborers in colonial enterprises, and in Southeast Asia the colonial powers set them up as middlemen. Overseas Chinese now form large populations in Indonesia, Malaysia, Singapore, and Thailand, and are active participants in the national economies of all Southeast Asian nations, except perhaps for Vietnam, from which many were expelled in the 1970s. The Overseas Chinese diaspora is diverse. Those who arrived and stayed before the 1850s often intermarried, and many of their descendants no longer identify themselves as ethnically Chinese. In the Philippines, Malaysia, Singapore, and Indonesia, syncretic Chinese-indigenous cultures developed, such as the Baba of Singapore and the Peranakans of Indonesia, which exist as distinct communities alongside the Chinese diaspora and the indigenous population. Chinese have assimilated most rapidly in Buddhist nations such as Thailand, where they are coreligionists with the indigenous population, and less so in the Muslim nations of Malaysia and Indonesia. Chinese solidarity and identity is maintained throughout the Southeast Asian diaspora by the building and maintenance of temples, communal halls, dialect associations, economic associations, and involvement in family-owned businesses, which today may take the form of multinational corporations. In some nations, such as Indonesia and Thailand, a majority of Overseas Chinese speak the host language at home, suggesting a future of permanent residence and weaker ties to the homeland and other diaspora communities.

Homeland

The notion of homeland is extremely important in diasporas, as symbolic, emotional, and material ties to the homeland may bond the diaspora community together and distinguish it from other groups in the host nation. However, within any diaspora there is often considerable internal variation based on social class, place of residence (urban or rural), length of residence in the host nation, region of emigration, language, and politics. These internal variations also affect the extent to which different subgroups within a diaspora feel and act on ties to the homeland. For example, Lubavitcher Hasidic Jews in the United States are closely linked to Israel and their leader actively tries to influence Israeli policies. The Satmar Hasidic Jews, though culturally similar to the Lubavitchers and also resident in New York City, reject the state of Israel and seek no contact with it. Similarly, younger Chinese in the Philippines who are prevented from learning Chinese have fewer ties to China and are more assimilated into Filipino life than are earlier generations.

As with variation within a diaspora, there is also marked variation when comparisons are made across diasporas. Jewish homeland ties go back 2,600 years, although for most of this time there was no physical homeland to which they could return. African-American homeland ties are not to a specific culture or place, but to an entire continent. The intensity of Indian ties range from those in the East African diaspora who retire in India to those in the United States who maintain ties but become U.S. citizens; Chinese ties are mainly to southern China, the area from which most Chinese emigrated.

The presence of homeland ties raises the issue of divided loyalties, which can create tension and conflict between diaspora and host communities. That is, the diaspora may be suspected of putting the interests of its homeland ahead of the interests of the host nation. This is one reason that diasporas are sometimes denied citizenship or scapegoated in times of political or economic unrest. The political relationships involving the diaspora, the homeland, and the host nation may take any of seven forms:

1. The diaspora may attempt to directly influence homeland policies

2. The diaspora may attempt to influence the host government to aid the homeland

3. The homeland government may seek assistance from the diaspora

4. The diaspora may seek protection from the homeland government

5. The host nation may try to use the diaspora to influence the homeland government

6. The diaspora may attempt to influence host-nation organizations to assist the homeland

7. The homeland government may ask the host nation to influence the diaspora

See also ANTI-SEMITISM; ASSIMILATION; IRREDENTISM; MIDDLEMAN MINORITIES; MIGRANT WORKERS; SLAVERY; SYNCRETIC CULTURES.

Cohen, Steven. (1983) *American Modernity and Jewish Identity*.

Harris, Joseph E., ed. (1982) *Global Dimensions of the African Diaspora*.

Kilson, Martin, and Robert Rotberg, eds. (1976) *African Diasporas: Interpretive Essays*.

Lim, Linda Y. C., and L. A. Peter Gosling. (1983) *The Chinese in Southeast Asia. Volume 1, Ethnicity and Economic Activity. Volume 2, Identity, Culture, and Politics.*

Murphy, Joseph M. (1993) *Working the Spirit: Ceremonies of the African Diaspora.*

Safran, William. (1991) "Diasporas in Modern Societies: Myths of Homeland and Return." *Diaspora* 1: 83–99.

Sheffer, Gabriel, ed. (1986) *Modern Diasporas in International Politics.*

Bosnian Muslims are a Slavic people who have resided in the region for centuries. Their ancestors converted to Islam during the four centuries of Ottoman rule.

Serbian ethnic cleansing, carried out by Serbs living in Bosnia and the Serbian-controlled former Yugoslavian military, has driven about 700,000 people from Bosnia, forced about 600,000 to relocate within the region, and killed tens of thousands. Those who fled went mainly to Croatia, with many sent on to refugee camps in Germany. Ethnic cleansing methods include rape of women and girls, murder of individuals, assassination of local political leaders, mass executions, seizure of property, house and barn burnings, placement in detention camps, and the seige of the capital city, Sarajevo. The Bosnians are opposed to and have resisted ethnic cleansing, preferring the continuation of Bosnia-Herzegovina as a multiethnic republic.

Beyond the Serbian desire for control of territory, factors cited as contributing to the ethnic cleansing campaign in Bosnia are the three distinct regional cultures (Bosnian, Croatian, Serbian) and religions (Islam, Catholicism, Orthodoxy); the loose confederation forged under Communist rule; Serbian control of the former Yugoslav military; historical conflict, dating most recently to Croat and Bosnian Muslim collaboration with Nazis during World War II in the killing of Serbs; and the failure of the European Community to intervene actively.

While the term *ethnic cleansing* has been applied specifically to Serbian actions in Bosnia, human history is filled with other instances of the same types of actions for the same purpose. In Europe, Nazi efforts to exterminate the Jews (called the "final solution" by the Nazis) and Gypsies are recent examples. Earlier attempts in Europe focused on the Armenians and Slavs. Some of the treatment of the native peoples of the New World by European colonizers also fits

ETHNIC CLEANSING

This term probably was first used in 1988 in the former USSR to describe the conflict between Armenians and Azerbaijanis in the Nagorno-Karabakh region. It was introduced to the international community by journalists quoting Serbian nationalists in 1992. In the context of the former Yugoslavia, the term refers to the Serbs' systematic effort to create purely Serbian areas in areas of Croatia, Serbia, and Bosnia-Herzegovina that were formerly multiethnic. In Serbia, the non-Serbian peoples were mainly Croats and Hungarians, most of whom fled to Croatia and Hungary following the dissolution of Yugoslavia. In Bosnia-Herzegovina, the non-Serbian peoples were Bosnian Muslims (about 41 percent of the republic population of 4.4 million) and Croats. As Croatia controls the northwestern areas of Bosnia-Herzegovina, Croatians found shelter there or in Croatia. Thus, Serbian ethnic cleansing was directed primarily at Bosnian Muslims. Like Serbs and Croats,

under the label of ethnic cleansing, as does the treatment of indigenous peoples in Asia and Africa.

See also ETHNOCIDE; GENOCIDE.

ETHNIC CONFLICT

Ethnic conflict means violent conflict among groups who differ from one another in terms of culture, religion, physical features, or language. For the last several years, ethnic conflict has been the most common form of collective violence in the world. In 1988 the majority of the 111 violent conflicts in the world involved minority and majority groups within nations. In July 1993 there were no less than 25 ethnic conflicts that involved the regular use of violence—mass killings, executions, terrorist bombings, assassinations, lootings, rapes, and forced expulsions—by one or both groups to achieve their aims. In addition, there are several dozen other conflicts that are mostly nonviolent, and hundreds of situations of political, economic, and cultural repression that may eventually erupt into open conflict and violence.

Although attention is always drawn to the bloodiest and most protracted of conflicts—Catholics and Protestants in Northern Ireland; Serbs, Bosnian Muslims, and Croats in the Balkans; Sri Lankan Tamils and Sinhalese in Sri Lanka; Kurds in the Middle East; Armenians and Azerbaijanis in Nagorno-Karabakh—the many nonviolent conflicts should not be ignored, as they are the seedbeds of future violent conflicts. Nonviolent ethnic conflict often takes the form of political, economic, or cultural repression of ethnic minorities, and includes restrictions on voting, burdensome taxes, exclusion from certain professions, residential isolation, educational quotas, prohibitions on the use of the ethnic language, and restrictions on religious worship. A 1989 survey lists 261 minority groups (many of which are ethnic groups) in 99 of 126 nations as the victims of such oppression, suggesting a long and troubled future for ethnic relations around the world.

Another form of ethnic conflict is legal conflict, which is occurring with some frequency in North America, Australia, and other areas where native peoples (American Indians, Inuit/Eskimos, and Aleuts in North America; aboriginal peoples in Australia; Maori in New Zealand; and Saami in Nordic nations, among others) are seeking to reestablish their legal, economic, political, cultural, and religious rights through petitions to the state and national governments, and through legal action. Their goals are to restore ownership of their ancestral lands or to receive compensation for the lands that are now owned almost always by nonindigenous people, official recognition as a distinct political entity, freedom from state and some federal laws, religious freedom, and the right to self-determination and self-government.

Ethnic conflict often involves more than just conflict among the groups; often there is conflict among factions within each group, and other nations and peoples often become involved. In Sri Lanka, for example, the conflict between the Sinhalese and Sri Lankan Tamils has been accompanied by assassinations, bombings, and riots by political factions in both groups, and violence directed at Muslim communities in Sri Lanka. Similar situations have occurred in Northern Ireland, Azerbaijan, and elsewhere as political rivals and their followers battle for influence and power. Often the key policy distinction between factions is the support for peaceful-accommodation resolutions to the conflict versus violent-conquest resolutions.

At the international level, ethnic conflicts also usually involve nations and citizens of nations who are not direct combatants in the conflict. Ethnic conflicts are a major cause of refugees and displaced persons who seek safety in noninvolved nations, nations that are supportive of their interests, or nations with large ethnic confederate populations. These large refugee populations (further discussed under "Refugees" in this volume) put heavy economic, social, and political stress on the host nation and may lead to ethnic conflict within that nation (as is the case in Germany), which gives the host nation a stake in seeing the external conflict quickly resolved. While those forced to flee are usually members of the warring groups, other noncombatants may be affected as well. In Sri Lanka, in addition to the Tamils who fled north and east and out of the country, and the Sinhalese who fled south, hundreds of thousands of Muslims not involved in the conflict fled from the eastern Tamil region to safety in the western region.

In addition to accepting refugees, nations with an interest in the conflict or ties to one of the groups may choose to become directly involved by assisting one ethnic group, as with the British in Northern Ireland, Turkey and Greece in Cyprus, and India in Sri Lanka, to name a few. Additionally, even if a government remains officially neutral or uninvolved, its citizens will often support members of their ethnic group in another nation, as can be seen in Jewish support for Israel and Irish-American support for Irish Catholics in Northern Ireland. For many people, mother country sentiments remain powerful, and feelings of ethnic solidarity quickly convert into political and economic support when the security of the homeland is threatened.

Types of Ethnic Conflict

Although students of ethnic conflict often lump all such conflicts together as a single type of human conflict, ethnic conflict actually takes a variety of forms. One key distinction is between conflicts that occur in unranked situations versus those in ranked situations. In an unranked situation the ethnic groups are relatively equal in power or perceive themselves to be so; in a ranked situation, the ethnic groups in a nation

are ordered in a hierarchy of power. Conventional wisdom holds that ethnic conflicts will be more common and less amenable to control in unranked situations where the groups are in competition for wealth and power, and where one group is not powerful enough to repress the other groups. Another distinction related to this first one is between conflicts in the developing world and those in the industrialized world. The former often center on competition between ethnic groups for political dominance, while the latter often involve separatist movements by ethnic minorities and repression by the government. A third distinction can be made among different types of violent ethnic conflict on the basis of the goals of the participants in the conflict. From this perspective, violent conflicts in the world today fall into five categories:

1. **Separatist Movements.** Violence occurs as part of an effort by an ethnic group to become politically independent, or as part of an effort by a nation to prevent the group from doing so. Such conflicts are quite common and most often involve minority groups seeking to establish an independent nation in their ancestral homeland, which is now controlled by the nation within which they live.

2. **Internal Rivalry for Autonomy, Political Power, or Territorial Control.** Violence occurs as part of a conflict between ethnic groups in one nation or between an ethnic group and the government over access to and control of economic resources, political power, territory, or political autonomy within the nation. When the goals of the group seeking autonomy or more power or wealth seem unattainable, they may shift their goal to separatism. Such conflicts are especially common in former colonies, and to a large degree result from colonial policies that purposefully created rivalries between indigenous peoples and also afforded

more education, status, and government or business responsibility to one group. Upon independence, these multiethnic nations are often faced with ethnic competition for political power that pits those who enjoyed more power under colonial rule with those now seeking power. Because of the historical link to colonial policies, such conflicts are most common in former colonized nations in South Asia and Africa.

3. **Conquest.** Violence occurs as part of a war between two or more nations where ethnic differences between the groups is a major factor in the animosity between the groups. The objective of the war might be the conquest of the other ethnic group, or the group's removal from all or some of its territory. Such conflicts are now quite rare.

4. **Survival.** Violence occurs as part of an attempt by a national government to forcibly assimilate, harm, remove, or drive out an ethnic minority or deprive them of social, religious, political, or economic rights granted other residents of the nation. While most such conflicts in the world today are mainly nonviolent (although political rioting is not uncommon), these conflicts have the potential to explode into violence in many nations around the world.

5. **Irredentist.** Violence occurs as part of an attempt by an ethnic group(s) or nation(s) to regain or retain territory on the basis of an alleged ancestral or historical right to the territory. Often the territory is controlled by another nation, but is located adjacent to, and the population is mainly of, the ethnic group dominant in the nation seeking ownership. Irredentist conflicts are very common today, and are often the result of national boundaries established during colonial times, or in eastern Europe during the era of Soviet dominance. These boundaries often ignored existing ethnic boundaries and

claims by local groups to their ethnic homelands.

The following table lists the major ethnic conflicts around the world as of January 1994—the ethnic groups involved, the nations in which they are occurring, and the type of conflict, based on this five-type typology. Some conflicts, of course, are of more than one type because the motivations of the conflicting groups are different or because political factions within one group may have different goals. Descriptive profiles of most of the conflicts listed below can be found in this volume. Nonviolent survival conflicts involving issues of minority rights are generally not included; a full list of these may be found in the publications by Gurr cited below.

Religious Conflict

Closely related to and sometimes indistinguishable from ethnic conflict is religious conflict—conflict between two groups who adhere to different religions. Since the religion of conflicting groups is often the most visible symbol of group differences to outsiders, many conflicts between ethnic groups are often assumed to be religious in nature. However, this is often only a misperception by outsiders unaware of long-standing hostility between the groups and competing territorial claims; not all ethnic conflicts result from religious differences, nor is all religious conflict considered ethnic conflict. Ethnic conflicts such as those involving the Kurds in the Middle East and the Basques in Spain involve groups of the same religion (Islam and Catholicism, respectively), although there are other cultural differences between the groups. In some conflicts, such as between the Protestant and Catholic Northern Irish, religious differences are present, but other factors—economic conditions and political repression—are more basic causes. In other conflicts, such as that between the Israelis and Palestinians, religious differences are a major barrier to peaceful

Ethnic Conflicts in 1994

Ethnic Group(s)	Nation	Conflict Type
Abkahzians, Georgians	Georgia	Separatist
Albanians, Serbs	Serbia	Survival, Irredentist
Armenians, Azerbaijani Turks	Azerbaijan	Irredentist
Assamese	India	Separatist, Survival
Baha'i	Iran	Survival
Basques	Spain	Separatist
Bodo	India	Survival
Bosnians, Serbs	Bosnia, Serbia	Survival, Conquest, Irredentist
Catalans	Spain	Survival
Catholics, Protestants	Northern Ireland	Separatist, Irredentist
Chakma	Bangladesh	Survival
Chechen-Ingush	Russia	Separatist
Copts	Egypt	Survival
Croats, Serbs	Croatia	Separatist, Conquest, Survival
Cypriots	Cyprus	Separatist
Indo-Fijians, Fijians	Fiji	Survival
Foreigners in Germany	Germany	Survival
French Canadians	Canada	Separatist, Internal
Gypsies and Travelers	Europe	Survival
Hausa, Yoruba, Igbo	Nigeria	Internal
Hindus, Muslims	India	Survival, Internal
Hungarians	Romania	Survival, Irredentist
Hutu, Tutsi	Burundi, Rwanda	Survival, Internal
Israelis, Palestinians	Middle East	Survival, Separatist, Irredentist
Jakun, Tiv	Nigeria	Survival
Kachin, Karen, Mon	Myanmar	Survival, Internal
Kashmiri	India	Separatist, Irredentist
Kurds	Iran, Iraq	Separatist
Kurds	Turkey	Survival, Irredentist
Luo, Kalejin	Kenya	Internal
Nagas	India	Separatist
Nepalese	Bhutan	Survival
Ossetes	Georgia	Separatist
Russians	Former Soviet Republics	Survival, Internal
Russians and Ukrainians	Moldova	Separatist
Shi'ite Muslims (Marsh Arabs)	Iraq	Survival
Sikhs	India	Separatist, Survival, Internal
Tamils, Sinhalese	Sri Lanka	Internal, Separatist
Tibetans	China	Survival, Separatist
Timorese	Indonesia	Survival
Vietnamese	Cambodia	Survival

relations, but are not the only cause of the conflict. Finally, there are some conflicts that are essentially religious in nature, such as between Muslims and Hindus in India, although in this case the two groups are actually quite similar culturally.

Perhaps the most common form of ethnic conflict is the persecution of religious minorities. Today, groups suffering from persecution caused mainly by religious differences (although issues of economic and political competition are rarely absent altogether) include Copts in Egypt, Baha'i in Iran, and Shi'ite Muslims (called Marsh Arabs) in southern Iraq.

One special form of religious conflict involves the efforts of religious fundamentalist movements to replace secular rule with religious rule. While Christian, Hindu, Jewish, and other fundamentalist movements can be found around the world, it is the Islamic fundamentalism movement that draws the most attention.

Islam is one of the major world religions, with over 950 million adherents worldwide in 1993, slightly less than half the number of Christians in the world. A follower of Islam is called a *Muslim* in English, a term now preferred to *Moslem*, which was conventionally used until about 20 years ago. Islam was founded by Muhammed in what is now Saudi Arabia between A.D. 610 and 632. The sacred book of Islam is the Qur'an (Koran), which is considered to be the one true statement of God's word and, in the view of Muslims, supersedes divine revelation as set forth in the Jewish and Christian bibles. Muslims follow the Five Pillars of Islam: (1) accepting and testifying that there is no god except Allah and that Muhammed is his true prophet; (2) praying five times daily, in the direction of Mecca; (3) fasting during the month of Ramadan; (4) giving alms to the poor; and (5) making a pilgrimage to Mecca, the holy land. Beyond a system of belief and worship, Islam is also a prescription for life, and Muslims live their lives in a manner consistent with Islamic

requirments. Thus, like Judaism, Islamic practice is filled with rules and prescriptions for daily life that go beyond religious practice. The two main branches of Islam are Sunni and Shi'ite; each, especially Shi'ite, has a number of distinct subsects.

Although its origins are in the Middle East, over the centuries Islam spread through trade, conquest, migration, and conversion to North Africa, northwest Africa, central Asia, south Asia, and Southeast Asia. Today, the four nations with the largest Muslim populations are not in the Middle East but in Asia—Indonesia, Bangladesh, Pakistan, and India. Of these, Pakistan, like Iran in the Middle East and the Sudan in Africa, is an Islamic rather than a secular nation. All other nations with majority Islamic populations are secular.

Although the nations with the largest Islamic populations are outside the Middle East and North Africa, Islamic fundamentalism is centered in the Middle East where Islamic and Arab identity are closely interrelated, contrasting with Christian and Western identity. At the same time, Islamic fundamentalism is global in that some Muslims in many nations adhere to the political agenda of the movement. In addition, whether fundamentalism is directly involved or not, Muslims are involved in ethnic conflicts in Bosnia, Serbia (Albanian Muslims), Cyprus (Turkish Muslims), Georgia, Azerbaijan, the Philippines (Muslim separatists on the island of Mindanao), India (Muslims in general and in Kashmir in particular), Sri Lanka, Israel, France, and Nigeria. In the United States, the bombing of the World Trade Center in New York City in 1993 produced a rise in anti-Muslim and anti-Arab feelings among the general U.S. population.

The fundamentalist movement in the Middle East centers on efforts by fundamentalists to replace secular governments in a number of—if not all—nations with Islamic governments, or governments that adhere to Islamic values. To achieve this end, Islamic organizations have sought power through elections and have resorted to violence, including assassinations, terrorism, riots, strikes, and the persecution of non-Muslim minorities. Fundamentalists have also mounted what are called "cultural offensives" in some nations, such as Egypt, to replace secular guidelines with Islamic principles. For example, efforts have been made to ban Western art and literature, change the school curriculum, and require women and girls to wear veils. In the affected nations, the responses to the perceived threat have varied—Tunisia, Algeria, and Egypt have reacted by forcibly repressing fundamentalist organizations; Jordan has allowed them political participation, and fundamentalists hold the majority in the Jordanian parliament; and Saudi Arabia has sought to placate them while the royal family maintains absolute control. In many nations outside the region, where fundamentalism is seen as a possible threat to order and secular rule, some ethnic conflicts are motivated at least in part by a desire to limit Muslim power.

The roots of the current Islamic fundamentalism movement go back 1,400 years to the founding of Islam and the ensuing and never-resolved conflict with the values of Western civilization and Christianity, and the frequent military battles between the Islamic world and the West. For the past 300 years Europe has had the upper hand, to the point that the political map of the modern Middle East is a product of European colonialism, and Western customs and products are found throughout. The fundamentalist movement, by creating independent Islamic nations and a unified Arab polity based on Islam as it existed in the past, is in large part a reaction to Western domination. Thus, the rhetoric of the movement stresses anti-Western, anticolonial, and anti-imperialism themes and targets governments, institutions, and individuals believed to be loyal to, or examples of, these Western themes. In accord with Islamic belief,

the movement is a Holy War, or struggle involving a battle over Good versus Evil, to many if not all Islamic participants, and an Islamic victory and the conversion of others to Islam is a triumph by Good.

Causes of Ethnic Conflict
As yet there is no complete answer to the question of cause and, given the different types of ethnic conflict and the various situations in which they occur, the question may ultimately require several, perhaps related, answers. In attempting to explain ethnic conflict in general as well as specific conflicts, one must consider the basic nature and strength of ethnic ties, situational factors that may encourage the development of ethnic solidarity and ethnic-based competition, and the actual motives articulated by the groups. As regards ethnicity, political scientist Donald Horowitz reminds us that ethnic solidarity is "powerful, permeative, passionate, and pervasive." Additionally, some biologically oriented researchers suggest that strong feelings of ethnic solidarity and ethnic conflict have their roots in human biological evolution, and thus it is not surprising that ethnic groups will fight to dominate other groups or to protect their own interests. Another not necessarily contradictory line of thought is that in many nations over the last several decades, ethnic groups have emerged or reemerged as interest groups whose members coalesce as a means of gaining political and economic power. Recently, a number of situational factors have drawn special attention as causes of ethnic conflict, including the end of centralized rule in former Communist nations; the end of colonial or colonial-style rule in Africa and Asia; the ideal of democracy, which places groups in direct competition for power and political control; and economic inequalities among ethnic groups both within and across nations.

In a recent attempt to explain rebellions by minority groups, political scientist Ted Gurr has suggested a complex theory incorporating many factors, in the most general sense, that may be related to ethnic conflict: (1) the minority group's history and current status, which includes the group's degree of disadvantage relative to other groups in the nation, the strength of the group's self-identity, the extent of group cohesion and its capacity to mobilize its resources, and the extent of repression by the dominant group; (2) the opportunities available to the group for political action including the control exercised by the ruling regime, the group leader's strategy and tactics, and shifts in state power that provide the opportunity for rebellion; (3) global processes that intensify grievances such as the modern state system, which stresses nationalism and centralized control, and the global economy, which has led to the economic exploitation of some groups; (4) the international spread of conflict, which may involve the same group such as the Kurds in a number of nations or the spread of conflict from one group to other groups; and (5) the effects of state power on political action such as the form of government, which may lead the government to try to resolve the minority group's grievance or alternatively to repress it.

Managing and Resolving Ethnic Conflicts
Many experts now believe that most ethnic conflicts are uniquely resistant to resolution and that the international community and national governments would be wiser to invest their resources in managing and controlling these conflicts rather than in trying to resolve them. Recent experience suggests that this is sound advice—while conflict-resolution efforts do sometimes produce formal accords, they rarely yield long-term peace and harmony. Ethnic conflicts in Cyprus, Northern Ireland, Bosnia, Sri Lanka, and northwest India were all "settled" by accords, but the conflicts quickly flared up anew and con-

Displacement of people is common in ethnic conflict, as with these Palestinians expelled into southern Lebanon by Israel in December 1992.

tinued. In most situations, ethnic conflicts end only through the subjugation or expulsion of one group by the other, a resolution likely to leave the loser unsatisfied and ready to resume the conflict when the opportunity presents itself in the future, which can be several decades away.

Ethnic conflicts are resolution-resistant for a number of reasons. First, we need to remember Donald Horowitz's point that ethnic solidarity is "powerful, permeative, passionate, and pervasive." Second, the stakes in ethnic conflicts are often, or are believed by the combatants to be, very high—the survival of their group, their domination by another group, or their domination of the other group. These are the very issues that precipitate the strong ethnic solidarity described by Horowitz, and are the reasons for which members of ethnic groups are willing to kill and die. Third, ethnic conflicts are usually not just disputes about tangible objectives, such as political control or access to employment, but also involve powerful xenophobic and ethnocentric feelings and symbols, and the resulting scapegoating and stereotyping tend to make such conflicts particularly impervious to rational resolution. Fourth, the international experience has so far produced few permanent alternatives to ethnic conflict in multiethnic nations and regions. The United States is perhaps the only nation that holds to the view that a nation will be stronger by assimilating all peoples into one national whole, although that goal has yet to be achieved. A few other nations adhere to a pluralism model with groups sharing power, but of these, Canada is burdened by the French-Canadian separatist movement and Switzerland by the Jura autonomy movement. While Belgium and the Mauritius seem free of protracted, violent conflict, they, along with Switzerland, are unique situations that do not provide a model for most other nations. Fifth, ethnic rights and ethnic conflict are neither legally recognized nor regulated at the international level and are still to a large extent treated as internal matters, to

be resolved by the nation itself. Unfortunately, in most situations the state itself is a party to the dispute or has a stake in the success of one group at the expense of another group. Thus, the state is often a self-interested and ineffective force for peaceful, long-term ethnic-conflict resolution that leaves all parties satisfied. Additionally, because ethnic conflicts are defined as internal matters, United Nations and multination alliances have generally restricted their involvement to peacekeeping and rescue missions designed to limit the fighting and have played a lesser role in long-term resolution. Similarly, the activities of nongovernmental organizations are mostly geared to assisting refugees and displaced persons, and sheltering, feeding, and treating the victims.

Ongoing Conflict

Violent ethnic conflict will likely continue and spread to other ethnic groups in the now-independent republics of the former Soviet Union, in south Asia, in developing nations in Africa, and in Europe. In the former Soviet republics, the conflict will most likely take two forms. First, it will continue to pit ethnic minorities against the majority groups such as the Abkhazians and the Georgians. Second, it will pit the national groups against the Russians who have settled in these nations since the seventeenth century and who occupied key economic and political positions during the Soviet period. Some of these Russian minorities will either be forced to give up power, assimilate, or leave for Russia. South Asia is already the arena for considerable ethnic unrest, including Tamils and Sinhalese in Sri Lanka, Assamese and Bodo in northeastern India, Chakma and other tribal peoples in Bangladesh, Sikhs in India and Pakistan, Kashmiri in the disputed Kashmir region, Muslims and Hindus in India, and Burmese and ethnic minorities such as the Karen and Mon in Myanmar. Because of the overwhelming social and economic change in south Asia and the complex mix of ethnic, occupational (caste), religious, and language groups, continuing escalation of conflicts over access to political power and economic opportunity is expected. In Africa, with 40 nations, over 700 ethnic groups, large Muslim and Christian populations in Western nations, and with groups in a number of nations already vying for political power, conflict will continue, although not all conflict is along ethnic lines. In Europe, a pattern of continuing conflict persists between ethnic minorities (including both linguistic minorities and national minorities) and the state in the former's quest for political autonomy or independence. Additionally, the emerging pattern of conflict and violence directed at non-European immigrants and refugees can be expected to continue. Finally, in South America, the violence directed at American Indians in the Amazon and elsewhere by those seeking to exploit the lumber, mineral, and other resources of the region are likely to continue.

See also COLONIALISM; ETHNOCENTRISM; ETHNOCIDE; GENOCIDE; HUMAN RIGHTS; INDIGENOUS PEOPLES; MINORITY RIGHTS; RACE AND RACISM; *SPECIFIC ETHNIC CONFLICTS.*

Binder, David, and Barbara Crossette. (1992) "As Ethnic Wars Multiply, U.S. Strives for a Policy." *New York Times.* 7 February: 1, 14.

de Silva, K. M., and S. W. R. de A. Samarasinghe. (1993) *Peace Accords and Ethnic Conflict.*

Elmer, Glaister A., and Evelyn A. Elmer. (1988) *Ethnic Conflicts Abroad: Clues to America's Future?* AICF Monograph Series, no. 8.

Esposito, John L. (1984) *The Islamic Threat: Myth or Reality.*

Gurr, Ted R. (1993) *Minorities at Risk: A Global View of Ethnopolitical Conflicts.*

Gurr, Ted R., and James R. Scarritt. (1989) "Minority Rights at Risk: A Global Survey." *Human Rights Quarterly* 11: 375–405.

Horowitz, Donald L. (1985) *Ethnic Groups in Conflict.*

Lewis, Bernard. (1990) "The Roots of Muslim Rage." *Atlantic Monthly.* September: 47–60.

Messina, Anthony M., et al., eds. (1992) *Ethnic and Racial Minorities in Advanced Industrial Democracies.*

Miller, Judith. (1992) "The Islamic Wave." *New York Times Magazine.* 31 May: 22–26, 38, 40, 42.

Minority Rights Group. (1990) *World Directory of Minorities.*

Rupesinghe, Kumar. (1987) "Theories of Conflict Resolution and Their Applicability to Protracted Ethnic Conflicts." *Bulletin of Peace Proposals* 18: 527–539.

Ryan, Stephen. (1990) *Ethnic Conflict and International Relations.*

Samarasinghe, S. W. R. de A., and Reed Coughlan, eds. (1991) *Economic Dimensions of Ethnic Conflict.*

Stavenhagen, Rodolfo. (1987) "Ethnic Conflict and Human Rights: Their Interrelationship." *Bulletin of Peace Proposals* 18: 507–514.

ETHNIC HUMOR

Ethnic humor is "a type of humor in which fun is made of the perceived behavior, customs, personality, or any other traits of a group or its members by virtue of their specific sociocultural identity." (Apte 1985, 108) Ethnic humor is a component of ethnocentrism as it serves to reinforce the values of the in-group by portraying the out-group in negative, stereotypical terms. Stereotyping is a key component of ethnic humor; the humor would not be understood nor considered funny unless the members of the culture all shared the same image of the group that is the butt of the humor.

Ethnic humor takes a variety of forms around the world and is usually expressed in the same ways other forms of humor are expressed in a culture. Common expressions of ethnic humor are through jokes, riddle-jokes (such as light bulb jokes in which the answer is a negative stereotype), imitative gestures, and rhymes, proverbs, and caricature. For example, the Taos imitate the dress of the Santa Clara and Navajo in ceremonies, Chicanos ridicule whites by translating Spanish names into their often-humorous English forms (for example, *María Dolores de la Barriga* becomes "Mary Stomach Pains"), and Hungarian children learn the following rhyme:

Stork, stork, turtle-dove,

Why are your feet bleeding?

Turkish children have cut them up,

Hungarian children will cure them,

With pipes, drums, and violins. . . .

Ethnic humor is a component of ethnic relations in all cultures, as some people in all cultures amuse themselves and others by ridiculing members of other cultures. It is likely that ethnic humor is more common, more cutting, and of greater social importance when it involves groups that are in conflict, such as those whose contact has resulted from colonization and large-scale immigration. The ethnic groups whose members constitute the American population have been brought together both by New World colonization and immigration, and ethnic conflict and competition have long been common features of American life, as indicated by the wealth of derogatory ethnic jokes told today and in the past. For example, a popular joke book published in 1921 titled *Jokes for All Occasions* contains jokes that portray and ridicule, in stereotypical terms, Americans of African, Latin

American, Jewish, Italian, Finnish, Japanese, Chinese, Dutch, American Indian, Scottish, Irish, and Asian Indian descent, as well as foreigners in general. A few of these jokes display the negative stereotypical images typical of early twentieth-century America. The following story depicts African-Americans as lazy and ridicules their speech:

The foreman of a Southern Mill, who was much troubled by the shiftlessness of his colored workers, called sharply to two of the men slouching past him.

"Hi, you! Where are you going?"

"Well, suh, boss," one of them answered, "we is goin' to de mill wid dis-heah plank."

"Plank! What plank? Where's the plank?" the foreman demanded.

The colored spokesman looked inquiringly and somewhat surprisedly at his own empty hands and those of his companion, whom he addressed good-naturedly:

"Now, if dat don't beat all, George! If we hain't gone an' clean forgitted dat plank!"

Another joke ridicules Latin Americans for the lack of political stability in their region as compared to the United States:

At a reception by the Daughters of the Revolution in New York City appeared a woman from one of the Latin-American States. She wore a large number of decorations and insignia. It was explained that she was a Daughter of all 238 revolutions in her own country.

A third joke ridicules the Italian immigrant, who was a frequent target of ethnic humor as part of a broader pattern of anti-Italian sentiment in the early twentieth century:

The Italian workman in the West was warned to look out for rattlesnakes. He was assured, however, that a snake would never strike until after sounding the rattles. One day, while seated on a log, eating his lunch, the Italian saw a rattlesnake coiled ready to strike. He lifted his legs carefully, with the intention of darting away on the other side of the log the moment the rattles should sound their warning. But just as his feet cleared the top of the log, the snake struck out and its fangs were buried in the wood only a fraction of an inch below the Italian's trousers. The frightened man fled madly, but he took breath to shriek over his shoulder:

"Son of a gun! Why you no ringa da bell?"

These three examples are of ethnic humor directed by the majority (white Americans of northern European ancestry) at ethnic minorities. Equally common is the reverse, where ethnic minorities make majority groups the butt of their humor. However, one key difference is that while the majority often expresses its humor openly, as in the book where these jokes were published, minorities are more careful and ridicule majority groups in private for fear of offending the more powerful group. The ethnic humor of minorities may also serve the function of releasing aggression and hostility. As with the ethnic humor of majority groups, the content of minority-group ethnic humor often portrays the majority in stereotypically negative ways, often emphasizing moral weakness or inappropriate social behavior. The following African-American joke emphasizes white immorality:

Two Negro women in domestic service are comparing notes.

"At my place," one complains, "I have a terrible time; all day it's 'Yes, Ma'am,' 'Yes, Ma'am,' 'Yes, Ma'am.'"

"Me, too," comments the other, "but with me it's 'No, Sir,' 'No, Sir,' 'No, Sir.'"

Mountain whites in Appalachia do not trust outsiders and delight in stories in which they take advantage of outsiders:

A middle-aged widow contracted with a large corporation to build herself a "shell house," a small frame building without interior partitions or finish. As security, she mortgaged a small tract of her land to the construction company.

As an informant related the story:

Well, Lucille had her a place all bulldozed off level, where she wanted them fellows to build her little house. When they brought the lumber,

they put it down the hill from the level place. Then about two days after that, the carpenters come and built the house where the lumber was. Well, let me tell you, they never did get Lucille to pay for that house. She got it free, because they didn't put it where she wanted it. Of course, they took that other piece—the one she put in the contract. But she got herself a house free and clear.

The western Apache often express their perception of "the Whiteman" through humor, including cartoons in the tribal newspaper, jokes, caricature, and clowning. One aspect of social interaction among western Apache men is joking imitations that portray whites such as teachers, doctors, and government workers, among others, as loud, aggressive, boorish, overly friendly, immodest social incompetents. This behavior, while not very common, serves to recount white mistreatment of the western Apache.

Ethnic humor is also sometimes used to define the boundary and clarify the relationship between different ethnic groups. The following Jicarilla Apache joke emphasizes the boundary between American Indians and whites and the historical basis of the inequality between the two:

An Indian comes into a bar, blanket, feather and all.

He puts two strings of cheap beads on the bar and orders a drink. The beads are to pay for the drink. The bartender refuses to accept. The Indian says, "Why not. Your ancestors sold my ancestors this stuff for one Manhattan."

This joke is similar in message to another in which treaties between American Indian nations and the U.S. government are described as containing this clause: "The (American Indian nation) shall keep the land for as far as the eye can see and for as long as the waters shall run or 90 days, whichever comes first." Ethnic humor is also used by individuals to establish ties with other members of the ethnic group and as an impression management technique in dealing with outsiders. For example, joking references by Italian-Americans to the Mafia or their ties to it play on the negative stereotype of Italian-Americans as gangsters, increasing their power and influence in encounters with non–Italian-Americans, who do not know if they should take these references seriously or not.

A final form of ethnic humor is derogatory humor directed at the group by members of the group. For example, ethnic comedians in the United States often imitate and mock the dress, mannerisms, and accents of immigrants in their own ethnic group. Such behavior perhaps allows the immigrants to laugh at their own sometimes difficult adjustment to the United States and also serves an assimilative function in publicly marking traditional customs that are not acceptable. Similarly, African-American comedians often tell poverty and Ku Klux Klan jokes to African-American audiences. Jokes such as "Down where I'm from the Klan is so bad they put a cross on your front yard and then they come and ask you for a match," or "We were so poor our daddy invented the limbo when he tried to enter a pay toilet" allow African-Americans to share in and express anger about their common experience of discrimination.

See also ETHNOCENTRISM.

Apte, Mahadev L. (1985) *Humor and Laughter: An Anthropological Approach.*

Basso, Keith H. (1979) *Portraits of "the White-man": Linguistic Play and Cultural Symbols among the Western Apache.*

Crocchiola, Stanley F. L. (1967) *The Jicarilla Apaches of New Mexico, 1540–1967.*

Di Leonardo, Micaela. (1984) *The Varieties of Ethnic Experience: Kinship, Class, and Gender among California Italian-Americans.*

Dundes, Alan. (1987) *Cracking Jokes: Studies of Sick Humor Cycles and Stereotypes.*

Fenton, William N. (1957) *Factionalism at Taos Pueblo, New Mexico.*

Hannerz, Ulf. (1969) *Soulside: Inquiries into Ghetto Culture and Community.*

Hicks, George L. (1976) *Appalachian Valley.*

Jokes for All Occasions (1921).

Pettigrew, Thomas F. (1964) *A Profile of the Negro American.*

Viski, Károly. (1932) *Hungarian Peasant Customs.*

West, Stanley A., and June Macklin, eds. (1979) *The Chicano Experience.*

ETHNIC IDENTITY AND SOLIDARITY

The basis of ethnic relations is the presence and interaction of members of different ethnic groups. *Ethnic identity* refers to the reality and the process through which people identify themselves and are identified by others as members of a specific ethnic group. *Ethnic solidarity* refers to the sense and degree of cohesion felt by members of an ethnic group.

Ethnic Identity

Ethnic identity involves self-identification as a member of an ethnic group and external ascription by others. The complexities resulting from this duality are indicated by perceptions of Gypsy ethnic identity in the United States. Outsiders (non-Gypsies) view all Gypsies as the same and often define them in stereotypical terms as dishonest and thieving, governed by a "king," and as engaged in certain occupations such as fortune-telling, prostitution, carnival work, and asphalt and auto-body repair. For Gypsies in North America, the distinctions they draw between themselves and others and among themselves are finer and multilayered. First of all, regardless of their affiliation, Gypsies distinguish between Gypsies and non-Gypsies (called *gaze* in the Rom language). Gypsies distinguish themselves from non-Gypsies on the basis of five core values held by all Gypsy groups: (1) the purity of Gypsies versus the pollution of non-Gypsies, which is played out behaviorally in various taboos and restrictions on contact with non-Gypsies; (2) ultimate loyalty to the family and kin group; (3) the restriction of group social life to group members only; (4) emphasis on using one's "wits" in economic relations with non-Gypsies; and (5) mobility. In addition to the Gypsy/non-Gypsy distinction, Gypsies also distinguish among different types of non-Gypsies, following the "racial" classification system typical of mainstream American society—whites and nonwhites, including African-Americans and Asians. Additionally, some Gypsy groups distinguish among eastern, southern, and western Europeans.

While non-Gypsies view all Gypsies as comprising one ethnic group, the Gypsies themselves see considerably more variation. In the United States, there are four Gypsy ethnic groups: Rom (with Lowara, Macwaia, and Kalderash subgroups), Rominchels, Ludari, and Black Dutch. In addition, Irish and Scottish Travelers, who are not Gypsies, are often perceived as such by non-Gypsies. Self-designation as a member of one of the Gypsy ethnic groups is based on descent from members of the group, use of the language of the group, following rules of purity and respect, adherence to appropriate social roles, participation in work requiring exploitation of non-Gypsies, and physical appearance. This belief in ethnic group identity is played out in the perceptions the groups have of one another and the rather limited interaction between groups. The Rom see themselves as the only real Gypsies; questioning whether all Rominchels and Ludari are actually Gypsies, they restrict interaction with them. The Ludari are more likely to interact with the Rominchels, but question

whether the Rominchels are real Gypsies; they tend to see the Rom as like themselves but more aggressive and better off financially. The Rominchels see all the groups as Gypsies; they acknowledge that the Rom follow traditional customs more closely than do the others, but at the same time resent the Rom view of them as not real Gypsies.

The Gypsies' self-ethnic identification system points to another salient feature of ethnic identity. Every ethnic group has its own classification system. Exactly where a given individual places himself or herself in the system varies, depending largely on the individual's relationship to the person with whom he or she is communicating and the context in which the question or issue is raised. For example, a Rom Gypsy male would identify himself as a Gypsy to a non-Gypsy, as a Rom to a Rominchel, as a Lowara to another Rom, and as a member of a particular kin group to another Lowara.

As has happened with the Rominchels, after the groups assimilate into American society they become defined as less Gypsy by more traditional Gypsy groups, although the ethnic identity situation of Gypsies in the United States is relatively static. That is, the identity of the groups and of individual group members tends to remain constant from one ethnic interaction situation to another. For other ethnic groups and in other parts of the world, the situation can be quite different, and one's ethnic identity can be changed.

In many parts of the world, ethnic identity change also requires migration to and settlement in a new locale where the individual's ethnic past is unknown or doesn't matter. This is true in much of Latin America and also India, where one's caste status is far less significant in the cities than in rural villages. One place where a shift in identity does not require relocation is the village of Saraguro in the Highland Ecuador. The community residents are defined as either whites (village or rural) or native Indians. The social category of *mestizo* so common throughout Latin America is not important in Saraguro. The option to switch identity is available to all residents, although it is not a step taken easily and any move is generally preceded by discussions with one's family. Most shifts are from Indian to white identity, and are described in the community as "He made himself white" or "He has turned himself white" or "He was Indian before, now he is white." Fewer numbers of individuals shift from being white to Indian, or from Indian to white and then back to Indian. One pattern of the Indian-to-white shift is for an Indian woman to marry a white man and take white identity at the time of the marriage. A second major pattern is for Indians who have little land or few cattle to move to town and take up white occupations, which they hope will be more lucrative. To become white means to speak Spanish (which most who convert already do), adopt white clothing styles, and cut one's hair short in the white style. While one motivation to becoming white is to overcome poverty, white status is also attractive because it allows fuller participation in the local society, including the freedom to run for political office.

In the modern world, political considerations often enter a group or individual's decision about how to define their or another group's ethnic identity. This is because in many postcolonial situations, ethnic identity can become a mechanism for access to power. In Colombia, for example, Afro-Colombians are seeking to assert their unique identity and ethnic status in the context of a national agenda that deemphasizes ethnic differences and stresses Colombian nationalism in its place. In a different situation, the Krymchaks of Crimea in the former Soviet Union, although clearly of Jewish origin and identified as Jewish by themselves and others, claimed in the face of religious persecution during the 1950s that they were not in fact Jewish, as they were descended from Crimean peoples who had converted to Judaism. For po-

litical reasons, the government accepted this redefinition of ethnic identity and considered Krymchaks a distinct ethnic group, a step that has hastened their assimilation into Russian society.

Interaction among members of different ethnic groups requires a sharing of mutually recognizable symbols of ethnic identity. These symbols serve as cues enabling the individuals to interact, often in stereotypical ways that reflect each individual's understanding of the other's culture. The major markers and symbols of ethnic identity are natural physical characteristics such as skin color, hair texture, facial features, and body shape; created markers include clothing style, jewelry, hairstyle, and alterations to the body in the form of tattoos, scarification, and piercing. Additionally, some markers might be imposed on the group; for example, Jews were required to wear distinctively styled hats and yellow badges in medieval Europe. A second primary marker is language, as different ethnic groups speak different native languages. Language can also be a symbol of ethnic identity for individuals in assimilated groups who now speak a language different from the native, and whose physical characteristics do not easily mark ethnic identity. For example, in the United States, members of many European-ancestry groups will use words or phrases from their native languages when communicating with other members of the same ethnic group, but not with or in the presence of outsiders.

Ethnic Solidarity

Ethnic solidarity can be thought of as composed of three elements, or, put another way, as manifesting itself in three major forms. First, ethnic solidarity might involve ethnic groups in a society distancing themselves from one another. Second, it might involve the development of a stronger sense of identity and cohesion within the group. And, third, it might involve the group's taking on the status of an interest group and thereby becoming an advocate for the

Azerbaijani Turks celebrating Nourooz, *the spring festival. Public ceremonies such as this one build ethnic solidarity in many ethnic communities around the world.*

interests of the group, often in competition with other ethnic groups.

A variety of explanations has been set forth by social scientists to explain continuing and re-emerging patterns of ethnic solidarity displayed by members of specific ethnic groups around the world. The three that continue to draw the most attention are primordialism, circumstantialism, and oppositionalism.

The basic assumption of *primordialism* is that feelings of ethnic solidarity and communality shared by members of a group persist over time and across space. For example, many Americans of Polish ancestry in some ways still "feel" Polish and often maintain some ties, perhaps only emotional but sometimes economic, political, and social as well, to the nation of Poland and to other people of Polish ancestry. These ties persist despite the reality that these people were born and live in the United States, speak English, see themselves as Americans, and expect to live their entire lives in the United States.

Many other Americans of other ancestries and, in fact, many people around the world maintain these same sorts of ties to "their" ethnic group, even though they spend much of their time apart from it or far from the "homeland."

The primordial approach seeks to explain this persisting sense of ethnic solidarity by identifying those factors that cause the sense of identity to continue. Anthropologist Clifford Geertz (1963, 259) lists a number of such factors:

> By a primordial attachment is meant one that stems from the "givens"...of social existence: immediate contiguity and kin connection mainly, but beyond them the giveness that stems from being born into a particular religious community, speaking a particular language...and following particular social practices.

Thus, people feel a sense of ethnic solidarity because they live near other members of the same group, are related to one another, share the same religious beliefs and practices, speak the same language, and/or share some common customs.

Most social scientists accept the primordial approach as a reasonable way to explain ethnic solidarity in groups where that solidarity has persisted at about the same level of intensity for a long time. Thus, the primordial approach can be seen as a valid way of explaining the high level of solidarity felt by members of the Amish community in the United States—they live near one another (mainly in rural farm communities in Ohio, Indiana, and Pennsylvania); many are related to one another, as evidenced by the few family names in the communities; they speak German at home; practice their own Anabaptist religion; and share numerous customs such as communal barn-raising, style of dress, preferences in art, and recipes. The primordial approach has also served well in explaining the solidarity felt by members of the 5,000 or so non-Western cultures of the world. In the past, though not so much today, these groups displayed all the features listed by Geertz.

Many social scientists, however, question the usefulness of the primordial approach as an explanation for ethnic solidarity in situations where the intensity level of solidarity felt by group members tends to wax and wane over time. Those who take this position argue, for example, that the primordial approach does not explain completely the very strong sense of ethnic solidarity that reemerged among members of the dozens of ethnic groups in the former Soviet Union in the 1990s. This reemergent solidarity (it had existed prior to Russian and Communist rule) led to the formation of distinct ethnic nations such as Lithuania, Georgia, Tajikistan, and at least 14 others. Social scientists suggest that while some primordial feelings may be involved here, it is other, more immediate factors that trigger the dramatic reemergence of ethnic solidarity displayed in this situation and others like it around the world. These immediate factors fall under the label of *circumstantialism*, the second major approach used by social scientists to explain ethnic solidarity.

As the name suggests, circumstantialism rests on the premise that ethnic solidarity results from either internal or external conditions. Ethnic solidarity might directly result from a change of circumstances, such as increased religious repression or economic opportunity in a society, or it might be the result of a rational choice by ethnic group leaders to use their ethnic identity to secure political, social, or economic benefits for the group. In this view, ethnic solidarity becomes most visible in situations of competition among ethnic groups, with the groups operating as interest groups. Situational ethnicity is a widespread form of this tendency. This view suggests that ethnic solidarity is not certain nor constant, and instead may be impermanent, flexible, and responsive to external forces, particularly the nature of relations with other ethnic groups and the opportunities and advantages members of one group expect to accrue through identification with another group. To some extent, the circumstantial approach assumes a degree of rational choice on the part of the participants; that is, individuals will affiliate with a group and act collectively when they think it is in their best interest to do so. In this regard, ethnic group leadership is of major importance; to be effective, leaders must show members how they will benefit.

In colonial and postcolonial situations, a number of conditions are likely to produce a heightened sense of ethnic solidarity and the use of that solidarity to achieve political and economic power. These include economic growth, political change, movement of one group into the traditional homeland of another group, and competition for employment opportunities. The Fulani of Nigeria provide an example of a group who changed their identity and the basis of their identity a number of times to ally themselves with the British colonists and thereby enhance their own political and economic position. The Fulani were recent arrivals in Nigeria, claimed to be Arabic in origin, and were practicing Muslims. Beginning in the early 1800s they spread Islam throughout northern Nigeria and became the rulers of the region, converting, and to some extent subjugating, the indigenous Hausa and other groups in the process. The Fulani self-identification as Arabian Muslims fit well with British racist ideology and the desire to control the local population through indirect rule, a role the British awarded the Fulani. The two groups collaborated in identifying the Fulani—because of tradition, religion, and race—as the natural rulers of the region. The British permitted the use of the name *Fulani,* and then *Hausa-Fulani,* which allowed them to keep the support of local pastoralists and to continue to claim traditional authority. In fact, the Fulani were not the traditional rulers of the region, were not from Arabia, were not ethnically Hausa, and had imposed Islam through often violent means on the local indigenous groups. However, their self-identification and the fictional basis of that identification served the purposes of the British rulers, who therefore supported it.

The third approach to ethnic solidarity merges some elements of the first two. Known as *oppositionalism,* it rests on the premise that the oppositional process between ethnic groups is the basic cause of the persistence of ethnic groups. Central to this interpretation are the concepts of *persistent identity systems* and the *oppositional process.* A persistent identity system is a culture that has survived over time in a cultural environment where it successfully resisted economic, political, and religious assimilation. Such cultures are also characterized by an identity that clearly differentiates them from other cultures. This identity is generally based on the real or symbolic notion of an ethnic homeland and the use of their indigenous language. For example, Basque identity is based in part on the concept of the Basque homeland and the use of the native Basque language. For Jews, on the other hand, in diaspora for some 1,500 years,

the ideas of homeland and ethnic language were largely symbolic, as they did not live in Israel and Hebrew was used only for religious purposes. An oppositional process, the second feature of oppositionalism, refers to attempts by one ethnic or national group to incorporate another ethnic group, and resistance by the latter to the former. It is this process of opposition that leads persistent oppositional systems to develop; and the ethnic groups then persist over time due to the use of a shared language in communication, a sharing of basic values, and a political organization or mechanism for the achievement of their group goals.

See also ASSIMILATION; DIASPORA; TRANSNATIONAL MIGRATION.

Barth, Frederick, ed. (1969) *Ethnic Groups and Boundaries: The Social Organization of Cultural Difference.*

Belote, Linda S. (1983) *Prejudice and Pride: Indian-White Relations in Saraguro, Ecuador.*

Geertz, Clifford. (1963) *The Interpretation of Culture: Selected Essays by Clifford Geertz.*

Hechter, Michael. (1986) "Rational Choice Theory and the Study of Race and Ethnic Relations." In *Theories of Race and Ethnic Relations,* edited by John Rex and David Mason, 264–279.

Khazanov, Anatoly. (1989) *The Krymchaks: A Vanishing Group in the Soviet Union.* Research Paper No. 71.

Royce, Anya Peterson. (1982) *Ethnic Identity: Strategies of Diversity.*

Salamone, Frank A. (1986) "Colonialism and the Emergence of Fulani Identity." In *Ethnic Identities and Prejudices: Perspectives from the Third World,* edited by Anand C. Paranjpe, 61–70.

Salo, Matt T. (1979) "Gypsy Ethnicity: Implications of Native Categories and Interaction for Ethnic Classification." In *Ethnicity* 6: 73–96.

Scott, George M., Jr. (1990) "A Resynthesis of the Primordial and Circumstantial Approaches to Ethnic Group Solidarity: Towards an Explanatory Model." *Ethnic and Racial Studies* 13: 147–171.

Shils, Edward. (1957) "Primordial, Personal, Sacred and Civil Ties." *British Journal of Sociology* 8: 130–145.

Spicer, Edward. (1971) "Persistent Identity Systems." *Science* 401: 795–800.

Stack, J. F., Jr., ed. (1986) *The Primordial Challenge: Ethnicity in the Contemporary World.*

Thompson, Richard H. (1989) *Theories of Ethnicity: A Critical Appraisal.*

van den Berghe, Pierre L. (1981) *The Ethnic Phenomenon.*

ETHNIC MEDIA

The term *ethnic media* refers to information communicated through mechanisms of mass communication directed at ethnic groups. The media employed include print media such as newspapers (dailies, biweeklies, weeklies), magazines, newsletters, calendars, political and educational reviews, religious tracts, and yearbooks; radio; television; and motion pictures.

Ethnic media potentially serve four major functions. First, they link scattered communities and help create a united cultural and political group. For example, Norwegian-language newspapers and magazines circulated to Norwegian communities through the United States in the late 1800s and early 1900s helped maintain a shared Norwegian identity despite geographic dispersal. More dramatically, radio and television in Greenland played a major role in uniting the dispersed Inuit population into a political unit, a group then able to achieve home rule. Second, ethnic media help maintain a sense of ethnic identity by linking diaspora communities to the homeland. In immigrant media, important focal points are reports and editorials about events in the homeland or effects on it from national and international developments. For example, Jewish English-language weeklies in the metropolitan New York City area regularly report on events in Israel and political developments in the United Nations, Middle East, and United States that affect Israel. Homeland ties are so important that homeland governments support some ethnic publications; an example is *Pakistan Affairs*, published by the Pakistan Embassy in Washington D.C., which reaches about 25 percent of Pakistanis in the United States. Third, ethnic media help revitalize and maintain the traditional culture and ethnic pluralism. This is the major function and often the explicit goal of ethnic media in contemporary indigenous cultures, particularly Eskimo and Inuit groups in Alaska, Canada, and Greenland, and ethnic minorities in the former Soviet Union. Ethnic media help maintain cultural identity and integrity in a number of ways:

1. The use of the native language—even if only for some programming or in some publications—increases the importance of the language in day-to-day communication, standardizes dialects, provides a model for those who do not speak the language, and distinguishes members of the indigenous community from outsiders.

2. Coverage of news and the presentation of information of interest to the community through news reports, essays, editorials, and informational, educational, and entertainment programming represents the agenda of the ethnic group and affords it priority over other news and information.

3. The community bulletin board function helps involve community members in community events.

4. Advertising by local merchants, many of whom are members of the ethnic community, strengthens the local economy and encourages members of the community to use local stores and services.

5. Ethnic media efforts that succeed become a public symbol of ethnic group vitality and the group's will and ability to survive and develop its own cultural institutions within a dominant society.

6. Ethnic journalists who are strongly supportive of ethnic solidarity and identity often become influential in the community due to their high visibility, speaking at public forums and serving as role models for children.

The fourth and final function of ethnic media is the opposite of the third function of cultural maintenance—to encourage assimilation into mainstream society. Ethnic media may serve this purpose, although not always by design, in a number of ways:

1. While ethnic journalists often support ethnic solidarity, they are also frequently in contact with mainstream society and use information from the mainstream press, which may reflect the interests of the dominant society.

2. Use of mainstream designs and styles, such as spot news, talk shows, quiz shows, soap operas, and standards of decency, may replace traditional ways of sharing information such as through gossip or group newspaper reading.

3. In order to survive, ethnic media must appeal to the widest possible audiences, which often include individuals or communities only marginally affiliated with the core ethnic community, and which may dilute the content of reports and programming with mainstream values and ideas.

4. Ethnic media are often published or presented in the dominant language either wholly or in part, thereby weakening the use of the native language.

5. The use of modern technology may disrupt traditional values, patterns of interaction, and music and art styles.

The ethnic media played a major role in maintaining group identity and ties to the homeland, and easing assimilation among most if not all immigrant groups in the United States. Tens of thousands of ethnic newspapers and magazines sprang up during the era of the great European and Asian immigration to the United States in the late 1800s and early 1900s, and in the mid-1960s ethnic media reappeared again in a great number of variations as part of the Latin American and Asian immigration. The contents usually feature news and opinion pieces about and events relevant to the homeland, social news, literature and literary criticism, and essays on American citizenship. Although many efforts were short-lived and only a few newspapers and magazines continue to appear, even failed efforts are a source of pride in ethnic communities. While some publications were meant for the entire ethnic group, many were published for localized communities in large cities such as Chicago and New York, and others were published as a means of communicating the views of particular political or religious factions within the larger ethnic community. For example, Armenian-Americans have access to two daily newspapers—*Hairenik* (Fatherland), established by the nationalistic Tashnag political party, and *Baiker* (Struggle), established by the more conservative Ramgavar party, as well as weeklies published by each party. Similarly, the Albanian-American community supports three magazines—*Jeta Musilmane Shqiptare* (Albanian

Muslim Life) for Muslim Albanians, *Drita Evërtetë* (The True Light) for Orthodox Albanians, and *Jeta Katholike Shqiptare* (Albanian Catholic Life) for Catholic Albanians. In large communities, a range of specialized publications might have enough readers to survive. In Chicago, for example, the large Czech community supported magazines aimed at Czech women and farmers, and a satirical review, in addition to the usual array of newspapers and magazines.

The success of immigrant publications rested on a core of intellectuals to found and write it, as well as a large, localized population to support it. Over time, as the second and third generations stopped using the native language, many immigrant publications shifted to English, and then declined in circulation or ceased publication as the population assimilated and dispersed. For example, in 1910 there were 58 weekly and 232 monthly Swedish-language publications in the United States with a circulation of 650,000. By the 1970s only 5 were left, with a circulation of no more than 15,000.

In the United States today, the Latino population supports active and growing ethnic media featuring Spanish- and English-language publications, as well as radio and television programs distributed to wide markets via satellite and cable. In general, the Latino ethnic media serve similar preservation and assimilation functions as did the earlier European ethnic media.

In recent years, a number of indigenous American Indian, Eskimo, and Inuit communities in North America have been actively developing native-language, bilingual, and English-language media featuring ethnic news, information, and entertainment. The media have taken the form of newspapers and other print publications, radio, and television, which is able to reach a very large audience via satellite. Many of these efforts are only just beginning and may not be successful, but nearly all are undertaken with the explicit goal of helping to preserve the native culture and providing balance to the as-

similative force of the mainstream media that appeal to the younger generation.

See also ASSIMILATION; ETHNIC IDENTITY AND SOLIDARITY; PLURALISM.

Riggins, Stephen H., ed. (1992) *Ethnic Minority Media: An International Perspective.*

Subervi-Vélez, F. A. (1986) "The Mass Media and Ethnic Assimilation and Pluralism: A Review and Research Proposal with Special Focus on Hispanics." *Communication Research* 13: 71–96.

Thernstrom, Stephan, ed. (1980) *Harvard Encylopedia of American Ethnic Groups.*

ETHNIC NATIONALISM

Any consideration of the concept of ethnic nationalism, and its application to ethnic relations across cultures, requires a definition of key concepts associated with the idea of ethnic nationalism. These include nationalism, nation, state, nation-state, national sentiment, national culture, national character, ethnic separatism, and ethnic nationalism. It must be noted that students of ethnicity and ethnic relations coming from a wide range of disciplines do not utilize a single definition of any of these concepts, and in fact the concepts are often used imprecisely, especially concerning ethnic relations in a global sense.

Nationalism is an ideology, a political strategy, and a type of social movement that developed following the French Revolution. As an ideology, nationalism encompasses the idea that a social group (a nation or nation-state) has the right to create its own laws and develop and support its own institutions, that each nation is unique, and that the world is composed of these nation-states. As a political strategy and social movement, nationalism has been a major force for the organization of the world into the 200 nations that exist today.

The rise and spread of nationalism is tied to industrialization, colonization, racism, and the spread of capitalism outside of Europe. In the post–World War II world, nationalism is linked to the end of colonialism and the beginning of state-building in the Third World, and to the demise of Communist governments in Europe. Contrary to the expectation of some experts, the spread of nationalism as both an ideology and movement has accompanied the expansion of the world system in which all nations are linked together economically, and to a lesser extent politically, as national borders have become more permeable in terms of the flow of people, goods, services, information, and culture. As a relatively recent phenomenon, nationalism is an "invented tradition" in that members of the nation-state (generally the elites) find, recall, make up, and stress visible symbols of cultural themes that signify their national cultural identity. These symbols are often expressed in language, music, dance, theater, literature, folklore, and other enduring symbols, as well as in more basic aspects of culture such as patterns in interpersonal relationships and social structure. For example, Danish society in the eighteenth century was much like other European societies, particularly for those who lived in feudal states and towns. However, a purer Danish culture existed among the rural peasantry, and this tradition forms the basis of modern Danish national identity. Key modern-day features of this cultural tradition include the Danish language, communalism and cooperative work organizations, sexual freedom, gender equality, participation in voluntary associations, citizenship, and folk arts and crafts. The notion of nationalism encompasses all citizens of a nation—rich and poor, urban and rural, men and women—and the only criterion is accep-

General Djokhar Dudayev among his supporters in the Chechen–Ingush independence movement. The status of the Chechen–Ingush region as an independent republic remains unresolved.

tance as a citizen of the nation-state. Through this process of nationalism, modern nations have come into existence with a clear sense of identity that distinguishes them from their neighbor nations. Thus, there is a Dutch nation, a Norwegian nation, and a Swedish nation, in both the political and cultural senses. This process is now nearly complete for most industrialized nations, and is a major issue for Third World postcolonial states seeking to develop nationalistic sentiments with a population composed of numerous ethnic groups with their own histories, traditions, and homelands.

The term *nation* is used with considerable imprecision and has a variety of meanings. In one usage it refers to an ethnic group (which defies easy definition as well) that is organized and mobilized for political action. In this usage, an ethnic group is one whose members feel a shared sense of identity and solidarity on the basis of a shared language, religion, culture, history, or race, or alternatively, a group that coalesces in the context of external oppositional forces. The term *state* can be used alone, and is sometimes used in conjunction with nation, as in nation-state. When used alone, state refers to a political entity with clear boundaries; sovereignty over its own territory; established criteria for citizenship; one system of law for all; state-backed institutions of socialization, such as an education system; and social and cultural mechanisms to promote the allegiance of its citizenry, such as a national flag or anthem. This same definition is also used by some for nation, creating confusion about the difference between the two. The difference is suggested by the definition of nation-state as a nation whose boundaries are the same as a state. Nation-states, so defined, are rare in the modern world, and those that qualify, or nearly qualify, such as Japan or Korea, are sometimes called culturally homogeneous states. Thus, nation-state is often used to mean a nation or state in the political sense, without regard for the degree of cultural homogeneity.

Associated with, and perhaps components of, nationalism and nation are *national sentiment, national culture,* and *national character.* National sentiment is a shared sense of group identity and cohesiveness among people residing within geographical and cultural boundaries. Patriotism, a related and more limited concept, refers to loyalty to the state. The national culture of a nation-state is the unique way of life of its people—their values, beliefs, customs, history—that distinguishes it from other nations. The concept is derived from anthropological research on non-Western cultures and the idea of cultural patterning, or consistency within cultures. Whether modern nations have a national culture shared by all members is questionable, especially in regard to ethnically heterogeneous societies. National character refers to the shared personality traits of members of the same nation. The notions of national culture and character are given much attention in ethnic humor and are components of ethnocentrism and stereotyping. For example, jokes about the titles of papers to be given at a conference on elephant research point to stereotypical views of national character (Dundes 1987, 109–111):

The Englishman gives his paper on "Elephant Hunting in India."

The Russian presents, "The Elephant and the Five-Year Plan."

The Italian offers, "The Elephant and the Renaissance."

The Frenchman delivers, "The Love Life of the Elephant."

The German gives, "The Elephant and the Renazification of Germany."

Finally, the American rises to give his paper on "How To Build a Bigger and Better Elephant."

Ethnic separatism refers to an acted-upon desire by an ethnic group (usually an ethnic minority) within a nation-state dominated by another ethnic group to become politically autonomous and form its own nation-state. The independence movements of the Basques in Spain, Sri Lankan Tamils in Sri Lanka, and Abkhazians in Georgia are examples of separatist movements.

Given these definitions, ethnic nationalism can be thought of as an ideology that supports political movement toward the formation and existence of a nation-state composed of either the members of a single ethnic group, or a group whose culture dominates the other ethnic groups resident in the nation-state. Most nation-states in the world today are of these types, with the majority in the second category. Only a few nations such as Japan and Saudi Arabia are ethnically homogeneous, and the presence of migrant workers, refugees, and indigenous minorities such as the Burakumin in Japan, and Bedouin and Palestinians in Saudi Arabia, suggests that even these nations are not demographically homogeneous. However, there are exceptions to these general patterns. In Mauritius, four ethnic groups have set aside differences in religion, language, and culture to form a nation-state. In Switzerland, regional ethnic autonomy (German, French, Italian) is emphasized and a strong sense of nationalism controlled.

In the world since World War II, three patterns of nationalism have been most obvious. First, following the end of the war—and more importantly, the end of colonialism in Asia and Africa—formerly colonized states became independent and faced the problem of building nation-states along boundaries created by the colonial powers from a cultural fabric often composed of dozens of cultures who had been united only in a political sense during the period of colonial domination. In Nigeria, for example, there are over 200 ethnolinguistic groups; in Kenya, several dozen; and in Indonesia, over 100. In some nations one group, such as the Javanese in Indonesia, are numerically and politically dominant, and maintain dominance by including in

the process some groups such as the Balinese, and violently repressing others such as the Timorese. In other nations politics are dominated by competition among different ethnic groups, such as the Hausa-Fulani and Yoruba in Nigeria, and when the political process fails, violent confrontation may result. In still other nations, groups numerically dominant or visible in one region may seek more power, or even independence, as exemplified by Muslims on Mindanao in the Philippines or Muslims in the Kashmir.

The second pattern is ethnic separatist movements in some Western nations where regionally localized ethnolinguistic groups seek political autonomy or complete independence and their own nation-state. Many of these movements predate World War II, although they have remained viable, and some have become even more active, as group leaders perceive threats to the group's autonomy from the national government. In movements of this type, as among the Québecois in Canada, Bretons in France, and Basques in Spain, a major concern is the loss of the use of one's native language through assimilation into a nation with another language (English in Canada, French in France, and Spanish in Spain).

The third pattern is the splitting up of the former Soviet Union and states of Eastern Europe (the former Yugoslavia and Czechoslovakia) and the reunification of Germany to form nation-states with one ethnic group numerically and politically dominant.

These three patterns are producing a world with more nation-states than in the past (almost 200 now compared to about 50 in 1900), with many of these nation-states built and governed on models that stress the primacy of one ethnic group.

See also CONSOCIATIONAL DEMOCRACY; ETHNIC CONFLICT; ETHNIC IDENTITY AND SOLIDARITY; INDIGENOUS PEOPLES; PLURALISM; TRIBE; WORLD SYSTEM AND ETHNIC RELATIONS.

Anderson, Benedict. (1991) *Imagined Community: Reflections on the Origin and Spread of Nationalism.* Rev. ed.

Anderson, Robert T. (1975) *Denmark: Success of a Developing Nation.*

Bendix, Regina. (1992) "National Sentiment in the Enactment and Discourse of Swiss Political Ritual." *American Ethnologist* 19: 768–779.

Conner, Walker. (1994) *Ethnonationalism: The Quest for Understanding.*

Dundes, Alan. (1987) *Cracking Jokes: Studies in Sick Humor Cycles and Stereotypes.*

Eriksen, Thomas H. (1993) *Ethnicity and Nationalism: Anthropological Perspectives.*

Foster, Robert J. (1991) "Making National Cultures in the Global Ecumene." *Annual Review of Anthropology* 20: 235–260.

Gellner, Ernest. (1983) *Nations and Nationalism.*

Handler, Richard. (1988) *Nationalism and the Politics of Culture in Quebec.*

Hobsbawm, Eric, and Terrence Ranger, eds. (1983) *The Invention of Tradition.*

McDonald, Maryon. (1989) *"We Are Not French!" Language, Culture and Identity in Brittany.*

Nagel, Joane. (1993) "Ethnic Nationalism: Politics, Ideology, and the World Order." *International Journal of Comparative Sociology* 34: 103–112.

Segal, Daniel A. (1988) "Nationalism, Comparatively Speaking." *Journal of Historical Sociology* 1: 301–321.

ETHNIC SEPARATISM

See ETHNIC CONFLICT; ETHNOCENTRISM; INDIGENOUS PEOPLES; MINORITY RIGHTS.

ETHNOCENTRISM

Ethnocentrism is the belief that one's own culture is superior to other cultures, and the judging of other cultures by the standards of one's own culture. Ethnocentrism is a cultural universal in that it is displayed to some degree by members of all cultures. Around the world, people in many ethnic groups tend to consider their groups to be more peaceful, friendlier, and more trustworthy than other groups; on the other hand, when comparing themselves to other groups, they are less concerned about being higher achievers, stronger, more attractive, or wealthier. When considered from a cross-cultural perspective, ethnocentrism is best viewed as a continuum, with some cultures displaying little ethnocentrism, others expressing some, and still others a great deal. In addition, a single culture may be more ethnocentric in regard to some groups and less ethnocentric in regard to others. In general, ethnic groups who are culturally and linguistically similar, or who live near one another and interact regularly, are less ethnocentric toward one another than are groups without such close ties.

However, even in situations of peaceful contact, ethnocentrism may not be completely absent. For example, the Toda, Badaga, and Kurumba peoples of South India are involved in a symbiotic trade network with one another. This does not, however, prevent the Badaga from seeing themselves as superior to the economically poorer Toda, the Toda as feeling superior because they do not eat meat, and both groups from viewing the Kurumbas as dangerous sorcerers. Similarly, in the various predominantly Catholic regional cultures of the Philippines, who all regard themselves as Filipinos, the members describe one another in ethnocentric, stereotypical terms—Tagalogs are proud and boastful, Pampangans are materialistic and self-centered, Ilocanos are hard-working and aggressive, and Bisayans are fun-loving and passionate.

In situations of open ethnic conflict, ethnocentric beliefs of superiority are often tied to feelings of mistrust and fear; actions are designed to limit contact with members of the other group and to discriminate against them. This is the situation between Jews and Arabs in Israel, where the Jews are the political, economic, and numerical majority and the Arabs are a discriminated-against minority. Arabs believe that Jews do not value the family and lack dignity, and see them as racists who discriminate against Arabs, do not trust Arabs, and do not want to live near Arabs or have them as friends. Jews, for their part, regard Arabs as primitive and limited, do not trust them, and do not want to live near them or have them as friends. In situations of violent ethnic conflict, as in Israel, Northern Ireland, and Sri Lanka, ethnocentrism is accompanied by xenophobia, discrimination, prejudice, physical separation of the groups, and extreme negative stereotyping. Ethnocentrism seems to be a component of all situations of violent conflict among ethnic groups, although the presence of ethnocentrism does not necessarily mean that violence will follow.

One very common pattern of ethnocentrism involves neighboring groups of different levels of economic development. The hill (tribal) and plains (peasant) Pathan of Afghanistan have very different images of themselves and each other. The hill Pathan see themselves as free, hospitable, brave, and never willing to compromise, while they view the plains Pathan as weak, quick to compromise, inhospitable, and under government control. The plains Pathan see themselves as not living up to traditional standards of Pathan behavior, but describe the hill Pathan as wild, petty, calculating, and unruly. The actual and perceived differences between the hill and plains Pathan are the result of nearly 30 years of separation and the gradual integration of the plains people into the wider Afghanistan society.

Today, ethnocentrism is a major cause of problems between the Western, industrialized portion of the world and developing nations in the Third World. The basic assumption underlying efforts of U.S. policymakers to provide assistance to Third World nations in developing stronger economies and more stable political systems is that what has worked in the West will work elsewhere. This is an ethnocentric assumption. Thus, following Western models, agricultural change centers on replacing extended families, or broader kin groups, with nuclear family farms; political succession is based on replacing hereditary succession with free elections; previously independent professional armies are placed under civilian control; and labor relations are based on collective bargaining rather than a client-patron system. Experience shows that many peoples in Africa and Asia do not accept these basic cultural changes simply because outsiders—no matter how well meaning—believe them to be "better" than traditional ways. As a result, many nations now reject Western-style economic and political development and search instead for solutions more in accord with their own beliefs and customs. Additionally, there has been a reemergence of traditional beliefs and practices such as Islamic fundamentalism and the assumption of power by traditional Fijian leaders in Fiji, as well as the persistence of cultural practices such as female genital mutilation practiced in Africa, despite external efforts to end such procedures.

Ethnocentrism is a universal feature of human life. Because it is present in all ethnic conflict situations, numerous explanations have been offered for its existence and persistence. One common explanation—which also applies to ethnic conflict—is that ethnocentrism is a rational choice made by members of an ethnic group who are competing with other ethnic groups for scarce resources such as political power or territory. Many other explanations emphasize the social-psychological aspects of ethnocentrism, and suggest that it reflects aggression displaced from the in-group to an out-group, or a projection of feelings of low self-worth or weakness onto others. Evolutionary explanations suggest that ethnocentrism is a biologically determined response to external threats against the group. Finally, explanations based in sociobiology point to a kin-group basis of ethnic groups and the role ethnocentrism plays in aiding the reproductive success of group members in competition with members of other groups for limited resources. At this point in time, all explanations are essentially conjectures that await careful testing—a difficult task because ethnocentrism is so common around the world.

Regardless of *why* ethnocentrism occurs, it is clear that one major way ethnocentric stereotypes of other peoples are spread and reinforced is through the mass media. In the past, reports by explorers and missionaries played the major role in shaping and reinforcing preconceived ideas of the "inferior" or "bizarre" ways of life of other cultures. Columbus returned from the New World to report on the cannibalism practiced by the native peoples he encountered. His reports—though untrue—were taken so seriously that the word *cannibalism* (taken from *Canib*, the name assigned the islanders) came into common usage. Columbus's first report was followed by centuries of untrue or exaggerated reports of cannibalism and human sacrifice practiced by non-Western peoples. In this case, these ethnocentric stereotypes were only one part of a pattern of genocide and ethnocide that ultimately destroyed many native cultures in the New World.

Ethnocentric descriptions have more recently been reinforced by portrayals of other peoples in literature and the popular press. The peoples of Africa, for example, are often portrayed in homogenized, stereotypical ways in Western literature: as uncivilized and devoid of humanity in Joseph Conrad's *Heart of Darkness*; as gentle and submissive in Hemingway's short stories; and as gentle, suffering, and in need of rescue in Alan Paton's *Cry, the Beloved Country*.

All of these images ignore the basic reality that Africa is the home of more than 700 cultural groups who differ widely in the extent to which they are gentle, submissive, suffering, or in need of rescue. More recently, as the television news media takes Westerners to non-Western places, ethnocentric portrayals are more immediate. For example, news coverage of the rescue mission in Somalia in 1992–1993 emphasized the use of *khat* (a mild narcotic) by Somali men, suggesting that it keeps them in a constant stupor. The reports failed to note that the use of *khat* more closely resembles the use of coffee by millions of Americans each morning than it does drug addiction.

Ahmed, Akbar S. (1980) *Pukhtun Economy and Society: Traditional Structure and Economic Development in a Tribal Society.*

Brewer, Marilynn B., and Donald T. Campbell. (1976) *Ethnocentrism and Intergroup Attitudes.*

Granqvist, Raoul. (1984) *Stereotypes in Western Fiction on Africa: A Study of Joseph Conrad, Joyce Cary, Ernest Hemingway, Karen Blixen, Graham Greene, and Alan Paton.* Umea, Sweden: *Umea Papers in English*, no. 7.

Hockings, Paul. (1980) *Ancient Hindu Refugees: Badaga Social History, 1550–1975.*

LeVine, Robert A., and Donald T. Campbell. (1972) *Ethnocentrism: Theories of Conflict, Ethnic Attitudes, and Group Behavior.*

Reynolds, Vernon, Vincent Falger, and Ian Vine. (1987) *The Sociobiology of Ethnocentrism.*

Smooha, Sammy. (1987) "Jewish and Arab Ethnocentrism in Israel." *Ethnic and Racial Studies* 10, no. 1.

Sumner, William Graham. (1979) *Folkways and Mores.*

Wiarda, Howard J. (1985) *Ethnocentrism in Foreign Policy: Can We Understand the Third World?*

ETHNOCIDE

Ethnocide is a term first used in print by French anthropologist Georges Condominas in 1965 to refer to French colonization in Vietnam. It is derived from the Latin *caedere* (to kill) and the Greek *ethnos* (nation). In general, it means the extermination of a culture, but not involving the physical extermination of the individual members of the culture. Forced assimilation, ethnicide, and cultural genocide are alternative names for ethnocide. The notion of ethnocide as something different from genocide was implied in Raphael Lemkin's 1944 definition of genocide, which brought the issue to the forefront of world debate. However, on a reality basis, it is often difficult to distinguish between genocide and ethnocide, and the two tend to co-occur in European settlement colonizations of the New World and Pacific.

Throughout human history, one common form of ethnocide has been the forced conversion of religious minorities, although this often involves genocidal actions as well, especially the threat of death if one does not convert. However, in many situations the ultimate goal of adherents to the majority religion was the eradication of the minority religion, not the killing of all its followers. Examples of ethnocide for religious purposes include Spain's forced conversion of Jews in 1492; the oppression of Old Believers in Russia; the persecution of Huguenots, Anabaptists, and others in Europe; the killing of Kazakh Islamic religious leaders (*mullahs*) by the Russians in the purges of the 1930s; and, more recently, the persecution of the followers of Baha'i in Iran. Although some adherents do convert and others are killed, for many the most common response is to flee and seek residence in nations where they will not be persecuted, and for those who stay to practice their religion in secret. In Spain after 1492, for example, many Jews (called *Conversos*) converted to Catholicism, but continued to practice Judaism in secret. Later, when some immigrated to lands of greater tolerance such as Brazil, they resumed the open practice of Judaism.

While ethnocide can be considered as a phenomenon distinct from genocide, behaviors and policies that fall within the rubric of one or the other often co-occur. This has been especially true in those regions of the world settled by Europeans in the last five centuries—the New World, southern Africa, and Australia. The indigenous cultures of these regions have been subjected to both genocidal and ethnocidal acts that have reduced the overall population from tens of millions or more to only a few million, and the number of distinct cultures from several thousand to less than a thousand. Most of these losses have resulted directly from the killing of the indigenous peoples and from the spread of European-introduced diseases, but ethnocide has also played a role. In this context of settlement colonization, ethnocidal acts include:

1. Banning the use of the native language

2. Forced relocation from the traditional homeland to a distant and environmentally different place

3. Economic disruption of the traditional economy (economic genocide), including the deliberate destruction of fields and orchards, damming or diversion of rivers, destruction of natural resources such as wild game, and exploitation of the people as slave labor or as low-wage laborers

4. Banning the practice of the indigenous religion and forced conversion to the religion of the settlers

5. Placement of the people on reservations or reserves

6. Mixing of peoples from different cultures and politically defining them as a single group

7. Removing children from their families and placing them in nonindigenous homes or schools

8. Instituting educational systems that ignore or denigrate the traditional culture and teach instead the language and culture of another society (while this was a common form of ethnocide in the past, definition of such behavior as ethnocide today is much more situationally specific, as in some polycultural settings where parents of indigenous children encourage the teaching of the dominant culture as a means of ensuring the economic viability of their children in the future)

9. Replacing traditional forms of government with others modeled on the government of the dominant culture

10. Policies or actions that ignore the social, cultural, economic, and health needs of the victims of ethnocide or genocide

11. Denial of the right of cultural and political self-determination

In the Russian Empire and then the former Soviet Union, ethnocide took the form of Russification. Russification was the formal policy of the Tsarist governments and the Communist party, whose goal was to replace regional and local cultures with Russian culture. Programs implemented to bring about the policy included settling large numbers of ethnic Russians in non-Russian regions (Russians form sizable minorities in Kazakhstan and Kyrgyzstan, for example), placing Russians in senior political and economic positions, banning the practice of native religions, forced settlement on collective farms or

in villages, and the use of Russian in the schools and as the official language. Current conflicts involving Russians and the indigenous inhabitants of many former Soviet republics such as Moldova, Lithuania, and Kazakhstan reflect long-repressed animosities felt toward the more powerful Russians, and a desire for cultural and political autonomy.

Beyond the means used, and the results of those means, a major difference between genocide and ethnocide is how the dominant group defines the victims. In genocide, the victims are usually defined as being subhuman, or somehow so different from the perpetrators that the genocide can be excused as not involving human beings. In ethnocide, the victims are not seen as subhuman or nonhuman, but rather as culturally, economically, or religiously inferior, and the ethnocidal acts are often justified as an effort to aid or civilize these inferior peoples. This reasoning has been a major justification for various relocation, reservation, boarding school, and missionary programs in the United States from the earliest contacts with American Indians through the 1990s. However, despite the good intentions of some individuals, these ethnocidal acts are almost always motivated by a desire to gain control of land or other resources controlled by native peoples.

The indigenous rights movements around the world today is a reaction to both genocidal and ethnocidal policies and practices of the past. These rights movements are motivated by a desire to revitalize cultures that were weakened by ethnocide. Various objectives include native control of indigeneous land; traditional forms of government; the teaching and use of the native language, which often involve deemphasizing the language of the dominant society; and the freedom to practice the traditional religion.

See also Ethnocentrism; Genocide; Human Rights; Indigenous Peoples; Minority Rights; Race and Racism.

Bodley, John. (1982) *Victims of Progress.*

Condominas, Georges. (1965) *L'Exotique est Quotidien.*

Cooper, Roger. (1982) *The Baha'is of Iran.*

Davis, Shelton H. (1977) *Victims of the Miracle: Development and the Indians of Brazil.*

Friedrich, Paul, and Norma Diamond. (1993) *Encyclopedia of World Cultures. Volume 6, Russia/Eurasia and China.*

Jonassohn, Kurt, and Frank Chalk. (1987) "A Typology of Genocide and Some Implications for the Human Rights Agenda." In *Genocide and the Modern Age,* edited by Isidor Wallimann and Michael N. Dobkowski, 3–20.

Lemkin, Raphael. (1944) *Axis Rule in Occupied Europe.*

Lincoln, W. Bruce. (1993) *The Conquest of a Continent: Siberia and the Russians.*

Stannard, David E. (1992) *American Holocaust: Columbus and the Conquest of the New World.*

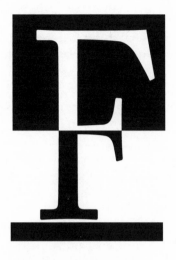

Fiji is an island nation composed of 322 islands (106 inhabited) in the Pacific Ocean. It is located between 15 and 22 degrees south latitude and 175 and 177 degrees west longitude, and covers about 18,400 square kilometers. In 1989 the population was 737,104, of whom 351,966 were Fijians and 337,557 Indo-Fijians (Fijians of Asian-Indian ancestry whose ancestors were brought to Fiji by the British colonists in the nineteenth century). Sixty percent of the population lives on the main island of Viti Levu, the location of the capital city of Suva. Fiji has been inhabited for over 3,500 years. Sustained contact with Europeans began in the early 1800s, and most Fijians were converted to Christianity by the middle of that century. Fiji was under British colonial rule from 1874 to 1970. From 1970 to 1987, Fiji was ruled by democratically elected governments, the last of which was overthrown and replaced in 1987 via two military coups. The current ethnic strife involves economic, political, and cultural conflict between the Fijians and the Indo-Fijians. The former, who seized control in the 1987 coups, have implemented and built on existing policies granting them preferential treatment and political power. The Indo-Fijians, on the other hand, now see themselves as a discriminated-against ethnic group, wrongly denied access to the political leadership achieved through the election of 1987.

Traditional Fijian society was based on a subsistence economy emphasizing the exploitation of root crops such as taro and cassava, and fishing. Life centered around the villages, and Fiji was organized into a number of chiefdoms, with each ruled by a chiefly clan. Other important groups were the extended family, subclan, clan, and clan federations. Under the British, the traditional Fijian culture (save for the religion) was largely ignored, with the British content to rule through influential chiefly clans and to allow most Fijians to lead a traditional life. Today, 60 percent of Fijians live in rural villages (where by law they own at least 83 percent of the land), although wage labor and migration to towns is becoming more common. Additionally, developments since 1987 have accelerated the availability of higher education and the number of government positions open to Fijians. Also, the British legal system is being modified to incorporate traditional elements, such as an emphasis on the avoidance of conflict and the fear of supernatural punishment.

Indo-Fijians were brought to Fiji by the British to work as indentured laborers on the islands' sugar and coconut plantations. The bulk of them, some 60,000, arrived between 1874 and 1920. Most members of the Indo-Fijian community are adherents of Hinduism, with Islam and Sikhism also present. Regardless of their place of origin in India and religion, all Indo-Fijians have been treated as a single ethnic group by the British and Fijians. Under British rule an ethnic-based division of labor was encouraged. Europeans managed the businesses and political affairs of the nation. Indo-Fijians worked on the sugar cane and coconut plantations, and later as traders. Fijians participated in traditional subsistence activities and the harvest of copra, which was processed into coconut oil for export. The small Chinese community was involved in retail trade. The British used ethnic rivalries to divide and maintain control of the population, and the ethnic division of labor was also reflected in housing, education, and political participation.

At the time of independence in 1970, Fiji was a nation divided along ethnic and social lines, with a history of nondemocratic rule (traditional chiefly clans and the British administrators), with a new constitution that called for a parliamentary democratic form of government. The new national constitution also preserved various traditional Fijian political and economic councils and alliances, afforded all Indo-Fijians full citizenship, and used ethnicity as a criterion in allotting seats in the parliament. From 1970 to 1987, elections generally left power with a coalition formed by Fijian chiefs and wealthy European and Indo-Fijian leaders. Most Indo-Fijians supported a rival party, which strove for a "one person, one vote" policy that favored the then numerically dominant Indo-Fijians and would serve to control Fijian power. During this same period, the Fijians, regarding themselves as the original inhabitants of the nation, began to assert their authority in order to reverse perceived inequities in education, housing, and economic opportunities, and also to reestablish the power of the chiefs. At the same time, increased wealth, the development of distinct wealth-based social classes, and the influence of labor unions established new political alliances that crossed ethnic lines, and in 1987 resulted in the election of a government supported by a coalition of Indo-Fijians and Fijian workers. This new government and its replacement were quickly overthrown by two coups led by the military. Under the ensuing governments, affirmative-action programs for Fijians have developed, chiefs and chiefly councils have been given increased power, and the military has been made exclusively

Fijian. In reaction, tens of thousands of Indo-Fijians have fled, making those who remain a numerical minority who claim to be the victims of religious, cultural, and economic discrimination, including the burning of Hindu temples and Islamic mosques, restriction of movement, and reverse discrimination in employment and education.

The current ethnic conflict in Fiji is caused by a mix of factors including the British colonial policies of importing foreign workers, not involving the Fijians in the developing economy, and using a divide-and-conquer strategy to rule; Fijian and Indo-Fijian unfamiliarity with democracy; the Fijian tradition of hereditary rule by chiefs, chiefly clans, and chiefly alliances; and postindependent economic growth that created wealth differentials as well as cross-ethnic patterns of economic and political interests. From the viewpoint of the Fijians, they are the indigenous people of the nation (and the victims of past colonialism as well), and as such are entitled to rule their nation; they also feel they have the right to preferential treatment to compensate for past wrongs. The Indo-Fijian perception is much different. They see themselves as losing their constitutionally guaranteed status as full citizens, with the result that they are now a discriminated-against minority in the nation where most were born and wish to remain. To date, the conflict has been mainly political and economic, with little violence, a development some attribute to the patience of the Indo-Fijians.

Hays, Terence, ed. (1992) *Encyclopedia of World Cultures. Volume 2, Oceania.* (See articles on Bau, Lau, and Rotuma).

Howard, Michael C. (1991) *Fiji: Race and Politics in an Island State.*

Lawson, Stephanie. (1991) *The Failure of Democratic Politics in Fiji.*

Naidu, Vijay. (1992) "Fiji: Ethnicity and the Post-Colonial State." In *Internal Conflict and Governance,* edited by Kumar Rupesinghe, 81–102.

Nayacakalou, R. R. (1975) *Leadership in Fiji.*

FORCED ASSIMILATION

See ETHNOCIDE; HUMAN RIGHTS; INDIGENOUS PEOPLES; MINORITY RIGHTS

FOREIGNERS IN GERMANY

The Federal Republic of Germany, located in central Europe, encompasses 137,838 square miles and borders Denmark, the Netherlands, Belgium, France, Switzerland, Austria, Czechoslovakia, and Poland. Germany is overwhelmingly inhabited by ethnic Germans (93 percent), most of whom are either Protestant or Roman Catholic. A very small minority (about 35,000) of German Jews is a mere fraction of the larger population that once existed in Germany, but who either fled or were destroyed by Hitler's Nazi regime in the 1930s and 1940s. The remaining 7 percent of Germany's population, approximately 6.5 million people, are considered foreigners, despite the fact that some have been in Germany for decades and many were born there. Of these, the largest minority is Turkish Muslims, numbering approximately 1.8 million. Because German citizenship is still defined by blood, officially Germany has no immigrants.

Historical records of German-speaking peoples begins when they came into contact with the Romans in approximately 55 B.C. For many years German-speakers inhabited a much larger portion of central Europe than present-day Germany. At its largest, prior to World War I, the German Empire consisted of 208,780 square miles. However, throughout its history, it had been fragmented into more than 300 smaller principalities. After World War I, Germany was forced to cede large portions of its land to France, Poland, and Denmark, and in addition, lost all of its colonies. In the decade preceding World War II, in what is known as the Third Reich, the National Socialist (Nazi) party came to power under Adolph Hitler. A second attempt at global hegemony was led by Hitler and the Third Reich, culminating in the Holocaust and World War II. After Germany's defeat in World War II, the victorious Allies administered zones of occupation. The Federal Republic of Germany (West Germany) was formed by the zones occupied by France, Britain, and the United States, and the German Democratic Republic (East Germany) was formed from the zone occupied by the Soviet Union. The city of Berlin, located within East Germany (but not part of it) was jointly occupied by the four powers until 1948, when the USSR withdrew to East Berlin and cut off supplies to the remainder of the city. This prompted a huge airlift by the Allies to West Berlin, and the USSR's erection of the Berlin Wall as a barrier separating the two sides in 1961. The two Germanies were reunited in 1990 after the collapse of communism in East Germany and the subsequent opening of the Berlin Wall. The unification of West Germany, which had experienced great economic growth since the end of World War II, and East Germany, which was economically stunted by communism, came as the result of negotiations by the United States, France, Britain, and the Soviet Union, as well as East and West Germany. The United Federal Republic of Germany is now a full member of the North American Treaty Organization (NATO).

The joining of two such economically polarized countries has presented great difficulties for the German government (led by Chancellor Helmut Kohl), with difficulties exacerbated by the simultaneous problem of dealing with a mass influx of foreign asylum-seekers from elsewhere in Europe, especially the former Yugoslavia. Until recently, these asylum-seekers had only to claim to be politically persecuted at home to receive government care in housing, clothing, and welfare. In a country already suffering from rising unemployment and other economic woes, some citizens have begun to focus their anger on the foreigners among them—those whom they feel are using resources that are rightfully theirs. This frustration has manifested itself in violent terrorism against those considered foreign. Although these right-wing extremists do not constitute a majority, and mass demonstrations against ethnic violence have been held by alarmed citizens, groups now referred to as neo-Nazis and Skinheads are particularly disturbing, considering Germany's recent history of intolerance and violence in the mid-twentieth century. Since the nineteenth century, Germany has based its citizenship solely on blood, and has largely considered its population to be an ethnic one, rather than defining nationality in legal terms. There are, in fact, many people that have resided in Germany for decades, some even born there, who have never been considered citizens because of a different ethnic background. These people, and not just the recently arrived asylum-seekers, have been the victims of an increase in crimes by right-wing extremists, who argue that they are "taking Germany back."

Since the 1989 collapse of communism and the Berlin Wall, the neo-Nazi youth movement and groups such as the Skinheads have been gaining momentum. Attacks such as the 1993 incident in Soligen, in which five Turkish women were burned to death in their home, have become increasingly common and have forced the government to recognize that these are not random acts of violence, but organized acts by such hate groups as the Skinheads. This neo-Nazi

reaction has been attributed, at least partly, to the mass influx of asylum-seekers since 1989. Critics say that the German government is not taking responsibility for social control, particularly of these young hate groups who seemingly have no political ideology other than anger and violence. Those right-wing politicians who point to the neo-Nazi hate groups as evidence of economic crisis have no official connection with them. However, in 1993 the German government passed a law that strongly restricted the right of foreigners to seek political asylum in Germany—a demand of both the political Right and the rightist hate groups. Although a majority is needed to amend the constitution in such a way, critics accuse the government of encouraging hate groups to believe that violence is an effective means of achieving political goals.

Previously, anyone who could get to Germany and claim political persecution at home was able to seek asylum. This is no longer the case under the constitution, and yet the violence continues. This is largely due to the fact that approximately 6.5 million foreigners reside in Germany without citizenship. Approximately 1.8 million of these are Turks, invited to Germany in the 1960s and 1970s as "guest workers," who have resided with their families in Germany for decades. Their sons and daughters, born and raised in Germany, are emerging as a new class of workers and sophisticated intellectuals who consider themselves to be more German than Turkish, and are increasingly demanding recognition as German citizens. The vast majority of these people are not relying on the government for welfare, and are in fact productive members of society. However, the neo-Nazi youth hate groups make no distinction between them and any other "foreigner." These groups also target those they call *Aussiedler*—people who are "ethnic Germans" and who, according to the German constitution, are automatically entitled to German citizenship under a "right of return." The Aussiedlers do not seem

Neo-Nazi rally in Halle, Germany, 1991, commemorating the fall of the Berlin Wall. The neo-Nazis have been charged with numerous attacks on nonethnic Germans in Germany.

very German to Skinhead gangs, who frequently target them as victims. Skinheads are subject to a gang mentality and apparently become more caught up in committing acts of violence than in carefully selecting their victims. In many cases, groups unsuccessful in finding the person they originally intended to victimize may instead focus their rage on the next non-German they find unacceptable on that particular day. Those especially at risk are anyone who appears physically different from themselves, including Turks, Africans, Asians, and anyone who "looks Jewish." "White Power" is a Skinhead cry not only in Germany, but in other countries as well. Germany, however, is under especially close watch by a world not entirely convinced that the unification of Germany—the largest country in Europe—is such a safe idea. In reaction to violence against foreigners, most recently including American athletes, the German government has taken steps toward loosening its citizenship requirements, publicly denouncing such violent assaults, and increasing the numer of police and investigators assigned to hate-crime cases. The government response may be having a positive effect, as the number of hate crimes declined from 2,366 in the first 11 months of 1992 to 1,699 in the first 11 months of 1993. At the same time, though, violence continues against a broad range of foreigners, including December 1993 attacks on Russians, Turks, and asylum-seekers.

Ardagh, John. (1987) *Germany and the Germans: An Anatomy of a Society Today.*

Craig, Gordon. (1982) *The Germans.*

Kramer, Jane. (1993) "Neo-Nazis: A Chaos in the Head." *The New Yorker,* 14 June: 52–70.

Peukert, Detlev. (1987) *Inside Nazi Germany: Conformity, Opposition and Racism in Everyday Life.*

FOURTH
WORLD

See INDIGENOUS PEOPLES.

FRENCH-
CANADIANS IN
CANADA

Canada is made up of ten provinces (Alberta, British Columbia, Manitoba, New Brunswick, Newfoundland, Nova Scotia, Ontario, Prince Edward Island, Quebec, and Saskatchewan) and two territories (Yukon and Northwest territories). Canada is a member of the British Commonwealth of Nations and became completely independent of British rule in 1982. The total population was estimated at 27.4 million in 1992. Canada is officially a bilingual (English and French) and multicultural society, and unlike in the United States, assimilation is not the model for ethnic relations. The two major ethnic groups are those of English ancestry (Anglophones), who make up the majority of the population, and those of French ancestry, who constitute about 24 percent of the population. French-Canadians are further subdivided ineo groups—Québecois (those who live in the Province of Quebec) and Francophones (those who live elsewhere in Canada); there is also a large French-Canadian diaspora in the northeastern United States dating to the mid-nineteenth century. The Canadian population also includes people who trace their ancestry to various European and Asian nations, and a group composed mainly of those who arrived from the Caribbean. The American Indian and Inuit populations are found mainly in the north and west.

The ongoing ethnic conflict centers on Québecois separatism, dating to the 1600s and the beginning of the English and French rivalry for control of Canada. Except for a revolt in 1837 and terrorist activity in 1970 (and swift reaction by the Canadian government), the conflict has been peaceful and now occupies a central place on the Canadian political agenda.

Quebec has a total population of 8 million, of whom about 90 percent are Québecois. It is the second largest province after Ontario, which has a population of about 10 million. Once largely agricultural, Quebec is now a highly industrialized province, with only 2 percent of the people engaged in agricultural work. The population is socially stratified into a powerful though minority Anglophone sector and French-Canadian business and professional, middle, and working classes, the last composed of unionized workers and agricultural laborers. Quebec has experienced economic difficulties since the early 1970s and has the highest unemployment rate of any Canadian province. In accord with the Canadian constitution, Quebec has its own parliament, which manages health, educational, economic, and social matters in the province, but as a part of Canada, other matters are under the jurisdiction of the national government. The legal system combines French civil law with British criminal law. French-Canadians are mainly Roman Catholic, although the influence of the church has weakened considerably since the 1960s. French is the official language of Quebec and is a key feature of French-Canadian autonomy. French-Canadians outside of Quebec have difficulty maintaining the use of French outside the home, while Anglophones in Quebec complain of discrimination based on their use of English. Thus, linguistic conflict between the French- and English-speaking communities is both a real struggle and one that symbolizes the underlying conflict between two different cultural traditions.

The first Europeans to reach what is now Canadian land were the Norse in about A.D. 1000. In 1497–1498, the Italian explorers John and Sebastian Cabot, sailing for England, were the first Europeans to make a landing in Canada with any subsequent ramifications. French navigator Jacques Cartier claimed eastern Quebec for France in 1534, and in 1608 Samuel de Champlain founded Quebec City. France ruled Canada until 1760, and nearly all contemporary French-Canadians trace their ancestry to French settlers who arrived during this 150-year period. The English were also active in settling the region during this time, and although they stayed mainly in the east, French and English conflict over Quebec and other territories was not uncommon. English-French conflict in Canada was part of a broader pattern of conflict and involved King William's War and the War of Spanish Succession in Europe. The French-and-Indian wars in Canada from 1756 to 1763 ended in English victory and control of the entire region, with New France becoming an English colony.

During the period of French settlement and independence, New France was a distinct society and culture based on the language, culture, and law of France. It had a powerful Roman Catholic clergy, a feudal economic and social system, and a fur trade exclusively with France. Thus, French-English conflict, both then and now, is not based simply on competition for land, but on the coexistence of two very different societies. In 1774 the English rulers recognized French distinctiveness in the Treaty of Quebec, which granted the latter cultural autonomy. Until the mid-1800s New France, or Lower Canada as it had come to be called, functioned as a semiautonomous region with its own culture and parliament, and church leaders maintained peaceful relations with the English rulers. In 1867 modern Canada began to emerge with the founding of a federation of five provinces; Lower Canada, mainly French in population and culture, was renamed Quebec. Canada continued to expand (adding five more provinces by 1949), evolving economically and politically into a modern industrial nation.

Although Quebec was, and continues to be, involved in Canadian development and growth, some Québecois felt left out of the process; others prefer to be separate, desiring that Quebec become an independent nation based on its French culture. Thus, the French-Canadian question in Canada is one that pits the separatists against the nationalists or federalists, who want Quebec to remain within the federation. This is an issue that divides not only Québecois but also English-speaking Canadians outside the province, some of whom (particularly those from the western provinces) question why Quebec is entitled to any type of distinct status.

The question of Quebec independence has been a major issue of Canadian politics since the mid-1940s. Major national political parties have generally opposed Quebec independence, with the Conservatives preferring assimilation and the Liberals generally granting concessions in the form of increased autonomy to keep Quebec in the federation. Opinion within Quebec has also been divided, and after much agitation for separation from Canada, in 1980 provincial voters rejected such a move, perhaps because of difficult economic conditions that led many to believe it would be more advantageous to remain a part of Canada. The Meech Lake Agreement of 1987 assured Quebec independent status within the Canadian federation, but it is seen as less than adequate by some separatists who want Quebec to have virtually complete authority over foreign policy, defense, and economic matters that are currently under the control of the national government. In 1994 the separatist Reform party forms the largest opposition party to the controlling Labor party in the national Parliament, which means that separatism is likely to remain a major political issue. It is expected that another referendum on separation will be held in 1995.

Hamilton, Roberta. (1988) *Feudal Society and Colonization: The Historiography of New France.*

Legendre, Camille. (1982) *French Canada in Crisis: A New Society in the Making?*

Pilon, Lise. (1990) "French Canadians." In *Encyclopedia of World Cultures. Volume 1, North America,* edited by Timothy J. O'Leary and David Levinson, 130–133.

Wade, Mason. (1968) *The French Canadians, 1760–1967.* 2 vols.

The term *genocide* was coined in 1944 by the Polish-American scholar Raphael Lemkin and is from the Greek *genos* (race or kind) and *cide* (to be killed). The 1948 United Nations Convention on Genocide provides the most generally accepted definition, one that has now been ratified by over 100 nations:

> In the present Convention, genocide means any of the following acts committed with intent to destroy, in whole or part, a national, ethnic, racial or religious group, as such:
>
> (a) Killing members of the group;
>
> (b) Causing serious bodily or mental harm to members of the group;
>
> (c) Deliberately inflicting on the group conditions of life calculated to bring about its physical destruction in whole or in part;
>
> (d) Imposing measures intended to prevent births within the group;
>
> (e) Forcibly transferring children of the group to another group.

To the categories covered in the U.N. Convention, some scholars add political and economic groups. By broadening the definition in this way, repression involving the killing or forced relocation of political opposition groups can also be considered a form of genocide. Examples of such acts in this century include the Soviet Union in World War II, the People's Republic of China during the Cultural Revolution, the Indonesian government against Indonesian Communists, and the El Salvador government against El Salvadorian Leftists. *Politicide* is the label sometimes used instead of genocide when the victims are political groups. Such acts, however, are not subject to U.N. intervention, although the U.N. has never directly intervened in any activity simply because it was considered genocide.

Various attempts have been made by social scientists to develop classification systems to help order and explain the numerous types of genocides that have occurred throughout human history. One classification scheme developed by Helen Fein differentiates among genocides that appeared before the rise of modern nation-states: (1) those to eliminate other faiths, (2) those to eliminate rival tribes, and those carried out by nation-states, (3) mass killings to legitimize political power, (4) to kill indigenous cultures, and (5) to kill rebellious elements. Another typology distinguishes among four major types, on the basis of the purpose of the genocide: "(1) to eliminate the threat of a rival; (2) to acquire economic wealth; (3) to create terror and (4) to implement a belief, theory or an ideology." (Jonassohn and Chalk 1987, 12) The fourth type is further subdivided into four subtypes based on whether the group targeted for genocide and the accusations against it are true or false. A third typology developed by Barbara Harff lists four types on the basis of the political context in which the genocide occurs: (1) postwar, postimperial, (2) postcolonial, (3) postcoup or postrevolution, and (4) conquest. This typology is also of explanatory importance as it suggests that a precondition for genocide is national upheaval due to lost wars, political consolidation, revolution, rebellion, or conquest. If such upheaval occurs in a society with marked ethnic, value, or religious variation, genocide might result, especially if no other societies intervene to prevent it. The presence of marked differences among cultural and religious groups in nearly all nations where genocide has occurred suggests that genocide is a product of plural societies.

Although much current attention is focused on genocides in the twentieth century, most genocides in human history have been perpetrated by colonial powers against the indigenous peoples of the New World, Australia, and southern Africa. The majority of victims have been the cultures and native peoples of the Caribbean, North America, Middle America, and South America who, beginning with Columbus's second expedition in 1494, were the target of genocidal and ethnocidal policies and acts that in some places continue today. These peoples were first targeted by the colonial governments—Portuguese, Spanish, French, and English—and then by the national cultures that succeeded the colonists as the rulers of the New World. Although the details vary from place to place, genocidal activities usually involved direct government involvement or support; a racist belief system that defined the native peoples as subhuman; raids and wars to kill native men, women, and children; the public execution of leaders; forced relocations; placement on reservations; removal of children; massacres; the purposeful spread of European diseases such as smallpox, from which the native people had no natural immunity; enslavement; and wars among native groups caused directly or indirectly by government policy or action.

Although the size of the pre-Columbian population is unknown, a comparison of historical estimates (now considered to be reasonably accurate) with more recent estimates and census figures indicates the enormity of the New World genocide. Within 100 years of Columbus's arrival, the Caribbean population, composed mainly of about 10 million Arawaks and Caribs, had disappeared entirely. In Mesoamerica, the population was reduced from about 30 million to under 300,000 in less than 100 years. In North America, an indigenous population of about 15 million declined to a low of 237,000 in 1900, and has now increased to about 2 million. In South America, a native population of nearly 40 million declined to 443,000 by 1570 and is now about 15 million. Some deaths resulted from the nonpurposeful spread of European diseases such as smallpox, measles, mumps, whooping cough, and cholera, but it is not unreasonable to assume that at least 50 percent were the direct result of genocide or the indirect result of ethnocide. In short, some 95 percent of the population of the New World was exterminated as a result of the arrival of and settlement by Europeans.

The situation is much the same in regard to the disappearance of New World cultures, although it is impossible to estimate how many actually existed in 1492. It is likely, though, that in North America at the time of European contact at least 1,000 different languages were spoken, a number that has decreased to about 100; efforts are under way to revive the use of some that have fallen into disuse. In South America and Middle America, numerous cultures disappeared, and in the Amazon they continue to disappear. In the Caribbean there are no remaining native cultures, although some survivors who fled to Middle America merged with others to form new cultures such as the Miskito. (See end of article for a list of extinct New World cultures.)

The situation in Australia was much the same, although because the number of aboriginal cultures and individuals was much less, there were fewer to be exterminated. The Australian genocide that has drawn the most attention was the extermination of the Tasmanians by the British. At the time of British arrival in 1803, Tasmania had been inhabited for some 23,000 years. In 1803 the total number of Tasmanians (the

Group of Tasmanians in the mid-1800s. Following English settlement in 1803, the 2,000–3,000 Tasmanians then living were hunted and killed. The culture has been extinct since the late 1800s.

island's inhabitants were actually a number of related though politically distinct groups) was between 2,000 and 5,000. By 1876 the last full-blooded Tasmanian was dead—the result of wars meant to kill them off and forced relocation.

In the twentieth century, the two genocides that have drawn the most attention are the kill-ing of about 1.5 million Armenians by the Turks in 1915–1917, and the killing of about 6 mil-lion Jews, 500,000 Gypsies, and other groups by Nazi Germany during World War II. The Nazi genocide of Jews led to the ongoing inter-est in genocide we see today. It has also become a matter of controversy as to whether this event, referred to as the Holocaust, is a singularly unique event in human history or the most extreme case of a human history filled with genocide. Both the Armenians and Jews were middleman minorities, a type of social group that is often the target of discrimination and genocide. (A middleman minority is a cultural group that serves in an economic middleman position in a society in which it is a cultural minority.) Some well-known middleman groups are the Overseas Chinese throughout Southeast Asia, Asians in Africa, and Jews in Europe. The following is a list of major genocides (not including politicides) of the twentieth century.

Major Genocides of the Twentieth Century

Perpetrator	Victim	Year
Germany	Herero	1904
Turks	Armenians	1915–1917
Germany	Jews, Gypsies	1938–1945
USSR	Chechen/Ingush, Karachay, Balkars, Jews, Meskhetian Turks, Crimean Tatars	1943–1968
Pakistan	Baluch	1958–1974
Iraq	Kurds	1959–
Angola	Kongo	1961–1962
Paraguay	Aché	1962–1972
Tutsi (Burundi)	Hutu	1965–
Nigeria	Igbo	1966
Uganda	Karamojong, Acholi, Lango, Asians	1971–1986
Indonesia	Timorese	1975
Myanmar (Burma)	Muslims	1978–
Iran	Baha'i, Kurds	1981–
Serbs	Bosnian Muslims	1992–

The following is a partial list of New World cultures that are physically or culturally extinct due to genocide and/or ethnocide.

North America

Alsea	Mugulasha
Apalachee	Nicola
Atakapa	Okelousa
Bayogoula	Pamilco
Beothuk	Pamunkey
Biloxi	Piro
Calusa	Quinipissa
Chakchiuma	Secotan
Chawaska	Siuslaw
Chimariko	Southhampton Inuit
Coahuilteco	Susquehanna
Conestoga	Takelma
Coos	Tangipahoa
Costano	Timucua
Cusabo	Tlatskanai
Edisto	Tolowa
Hitchiti	Tsetsaut
Jumano	Tutelo
Kamia	Umpqua
Karankawa	Wappinger
Kwalhiokwa	Washa
Mackenzie Inuit	Wenrohonron
Manso	Yamasee
Mobile	Yana
Molala	Yuki
Mosopelea	

Middle America and the Caribbean

Acaxee	Boyaca
Aguacadibe	Cahibo
Ameyao	Caizcimu
Arawak	Camaguey
Bainoa	Carib
Bani	Cayaguayo
Barbacoa	Chiapanec
Bayamo	Ciboney
Bayaquitiri	Ciguayo

Cochimi
Cubanacan
Cuciba
Guaimaro
Guamahaya
Guanachahibe
Guaniguanico
Hanamana
Havana
Hubabo
Huereo
Igneri
Jaqua
Lucayans

Macorize
Maguan
Maguana
Marien
Marisi
Mayaguez
Ornoray
Pai-Pai
Paya
Sabaneque
Tahue
Taino
Totorame
Xixime

Toromona
Tupinamba
Uantuya
Urumi
Wainumá
Warpe

Yabaana
Yahgan
Yakaroa
Yapua
Yura

See also ANTI-SEMITISM; APARTHEID; ETHNOCIDE; HATE (BIAS) CRIMES; RACE AND RACISM.

South America

Arikêm
Atsawaka
Ayomén
Bisaniwa
Boanarí
Botocudos
Buijana-Piri
Care
Chaima
Chandinawa
Ciguaje
Eno
Fa-al
Garú
Genambi
Icaguate
Imihita
Iñapari
Jurí
Kabixiéna
Kamaka
Karamanta
Karirí
Kénkateye
Kiyasinga
Koëruna

Kokonuko
Kueretú
Makawahe
Makusa
Manitsawá
Mariaté
Mekka
Mongoyó
Morike
Mura
Nobenidza
Ona
Pamiwa
Pasé
Purí
Riama
Shaninawa
Shereu
Siary
Sura
Tamanako
Tapiira
Tapuya
Taruma
Tekiraka
Tiniwa

Davis, Shelton H. (1977) *Victims of the Miracle: Development and the Indians of Brazil.*

Dobyns, Henry F. (1966) "Estimating Aboriginal American Population." *Current Anthropology 7:* 395–416.

Dow, James. (1995) *The Encyclopedia of World Cultures. Volume 8, Middle America and the Caribbean.*

Fein, Helen, ed. (1992) *Genocide Watch.*

Gutman, Israel, ed. (1990) *The Encyclopedia of the Holocaust.* 4 vols.

Harff, Barbara. (1987) "The Etiology of Genocide." In Walliman and Dobkowski, 41–59.

Jaimes, M. Annette, ed. (1992) *The State of Native America: Genocide, Colonization, and Resistance.*

Jonassohn, Kurt, and Frank Chalk. (1987) "A Typology of Genocide and Some Implications for the Human Rights Agenda." In Walliman and Dobkowski, 3–20.

Kuper, Leo. (1985) *The Prevention of Genocide.*

Lemkin, Raphael. (1944) *Axis Rule in Occupied Europe.*

Lizarralde, Manuel. (1992) *Index and Map of the Contemporary South American Indigenous Peoples.* Unpublished manuscript, University of California at Berkeley.

O'Leary, Timothy J., and David Levinson, eds. (1990) *The Encyclopedia of World Cultures. Volume 1, North America.*

Reynolds, Henry. (1981) *The Other Side of the Frontier.*

Rummel, R. J. (1991) *China's Bloody Century: Genocide and Mass Murder since 1900.*

Stannard, David E. (1992) *American Holocaust: Columbus and the Conquest of the New World.*

Ternon, Yves. (1981) *The Armenians: History of a Genocide.*

Walliman, Isidor, and Michael N. Dobkowski, eds. (1987) *Genocide and the Modern Age.*

GHETTO Ghetto refers to an area within a city occupied by a distinct ethnic group. The term is evidently derived from the Italian *geto vecchio* meaning "old foundry," referring to the former use of the site of the Jewish ghetto established in Venice in 1516. The Venice ghetto was one of a number established in European cities in the fifteenth through seventeenth centuries designed to keep Jews physically separate from the predominantly Christian population. In towns and villages too small to house a ghetto, all Jews were required to live on a single street. In a city, the Jewish ghetto was usually surrounded by a wall; a locked gate closed Jews in at night. During the day they were permitted to leave the ghetto and interact openly with non-Jews. The question of whether Jews preferred living in ghettos (as it was safer for them to live there) or were forced to do so is a matter of debate, although it is clear that segregation in ghettos was part of a larger pattern of persecution including the wearing of special clothing or markers of ethnic identity, exclusion from many occupations, and the payment of special taxes. Jewish ghettos largely disappeared in western Europe as a result of the French Revolution and reforms in the 1800s.

In the twentieth century the label *ghetto* has been applied to urban neighborhoods occupied mainly by members of a distinct ethnic group, especially African-American neighborhoods in the United States, immigrant Turk and Greek neighborhoods in Germany, and aboriginal neighborhoods on the edges of cities in Australia. A strict definition of ghetto, and classification of an area as a ghetto, requires that a specific ethnic group be the sole or majority population in the ghetto. Exactly what spatially constitutes a ghetto is unclear; it may be an entire neighborhood, a block, or perhaps even a single building. A ghettoized ethnic group is one in which all or most of the group resides in a ghetto. In the United States in 1980, for example, 60 percent of African-Americans lived in cities, the majority in neighborhoods that were mainly African-American. Another 22 percent lived in suburban neighborhoods, again mainly African-American in population, adjacent to the city neighborhoods. Thus, some 82 percent of African-Americans, a large majority, lived in mainly African-American neighborhoods, meeting the strict definition of ghetto and ghettoization.

While a salient feature of communities called *ghettos* is occupation by a single ethnic group, a neighborhood is rarely labeled *ghetto* unless the residential group is a discriminated-against minority who are poorer than the general population. In fact, the term *ghetto* carries with it the assumption that those who reside in the ghetto are socioeconomically inferior to the general population and socially isolated from it to a large extent. While, and perhaps because, ghettos are the home of disadvantaged ethnic outsiders, they are also often the center for the expression of ethnic identity in the form of local economic institutions, churches, schools, restaurants, and entertainment.

Cross-culturally, neighborhoods called ghettos take a variety of forms including the one-ethnic-group form in the United States, neighborhoods occupied by a number of distinct economically disadvantaged groups, and immigrant communities in cities. In addition, the pattern of residential segregation is often accompanied by considerable economic interaction between ghetto residents and outsiders, and the movement of individuals or families to mixed communities outside the ghetto.

See also ANTI-SEMITISM.

Eban, Abba. (1984) *Heritage: Civilization and the Jews.*

Grimes, Seamus. (1993) "Residential Segregation in Australian Cities: A Literature Review." *International Migration Review* 27: 103–120.

O'Laughlin, J., and G. Glebe. (1984) "Residential Segregation of Foreigners in German Cities." *Tijdschrift voor Economische en Sociale Geografie* 74: 373–384.

Peach, Ceri, Vaughan Robinson, and Susan Smith, eds. (1983) *Ethnic Segregation in Cities.*

Wirth, Louis. (1928) *The Ghetto.*

GYPSIES AND TRAVELERS IN EUROPE

An exact definition of Gypsy or Traveler is impossible, although in most countries in which they live, identification of an individual or community as Gypsy is relatively easy. The three defining characteristics of Gypsy are a nomadic or formerly nomadic lifestyle, an economic system based on the provision of products or services to non-Gypsies, and marriage within the group, which reflects the powerful dichotomy Gypsies make between themselves and non-Gypsies. Gypsies are people whose place of origin is outside Europe—presumably India—while Travelers are peoples indigenous to Europe such as Irish and Scottish Travelers, Jenischen in Switzerland, and Woonwagenbewoners in the Netherlands. Intermarriage between the two categories has in some places made the distinction problematic, and some experts now prefer the designation Gypsy-Travelers, while others prefer Roma or Romany peoples for Gypsies, and for the rest the more generic term peripatetics. Population estimates vary widely, placing the number of Gypsies and Travelers in Europe between 2 and 9 million. Recent estimates indicate the following countries have the largest Gypsy populations: Romania (3.5 million), Hungary (900,000), Slovakia (750,000), Croatia (750,000), Bulgaria (750,000), Spain (650,000), Russia (500,000), and France (500,000).

Experts generally believe that Gypsies first entered Europe about A.D. 1000, having migrated from northern India through the northern Middle East. Some bands moved west and north, while others remained in southeastern Europe. These latter groups, the ancestors of the modern-day Rom, spread out from southeastern Europe in the mid-nineteenth century and are now found throughout the world.

European reaction to Gypsies was of two major types. In western Europe, Gypsies were a regular target of genocidal and ethnocidal government policies and actions designed to exterminate or deport them. They were considered pariah communities and were excluded from any meaningful participation in society. In the Netherlands, for example, from 1420 to 1750 they were persecuted, expelled, and even hunted for bounties offered by the government. From 1750 to 1868 they were assumed to have disappeared. From 1868 to today, when Gypsy groups immigrated to the Netherlands, they were again persecuted (the Dutch turned over several hundred Gypsies to the Nazis for execution during World War II). In England, up to recent times, Gypsies were frequently expelled; at times, those

Gypsies fleeing from Romania in front of the Prague main railway station in the Czech Republic.

dom, then as middlemen, and in specialized occupations such as musicians and performers.

Since the fall of the Communist governments in eastern Europe, Gypsies have become frequent victims of hatred, persecution, and discrimination, and many have fled west—a departure from history, when they were generally safer in the east. In general, the old stereotype of Gypsies as lazy, dirty, dishonest, criminal, and sickly has reemerged following the end of centralized control of free speech and ethnic rivalries. In Hungary, the unemployment rate among Gypsies is 40–45 percent, three times the national average. In Slovakia they are blamed by government officials for half the crime in the country and are described as having a high alcoholism rate. In Germany, Slovakia, the Czech Republic, Poland, Hungary, Romania, and Croatia there have been assaults on Gypsies and their property in the last several years. In Romania, in one of the worst incidents, 4 Gypsies were killed, 17 of their homes were destroyed, and 130 people—the entire community—were forced to flee in fear for their lives. There is also evidence that some governments are lax in cracking down on those who attack Gypsies. For example, again in Romania, of 16 recent incidents involving Gypsies, only the Gypsies have been prosecuted. Anti-Gypsy sentiment is not confined to eastern Europe; a recent survey in England, for example, indicates that 66 percent of the population do not want Gypsies as neighbors. In fact, the condition of life for Gypsies across Europe is generally worse than that of the general population. In eastern Europe, many Gypsies have become unemployed as the demand for low-skill labor has declined, and the Gypsy literacy rate is often below the national average. In most nations Gypsies are blamed for the problems of others and are not perceived as victims; little effort is being made to deal with Gypsy social and economic problems. Efforts

caught associating with them were subject to criminal punishment. In southern and eastern Europe the situation was different, and Gypsies were often integrated into the economy and treated better, although they were never fully assimilated in any country. In Slovakia, which always had a large Gypsy population, they worked as craftsmen and musicians for both barons and peasants, and served as soldiers in the army. Such occupations meant that they were largely settled and economically assimilated into Slovak society. In Bulgaria, Gypsies worked as serfs during the period of the Romanian king-by Gypsy organizations and those working on behalf of Gypsy rights have not led to meaningful reform.

—————

Cottaar, Annemarie, Leo Lucassen, and Wim Willems. (1992) "Justice or Injustice? A Survey of Government Policy towards Gypsies and Caravan Dwellers in Western Europe in the Nineteenth and Twentieth Centuries." *Immigrants and Minorities* 11: 42–66.

Gmelch, Sharon B. (1986) "Groups that Don't Want In: Gypsies and Other Artisan, Trader, and Entertainer Minorities." *Annual Review of Anthropology* 15: 307–330.

Hancock, Ian F. (1992) "The Roots of Inequality: Romani Cultural Rights in Their Historical and Social Context." *Immigrants and Minorities* 11: 3–30.

Liégeois, Jean-Pierre. (1986) *Gypsies and Travelers.*

Piasere, Leonardo. (1992) "Peripatetics." In *Encyclopedia of World Cultures. Volume 4, Europe,* edited by Linda A. Bennett, 195–197.

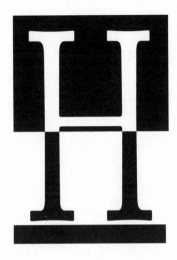

HATE (BIAS) CRIMES

Hate or bias crimes are behaviors defined by the state to be illegal and subject to criminal punishment if they cause or are meant to cause harm to an individual or group because that individual or group is different. Difference can be defined broadly or narrowly, but generally involves differences based on physical characteristics (including those based on race or physical disability), religion, ethnicity, and sexual orientation. Cross-culturally, and even within a single nation, the concept of hate crime has little meaning. In many nations "hate" crimes are not differentiated as a distinct type of crime as they are in the United States. What may be considered hate crimes may be tolerated when directed against some groups but not against others, and the degree of acceptability of attacking typical victims of hate crimes may also change over time. The cross-cultural difficulties in dealing with the notion of hate crimes are varied; for example, in Romania those who attack Gypsies rarely if ever face arrest and trial, while similar attacks on ethnic Romanians do lead to arrest and trial. In Japan, until 1992, non-Japanese residents (most of whom are Koreans and Taiwanese) were routinely fingerprinted. Acts that Germany calls hate or bias crimes are called Rightist crimes in the United States. Verbal insults hurled by American teenagers at teenagers of other ethnic groups, acts widely accepted as a part of adolescent life in the 1950s, are now reported to authorities as bias crimes. In all cultures, the notion of bias crimes is also confused by issues of free speech and assembly rights, and by the relationship between bias crimes and government-sanctioned discrimination, which is not considered a crime. Finally, bias crimes are difficult to identify and count accurately because many (especially verbal assaults) are never reported, reports by activist groups may inflate the counts, reports by police may deflate the counts, and defining a crime as a bias crime requires a police or judicial official to make a judgment about the motivation of the alleged perpetrator.

Bias crimes include a wide range of behaviors, all of which are defined as misdemeanors or crimes even if they are not motivated by bias or hatred. In the United States they generally include verbal harassment; physical assaults; vandalism, including the destruction or defacing of property such as religious buildings; threatening through acts such as cross burnings; insults delivered through the mail or by phone; and homicide. Defining a crime as a hate crime might bring with it a harsher punishment, as in Germany, where concern over neo-Nazi violence directed at Turks and others has led to increased surveillance of alleged neo-Nazi groups, more arrests, and longer jail sentences than would otherwise be meted out for convicted perpetrators.

Although little is known about the patterns and causes of hate crimes, some information from a few states in the United States and Germany indicates that the crimes are usually committed by young men who feel economically victimized by others who have taken jobs and opportunities the young men believe are rightfully theirs. The "others" are often members of other ethnic groups, particularly those who can be marked as different by their physical appearance—African- and Asian-Americans in the United States, Jews (whose institutions such as the synagogue mark them as different), and Turks and other non-Germans in Germany. However, one frequent target of hate crimes is homosexuals, with ethnic or racial difference irrelevant. In fact, what is important about hate crime in terms of the perpetrator's motivation is not that other groups have actually caused the perpetrator harm, but that they are perceived as so doing. Thus, blaming members of other groups is often irrational, suggesting that strong ethnocentric, xenophobic, and racist sentiments are involved in hate crimes.

Perpetrators are often described as people who have low self-esteem, have divorced parents, have no high school diploma, are unemployed, and who view violence as an appropriate means of settling conflicts. Although numerous groups associated with bias crimes exist in the United States and elsewhere, most attention has been drawn to so-called Skinheads—groups of young men whose individual life profiles fit the model noted above. However, the targets of Skinhead groups are not predictable. In the United States, for example, persons of Asian or African ancestry and homosexuals are common victims, while Jews are rarely targeted.

While the targets of hate crimes are known in a general sense to the perpetrators, most attacks evidently arise spontaneously, not uncommonly following group meetings and the consumption of alcoholic beverages. Thus, the victims are often selected randomly—often the first person or persons from a possible target group the perpetrators encounter. Even then, the definition of a target might be quite flexible, as for some German Skinheads for whom "anyone who looks like a Jew" is an appropriate target. Due to the often random nature of the attacks, weapons are rarely used and damage to property tends to be minimal. Of course, some assaults are planned, such as attacks on Turkish houses in some German cities.

In addition to stiffer punishments for bias crimes, programs to control the problem in the United States and Germany have also focused on changing the behavior of the perpetrators through counseling, social skills training, boot camp–type training, and behavioral confrontation. To control violence against foreigners, the German government has taken steps toward loosening its citizenship requirements, publicly denounced such violent assaults, increased the number of police and investigators assigned to hate crime cases, and initiated training programs for perpetrators. What effect these programs are having is unclear; in 1993, according to the FBI, there were 7,684 reported hate crimes in the United States, and a large but unknown number of unreported crimes. Sixty-two percent of the crimes involved racial bias, 18 percent religion, 12 percent sexual orientation, and 8 percent ethnicity.

See also ETHNOCENTRISM; FOREIGNERS IN GERMANY; RACE AND RACISM; SCAPEGOAT; XENOPHOBIA.

Kramer, Jane. (1993) "Neo-Nazis: A Chaos in the Head." *The New Yorker,* 14 June: 52–70.

Mock, Stephan, and Guide Meyer. (1993) "Breaking the Cycle of Violence." *Refugees* 93: 22–23.

Moore, Jack B. (1993) *Skinheads, Shaved for Battle: A Cultural History of American Skinheads.*

HINDUS AND MUSLIMS IN INDIA

The Republic of India is a nation with a 1993 estimated population of 897 million. The capital is New Delhi, with a population of 8.3 million, ranking third in size in the world behind Bombay at 12.5 million and Calcutta at 10.8 million. India is bordered by Pakistan on the northwest; China, Nepal, and Bhutan on the north; and Myanmar and Bangladesh on the northeast. It is now a federal republic composed of 25 states and 7 union territories. India's official languages are Hindi and English, although there are at least 16 major languages and numerous dialects presently spoken throughout the country. Many modern Indians are descendants of the interbreeding of earlier inhabitants of the region with Aryan tribes who invaded the subcontinent around 1500 B.C.

The Indian population is composed of two major religious groups: Hindus and Muslims, with small numbers of Christians, Sikhs, and Jains. Hindus comprise about 82.6 percent of the population and number about 760 million, while Muslims comprise 11.3 percent and number some 95 million. India is today the locale for a number of ongoing ethnic conflicts, the most widespread and perhaps most threatening to Indian development and stability being one between segments of the Hindu and Muslim populations, particularly in the north.

Hinduism itself has been described as more a way of life than a faith, although it is certainly one of the world's oldest religions. In fact, Hinduism predates almost all others (except Judaism, for example). It is difficult to give a concise definition of what it means to be a Hindu. With 330 million gods (Krishna, Shiva, Shakti, and Rama are among the best known) and only a few precepts to live by, it is easier to describe Hinduism as it contrasts to Islam than by itself. It is important to note that Hinduism is more than a religion in India, as its tenets (ritual purity and rebirth, for example) are guiding principles that provide the framework for social, political, and economic relations between individuals and communities, especially in rural India.

Islamic peoples (variously called Muslim, Moslem, Mahommedan, Mohommedan, Musulman) in India are actually not ethnically different from Hindus; the large majority of today's Muslims are descendants of Hindus who converted to Islam. To a large extent, Muslim and Hindu communities in India interact peacefully, with both following a castelike structure in rural communities. At the same time, Muslims of south Asia (India, Pakistan, and Bangladesh) are different culturally from Muslims of the Middle East, largely because they live among or near the majority Hindu population and interact with it on a daily basis. Still, the religious beliefs and practices among the various Muslims remain the same, as there is little room for variation in the Islamic religion. As elsewhere, the Five Pillars of Islam are followed by Muslims in India: (1) accepting and testifying that there is no god except Allah and that Muhammed is his true prophet; (2) praying five times daily, in the direction of Mecca; (3) fasting during the month of Ramadan; (4) giving alms to the poor; and (5) making a pilgrimage to Mecca, the holy land.

Hinduism became the dominant religion on the Indian subcontinent after the third century. Control over the subcontinent shifted repeatedly until the seventeenth century, when the British gained control over most of it. India remained a British colony until the first half of the twentieth century, when Indian demand for constitutional reform found a leader in Mahatma Gandhi. In 1947 England partitioned their colony into the dominions of India and Pakistan; the latter became a Muslim nation. India was established as a secular state, housing several religions, but the large majority was, and still is, Hindu. Although Mahatma Gandhi

Militant Hindus at Babri mosque in Ayodhya, India, 1992. The Hindu extremists razed the 430-year-old mosque to clear a site for a proposed Hindu temple.

advocated nonviolence, the sundering of colonial India into present-day India and Pakistan was done amid bloody Hindu-Muslim rioting in which nearly 200,000 people were killed.

From its inception, India has been plagued with periods of unrest, rioting, massacres, and demonstrations between Muslims and Hindus, although on a smaller scale the two groups do integrate daily. Despite the periodic unrest, the Congress party, embodiment of the ideal of secular democracy, ruled India virtually unchallenged until recent years. A Hindu Nationalist movement (with the aim that India be a Hindu nation rather than a secular state) has taken shape in the form of both a political party and a violent conflict. The Bharatiya Janata party (BJP), led by L. K. Advani, has campaigned on the issue of Hindu nationalism. The BJP has grown at a remarkable rate; merely a fringe political organization in the 1970s, they gained 2 seats in parliament in 1984, and in 1993 held not less than 119 (out of 533). The BJP gained much of its momentum around the issue of building a

Hindu temple on the site of a sixteenth-century Muslim mosque in 1990. The Hindu nationalists led by the right-wing BJP, maintained that the mosque was built on the exact site of the birthplace of the Hindu god Rama. The effort to remove the mosque was challenged by V. P. Singh, then prime minister of India. In response, the BJP withdrew its parliamentary support for the government during a crucial vote of confidence in November 1990, causing it to lose its majority. Hundreds were killed across the country in a series of protests and riots related to the removal of the mosque, finally resulting in its destruction in a bloody raid by Hindu nationalists in December 1992. Throughout this time the BJP has maneuvered its way to a position of recognition as a national party, and is certainly a political force to be reckoned with in the northern states.

Critics have accused the BJP of fanning the fears of paranoid Hindus who believe that the large Muslim minority has been given special treatment and too much power and leverage. Fears stem also from acute violence in the Muslim-majority state

112

of Jammu and Kashmir, where a Kashmir separatist movement has gained momentum in the past few years. The BJP has been accused of posing a severe threat to the secular principles on which the nation was founded.

The BJP finds a large base of support in Hindu youths, particularly students. The young people have also joined activist groups such as the Shiv Sena in Bombay, which has an unprecedented 40,000 members. In the past the Shiv Sena campaigned in Maharastra State (of which Bombay is the capital) on a platform in which they proposed to prevent outsiders from migrating to the state in search of employment in order to preserve such opportunities for current residents. In its latest and most violent campaign, Hindu nationalism, the Shiv Sena instigated a nine-day-long attack on the Muslims of Bombay, firebombing and charging Muslim residential and business communities, and killing more than 600 Muslims. In February 1993 the government, led by P. V. Narashima Rao, responded effectively for the first time by suppressing a massive demonstration by the BJP and Hindu nationalist forces in New Delhi. Over 100,000 people were arrested across the country and over 1,000 in the capital alone. Election results in December 1993 suggest a lessening of anti-Muslim sentiment; the BJP suffered wholesale defeats and lost control of the state assemblies in the northern states of Uttar Pradesh, Madhya Pradesh, Rajasthan, and Himachal Pradesh.

Ahmad, Imtiaz, ed. (1981) *Ritual and Religion among Muslims in India.*

Chaudhuri, Nirad C. (1979) *Hinduism: A Religion To Live By.*

Hockings, Paul, ed. (1992) *The Encyclopedia of World Cultures. Volume 3, South Asia.*

Mann, E. A. (1992) *Boundaries and Identities: Muslims, Work and Status in Aligarh.*

Zaehner, R. C. (1962) *Hinduism.*

HOMELAND

See DIASPORA; IRREDENTISM.

HOPI AND NAVAJO

The Hopi (also called Moqui or Tusayan) are an American Indian nation who live on their reservation in the northeastern portion of Arizona. In 1988 the Hopi tribal enrollment was 6,624; today there may be as many as 10,000. Their language is part of the Shoshonean branch of Uto-Aztecan. The Hopi peoples' first contact with Europeans came in 1540 with the Spanish explorer Francisco Vasquez de Coronado. In the seventeenth century attempts were made to convert the Hopi to Christianity, but following the destruction of Spanish missions toward the end of the century there was little contact between Hopi and settlers. In the latter half of the nineteenth century, there was further contact with Americans, and the first reservation was established in 1882. Today there are approximately 11 compact villages in which the Hopi live. Each village has elected representatives who convene a tribal council, in accordance with the tribal constitution adopted in 1936, to adjudicate clan land disputes and warfare. Religion is central to Hopi life; kivas, or ceremonial chambers, are scattered throughout villages and among houses, and are used for sacred ceremonial purposes and as clubhouses for men. Additionally, there are several other natural shrines outside the village to which Hopi make pilgrimages to offer prayers to their deities. The Hopi are a farming people with a reputation for nonviolence.

The Navajo (also called Apaches de Nabaju, Dine, Dineh, Dinneh, Nabajo, Nabaju) are located in Arizona and New Mexico. Their traditional home had been on the Colorado Plateau, and the present Navajo reservation encompasses approximately 25,000 square miles in the Four Corners area of the Southwest (Arizona, Utah, Colorado, and New Mexico). In 1988 their total population was estimated at approximately 200,000, making them one of the largest American Indian nations in North America. While most remain on the Navajo Reservation (about 150,000) there are substantial Navajo populations in Southwest cities as well. Their language belongs to the Apachean branch of the Athapaskan family.

Originally hunters and gatherers, after their migration from Canada to the Southwest the Navajo adopted agriculture and became nomadic sheepherders. Although in the sixteenth century the Spanish managed to subjugate other American Indian tribes, the Navajo resisted conquest. The annexation of New Mexico in 1848 led to an American military campaign in 1874 that eventually ended the Navajo wars. In 1868 a treaty was signed that allowed the Navajo to return to their original homeland and established a reservation. The Navajo have not traditionally been town dwellers, preferring instead a semimobile existence. Only since the nineteenth century, following the establishment of the reservation, have the Navajo lived in extended family encampments. Until political organization of the tribe was instituted in 1923 (modeled after U.S. parliamentary democracy), there was no system of formal ranking of authority other than kinship relationships.

For more than a century the Hopi and the Navajo have been trying to resolve a land dispute. In 1868, following the pacification of the Navajo and their release from federal internment, they returned to the northeast area of Arizona that, in 1882, became the Hopi Reservation. The Hopi Reservation is surrounded entirely by Navajo land, and the federal government has had no success in keeping Navajos from settling in Hopi territory. This eventually led to a lawsuit in 1962, and a federal district court declared the land a Joint Use Area. After the Hopi pressed the matter further, claiming that the Navajo refused to share the land, Congress passed the Navajo-Hopi Resettlement Act in 1974. The Resettlement Act called for negotiations to determine the repartitioning of the land into clearly defined Hopi and Navajo sections. A resettlement commission was also established to organize relocation. The issue finally went back to the courts, where the land was divided in half (between 10,000 Hopi and 200,000 Navajo). Relocation, which mainly affects the Navajo, has been long and costly; as of 1992, 3,000 Navajo remained to be moved. For the Navajo, relocation means a disruption to their culture, and hardship for many elderly residents of the region. Mediation has continued in order to determine the use of sacred shrines located on each tribe's property—a major issue of dispute and one whose violation quickly opens old wounds and hinders progress toward a final settlement.

Kluckhohn, Clyde, and Dorothea Leighton. (1946) *The Navaho.*

Nagata, Shuichi. (1960) *Modern Transformations of Moenkopi Pueblo.*

Ortiz, Alfonso, ed. (1983) *Handbook of North American Indians. Volume 10, Southwest.*

Titiev, Mischa. (1944) *Old Oraibi: A Study of the Hopi Indians of Third Mesa.* Papers of the Peabody Museum, Harvard University 22(1).

HUMAN RIGHTS Interest in the basic rights of individuals goes far back in human history, and such rights are mentioned in the Old Testament, the Magna Carta, and the U.S. Declaration of Independence. However, only since the end of World War II has the issue of human rights emerged as a major focus of worldwide concern and international relations, and only since the 1940s have such rights been viewed by the world community as protected by international law. The emergence of the human rights issue and its continuation as a major worldwide issue are the result of a number of factors. These include the genocide and other large-scale human rights violations of World War II; the erosion of colonialism; the demand for rights by indigenous and minority peoples; and the very common human rights violations of torturing political prisoners, political repression, and mass rapes that have occurred in numerous nations in the last 50 years.

The basic definition and framework for the subsequent consideration of human rights is contained in the Universal Declaration of Human Rights adopted and proclaimed by the United Nations General Assembly resolution 217 A (III) of 10 December 1948. This document, reprinted in full below, establishes as a moral principle that all human beings are entitled to certain rights and freedoms. The Universal Declaration has been followed by numerous other documents focusing on specific rights or categories of rights pertaining to genocide, protection of war captives and victims, collective bargaining, prostitution, children, refugees, prisoners, slavery, marriage, forced labor, racial discrimination, cultural rights, political asylum, mental retardation, hunger and malnutrition, disabled persons, religion, and medical care.

From the viewpoint of ethnic relations, human rights violations against entire ethnic groups are fundamentally different from those against individuals. Human rights violations involving ethnic groups are purposeful acts intended to harm both individuals who are members of a specific ethnic group and the group itself. Such violations commonly include mass killings, deportations, rapes, denial of food and housing, torture, detention without due process, destruction of dwellings and material possessions, and

destruction of cultural, educational, and religious institutions. When a national government is directly involved in ethnic conflict, it may be a perpetrator of rights violations and simultaneously render itself unavailable as a protector of victims' rights. Similarly, when ethnic groups engage in terrorism against civilian populations, they too are guilty of human rights violations.

Efforts to apply the concept of human rights to ethnic groups have produced three controversies in the international community. The first is whether the concept of human rights as set forth in the Universal Declaration and subsequent documents applies only to individuals or whether it also applies collectively to religious groups, ethnic minority groups, and indigenous peoples. It is clear from the policy and practice in many nations that, as regards certain matters, ethnic groups do have a collective, corporate identity. For example, land claims and other rights asserted by American Indians have been adjudicated in courts or settled by administrative bodies within the framework of the group's rights. Similarly, in New Zealand, the Maori right to political representation is a group right, not an individual right. However, when it comes to rights defined as human rights, the question of whether those rights apply only to individuals or to groups as well is not clear. Human rights advocates argue for the latter view as a way of more broadly protecting human rights, while many national governments adhere to the individual-rights-only position as a means of defining human rights as an internal matter. Efforts at applying rights protection to entire groups has led to many unanswered questions such as: What is an ethnic minority? Is group size a reasonable criterion for measuring group existence? Does a group need to be localized to exist? How does one measure group cohesiveness?

The second controversy concerns the issue of differentiation versus discrimination, which often arises when one group is afforded some rights denied to other groups. The controversy arises because in many nations ethnic minority groups want to be treated differently, often to maintain their cultural integrity or regain rights lost during times of colonial domination. The question is whether this differential treatment of groups, as in affirmative-action programs for African-Americans in the United States or like programs for Untouchables in India, is a form of discrimination, either against individual members of the group or against members of other groups who are not eligible for differential treatment. Outsiders sometimes see these special group rights (designed to reverse the effects of past discrimination) as a form of reverse discrimination. In general, when groups are given collective rights, these groups tend to have

a clear ethnic identity and membership, are different from other groups, and can be awarded rights on the basis of objective criteria that also can be applied to other groups.

The third controversy concerns the cross-cultural validity of current conceptions of human rights; some non-Western nations regard these views as reflecting Western values and therefore ethnocentric. Some experts consider this ethnocentrism a hurdle to the universal adoption and enforcement of human rights protections. From a cross-cultural perspective, much attention has been focused lately on Islam and Islamic nations and the need to balance universal human rights concepts with Islamic practices such as the use of amputation as a punishment for crime.

UNIVERSAL DECLARATION OF HUMAN RIGHTS

PREAMBLE

Whereas recognition of the inherent dignity and of the equal and inalienable rights of all members of the human family is the foundation of freedom, justice and peace in the world,

Whereas disregard and contempt for human rights have resulted in barbarous acts which have outraged the conscience of mankind, and the advent of a world in which human beings shall enjoy freedom of speech and belief and freedom from fear and want has been proclaimed as the highest aspiration of the common people,

Whereas it is essential, if man is not to be compelled to have recourse, as a last resort, to rebellion against tyranny and oppression, that human rights should be protected by the rule of law,

Whereas it is essential to promote the development of friendly relations between nations,

Whereas the peoples of the United Nations have in the Charter reaffirmed their faith in fundamental human rights, in the dignity and worth of the human person and in the equal rights of men and women and have determined to promote social progress and better standards of life in larger freedom,

Whereas Member States have pledged themselves to achieve, in cooperation with the United Nations, the promotion of universal respect for and observance of human rights and fundamental freedoms,

Whereas a common understanding of these rights and freedoms is of the greatest importance for the full realization of this pledge,

Now, therefore,

The General Assembly,

Proclaims this Universal Declaration of Human Rights as a common standard of achievement for all peoples and all nations, to the end that every individual and every organ of society, keeping this Declaration constantly in mind, shall strive by teaching and education to promote respect for these rights and freedoms and by progressive measures, national and international, to secure their universal and effective recognition and observance, both among the peoples of Member States themselves and among the peoples of territories under their jurisdiction.

Article 1

All human beings are born free and equal in dignity and rights. They are endowed with reason and conscience and should act towards one another in a spirit of brotherhood.

Article 2

Everyone is entitled to all the rights and freedoms set forth in this Declaration, without distinction of any kind, such as race, color, sex, language, religion, political or other opinion, national or social origin, property, birth or other status.

Furthermore, no distinction shall be made on the basis of the political, jurisdictional or international status of the country or territory to which a person belongs, whether it be independent, trust, non-self-governing or under any other limitation of sovereignty.

Article 3

Everyone has the right to life, liberty and security of person.

Article 4

No one shall be held in slavery or servitude; slavery and the slave trade shall be prohibited in all their forms.

Article 5

No one shall be subjected to torture or to cruel, inhuman or degrading treatment or punishment.

Article 6

Everyone has the right to recognition everywhere as a person before the law.

Article 7

All are equal before the law and are entitled without any discrimination to equal protection of the law. All are entitled to equal protection against any discrimination in violation of this Declaration and against any incitement to such discrimination.

Article 8

Everyone has the right to an effective remedy by the competent national tribunals for acts violating the fundamental rights granted him by the constitution or by law.

Article 9

No one shall be subjected to arbitrary arrest, detention or exile.

Article 10

Everyone is entitled in full equality to a fair and public hearing by an independent and impartial tribunal, in the determination of his rights and obligations and of any criminal charge against him.

Article 11

1. Everyone charged with a penal offense has the right to be presumed innocent until proved guilty according to law in a public trial at which he has had all the guarantees necessary for his defense.

2. No one shall be held guilty of any penal offense on account of any act or omission which did not constitute a penal offense, under national or international law, at the time when it was committed. Nor shall a heavier penalty be imposed than the one that was applicable at the time the penal offense was committed.

Article 12

No one shall be subjected to arbitrary interference with his privacy, family, home or correspondence, nor to attacks upon his honor and reputation. Everyone has the right to the protection of the law against such interference or attacks.

Article 13

1. Everyone has the right to freedom of movement and residence within the borders of each State.

2. Everyone has the right to leave any country, including his own, and to return to his country.

Article 14

1. Everyone has the right to seek and to enjoy in other countries asylum from persecution.

2. This right may not be invoked in the case of prosecutions genuinely arising from non-political crimes or from acts contrary to the purposes and principles of the United Nations.

Article 15

1. Everyone has the right to a nationality.

2. No one shall be arbitrarily deprived of his nationality nor denied the right to change his nationality.

Article 16

1. Men and women of full age, without any limitation due to race, nationality or religion, have the right to marry and to found a family. They are entitled to equal rights as to marriage, during marriage and at its dissolution.

2. Marriage shall be entered into only with the free and full consent of the intending spouses.

3. The family is the natural and fundamental group unit of society and is entitled to protection by society and the State.

Article 17

1. Everyone has the right to own property alone as well as in association with others.

2. No one shall be arbitrarily deprived of his property.

Article 18

Everyone has the right to freedom of thought, conscience and religion; this right includes freedom to change his religion or belief, and freedom, either alone or in community with others and in public or private, to manifest his religion or belief in teaching, practice, worship and observance.

Article 19

Everyone has the right to freedom of opinion and expression; this right includes freedom to hold opinions without interference and to seek, receive and impart information and ideas through any media and regardless of frontiers.

Article 20

1. Everyone has the right to freedom of peaceful assembly and association.

2. No one may be compelled to belong to an association.

Article 21

1. Everyone has the right to take part in the government of his country, directly or through freely chosen representatives.

2. Everyone has the right to equal access to public service in his country.

3. The will of the people shall be the basis of the authority of government: this will shall be expressed in periodic and genuine elections which shall be by universal and equal suffrage and shall be held by secret vote or by equivalent free voting procedures.

Article 22

Everyone, as a member of society, has the right to social security and is entitled to realization, through national effort and international co-operation and in accordance with the organization and resources of each State, of the economic, social and cultural rights indispensable for his dignity and the free development of his personality.

Article 23

1. Everyone has the right to work, to free choice of employment, to just and favorable conditions of work and to protection against unemployment.

2. Everyone, without any discrimination, has the right to equal pay for equal work.

3. Everyone who works has the right to just and favorable remuneration ensuring for himself and his family an existence worthy of human dignity, and supplemented, if necessary, by other means of social protection.

4. Everyone has the right to form and to join trade unions for the protection of his interests.

Article 24

Everyone has the right to rest and leisure, including reasonable limitation of working hours and periodic holidays with pay.

Article 25

1. Everyone has the right to a standard of living adequate for the health and well-being of himself and of his family, including food, clothing, housing and medical care and necessary social services, and the right to security in the event of unemployment, sickness, disability, widowhood, old age or other lack of livelihood in circumstances beyond his control.

2. Motherhood and childhood are entitled to special care and assistance. All children, whether born in or out of wedlock, shall enjoy the same social protection.

Article 26

1. Everyone has the right to education. Education shall be free, at least in the elementary and fundamental stages. Elementary education shall be compulsory. Technical and professional education shall be made generally available and higher education shall be equally accessible to all on the basis of merit.

2. Education shall be directed to the full development of the human personality and to the strengthening of respect for human rights and fundamental freedoms. It shall promote understanding, tolerance and friendship among all nations, racial or religious groups, and shall further the activities of the United Nations for the maintenance of peace.

3. Parents have a prior right to choose the kind of education that shall be given to their children.

Article 27

1. Everyone has the right freely to participate in the cultural life of the community, to enjoy the arts and to

share in scientific advancement and its benefits.

2. Everyone has the right to the protection of the moral and material interests resulting from any scientific, literary or artistic production of which he is the author.

Article 28

Everyone is entitled to a social and international order in which the rights and freedoms set forth in this Declaration can be fully realized.

Article 29

1. Everyone has duties to the community in which alone the free and full development of his personality is possible.

2. In the exercise of his rights and freedoms, everyone shall be subject only to such limitations as are determined by law solely for the purpose of securing due recognition and respect for the rights and freedoms of others and of meeting the just requirements of morality, public order and the general welfare in a democratic society.

3. These rights and freedoms may in no case be exercised contrary to the purposes and principles of the United Nations.

Article 30

Nothing in this Declaration may be interpreted as implying for any State, group or person any right to engage in any activity or to perform any act aimed at the destruction of any of the rights and freedoms set forth herein.

See also ANTI-SEMITISM; APARTHEID; ETHNOCIDE; GENOCIDE; INDIGENOUS PEOPLES; MINORITY RIGHTS.

An-Na'im, Abdullahi A., ed. (1992) *Human Rights in Cross-Cultural Perspective: A Quest for Consensus.*

Brownlie, Ian. (1992) *Basic Documents on Human Rights.*

Felice, William. (1992) *The Emergence of Peoples' Rights in International Relations.*

Heinz, Wolfgang S. (1991) *Indigenous Populations, Ethnic Minorities and Human Rights.*

Lawson, Edward, ed. (1991) *Encyclopedia of Human Rights.*

Ramaga, Philip V. (1993) "The Group Concept in Minority Protection." *Human Rights Quarterly* 15: 575–588.

Stavenhagen, Rodolfo. (1987) "Ethnic Conflict and Human Rights: Their Interrelationship." *Bulletin of Peace Proposals* 18: 507–514.

Van Dyke, Vernon. (1985) *Human Rights, Ethnicity, and Discrimination.*

Whalen, Lucille. (1989) *Human Rights: A Reference Handbook.*

HUNGARIANS IN ROMANIA (TRANSYLVANIA)

Transylvania is a region in Romania. Its population of about 8 million (35 percent of the population of Romania) is multiethnic—about 70 percent Romanian, 22 percent Hungarian, 4 percent German, and less than 1 percent Serbian. Hungarians dispute these numbers as underestimates, and the Hungarian population in Transylvania may actually be as high as 25 percent. This disagreement is only one of many conflicts between the two groups; perhaps the most important disagreement concerns the settlement history of the region. Although Transylvania currently has no political boundaries and is therefore not officially designated, the area is usually defined as including all the territory of Romania west and north of the southern and eastern Carpathian Mountains, extending to the borders of Hungary and the Ukraine; it therefore occupies 41.9 percent of the land area of Romania. For the Hungarians, interest in Transylvania is twofold. First, they have an irredentist interest; Hungarians regard Transylvania as a region of Hungary that should be returned to it. Second, Hungarians are an ethnic minority in the region, and both during and following Communist rule their rights have been threatened by Romanian ethnic nationalism. Romanian concerns include maintaining control of a territory they view as a part of Romania and the home of a Romanian majority, and building a modern nation in the post-Communist era. The Romanians perceive the presence of a large Hungarian minority as interfering with ethnic solidarity in nation-building.

The official language in the Transylvanian region is Romanian, although the version spoken there is slightly different from that spoken elsewhere in the country. Likewise, the Hungarians in Transylvania speak Hungarian, also slightly different from that spoken in Hungary. Hungarians are predominantly Roman Catholic, with large minorities of Calvinists and Unitarians. Romanians have a small minority of Roman Catholics (about 6 percent), but most are followers of the Eastern Orthodox Church.

The Hungarian and Romanian versions of the history of the Transylvanian region are markedly different and constitute a major factor in the current ethnic strife. Modern Romanian ancestry can be traced to the intermarriage of Romans and Dacians after the Roman conquest of Dacia in A.D. 105–106. According to Romanian history, this population has been the continual inhabitant of the Transylvanian region, retreating only briefly from the open spaces to escape the invasions of different nomadic groups. Hungarians maintain that they gradually expanded into the Transylvanian region after firmly establishing control in present-day central Hungary. They claim that Transylvania was not inhabited by Romanians during the tenth and eleventh centuries when Hungarians established settlements there. Current archaeological evidence is not of sufficient quantity nor trustworthiness to support either version. Additionally, since the Hungarian and Romanian ethnic groups as now defined did not exist 1,000 years ago, it is difficult to decide claims in the present

on the basis of ties to a murky past.

Transylvania was, in any case, conquered by the Hungarians and became an integral part of the kingdom after 1526, when the Ottoman Turks defeated Hungary and occupied its central region for more than a century. During this time the Transylvanian region became a semi-independent principality, attracting many Romanians and others seeking refuge from the Turkish-occupied Balkans. It was not until the late 1600s that the Austrian Hapsburgs, who had been occupying the western and northern regions of Hungary, defeated the Turks and established control. After several unsuccessful uprisings, revolts, and attacks by revolutionary Hungarians, the dual monarchy of Austria-Hungary was established. Austria-Hungary was defeated in World War I and forced to sign the Treaty of Trianon at Versailles in 1920. As a result of this treaty, Hungary lost 68 percent of its total surface area to various surrounding countries, and Transylvania was ceded to Romania, who had long viewed Transylvania as rightfully theirs. This shift of control is a basic factor in the ongoing disupute between Hungary and Romania.

Under Communist control, the relations between Hungarians and Romanians in Transylvania were often tense, but violent confrontation was controlled by the government security apparatus. Following the overthrow of Communist leader Nicolae Ceausescu in 1989 and continuing into the mid-1990s, tensions increased as the Hungarians demanded political, educational, and cultural rights denied them under the Communist policy of forced assimilation, while the Romanians are more concerned with forging a unified Romanian nation.

Kligman, Gail. (1988) *Wedding of the Dead: Ritual, Poetics, and Popular Culture in Transylvania.*

Verdery, Katherine. (1983) *Transylvanian Villages: Three Centuries of Political, Economic, and Ethnic Change.*

HUTU AND TUTSI IN BURUNDI AND RWANDA

The Hutu and the Tutsi are the major ethnic groups in the East African nations of Rwanda and Burundi. Prior to colonization (and as is currently the case), the Tutsi were the numerical minority and the Hutu were the majority. The Tutsi were traditionally herders and the Hutu were farmers, with the latter considered socially inferior by the former. In fact, traditional social and political organizations were more complicated, and the dominant Tutsi group was the Tutsi-Hima, found mainly in the south. Both the Tutsi and Hutu were organized on the basis of patrilineal clans that existed as corporate groups. The Hutu and Tutsi were closely linked to one another by a series of interlocking patron-client relationships at all levels of the social hierarchy. Ethnic conflict was rare, and disputes more commonly involved clans or ruling lineages called *ganwa*. Much attention has been paid to the difference in physical appearance—the tall, thin Tutsi and the shorter, stout Hutu. Whether this dissimilarity had a role in precolonial Tutsi dominance is unclear, although it is evident that the colonial powers favored the appearance of the Tutsi.

In both nations, the Hutu form a large majority of the population, but the relative statuses of the groups and the nature of ethnic conflict in the two nations have been quite different. Once part of German East Africa, Rwanda and Burundi became Belgium mandates in 1923 and shared one administration (known as Ruanda-Urundi). In 1962 Urundi gained full independence and became Burundi, and Rwanda followed. Violent ethnic conflict has been an ongoing problem in each nation since independence, fueled in part by Hutu-Tutsi rivalries that predated colonial rule, a regime that placed the minority Tutsi in key government and economic positions, and postcolonial rivalry for political and economic dominance. In addition to hundreds of thousands of dead, the conflict has brought about refugees and internally displaced persons. With world attention drawn to the crisis in the 1990s and political reform in both countries, the conflict was moving toward peaceful resolution until April 1994. The problems of displaced persons and refugees, who have lived in neighboring nations for as much as 30 years, have not yet been resolved completely.

The Republic of Rwanda has an area of 10,162 square miles and is located in the central African rift valley. It is bounded by Uganda on the north, Zaire on the west, Burundi on the south, and Tanzania on the east. In 1993 the population was estimated at 7.4 million, composed of 90 percent Hutu, 9 percent Tutsi, and 1 percent Twa. About 74 percent of the population are Christian, 25 percent follow traditional religions, and 1 percent are Muslim. The official languages are French and Rwanda. Both before and during colonial rule, the Tutsi minority maintained dominance over the large Hutu majority. In 1959, during Belgium administration, the Hutu mounted a bloody revolt against the Tutsi, leaving approximately 12,000 dead. Nearly 120,000 Rwandians fled to Burundi and other neighboring countries. By the 1990s some 250,000 Rwandians (mainly Tutsi) were living as refugees in neighboring nations, and some 350,000 were internally displaced in Rwanda. Since independence in 1962, Rwanda has been ruled by the majority Hutu. Throughout the 1980s the Hutu refused requests by the Tutsi refugees to return to Rwanda. Civil war broke out in October 1990, precipitated by the formation of the Rwandan Patriotic Front, a rebel force composed largely of Tutsi refugees in Uganda. The Tutsi rebels invaded Rwanda,

A group of Rwanda refugees watches a French armored vehicle in southern Rwanda. The French presence points to the often transnational nature of ethnic conflicts.

demanding greater freedoms for Tutsi in Rwanda and the right of refugees to return. The civil war resulted in more deaths and refugees, and at least 80,000 displaced persons within the nation. However, it also led to talks between the Hutu government and Tutsi rebels that, along with political reforms already under way, created an opportunity for peaceful coexistence between the groups. Among major changes were tentative agreements by the two groups to share power eventually, allow all refugees to return, and hold multiparty elections in 1993. However, violence directed by conservative Hutu against Tutsi in 1993 disrupted the peace process and real, permanent change has yet to take place. In June 1993 the United Nations Security Council adopted a resolution establishing a small peacekeeping force to monitor the border of Uganda and Rwanda, in hopes of stopping the violence by preventing the smuggling of weapons.

President Juvénal Habyarimana was killed in a plane crash in April 1994, and civil war involving the Tutsi Rwandan Patriotic Front and the Hutu-dominated government resumed. In a few months, the war has produced hundreds of thousands of deaths and massive refugee problems in neighboring nations. In June 1994 a French force of 2,500 soldiers entered the nation to protect civilians from further massacres.

The Republic of Burundi is an area of 10,759 square miles, roughly the same size as Rwanda. It borders Rwanda on the north, Zaire on the west, and Tanzania on the east. As of 1991, the population was 5,831,000, composed of 85 percent Hutu, 14 percent Tutsi, and 1 percent Twa. French and Rundi are both official languages. About 62 percent of the population is Roman Catholic and 32 percent follow traditional religions. Like Rwanda, Burundi has been the scene of violent ethnic conflict involving the Hutu and Tutsi. Tutsi remain the ruling group in Burundi despite the fact that they are greatly outnumbered by the Hutu. In 1972 an unsuccessful Hutu uprising (which itself claimed at least 2,000 Tutsi lives) led to a Tutsi counterattack of mass proportions. Perhaps fearing the same fate as the Tutsi in Rwanda and in order to consolidate their power in the postcolonial era, Burundi Tutsi systematically killed off much of the educated or semieducated strata of Hutu society, thereby lessening the possibility of further challenges from the Hutu community. Some 150,000 Hutu fled their homeland and became refugees in Zaire, Rwanda, and Tanzania, where they were joined by another 40,000 who fled following unrest in 1988–1991. With only limited leadership, the Hutu within Burundi were effectively silenced for at least a generation. The Burundi government, led by the Tutsi, had killed nearly 100,000 Hutu. From 1990 to 1992 a series of political reforms was instituted including the ratification of a multiparty constitution, the granting of more representation to the Hutu, and guaranteed safe return and the promise of land for all returning refugees. To date, some 57,000 Hutu refugees have returned. In June 1993 in the first free elections, a Hutu, Melchior Ndadaye, was elected president. He sought to encourage bicultural rule by appointing 9 Tutsi to ministerial positions (the other 14 were Hutu) and a Tutsi as prime minister. However, his efforts to weaken Tutsi control of the military and to repatriate refugee Hutu led to a military coup and his assassination in October 1993. The coup was followed by raids destroying villages, the killing of civilians by both the Hutu and Tutsi, and the dislocation of some 200,000 Tutsi. Despite efforts by the military to withdraw from the situation and allow the restoration of civilian rule, full-scale Hutu-Tutsi warfare remains a possibility.

Lemarchand, René. (1970) *Rwanda and Burundi.*

———. (1974) *Selective Genocide in Burundi.*

Trouwborst, Albert. (1965) "Kinship and Geographical Mobility in Burundi." *International Journal of Comparative Sociology* 4: 166–182.

U.S. Committee for Refugees. (1993) *World Refugee Survey.*

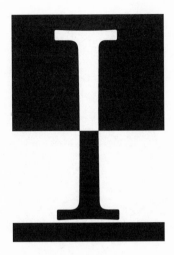

of which they now form a part, under a State structure which incorporates mainly the national, social and cultural characteristics of other segments of the population which are predominant.

A composite definition, suggested by Julian Burger, combines elements from earlier definitions proposed by the U.N., World Bank, and the World Council of Indigenous Peoples, among others. Burger's definition suggests that people are indigenous if they display all or some of the following characteristics:

1. Are descended from the original inhabitants of a territory who were conquered
2. Are nomadic or seminomadic
3. Have a subsistence-level economy
4. Have no political organization above the community level
5. Share a common language, religion, and customs
6. Are subjugated by a dominant culture
7. Have a different worldview from the dominant culture
8. Consider themselves to be an indigenous people

INDIGENOUS PEOPLES Indigenous peoples is a term that has come into common usage in the last few decades as a generic label for ethnic groups who were, and sometimes continue to be, labeled tribal peoples, national minorities, native peoples, tribal minorities, scheduled tribes, autochthones, and the Fourth World.

Despite its increasingly widespread use, there is no single agreed-upon definition of what the term indigenous people means and what specific groups should be so classified. The key elements of the United Nations Working Definition of Indigenous Peoples are:

> Indigenous populations are composed of the existing descendants of peoples who inhabited the present territory of a country wholly or partially at the time when persons of a different culture or ethnic origin arrived there from other parts of the world, overcame them, and by conquest, settlement or other means, reduced them to a non-dominant or colonial situation; who today live more in conformity with their particular social, economic and cultural customs and traditions than with the institutions of the country

Given the large variety of cultures in the world and the change they are experiencing, this definition does not neatly fit every culture that might be considered an indigenous one. However, it does provide a helpful framework for classifying cultures as indigenous or not. In general, the criteria considered most often are: descent from the original inhabitants of a region, conquest and continued domination by another group, and self-definition as indigenous.

With this definition in mind, the cultures falling within the following categories (although not necessarily all cultures in each category) are indigenous peoples.

North America
Aleutian Islanders
Eskimo and Inuit Peoples

Aboriginal people in Australia perform a traditional dance in 1992 to launch the International Year of Indigenous Peoples.

North American Indian Nations

Central and South America

Central American Indian Nations

South American Indian Groups

Europe and Russia

Ethnic Minorities

Linguistic Minorities

Peoples of the North

Middle East

Bedouin

Africa

Foragers

Nomadic Pastoralists

Oceania and Australia

Aboriginal Peoples

Maori

Pacific Islanders

Asia

Aboriginal Peoples

Ethnic Minorities

Hill Tribes

National Minorities

Nomadic Pastoralists

Scheduled Tribes

The number of indigenous people in the world is estimated at between 200 and 300 million. The number of indigenous groups is unknown, but certainly is more than 1,000, and probably several thousand. Consideration of the more than 500 American Indian nations in the New World, the Scheduled Tribes of India, the Hill Tribes elsewhere in Asia, and the dozens of Australian aboriginal groups makes an estimate of several thousand reasonable.

In the last two decades, as indigenous peoples have been seeking to reclaim their rights in the New World, Australia, New Zealand,

Norway, and Russia, the concept of indigenous people has become politically important. From a political perspective, defining a people as indigenous implies encapsulation within a dominant nation, awareness by the indigenous people of their unique identity, a peripheral place in the dominant society, moral opposition to continued dominance by the nation, and dependence on the good will of the nation to grant the indigenous people their rights.

See also INDIGENOUS RIGHTS; MINORITY; PEOPLES OF THE NORTH; TRIBE.

Burger, Julian. (1987) *Report from the Frontier: The State of the World's Indigenous Peoples.*

Graburn, Nelson H. H. (1981) "1, 2, 3, 4…Anthropology and the Fourth World." *Culture* 1: 66–70.

Paine, Robert. (1985) "The Claim of the Fourth World." In *Native Power*, edited by Jens Brostad, et al., 49–66.

Wilmer, Franke. (1993) *The Indigenous Voice in World Politics: Since Time Immemorial.*

World Bank. (1982) *Tribal Peoples and Economic Development: Human Ecological Considerations.*

INDIGENOUS RIGHTS

The quest by indigenous peoples around the world to regain or establish their rights is the defining feature of the relationship between various national governments and indigenous peoples in the 1990s. It is also an important motivating force behind the increasingly strong ties forged among indigenous peoples both within and across regions in the last several decades. Indigenous rights are also a central concern of the international community, as reflected in the

United Nations (U.N.) declaration of 1993 as the Year of Indigenous Peoples and the mission of protecting indigenous rights taken on by many nongovernmental organizations. Indigenous rights encompass two very general categories: (1) rights to which individual members of indigenous nations are entitled because they are also citizens or residents of a dominant nation-state within whose borders they reside (that is, the same rights enjoyed by other citizens of the nation) and (2) rights that accrue to both indigenous nations and their individual members because of their status as indigenous people or "First Nations" within the dominant nation-state. For example, the Taos Indians of New Mexico are entitled to the same rights as other citizens of the state of New Mexico and the United States of America, and also to special rights because of their status as an indigenous people in New Mexico and in the United States. This same dual status as regards rights pertains to all indigenous peoples around the world. Over the centuries of contact with dominant societies, these rights have been ignored, done away with, or eroded. The current quest for indigenous rights is an effort to reverse this situation.

The topic of indigenous rights is a very broad and complex one involving numerous legal, political, economic, cultural, social, and religious concepts, the definitions and applications of which vary widely over place and time. Thus, the situation regarding their indigenous rights differs for every indigenous people in the world. At the same time, there are some similarities across peoples and nations—in how those rights were lost, what the rights are, and how they are being regained.

Theoretically, the lack of, and efforts to regain, indigenous rights affects and is of concern to all indigenous peoples and the governments of the nations in which they reside. However, as a practical matter at this point in history, indigenous rights as discussed here is of greater concern in democratic, highly industrialized nations

that are in a postcolonial stage, and thus are redefining the relationship between indigenous peoples and the nation-state. These include Canada, Greenland, the United States, Australia, New Zealand, and Norway. In other nations, such as those in Latin America and some in Southeast Asia, rights are naturally of concern to indigenous peoples, but often more pressing are direct threats to their physical and cultural survival. In China and the former Soviet Union, indigenous rights are subordinate to the national agenda, although the breakup of the latter brings with it the hope that the rights of indigenous people, mainly in Siberia and the Caucasus, as well as minority groups will be established and protected. In Oceania and Africa, where indigenous peoples have taken power in many nations, indigenous rights are less of a concern; the rights of nonindigenous minorities (such as Indo-Fijians) are perhaps a more crucial issue.

The loss of rights by indigenous peoples around the world is a direct result of Western colonization. Those nations whose indigenous peoples are in the forefront of battles for indigenous rights are primarily those with a history of settlement colonization, such as Australia and the United States, where most indigenous peoples lost all or most of their land and other rights as the result of settlement and political and economic domination by Europeans. However, the philosophical and legal rationale for European dominance and indigenous displacement predates settlement of the New World, dating to the early medieval period and the reinterpretation of the Roman legal principle of *territorium (res) nullius* to mean that "a discoverer could legally occupy a territory that was already inhabited [by 'infidels'] and extend Christian sovereignty over it." Spanish and English colonization policy and practice, although the subjects of much debate in the home nations, proceeded in this way even though they conflicted with other established legal principles such as the concept of immemorial possession.

In general, economic goals outweighed legal and moral concerns, and over time most indigenous peoples lost all or most of their land base and other rights through treaties, agreements, laws, and various genocidal and ethnocidal policies, often backed or allowed by the colonial governments, and later by the national governments in the United States, Canada, Australia, and New Zealand.

The current battle for indigenous rights around the world is essentially a post–World War II phenomenon. It has emerged following the disintegration of colonial systems around the world and has accompanied the emergence of human rights as a major international issue. The U.N., through its charter, declarations, reports, and agencies, has been a major force in first exposing the problems faced by indigenous peoples and then providing a framework and mechanisms for securing indigenous rights. In both a general sense and in specific situations, the overall U.N. effort has been augmented and sometimes surpassed by the efforts of international, regional, and local organizations devoted to restoring rights to indigenous peoples. In nearly all cases, however, it is basically the efforts of the people themselves, and the moral and legal pressure they can exert on national and state governments, that determine whether or not they achieve their goals. Encouraged by the Civil Rights and Womens' Rights movements, among others in the United States, and depending on the rights being sought and local circumstances, a very broad array of techniques has been used. These include attention gained by influential leaders or spokesman; lobbying efforts by indigenous organizations, acting both alone and in alliance with other indigenous or nonindigenous organizations; support by nonindigenous advocacy organizations; alliances with other interest groups, especially environmental groups; exposure through the national media and indigenous media outlets; protests such as hunger strikes and sit-ins; participation in the political process; litigation; and appeals to international organizations. At this point, about 30 percent of indigenous peoples around the world have achieved restoration of some rights.

As in political conflicts, both sides in the indigenous rights movement generally tend to use the resources available to them in ways that are most likely to help their cause. The two sides in the conflict are, on the one hand, the indigenous peoples and their supporters, which include various local, regional, and international nongovernmental organizations; various agencies of the U.N.; wealthy and/or influential individuals; and sometimes government officials or elected representatives. On the other side, from the viewpoint of indigenous peoples, are the local, state/provincial, and national governments; political parties; local landowners; and economic interests including developers and energy companies. Within each group are numerous factions based on differing philosophies, goals, and tactics. One hurdle to resolving some indigenous rights situations has been the difficulty in sorting out who speaks for each side and who will enforce any decisions made and agreed to by the parties.

The following section provides brief overviews of seven general categories of rights sought by many indigenous peoples around the world. The issue of indigenous rights is extremely varied and complex, and no attempt is made here to provide all the details, possibilities, or explanations, but instead to give a general introduction to some of the most basic issues using a few specific examples.

Right to Recognition as an Independent Nation or Political Entity

Underlying the quest for indigenous rights around the world is a belief by indigenous peoples that they are each an independent nation or political entity, and must be so recognized and dealt with by the nation within which they now reside. For the Saami of Sweden,

Finland, and Norway, this means recognition as a distinct minority within those nations, maintenance of a separate cultural identity, and the right to use the Saami language. In Canada in 1991, some degree of autonomy was achieved by Inuit peoples with the formal establishment of a new political region in Arctic northeastern Canada called *Nunavut* ("our land" in the Inuit language), which brought with it political autonomy, land, and economic rights. In the United States, the situation regarding the independent national status of various American Indian peoples is being sorted out through administrative procedures and litigation. The issue is being monitored carefully by the world community as perhaps a model for other nations because of a variety of factors that include U.S. international status, the recognition and implication of national autonomy given or implied in various treaties with American Indian peoples, and an already existing degree of self-rule on a reservation land base by many of the American Indian peoples.

Right to Self-Definition and Accurate Enumeration

The right of an indigenous people to set for itself the criteria by which it recognizes its citizenry is vital for the survival of indigenous peoples and for maintenance of their unique cultural identities. In North America this right was traditionally held, and to some extent still is, by the national governments. In the United States, for example, the "blood quantum" measure of "Indianness" was established in the 1867 General Allotment Act when persons of 50 percent or more "Indian blood" were allotted land and those with less than 50 percent were not so allotted. The usurpation of their right to determine their own citizenry and the use of "blood quantum" type criteria are seen by indigenous peoples as inherently racist, and are widely believed to be motivated by economic and political colonial interests. External rather than self-designation is seen as a mechanism used by colonial powers to take land from indigenous peoples, to prevent them from regaining the land, to control the cost of material support and services promised in treaties and laws, and to gain access to natural resources. Politically, external control creates conflict among different indigenous groups as to who is and who is not indigenous, and can be used to define groups out of existence or prevent them from gaining recognition as an indigenous people.

Criteria commonly employed by indigenous peoples themselves include degree of adherence to traditional beliefs and practices, descent from a member of the group, socialization into the group, and a commitment to be a productive member of the nation. For example, the Cherokee of Oklahoma, who lacked a land base in the 1970s, defined themselves as composed of individuals who could trace descent along Cherokee lines. This caused their population to increase from 12,000 to 64,000 by 1985 and made them a politically powerful group in the region.

Right of Self-Determination and Self-Governance

Prior to colonization, indigenous peoples were self-governing and, from a cross-cultural perspective, used a very wide range of governmental institutions and political mechanisms to manage their internal and external affairs. These traditional systems were largely destroyed, weakened, or altered by colonization, assimilation, and ethnocide; by the twentieth century, indigenous peoples around the world were almost entirely under the control of the nations in which they lived, and sometimes also under state/provincial, county, and local control as well. This condition is called internal colonialism.

The right of self-determination includes, for most peoples, the following:

1. Independent control of their affairs
2. Control of all material and financial assets

3. Freedom to engage in foreign relations

4. Freedom to decide the extent of control they cede to outsiders

5. Freedom to choose their own form of self-government

6. Adherence to agreements between the indigenous nation and other nations only when those agreements are entered into by recognized indigenous governmental bodies or individuals

In addition, the right of self-determination carries with it all other rights demanded by indigenous peoples.

Achieving the right of self-determination, or progress toward that end, always requires large-scale change in the basis and nature of the relationship between the indigenous people and the national government. In virtually all nations where indigenous rights are an issue today, traditional indigenous-state relations were characterized by a genocidal–forced assimilation (ethnocide) policy and colonial/paternalistic practices on the part of the national government. Governments typically acted as hosts in allowing indigenous peoples to live on government-controlled land, as patrons in providing material support and services to the indigenous communities, and as guardians in directing indigenous affairs. For their part, indigenous peoples existed mostly as wards and clients of the state.

Traditionally, state policy was usually carried out by government agencies charged with managing indigenous affairs—the Bureau of Indian Affairs in the United States, the Department of Indian Affairs in Canada, and the Maori Affairs Department in New Zealand, among others. In establishing policy and managing programs, there was rarely any indigenous input. Typically, the advice and needs of groups whose goals were in opposition to those of indigenous peoples (such as land developers, farmers, ranchers, and missionaries) were instead given considerable weight.

In nations where native peoples have achieved some of the rights they seek, a shift in indigenous-government relations has been a key element in this process. In New Zealand, for example, Maori demands for their rights eventually resulted in a government policy shift from assimilation of the Maori into white society to biculturalism, where the Maori would be full participants in white society, but would also be able to maintain their indigenous culture. This policy shift was backed up by various practical changes, including recognition of Maori administrative units, replacement of the assimilationist Maori Affairs Department with the Iwi Transitional Agency, creation of an Advisory Ministry of Maori Affairs, increased and more rapid response to Maori requests for public services, and an acceptance of the Treaty of Waitanga (1840) as the framework for Maori-white relations. Similarly, in Canada, in 1867 the Department of Indian Affairs began managing American Indian matters, including but not limited to deciding who was or was not an Indian, who could vote as a Canadian citizen, how Indian land was used, the form of government in Indian communities, and whether or not traditional religious rituals could be practiced. In 1966 the Department of Indian Affairs was replaced with the Department of Indian Affairs and Northern Development, with a shift in policy from control and assimilation to assistance in economic development and Indian community participation in decision-making toward a goal of indigenous self-sufficiency. While progress toward the realization of full rights has been too slow for some, programs such as community negotiation and block funding with limited local control are marked departures from past government practices.

Land Rights

For many indigenous peoples, their attitudes and beliefs about the land are different from those of nonindigenous peoples. People in many indigenous cultures believe that the land has a sacred quality; that it is a link to the past, the history of their people, and their unique identity; and that it is their obligation to preserve the land for future generations. Thus, land is not just a material object to be used, consumed, sold, or owned. For example, the Blue Lake area is of such sacred importance to the Taos of northern New Mexico that they spent nearly half a century attempting to regain ownership and control from the federal government, which had incorporated it into the Carson National Forest in 1906. In 1971 the Taos succeeded, the first time that American Indians had regained their land on the basis of the right to religious expression rather than as a financial settlement.

Outsiders have long assumed that indigenous peoples have no concept of land ownership because of the views that many indigenous people hold about their relationship to the land. This is not the case; all cultures have rules and practices about ownership and the use of natural resources, land, and the products of the environment. The indigenous peoples of northern Luzon Island in the Philippines, such as the Bontok and Kalinga, for example, distinguish among the following types of natural resources that can be owned or controlled: forest and forest products, water from springs, rivers, land for horticulture, pastureland, land with minerals, clay soil, terraced land for agriculture, and residential land. Three types of land rights govern the use of these types of land and the extraction of raw materials from them: (1) communal land rights held by all members of a village community; (2) indigenous corporate rights, which are rights to common land held by a specific family, kin group, or neighborhood, and (3) individual rights. It is not that indigenous people do not have concepts of land ownership, but rather that their concepts differ and are in conflict with those of the dominant society, such as exclusive individual ownership, restricted or specialized use, renting, leases, sales, and state ownership.

In a most general sense, indigenous peoples are demanding

1. Ownership and control of the land and its resources, which had been theirs at the time of Western contact (their ancestral domain)
2. Return of land ownership or, in some cases, monetary or other compensation for lands taken from them illegally—that is, in violation of treaties and agreements, and international, national, or state/provincial laws
3. Control of access to and use of their land by outsiders
4. The right to stop destruction of their land or natural resources
5. The establishment of public policies and programs that prevent the destruction of the environment
6. The right to use the land in accord with their cultural traditions

Underlying these wishes is the belief of virtually all indigenous peoples that their very survival rests on their ability to regain control of their land and live on it as sovereign peoples. Possession of their land affords indigenous peoples both independent status as a nation and an economic base. For example, mining operations are a major threat to aboriginal freedom in Australia, and control of their land would bring with it the right to control environmental damage from mining and the right to extract fees and royalties from mining operations.

Most state/provincial and national governments have generally resisted returning aboriginal lands or broadening indigenous control of their land. In the United States, where American Indian land claims and court cases number in the thousands, opposition rests on the beliefs that there is not enough land to give back, non-Indian property owners will be damaged, and that domestic natural resources will be removed for use by others. These arguments are seen as less than credible by indigenous peoples, who generally believe that compromises can be reached in which no one's interest is harmed and perhaps all gain by developing a deeper respect for the land.

Right to Protection and Use of Natural Resources

Along with loss of land and political autonomy, indigenous people also lost control over natural resources on their land, exclusive use of the land, and control over the use of their land by outsiders. Indigenous people are now seeking to regain these rights, which include water rights, ownership and control of mineral extraction on their land, and unlimited access to traditional sources of food such as fishing, hunting, and herding.

The building of dams to create a source of hydroelectric power in North America, South America, Scandinavia, and elsewhere has had damaging effects on both the environment and the economic viability of indigenous peoples. These effects include land lost to lakes and flood plains, pollution of the waters, water shortages, and road and related construction that damages the environment. Mining has also had damaging effects, particularly in Australia and some parts of the western United States, where strip mining has destroyed the soil, hunting territories, and sacred sites, and provided indigenous peoples with little income from minerals taken from their ancestral lands. In order to regain control of their natural resources, indigenous peoples are seeking the rights to exclusive control over outside use of their land, to develop means to protect the land, and to sell rights to the use of the land to outsiders for a fair market price.

Rights of Religious Expression

Partly through government action and partly through the actions of missionaries who sought to replace the traditional religion with their own, the religious systems of many indigenous peoples have been altered or have nearly disappeared. For example, in Russian Siberia the shamanistic religions of dozens of indigenous peoples were suppressed by Russian and Soviet authorities, who preferred that people adopt Russian Orthodoxy in the former case, and atheism in the latter. Shamanistic belief and ritual were transmitted orally from generation to generation, and there is now some doubt about the revival of shamanism in the post-Soviet period because many shamans were killed in an effort to destroy the belief system. While the suppression of shamanism may be extreme, it is typical of many colonial situations where native religious practices were outlawed and those who practiced them were punished or even killed. Similarly, in many places the taking of indigenous lands and their use by outsiders have led to native peoples' loss of the use of traditional sacred sites; in some cases, sacred sites have even been destroyed. The turning of these sites into public-use sites, as was the case with Blue Lake in New Mexico, is particularly offensive to native peoples; they view this act as no different from turning a cathedral into a picnic area. To reverse this situation, indigenous peoples are seeking full religious freedom that includes not just the right to freedom of worship, but also the return and control of sacred sites.

Right To Manage and Recover Cultural Resources

Cultural resources are material manifestations of the beliefs and customs of a cultural group. They include sites of archaeological, historical, and ethnographic importance to both the people themselves and outsiders, as well as specific objects such as religious artifacts, clothing, weapons, tools, dwellings, and art. Also falling within the rubric of cultural resources are skeletal remains of ancestors, both those *in situ* and those removed and stored elsewhere.

One part of the vigorous study of indigenous peoples by archaeologists, anthropologists, sociologists, historians, explorers, and others for well over 100 years has been the identification of indigenous sites and the collection and removal of items of cultural significance. Indigenous peoples are now demanding a role in cultural resource management; that is, in protecting, preserving, and conserving sites. Specifically, they desire a role in (1) designating a site and determining its importance, (2) controlling the activities of the archaeologists who excavate and study the site, and (3) determining the subsequent use of the site. Sites of concern include villages or dwellings occupied by ancestral peoples, art sites containing pictographs or petroglyphs, sites of historical importance such as massacre scenes and the locales of missions or forts, and sacred sites or places of mythical or ceremonial importance. Places of sacred importance may be specific places, environmental features such as a marked tree, or places with no discernible physical features to an outsider, such as the *bosra* sites of indigenous Australians.

As regards items of material culture now displayed in museums or private collections, and skeletal remains (there are several thousand American Indian skeletons stored for study in U.S. museums), indigenous peoples are seeking the return of items of special importance to them as well as an active role in the display of objects to ensure that their culture is portrayed accurately, with both the present situation and the traditional culture described. Efforts to regain objects have met with considerable resistance from scientists, who see them as objects of study; museum curators, who see them as both scientifically and aesthetically valuable; and collectors, who see them as economically valuable. Thus, for example, in an effort that began in 1978, by 1992 the Zuni had repatriated 69 *Ahayu:da* (twin gods or war gods) from museums and private collectors. When the Zuni, in accord with their beliefs, placed the objects in the New Mexico desert to disintegrate slowly and return to the earth from which they came, some outsiders bemoaned the loss to the art world, ignoring the religious right of the Zuni to handle these sacred objects in their traditional way.

See also ETHNOCIDE; GENOCIDE; INDIGENOUS PEOPLES; MIGRANT WORKERS; MINORITY RIGHTS; RACE AND RACISM.

Berndt, Ronald M., and Catherine H. Berndt, eds. (1984–1985) *Collection of Essays on Aboriginal Land Rights for the Guidance of the Government of Western Australia Aboriginal Land Inquiry 1983–1984. Anthropological Forum* 5 (3).

Brosted, Jens, et al., eds. (1985) *Native Power: The Quest for Autonomy and Nationhood of Indigenous Peoples.*

Burger, Julian. (1987) *Report from the Frontier: The State of the World's Indigenous Peoples.*

Fleras, Augies, and Jean Leonard Elliott. (1992) *The "Nations Within": Aboriginal-State Relations in Canada, the United States, and New Zealand.*

Jaimes, M. Annette, ed. (1992) *The State of Native America: Genocide, Colonization, and Resistance.*

Merrill, William L., Edmund J. Ladd, and T. J. Ferguson. (1993) "The Return of the *Ahayu:da.*" *Current Anthropology* 34: 523–567.

Olson, Paul A. (1989) *The Struggle for the Land: Indigenous Insight and Industrial Empire in the Semiarid World.*

Prill-Brett, June. (1988) *Preliminary Perspectives on Local Territorial Boundaries and Resource Control.* Cordillera Studies Center Working Paper 6.

Wilmer, Franke. (1993) *The Indigenous Voice in World Politics: Since Time Immemorial.*

IRREDENTISM Conflicting claims on territory have always been a major feature of ethnic disputes around the world. Irredentism refers to a specific type of territorial dispute, in which a nation seeks the return of usually adjacent territory from another nation that is or was historically controlled by members of the ethnic group who inhabit the first nation. Thus, irredentism concerns reestablishing ethnic nations through the linking of all adjacent territories occupied by members of the ethnic group. Irredentism becomes an issue and a goal of ethnic groups and governments when national boundaries do not follow ethnic ones, and is often precipitated by strong ethnic, nationalistic sentiments. For example, Nazi Germany expansion was motivated in part by a desire for the German-occupied Sudetenland and German-speaking Austria. More recently, the ongoing violent conflict among Serbs, Bosnians, and Croats in the former Yugoslavia is motivated by the Serbs' and Croats' desire to amalgamate all territories occupied by members of their groups, now or in the past. The mixing of the populations over the past 50 years has distorted previous ethnic boundaries, and because some of those boundaries were already disputed, both the Serbs and Croats have used violence to remove the other groups. By contrast, when Slovenia separated from Yugoslavia, there was little conflict, as most Slovenes already lived in the territory of Slovenia and few lived in adjacent regions.

Irredentism around the world today is mainly a product of Western wars, colonialism, and treaties that created nations and national boundaries not in accord with the already-existing ethnic boundaries in the region. Current movements and conflicts that have this genesis include those involving Romania and Moldova (formerly the Moldavia Soviet Socialist Republic); Hungarian interest in the Transylvania region of Romania, with its sizable Hungarian population and former status as a region of Hungary; Albanian interest in the adjacent Kosovo region of Serbia; Somalia interest in Somali-inhabited regions of Kenya and Ethiopia; Pakistani interest in the heavily Muslim Kashmiri region disputed with India; Armenian interest in uniting communities in the former Soviet Union, Turkey, and Iran; and Navajo resistance to relocation from land that has been ruled part of the Hopi Reservation in Arizona.

The situation regarding Romania and Moldova displays many elements typical of irredentism. Moldovans and Romanians both speak Romanian and are culturally Romanian. The designation *Romanian* refers to both a nationality and an ethnic group. Moldovans, on the other hand, are a nationality but not a distinct ethnic group. Ethnic Romanians constitute 65 percent of the population of Moldova and 75 percent of the population of Romania. After a long history of shifting borders and domination by outsiders such as Turks and Russians, what are now essentially Romania and Moldova were unified in 1918, although the Soviet Union kept a small strip that became the Moldavian Autonomous Republic. In 1940, with German support, the Soviet Union obtained more territory from Romania, and established the Moldavia Soviet Socialist Republic. In 1947, Moldavia was again divided, with a segment added to the Ukraine and a small strip added to what remained of the Moldavia SSR. With the demise of the USSR beginning in 1989, Moldova became an independent republic and then one of the 18 members of the Commonwealth of Independent States (CIS) of the former Soviet Union. Since then, the Latin alphabet has been reintroduced, numerous publications have been printed in Romanian, the Romanian majority has achieved political control, and cultural and economic ties have been established with Romania. While the Romanian majority population in Moldava prefers unification with Romania, that wish has not yet been achieved because of the threat of political and economic instability in Romania.

As with other forms of ethnic land disputes such as ethnic separatist movements and efforts by indigenous peoples to regain their homelands, irredentism points to the central role played by land and beliefs about the homeland in ethnic identity, solidarity, and conflict.

See also ETHNIC CONFLICT; TRANSNATIONAL MIGRATION.

Dimi, Nicholas. (1991) *From Moldavia to Moldova: The Soviet-Romanian Territorial Dispute.*

Landau, Jacob. (1990) "Irredentism and Minorities in the Middle East." *Immigrants and Minorities* 9: 242–248.

ISRAELIS AND PALESTINIANS

The ongoing conflict between Israelis and Palestinians in the Middle East is one of the most—if not the most—complex of all ethnic conflicts. On the surface, it is a conflict about rival claims to the same homeland—the modern state of Israel, formerly Palestine. However, the conflict also involves the displacement of Palestinians from Israel after 1948, Israeli control of the Gaza and West Bank territories, Palestinian resistance to Israeli control, second-class status for Palestinians and other Islamic Arabs in Israel, the displacement of Jews from Arab nations, and the desire of Jews for a homeland. To complicate matters further, the conflict has taken place in the context of considerable unrest in the Middle East, including four Arab-Israeli wars (1948, 1956, 1967, 1973), Cold War politics, oil politics, sporadic efforts at forging unity among the Arab nations of the region, the rise of Islamic fundamentalism, anti-Western sentiments, lingering effects of European colonialism, the Iran-Iraq war in the 1980s, the Gulf War in 1991, and the ongoing conflict with the Kurds in Turkey, Iraq, and Iran.

There are about 6 million Palestinians in the world, with about 31 percent in Jordan, where they have been granted citizenship; 19 percent on the West Bank; 11 percent in Gaza; 12 percent in Israel; 18 percent in other Arab countries, especially Syria and Lebanon; and 8 percent elsewhere in the world, mainly in Europe and the United States. About a third of Palestinians on the West Bank and in Gaza commute to work in Israel, although the actual number fluctuates greatly depending on Israeli labor demands and admission policies. Palestinians do not form an ethnic group according to traditional criteria. At this time they are not a localized community; instead, they live in diaspora and share a common language (Arabic) and religion (Islam) with the majority of their Arab neighbors in the Middle East. However, Islam and Arabic do distinguish them from the Israelis and are important components of Palestinian identity vis-à-vis the Israelis. The strong sense of solidarity and nationalism expressed by Palestinians today is largely the result of the displacement and the crises they have endured in the twentieth century, including British control of Palestine, the establishment of the state of Israel in 1948, Israeli victories in the Arab-Israeli wars, the dispersal of most Palestinians from their homeland, settlement in refugees camps, Israeli control of the West Bank and Gaza, second-class status in Israel, and lack of full acceptance and support by other Arab nations. Since 1948 various factions have vied for and held power within the Palestinian community. The Palestinian Liberation Organization (PLO), which came into existence in 1964, now serves as the Palestinian government, providing services for its citizens, representing Palestinians in negotiations with

Israel and other nations, and as an envoy to international organizations. Palestinian nationalism centers on their perceived rights to return to their homeland and to establish an independent Palestinian state. Palestinian nationalism solidified after the 1987 uprising *(Intifada)* in Gaza and the West Bank. More recently, the goal has focused on establishing an independent Palestinian state in Gaza and on the West Bank.

Israel is a nation of 5.8 million people and comprises a territory of 8,020 square miles. In addition to Israel proper, Israel currently controls territory taken from Arab nations in the previous wars—the West Bank of the Jordan River, the Old City in Jerusalem, the Golan Heights, and the Gaza Strip. While Israel is a secular state and theoretically accepting of non-Jews, it is a Jewish state in that the population is mainly Jewish (82 percent), Jews consider it the Jewish homeland, and all Jews are allowed to immigrate to and settle in Israel. Before becoming a state in 1948, what is now Israel was inhabited by a mixed population of Arab Palestinians and Jews, the majority of the latter from eastern and central Europe, and about 25 percent from the Middle East. Postindependence immigration to Israel was from Europe, North Africa, the Middle East, and India. More recently, immigrants have arrived from Ethiopia (Beta Israel) and Russia. Although the population is about evenly split between Jews of European and non-European origin (mainly North African and Middle Eastern), the European-ancestry Jews are politically and economically dominant. Unity is formed amid this diversity of background by a number of factors: (1) a shared belief that Jews are "one people"; (2) a belief that Israel is the Jewish homeland; (3) use of Hebrew as the national language (it was not the daily language of any of the constituent groups); (4) the ideal of integration through intermarriage within the Jewish community; and

Israeli soldiers in Jericho plead with Palestinian residents to clear the road for the visit of Police Minister Moshe Shahal, September 1993. Under the Jericho-Gaza peace plan, control has been transferred to the Palestinians.

137

(5) adherence to generally accepted standards of public behavior accompanied by acceptance of individuality.

Israeli Jews, and sometimes all Jews, are labeled as Zionists, although not all Zionists are Jews and not all Jews are Zionists. Zionism is a nationalistic political philosophy that calls for a Jewish homeland, and was an important motivating force in the establishment of Israel as an independent state. Like all philosophies, it defies easy description and takes a variety of forms. Once labeled as a form of racism by the United Nations, it has now faded as an issue of importance in Israeli-Palestinian relations. Zionism was developed in Europe by Jewish intellectuals in the late 1880s in reaction to, and as a solution to, the centuries of persecution Jews endured in Europe. The goal was a secular Jewish state that would use such modern principles as technology, rationality, socialism, and nationalism to build prosperity for itself and the entire region. Thus, the goal was not just a Jewish state, but a modern state that would create a way of life and opportunities that Jews had been denied in the past. This goal was pursued through emigration from Europe to Palestine beginning in the 1880s, and the establishment of Jewish settlements in the region alongside the Arab population already resident there.

The territory that is now Israel was the birthplace of both Judaism and Christianity, and is also of importance to Islam. The Hebrews, the ancestors of Jews today, inhabited the region as early as several thousand years ago, and had established a kingdom there by 1000 B.C. that later divided into the kingdoms of Judea and Israel. Both were invaded and conquered in subsequent centuries by various groups, and eventually the Jewish population was expelled from the region, first by the Babylonians and later by the Romans. This led to centuries of exile and Jews lived in other lands without a homeland of their own (a few remained in present-day Israel). The name Jew is derived from the region of Judea, in which

Jerusalem was located. The Arabs gained control of the region from the Byzantine Empire in A.D. 640 and ruled until 1516, when it fell under Turkish (though still Islamic) rule. In 1917 the British defeated the Turks and were given a mandate to govern the region by the League of Nations in 1923. British rule was inconsistent (in international circles they backed Jewish control, while in Palestine they supported the Arab population). Various plans failed to either unite the Jewish and Arab residents into one nation or create separate nations, and conflict between the two groups deepened and often erupted into violence. World War II brought an increased number of Jews fleeing to the region from Europe, and in 1946 they numbered 678,000 alongside 1.3 million Arabs. In 1947 the U.N. voted to partition the region, and when the British withdrew in 1948, the Jews declared the establishment of the state of Israel. The first of the four Arab-Israeli wars ensued, ending in a ceasefire in 1949. It was the establishment of Israel, the war, and the expulsion of the majority of the Arab population that ultimately led to the emergence of the Palestinians as a distinct group in the region. By 1948 there were between 550,000–800,000 Palestinian refugees living on the West Bank of the Jordan River, in the Gaza Strip, and in other Arab nations such as Syria and Lebanon.

From then on, Israeli-Palestinian relations existed within the context of the broader Israel-Arab conflict. However, after Israel annexed the West Bank and the Gaza Strip in 1967, hostilities with the Palestinian population escalated into a pattern of cyclical violence that persists to this day. Because Israel refused to recognize the Palestinians and the PLO as political units, the Palestinians were left out of the various negotiations among the parties in the region. However, in late 1993, direct negotiations led to an agreement that called for limited Palestinian rule of the Gaza Strip and the city of Jericho on the West Bank, steps implemented in 1994, and a timetable for negotiations to produce peace by the end of the century.

Binur, Yoram. (1990) *My Enemy, My Self.*

Black, Eric. (1992) *Parallel Realities: A Jewish/Arab History of Israel/Palestine.*

Fuller, Graham E. (1989) *The West Bank of Israel: Point of No Return.*

Gerner, Deborah. (1991) *One Land, Two Peoples: The Conflict over Palestine.*

Goldschmidt, Arthur, Jr. (1991) *A Concise History of the Middle East.* 4th ed.

Hertzberg, Arthur, ed. (1960) *The Zionist Idea.*

Lewis, Herbert S. (1993) Jewish Ethnicity in Israel: Ideologies, Policies and Outcomes." In *Ethnicity and the State,* edited by Judith D. Toland, 201–230.

Muslih, Muhammad Y. (1988) *The Origins of Palestinian Nationalism.*

Peretz, Don. (1990) *Intifada: The Palestinian Uprising.*

Sahliyeh, Emile. (1993) "Ethnicity and State-Building: The Case of the Palestinians in the Middle East." In *Ethnicity and the State,* edited by Judith D. Toland, 177–200.

vive to this day. When the British displaced the Mughuls, Kashmir became part of the British Empire.

At the time of Indian and Pakistani independence, hundreds of thousands of civilians and soldiers were killed in the fight between India and Pakistan, both of whom laid claim to the Kashmiri region. Since 1947 there have been three Indo-Pakistan wars (1948, 1965, 1971), at least two of which have been fought for control of Kashmir. The current ethnic strife in Kashmir remains a violent separatist or irredentist (depending on the viewpoint of the opposing sides) conflict, as Muslim Kashmiris continue to fight for independence from India. The current conflict dates to 1990 and centers on Muslim efforts in the Vale of Kashmir to push the Indian army out of Kashmir, and army efforts to eradicate the Muslim separatists through torture, rape, murder, and destruction of Muslim property. Since 1990 nearly 6,000 combatants and civilians have died in the struggle.

Although the traditional aim of such groups as the Jammu and Kashmir Liberation Front and Hezbol Mujahedeen has been to achieve independence and autonomy, most separatists would opt for mergence with Islamic Pakistan rather than remain part of India. India seeks to retain control of the region partly because of its historical ties to India, and in part because of the tourist potential of the region, with its mountains, lush valleys, and the central Vale of Kashmir. Violent conflict, including the abduction of tourists, has so far limited tourism and economic development in Kashmir. The situation has been aggravated by Pakistan's (denied) involvement in arming militant separatist groups and providing training in guerrilla warfare on the Pakistani side of the border. Both India and Pakistan have been criticized for their policies in this situation, India for resorting to torture and murder of suspected militant rebels. India's government officially denies the use of any unnecessary violence in attempting to suppress the

KASHMIRI   Kashmiri are the inhabitants of Jammu and Kashmir, the only Muslim-majority state in predominantly Hindu India, as well as Azad Kashmir (the Pakistan-controlled portion of Kashmir). The estimated population in 1991 was 7.5 million in the 222,236-square-kilometer Indian state of Jammu and Kashmir. In 1947 when the region was partitioned by Great Britain into India (a secular nation) and Pakistan (a Muslim nation), 77.1 percent of Kashmiris were Muslim. Only 20.1 percent, including the former maharaja of Kashmir, were Hindu. Of the groups currently residing in Kashmir, Hindus were the first inhabitants and ruled the region until the fourteenth century, although Hindu influence was somewhat mitigated by the influence of Buddhism. Islam came to Kashmir in the fourteenth century from central Asia, and the Hindu population declined as many converted to Islam and others fled or were killed. In the sixteenth century, Kashmir came under the control of the Islamic Mughul Empire, with many Hindus fleeing, creating diaspora communities in Indian cities that sur-

rebellion. Pakistan likewise denies allegations of funding separatists.

The situation has become more critical in this latest movement for independence. While Indian and Pakistani leaders have promised to avoid war, and thus far have done so, the fact that both countries have nuclear capability heightens the concern surrounding the conflict. Whatever Pakistan may be doing to assist the movement behind closed doors, its official stance is to discourage militant efforts for independence and such displays as mass marches across the border. This is evidenced by the February 1992 incident, in which Pakistani police opened fire on Pakistani Kashmiri marching into India.

Bamzai, P. N. K. (1962) *A History of Kashmir.*
Sender, Henry. (1988) *The Kashmiri Pandits: A Study of Cultural Choice in North India.*

KURDS

The Kurds have inhabited *Kurdistan,* the "Land of the Kurds," for over 2,000 years. Kurdistan includes territory located in the modern nations of Turkey, Iran, Iraq, and Syria. In addition to Kurds in Kurdistan proper, sizable populations can be found in Armenia, Azerbaijan (although many have fled the Armenian-Azerbaijani conflict), central Asia, and western Turkey. There is also a diaspora community outside the Middle East numbering at least 400,000. Never in the past, nor at this time, has Kurdistan been a unified political entity. Rather, the image of a unified Kurdistan as the homeland for all Kurds is a goal of some Kurds and Kurdish political organizations, while others seek the end of political and cultural repression, and autonomy in the nations where they live. Thus, the Kurds, numbering perhaps as many as 26 million, are the largest ethnic group in the world without a national homeland.

Because of the census policies in some nations (Turkey, for example, does not consider Kurds a distinct ethnic group), inaccurate census figures, and the movement of large numbers of Kurds in recent years, the total Kurdish population and the percentage in any nation are difficult to measure. Figures for 1990 suggest the following:

Turkey	13.65 million (24.1 percent of the national population)
Iran	6.60 million (6.6 percent of the national population)
Iraq	4.40 million (23.5 percent of the national population)
Syria	1.16 million (9.3 percent of the national population)

Including those in the former Soviet Union, the total estimated Kurdish population in 1990 was 26.15 million, representing a 37 percent population increase since 1980.

Shared ethnic identity among the Kurds is based on common ancestry, a common history, economic cooperation (especially in the past), and a common homeland. There is also some commonality based on religion (nearly all Kurds are Muslim), and language, although religious and language differences just as easily tend to divide the Kurds. Critics of Kurdish ethnicity question whether the Kurds of today are the same as the people called Kurds in antiquity and whether the label *Kurd* actually referred to a distinct group in antiquity or simply meant "shepherd." Critics also point to the absence of a common language and unique religion, two markers of ethnic cohesiveness in many other groups.

While there is little doubt that a Kurd ethnic group exists (although some Kurds have assimilated into the non-Kurd populations of the nations where they live), there are significant cleavages within the Kurdish community that, in the past and today, make it difficult if not impossible for the Kurds to organize as a single political entity. The most important cleavages are those based on region, nation of residence, language, religion, economics, and political-party affiliation. Because of historical and geographical factors, traditional Kurdistan could be divided into five rather distinct regions—southern, central, eastern, northern, and western. Today, the urban-rural, herding-agriculture distinctions among these regions are perhaps less important than variation based on nation of residence. While the Kurds remain, at best, a discriminated-against minority in all four nations in which Kurdistan is located, their treatment and status has varied over this century both within and across these nations. For example, Kurdish culture is repressed in Turkey to the point where they are not identified as a distinct group, while in Iran, following a period of repression, public displays of Kurdish culture, including publications in Kurdish, are again permitted. Nation of residence also determines Kurdish political-party affiliation, with different parties having different goals and espousing different methods for achieving those goals. Major political parties by nation include: in Iran, Kurdish Democratic party (KDP) or Kurdish Democratic party of Iran (KDPI) and Komala; in Iraq, Kurdish Democratic party (KDP), Patriotic Union of Kurdistan (PUK), and the Socialist party of Kurdistan (SPK); in Turkey, Kurdish Democratic party (KDP-T), Workers' Party of Kurdistan (PKK), and Komkar; and in Syria, Kurdish Democratic Party of Syria (KDP-S). In September 1993, in a move toward unity, the two main Kurdish parties in northern Iraq unified in an attempt to solidify Kurdish control of northern Iraq.

The Kurdish language is an Indo-European language with two major branches and a number of dialects and subdialects, most of which are mutually unintelligible. Language and dialect variation is, of course, closely related to regional and national population distribution patterns. About 60 percent of Kurds are Sunni Muslim. Shi'ite Muslim Kurds predominate only in Iran, itself a Shi'ite Muslim nation. Most non-Muslim Kurds are adherents of ancient religions, commonly called the Cult of Angels, including Yezidism, Alevism, and Yarsanism. Traditionally and today, Kurds have been involved in a variety of occupations including nomadic herding, settled agriculture, trade, crafts, and serving the kingdoms and nations under whose rule they lived. This variation has been further broadened by growing gaps between urban and rural residents. Urban Kurds (there are, for example, about 3 million Kurds in Istanbul), on the one hand, are more readily exposed to assimilative pressures of the dominant national culture, but on the other hand, through easier contacts with other Kurd groups, international organizations, and the media, are better able to work for autonomy.

A final factor influencing the failed efforts by the Kurds to establish a unified Kurdistan, or even to achieve political autonomy within another nation, is Kurdish reliance on outside nations for assistance. In various times and places during the twentieth century, Kurds have looked to the British, Soviets, and Americans for political and/or military support, which has failed to materialize. Additionally, Kurds have sometimes tried to use international situations, such as the Iran-Iraq War from 1980–1987 and the Gulf War in 1990–1991, to their advantage by revolting or supporting one side in the war. However, all of these revolts have been harshly repressed. Currently, the large refugee population in northern Iraq is supported by the United Nations, and is protected to some extent by U.N. sanctions on Iraq and a prohibition on flights above the 36th parallel. Recent protests by Kurds in France and Germany and attacks on overseas Turkish citizens, businesses, and consulates have led to crackdowns on suspected Kurd leaders in those nations.

Recent and Current Situation

In the twentieth century, most developments relevant to Kurd efforts to form an independent nation or autonomous regions have centered on the nations of Turkey, Iran, and Iraq. All of these nations reached independent status in their current form following the breakup of the Ottoman Empire, the end of British rule in the region, and partitioning of the region into separate nations. These major events, as well as others such as World Wars I and II, the founding of the state of Israel, and the Gulf War of 1990–1991, have had an enormous political and economic impact on the region and the nations in it, and consequently on the Kurds and their search for independence.

In Turkey, despite comprising nearly a quarter of the national population, Kurds do not enjoy the status of a protected official minority. The Turkish constitution denies their claim to a separate political identity. The first half of the twentieth century, following the defeat of the Ottoman Empire and during the period of Turkish development as an independent nation, was one of generally severe repression for the Kurds, who were denied rights afforded other residents, displaced from their traditional territory and villages, and killed when they resisted. After free elections in 1950, the Kurds became more active and freer participants in Turkish society, the number of those living in cities increased, and a Kurdish middle class active in business, education, and politics emerged. In the 1960s a movement for Kurdish autonomy gained strength, and beginning in 1967 the government moved to repress these demands. A military coup in 1971 marked the beginning of harsh repression of Kurdish demands for fuller rights and autonomy, and another coup in 1980 led to mass arrests of Kurd leaders and activists, and a formal policy of not only denying Kurd identity, but instead

officially defining them as Turks. In the late 1970s the Workers' Party of Kurdistan (PKK) emerged as the major supporter of Kurd autonomy and resister of government repression, and the Turkish military government reacted with mass arrests, illegal detention, torture, and execution of alleged leaders and collaborators, and the stationing of Turkish army units in the Kurd region. The government was able to rely on those in the Kurd community who opposed the PKK to assist them in monitoring and controlling PKK activities, which, as they became more violent, included killing civilians and destroying villages. Government-PKK fighting continued through the 1980s and into the 1990s, and was complicated by the arrival of 60,000 Iraqi Kurd refugees in 1988 and the relocation of some 400,000 Iraqi Kurds in 1991 during the Gulf War to the Iraq-Turkey border, where many lived in refugee camps. In 1991 these Iraqi Kurds, motivated by a need to ensure a steady flow of food and heating fuel to their camps and settlements, joined the Turks in driving the PKK from the border region. From 1984 to 1992 the PKK-Turkish conflict produced over 3,500 deaths and at least 20,000 displaced persons in Turkey. Within Turkey, the Kurd desire for autonomy is motivated by their experience of repression and their perception of themselves as second-class citizens whose region is grossly underdeveloped in comparison to the rest of Turkey.

Prior to the twentieth century, Kurdish experience in Iran was a combination of periods of self-rule, service to various kingdoms and shahs, and separatist movements, usually involving only a few Kurdish communities. In the political confusion produced by World Wars I and II, the Kurds were able to establish the Mahabad Republic, an autonomous republic within Iran. The republic lasted one year, from December 1945 to December 1946, when it was defeated by the Iranian army. To control future autonomy movements, the Iranian government banned public displays of Kurdish identity, quickly and

Armenian Kurds protesting Iraq's policy against Kurds, April 1991.

harshly put down any incipient revolts, arrested and executed political leaders, and used the secret police to monitor Kurd activity. The replacement of the shah with an Islamic government in 1979 encouraged the Iranian Kurds to believe that autonomy was a reachable goal. However, the fundamental principle of the new Iran—that it be a unified Islamic state—meant that autonomy for the Islamic Kurds was impossible. The result was open warfare between the Kurds and the Iranian government, beginning in 1979 and effectively ending in 1984 with Iran in control of nearly all of Iranian Kurdistan and some 27,000 Kurds killed. Since then the region has remained under military control, and political leaders have been imprisoned or executed. Attempts at a negotiated settlement and a peaceful redefining of Kurd-Iranian relations by the government and the Kurdish Democratic party

of Iran have been hampered by political assassinations. Although political repression continues, there has been a relaxation of bans on expressions of Kurdish culture. A 1992 agreement between Iran and Turkey was designed to control the border activities of the PKK in Turkey and the Mojahedin-e Khalq in Iran; both groups were seen as threats to the internal security of the two nations.

During the period of Iraq's transition to nationhood from 1918 to 1932, the Iraqi Kurds had great hopes of establishing an independent nation or an autonomous region within what was to become Iraq. However, there was a lack of Kurd unity; internal splits were based on urban-rural residence, agricultural-herding economy, political rivalries, and conflicting goals among Kurd leaders. Partly because of these divisions, neither independence nor autonomy was achieved, and instead the Kurdish region came under Iraqi control. This led to an unstable situation that lasted until 1970, in which the Kurds existed as a fragmented political entity within Iraq. Various attempts at autonomy or separatism were put down by the government, and the Kurdish Democratic party was established in Iraq. It was during this period that Mulla Mustafa Barzini emerged (although not without continual rivalries in the community) as the Kurd leader, a role he maintained both in Iraq and during exile until his death in the United States in 1979. Fighting between the Kurds and the government in the 1960s produced perhaps as many as 60,000 deaths, destroyed over 700 villages, and displaced 300,000 Kurds. In 1970 the Iraqi government signed an agreement that for all practical purposes committed it to recognize and treat the Kurds as equals in a bicultural Iraq, by far the broadest recognition of Kurd autonomy offered by any nation. However, disagreements quickly escalated over various details of the agreement, and in 1974 it was replaced by the watered-down Autonomy Declaration. That was followed by warfare between Kurdish and government forces, which led to at least 40,000 more deaths and 300,000 displaced persons, and ended with a decisive government victory in 1975. Since then, Kurd autonomy efforts have generally coincided with events that kept Iraqi military forces busy elsewhere. During the Iran-Iraq war, the five major political factions joined forces as the Iraqi Kurdistan Front and were successful enough in occupying Iraqi forces needed on the Iranian front that a cease-fire was negotiated in 1983, although never fully agreed to nor implemented. Desperate to end the Kurd military activity, in 1983 the Iraqis began a six-year campaign called the *Anfal*, which included razing villages, mass deportation, the establishment of detention camps, mass executions, and, at its height in 1988 following the end of hostilities with Iran, an all-out assault on Kurd positions and the use of chemical warfare. The result was mass Kurdish casualties and displacements, and the reduction of Kurd-controlled territory by about 60 percent. In 1991, with Iraq occupied by the Gulf War and then defeated by the Allied forces, the Kurds again revolted. The revolt was put down by the Iraqis, and approximately 1.5 million Kurds fled to the Turkish border, where many still live in camps under international protection. At this point, Kurdish separatism in Iraq is extremely unlikely, and the Kurds are attempting to coalesce and establish control of the northern region above the 36th parallel, where many reside as displaced persons.

Chaliand, Gerard. (1980) *People without a Country: The Kurds and Kurdistan.*

Izady, Mehrdad R. (1992) *The Kurds: Concise Handbook.*

McDowall, David. (1992) *The Kurds: A Nation Denied.*

The term martial races refers to groups within a nation who are defined on the basis of their reputation as soldiers. They are not "races" in any sense of the word. Sometimes they are distinct ethnic groups, such as the Iban (known as the Sarawak Rangers) in Malaysia, or the Highland Scots. They can be drawn from a distinct cultural category, such as the Bedouin nomadic pastoralists in Saudi Arabia, or they can be formed by members of a number of ethnic groups, such as the Gurkha of Nepal. They may be members of the dominant ethnic group, such as the Cossacks in Russia, who were primarily of Russian and Ukrainian ancestry. So-called military races have essentially disappeared since the end of World War II.

Political scientist Cynthia Enloe characterizes military race in terms of what she calls the *Gurkha Syndrome*. That is, they are created as distinct groups by the nation-state in order to take advantage of their military ability, and then made dependent on the state in order to maintain their loyalty. For example, in India the Brit-

ish sought the services of the Gurkhas after 1815, when Britain took control of northern India and stopped incursions by the Gurkha Kingdom from Nepal to the north. The British were impressed by the Gurkha military performance, and recruited men into Gurhka regiments who served British interests from the 1850s through World War II. In fact, the Gurkha are neither a racial nor an ethnic group, but are Nepalese nationals (including Gurung, Magar, Tamang, and other ethnic groups) who formed the Gurkha military units within the British army. Gurkha loyalty to the British was based on their unique identity and status within the British army, and their relatively high salaries and pensions, which made Gurkha soldiers and their families socially and economically powerful in their home villages. Similarily, the Cossacks in Russia were at first social bandits who defended peasant interests, then mercenaries, and finally military irregulars who defended the Russian Empire from Turkish invasions from the south and internal peasant uprisings. The Cossacks were mainly ethnic Russians and Ukrainians, although there were also some Turkic and Kalmyk Cossack communities. Until the eighteenth century the Cossacks were largely supported by the Russian government, which supplied them with grain, ammunition, and liquor; paid them for their services; and allowed them to keep booty taken from the Turks. In later years, as the population increased, the Cossacks became essentially self-supporting.

Both the Gurkhas and Cossacks display another key feature of the Gurkha Syndrome—they are ethnically different from the enemies of the state that they support. For the Cossacks, the primary enemy was the Turks, while the Gurkhas served British interests in various places outside Nepal; some are still stationed in Hong Kong. Thus, the basic value of martial races may reside in their willingness to more readily attack people of another ethnic group than are the members of the ethnic groups that retain their services.

Enloe, Cynthia. (1980) *Ethnic Soldiers: State Security in Divided Societies.*

Longworth, Philip. (1969) *The Cossacks.*

Vansittart, Eden, and B. V. Nicolay. (1915) *Gurkas.*

MIDDLEMAN MINORITIES

Middleman minorities is a label used for a socioeconomic category composed of ethnic and religious groups who occupy specialized economic niches in a society. The term is derived from the economic role played by Jews in medieval Europe, where they specialized in mediation activities between marketplace providers and consumers such as trading, peddling, moneylending, and pawnbroking—economic activities generally not engaged in by non-Jews. The term *middleman minorities* was coined by sociologist Howard Becker in an attempt to extend the discussion from Jews to other middleman groups such as Scots, Overseas Chinese, and Armenians. Other labels now used for the middleman minority phenomenon include *pariahs* (although this refers to nonmiddleman outcaste groups as well), *pariah capitalism, trading diaspora, marginal trading minorities, outcaste traders,* and *guest peoples.*

The label *middleman minorities* summarizes the two essential features of such groups that set them apart from other groups in a society. First, they are *middlemen* in that they occupy economic niches that place them between those who produce goods and services and those who consume them. For example, for centuries in Europe Jews were traders and moneylenders, Korean-Americans in New York and Los Angeles are grocers, Chinese in Southeast Asia and the West Indies are traders, and Asian Indians in East Africa were low- and mid-level government officials. Second, they are nearly always numerical and socioeconomic minorities in the nations in which they live. With the exception of Chinese in some Asian nations such as Malaysia, they often number no more than 5 percent of the total population. Other major characteristics of middleman groups are: (1) they are not native to the nation; (2) they have strong, patriarchal, extended families, with a high tendency to marry within the group; (3) they usually live apart from the general population in ghettos or in their own ethnic neighborhoods; (4) they tend to assimilate more slowly than do other groups; (5) though they do not display their wealth, they are often better off financially than the population they serve.

The work performed by middleman minorities also has a number of distinct features common to all middleman minority situations. Most importantly, the work they perform fills a status or economic gap in the socioeconomic structure of the society. The gap is one that for varying reasons is not filled by members of the wealthy or ruling segment of the society, nor by members of the general population. In agricultural societies, the gap is usually between the wealthy-and-powerful and the poor-and-weak. For example, in medieval Europe the Christian population was prohibited from engaging in moneylending, so Jews occupied that niche. In Southeast Asia, Chinese who immigrated from the north serve as store owners in villages and towns, where they sell goods supplied by larger companies to rural farmers. In nations under colonial domination, the gap was created by the need for local government officials and the reluctance of the colonial government to use local peoples for that purpose. Instead, outsiders were employed, such as Asian Indians in East Africa.

In modern capitalist nations, the gap is often found in rural areas and urban neighborhoods where large chain stores choose not to do business. This gap leaves a need for retail sales outlets, often filled by recent immigrants such as Korean-Americans, who own and operate grocery and other markets. In socialist nations the gap is created by government inefficiency, creating a product-supply gap filled by a gray or black market, often managed by middleman minorities. In the former Soviet Union, for example, black-market traders were often Georgians. Aside from the great advantage that middleman businesses require little capital investment, certain qualities enable minority groups to fill these gaps and perform these types of work: The minority group members often possess specialized skills (such as literacy in English in colonial East Africa), are often hard-working, are willing to delay gratification, and have a network of kin or other group members with whom to exchange products and services. The economic success of middleman minorities has been described by sociologist Pierre van den Berghe as "nepotism in the service of capitalism." This means that their success comes from the extensive use of unpaid family labor, the extension of credit within the group, and their ability to maintain a supply of goods for the marketplace.

While middlemen minorities often experience short-term financial success, and in some situations many members of the group eventually assimilate into the dominant society, they are often in a weak and defenseless position in relation to other groups in the society—they are seen as a necessary evil by the ruling class, which is threatened by their economic success, and they are often despised by the population they serve as aggressive outsiders who overcharge their customers and take jobs from economically disadvantaged members of the society. Recent tensions between and occasional violence directed at middleman groups in U.S. cities such as New York and Los Angeles is a result of this view of middleman minority business located in African-American communities.

When the society is under stress from economic deterioration or war, middleman groups are often scapegoated and victimized. The expulsion of Jews from various European countries and violence directed against them, the expulsion of Asian Indians from Uganda, the genocidal massacre of Armenians in Turkey, and the expulsion of the Chinese ("boat people") from Vietnam are all examples of the victimization of middleman groups and suggest the tenuous position they often occupy in a society. However, middleman minorities do not always suffer such a fate, and in nations that stress assimilation, groups will often assimilate into mainstream society, and few individuals will be involved in the traditional occupation.

Bonacich, Edna. (1973) "Theory of Middleman Minorities." *American Sociological Review* 38: 583–594.

van den Berghe, Pierre L. (1981) *The Ethnic Phenomenon.*

Zenner, Walter. (1991) *Minorities in the Middle: A Cross-Cultural Analysis.*

MIGRANT WORKERS

The exploitation of the labor of the members of one ethnic group by another ethnic group has a long history in the human experience. Around the world the labor of other ethnic groups has always been used to perform undesirable work or to augment the labor pool so as to enhance productivity and economic growth. Domestic slavery practiced by indigenous peoples in Asia, Africa, and the New World; the economic slavery of colonial domination; contract laborers in Oceania; migrant farm workers in the United States; guest workers in Europe; and middleman minorities are a few forms of this widespread pattern. As stated by Max Frisch, the goal of the receiving nations in all of these activities has been "acquiring workers but not human beings."

A wide variety of terms is used around the world for peoples grouped here under the generic label *migrant workers*. The governments of receiving nations, the citizens of these nations, social scientists who study them, organizations that assist them, and the people themselves all have different labels. These terms include *immigrants, guest workers, migrant workers, seasonal workers, illegal workers, denizens, native-born second generation, foreign workers, colonial workers, postcolonial migrants, economic refugees, refugees, contract laborers, foreigners, foreign labor,* and *foreigner fellow citizens*. Definitions of some of the more inclusive terms are:

> *immigrant worker* An individual, and often his or her immediate family, who has been granted resident status in the receiving nation or who, because of the laws in the receiving nation, has a reasonable expectation that such status will be granted.

> *year-round migrant worker* An individual who has been granted a one-year work permit by the receiving nation, with the nation having the right to extend the permit indefinitely.

> *seasonal or circular labor migrant* An individual under a labor contract that limits his or her work to a specific time period or season of the year. In some nations, the worker may be required to leave the host nation during nonwork periods; in other nations, the migrant might move from region to region in search of seasonal work.

> *commuting or frontier worker* An individual who crosses an international border on a daily basis to work in a country different from that of residence.

> *asylum-seeker and refugee* From the perspective of labor migration, an individual fleeing his or her homeland who falsely claims political persecution in order to settle and work in the receiving nation. These individuals, now common around the world, are sometimes called economic refugees to distinguish them from political refugees who flee their homeland to escape political persecution.

> *illegal immigrant* An individual who enters or stays in a nation illegally, often in search of work.

> *denizen* An individual, whether or not a citizen of the receiving nation, who has established deep and long-standing ties with that nation and is very likely to remain resident in it.

> *transmigrant* A term now used in the popular press with considerable imprecision that refers to any person who has moved from one nation to another.

Whatever they are called, the primary distinguishing features of these groups today are that (1) they are members of ethnic groups different from the dominant ethnic groups in the nations in which they have settled, either temporarily or permanently; (2) they are numerical minorities; (3) many become or wish to become permanent residents of the receiving nation, including a sizable proportion born there who form the second and now third generations; (4) the receiving nation is not desirous of them being permanent residents or citizens; (5) with the exception of nations with an assimilation ideology such as the United States, few members of the groups do become citizens of the receiving nation; (6) most work at low-paying, low-skilled jobs that citizens of the receiving nation do not want to perform; and (7) most are denied some rights that are afforded citizens of the receiving nation. In addition to these seven characteristics, there are other difficulties. The expectations of many receiving nations were that these people would not stay permanently; however, many have stayed and formed ethnic communities. The economic repression and high unemployment from the late 1980s into the mid-1990s, coupled with ethnocentrism, stereotyping, scapegoating, and racism present in some nations, has led to conflict between migrant workers and the ethnic majorities in the receiving nations, and difficult times for many migrant workers around the world.

Migrant Workers around the World

The use of individuals from ethnic groups different from that dominant in the host nation is a worldwide phenomenon. In the Middle East, a substantial percentage of the labor force in oil-rich nations such as Saudi Arabia, Kuwait, and Bahrain is composed of those from other Middle East nations, Palestinians, and peoples from the Philippines, South Korea, and Taiwan. Egyptians are now a major migrant-worker group in the Middle East. In Saudi Arabia, approximately 180,000 Egyptians are farmers, 150,000 Egyptians are skilled workers, 150,000 are unskilled workers, and 110,000 are professional and clerical employees. In the United States, many legal immigrants from Asia, and legal and illegal immigrants from Mexico and the Caribbean region, form a sizable percentage of the work force. In Singapore, Malaysians and Indonesians fill many low-level jobs on the Chinese-controlled island. Nigeria formerly employed several million people from neighboring Benin and Ghana who were expelled during the early 1980s in reaction to a serious internal economic crisis. In 1992 Congo expelled several hundred thousand so-called illegal workers from Zaire. Although technically labeled *illegal* in Congo, the Zairian workers held many low-level positions; many had been long-time residents and had children born in Congo. They were forced to return to Zaire because of political unrest in Zaire, and the Congo government's fear that the unrest would

Filipino farm worker in Delano, California, 1970.

spread to Zairians in Congo and that more Zairians fleeing the conflict would enter Congo. In the last decade of the twentieth century, migrant workers in western Europe have become a major focus of ethnic conflict.

The fall of communism in eastern Europe and the demand for workers in developing or expanding South American industries have combined to create a flow of eastern European workers to nations such as Venezuela, Chile, Argentina, and Uruguay. However, rather than low-paid, low-skilled workers, the demand is for trained technicians, engineers, scientists, and other skilled occupations. Venezuela, for example, has been especially aggressive in recruiting eastern Europeans by providing labor contracts with employers, paying the workers' airfares, offering Spanish-language education, and providing free housing for a short period. By contrast, Argentina's method of controlling the type of worker who migrates there has been to restrict immigration to only those who can bring $20,000 with them—an impossibile requirement for virtually all eastern European workers. As in Argentina, much caution is expressed in South American nations due to concerns about deflating wages in general, losing jobs to outsiders, creating multiethnic socities, and burdening the national and regional social-support systems.

Although the motivation for using ethnically different migrant workers varies from country to country, a number of factors are often of primary importance. First, migrant workers fill an employment niche created when local workers refuse to do work that is low paid or dangerous, such as service work, mining, and agriculture. Second, migrant workers are often less expensive to recruit, train, and terminate than are local workers. Third, demographic factors may create a labor shortage that can be filled only by importing workers. For example, post–World War II Europe experienced a labor shortage caused by the low fertility rates of the 1930s, deaths during World War II, and rural-to-urban migration that shrank the pool of rural workers. In Saudia Arabia, a labor shortage was caused by women not being permitted to work, and the small but wealthy population demanding many products and services. Fourth, migrant workers traditionally have been viewed as a low-cost cure to what are perceived as temporary labor shortages, such as the post–World War II situation in Europe, the postindependence period in some African nations, and the 1973 oil boom in the Middle East. Fifth, the use of non-native workers is thought to encourage political stability in nations by reducing wealth differences, since migrants take the bulk of low-paying jobs; by maintaining ethnic homogeneity; and, because migrants often have no politi-

cal rights, by controlling threats to government stability.

Migrant Worker Crises in Europe

Before 1945 Europe was a continent of emigration; that is, far more people left Europe to settle elsewhere, particularly in the New World, than moved to Europe. After 1945 the collapse of overseas colonial empires and political realignment at the start of the Cold War era forced the return of many Europeans to their native countries. Germans returned from the USSR and Poland, French from North Africa, Portuguese from Angola and Mozambique, British from India, and Dutch from Indonesia, all of whom were rapidly and easily absorbed into their respective homeland populations. In order to meet the demand for labor caused by a labor shortage, rapid economic expansion, postwar reconstruction, and consumer demand, some western European nations began importing temporary workers from other European nations. However, the labor demand was so great that by the early 1950s, workers were being brought in from outside Europe—from North and Sub-Saharan Africa, Turkey, Caribbean nations, south Asia, and in increased numbers from Greece and Italy. While in the early 1950s the non-European population in Europe was about 350,000, by the early 1960s it had increased to around 4 million. Although these migrant workers provided cheap, low-level labor, western European nations were ill equipped to handle the social, political, and legal challenges presented by the presence of large, non-European populations in what had been essentially ethnically or linguistically homogeneous or pluralistic nations. The immigration of non-European migrant workers in most receiving nations was halted by 1973–1974, and only family members of resident migrants were allowed entrance. Since then, the increase in the number of non-Europeans has been mostly the result of children born in Europe and the arrival of family members from the countries of origination. The actual number of migrant workers and family members in Europe since 1945 is estimated at between 15 and 30 million, and presently there are about 6 million migrant workers of non-European origin. Rather than return to their homeland when their labor migration was halted, these migrants created permanent communities, thereby turning many western European nations into multiethnic societies. The major non-European communities and other European communities in the principal receiving nations are:

Belgium	Turks, Moroccans
Britain	Irish, West Indians, Pakistanis, Indians, Sri Lankans
France	Algerians, Moroccans, Tunisians, Italians, Portuguese, Spanish, Vietnamese, Sub-Saharan Africans, Pakistanis
Germany	Turks, Italians, Greeks, Spanish, Yugoslavians
Netherlands	Turks, Moroccans, Spanish, Dutch Antillians, Indonesians, Surinamese
Sweden	Turks, Finns, Yugoslavians, Estonians, Poles
Switzerland	Italians, Spanish

Particularly in France, Germany, and Britain, both non-European and European migrants formed distinct ethnic communities by the 1980s. The communities are composed primarily of families, with most of the children born in the receiving nation. They differ in language, occupation, place of residence, homeland, and often in religion and physical appearance from the native population. They are likely to occupy poor inner-city or industrial neighborhoods characterized by substandard housing and high crime rates. Each ethnic group tends to be segregated, not only from the dominant population, but also from other migrant ethnic groups.

The many ethnic voluntary associations are an important feature of ethnic migrant communities; they create solidarity within the community, maintain ties to the homeland, provide assistance to migrants and migrant families, and assist in dealing with receiving-nation political and economic structures. Among these associations are religious institutions, language schools, social clubs, banks, lending societies, newspapers, radio shows, advice centers, sports clubs, social clubs, housing associations, and political parties. During the 1980s, in London there were 750 ethnic associations; in Sweden, there were 1,200; in France, there were 770 ethnic associations serving the Portuguese community, and 325 associations for the Italian community; and in Switzerland, there were 175 serving the Spanish community. Community solidarity and ties to the homeland are further strengthened in some ethnic communities by extensive extended family and kinship networks, endogamous and arranged marriages, and chain migration from the same families, villages, or regions in the sending nation.

As these ethnic communities grew and became more visible—with residents demanding educational, social, and health services and their teenage children entering the labor market—resentment and hostility within the host societies increased—rising at an especially rapid rate in the late 1980s in reaction to recession and high unemployment in western Europe and an influx of political refugees from eastern Europe—straining resources in countries such as Germany and France.

Government responses to "overforeignization," "the foreigner problem," and "the social time bomb" included restrictions on the renewal of residence permits, restrictions on further immigration, and expulsion or repatriation programs. Responses of the European nations have varied, with Sweden and the Netherlands placing the least restrictions on migrants, while Germany and France have been the most restrictive. In France, for example, a strong antiforeigner sentiment has developed and there has been a rise in neo-Nazi political parties; animosities are directed mainly at North Africans and especially toward Muslims, who have shown little interest in assimilating into mainstream French society. Among actions taken or attempted by the French government are a zero immigration policy enacted in 1993, tighter criteria for granting French citizenship, identity checks on persons appearing foreign, a three-month jail sentence for migrants who refuse identity checks, a two-year waiting period for the immigration of migrant family members, a reversal of the law awarding citizenship to those born in France, and the mass arrests of those thought to be supporters of Islamic fundamentalist political movements.

Even in eastern Europe a migrant worker population exists. In Bulgaria, for example, both Vietnamese and Turks have been the object of antimigrant programs. Vietnamese were recruited to work on large construction projects, but as the economy declined in the 1980s many lost their jobs and were forced to live through black-market enterprises or to seek employment in neighboring nations. With a complete halt to Vietnamese immigration and all existing contracts expiring in 1992, Bulgaria was then able to rid itself of the unwanted Vietnamese migrants. Turks (who form 15 percent of the population in Bulgaria) have been resident there for many generations, but beginning in 1989 several hundred thousand left for resettlement in Turkey. Bulgarian assimilation policies, which included repression of Islam, a ban on speaking Turkish in public, and violent repression of Turkish protests, were perhaps motivated by a desire to force the Turks to leave, and were the main factor in the Turkish exodus.

Rights of Migrants

As it has become apparent that the 6 million or so non-European migrant workers in western Europe are permanent rather than temporary residents, their status in the host nations has become a difficult political issue. On the one hand, western European nations are all democracies, with very broad political and civil rights afforded their citizens. Non-European residents, particularly in times of economic hardship, are seen as outsiders who at one point fit in, but who now draw on already scarce resources. In western Europe today, the rights afforded noncitizen migrants varies from nation to nation. The basic right from which all other rights flow is citizenship. Sweden, Great Britain, and the Netherlands have liberal citizenship policies, while Germany, France, Belgium, and Switzerland have protectionist policies; not many migrants in these latter nations ever become citizens. Since noncitizens usually cannot vote, few migrants in these nations are allowed to vote, either; however, in the Nordic nations, the Netherlands, and Britain, certain categories of noncitizen migrants are allowed to vote. In Nordic nations, these are citizens of other Nordic nations, while in England, some voting rights are extended to citizens of other Commonwealth nations. Civil rights have been extended to foreigners in Europe since the 1970s, and now most countries have liberal policies. However, in Germany, France, and Switzerland, some rights to association and opinion may be curtailed, especially in times of national emergency. In general, the rights of migrant workers in western Europe can be viewed as a continuum, with illegal workers having the fewest rights, seasonal and temporary workers having a few rights, permanent residents having many rights, and citizens having full rights.

The treatment of migrants in the Middle East is far more uniform and restrictive than in Europe. Migrant workers are essentially without rights. They may not become citizens, nor may their children. They may not own property, and their work is carefully controlled by the government. They are denied virtually all basic political rights, including the right to due process, the right to vote, the right of assembly, and the right to form labor organizations. Non-Muslims are forbidden to display religious symbols (a restriction that was extended to American servicemen and women serving in the Gulf War in Saudi Arabia). Migrant workers are also denied access to the free education and health care offered citizens, and most unskilled and low-skilled workers do not earn enough to bring their families with them.

See also FOREIGNERS IN GERMANY; MIDDLEMAN MINORITIES; RACE AND RACISM; REFUGEES; SLAVERY; TRANSNATIONAL MIGRATION.

Berger, John, and Jean Mohr. (1975) *A Seventh Man.*

Castles, Stephen, H. Booth, and T. Wallace. (1984) *Here for Good.*

Cross, Malcolm, ed. (1992) *Ethnic Minorities and Industrial Change in Europe and North America.*

Extra, G., and L. Verhoeven, eds. (1993) *Immigrant Languages in Europe.*

Layton-Henry, Zig, ed. (1990) *The Rights of Migrant Workers in Western Europe.*

Miller, Judith. (1991) "Strangers at the Gate: Europe's Immigration Crisis." *The New York Times Magazine*, 15 September: 32–37, 49, 80–81.

Murphy, Dervla. (1987) *Tales from Two Cities: Travel of Another Sort.*

"The New Face of America: How Immigrants Are Shaping the World's First Multicultural Society. Special Issue of *Time*, Fall 1993.

Rex, John, D. Joly, and C. Wilpert, eds. (1988) *Immigrant Associations in Europe.*

Rogers, Rosemarie, ed. (1985) *Guests Come To Stay: The Effects of European Labor Migration on Sending and Receiving Nations.*

Solomos, John, and John Wrench, eds. (1992) *Racism and Migration in Contemporary Europe.*

Weiner, Myron. (1986) "Labor Migrations as Incipient Diasporas." In *Modern Diasporas in International Politics,* edited by Gabriel Sheffer, 47–74.

MINORITY

Within the context of ethnic relations, a minority or minority group is a social category within a nation that has a collective, ascribed status in relation to other groups, and is the object of differential treatment. This differential treatment may be the result of government policy, social practice, or both, and is usually negative, taking the form of discrimination or persecution; it may also be positive, as in affirmative-action programs meant to reverse the effects of previous negative treatment. Discrimination often includes denial of access to jobs or certain categories of employment, education, housing, medical care, the legal system, and other social and economic forms. Minority groups may be differentiated as *sociological minorities,* who are defined as such because they are discriminated against, and *elite minorities* who, though a numerical minority, comprise the ruling class. In general, minorities are usually numerical minorities, although in a few nations such as Burundi and South Africa, they are actually numerical majorities. In Burundi, the majority Tutsi are dominated by the Hutu. In South Africa, under the former system of apartheid, Bantu-speaking Africans were subordinate to the small population of whites.

In addition to differential treatment, criteria commonly employed in nations around the world to indicate minority status include physical features such as skin color, ethnicity, religion, language, occupational specialization, historical status, region of residence, and degree of political autonomy. Political scientist Ted Gurr distinguished among three categories of minority groups: ethnoclasses, militant sects, and communal contenders. Ethnoclasses are groups who are physically, religiously, or culturally distinct, and who fill specialized economic niches in the dominant society, such as Muslims in France, Gypsies in Europe, and Koreans in Japan. Militant sects are groups who are differentiated primarily on the basis of religion, such as Copts in Egypt, Druze in Lebanon, and Jews in Argentina. Communal contenders are groups in multicultural nations who share or seek to share power. They are of two types: (1) disadvantaged communal contenders, which are groups who are discriminated against, such as the Luo in Kenya, and (2) advantaged communal contenders, which are groups who hold all or large shares of political power, such as Tutsi in Burundi or Maronites

in Lebanon. In this scheme, minority groups or peoples who hold political power are distinguished from national peoples, with the latter including ethnonationalists and indigenous peoples whose defining feature is the desire for political autonomy.

There is much variation across nations as to what is officially considered a minority group. Thus, in the United States, African-Americans and Latinos in general are considered minorities, while others are not (the status of Asian-Americans is unclear). In the former Soviet Union, groups that would be considered minorities elsewhere were called *nationalities*. In China, the government has designated 55 official minorities, using a mix of criteria that do not always conform to the people's own views as to which groups are ethnically distinct. In Turkey, minorities do not exist because the government has simply decreed that Turkey is ethnically and religiously homogeneous. While minority sta-

Amish farmers hauling a load of corn from their farm in Bird in Hand, Pennsylvania, 1990.

tus is often ascribed and by birth, many minority groups prefer to maintain their unique identity, sometimes through ethnic separatism (as with the Basques in Spain and France), or through resisting assimilation (as with Croats in the former Yugoslavia and Latinos in the United States), or by supporting a pluralistic political system (as with the Walloons in Belgium). For individuals, their minority status is often fluid and can change, depending on the social situation in which they are involved. In addition, one can hide or lose ethnic identity through migration and settlement elsewhere, or through intermarriage.

See also CASTE; INDIGENOUS PEOPLES; INDIGENOUS RIGHTS; MINORITY RIGHTS; RACE AND RACISM.

Gurr, Ted R. (1993) *Minorities at Risk: A Global View of Ethnopolitical Conflicts.*

Gurr, Ted R., and James R. Scarritt. (1989) "Minorities at Risk: A Global Survey." *Human Rights Quarterly* 11: 375–405.

Sigler, Jay A. (1983) *Minority Rights: A Comparative Analysis.*

Wirsing, Robert G., ed. (1981) *Protection of Ethnic Minorities: Comparative Perspectives.*

MINORITY RIGHTS

Minority rights are rights of minority groups, and accrue to the group as a whole, although individual members of the group can claim those rights based on their status as members of the group. Underlying the concept of minority rights are two general principles of the human condition shared by many nations in the world community: All peoples have the right of self-determination, and discrimination against any category of people is wrong. Of course, if these principles were the basis of universal government policy and action, minority rights would not be a concern. Since these principles are so often ignored, the denial or removal of such rights to minority groups is a major human problem in the world today. Because many minority groups are ethnic groups, it is also an important aspect of ethnic relations. In a survey of 126 larger nations, at least one minority group was without some rights in nearly 75 percent of the nations, and in 42 nations, at least 25 percent were denied some rights.

Nations employ many different strategies and policies to deal with the rights of minority groups within their society. In the United States, an assimilation policy is dominant; assimilation into mainstream society and the assumption of an American cultural and political identity is believed to be the route to equal status for all citizens. At the same time, since 1968 the United States has employed timetables for increasing minority representation in employment. Canada's official bilingual/multicultural policy supports the use of both the English and French languages and the cultural autonomy of all minority groups; but, again, affirmative-action programs for the benefit of French-Canadians have been instituted to alleviate past inequities. In India, the policy with regard to the thousands of minority outcaste and tribal groups has been one of compensatory group rights through affirmative-action programs that provide opportunities in education and employment. In China, the 55 officially recognized national minorities enjoy limited cultural and religious autonomy, and some rights denied the majority Han Chinese, while living within the framework of centralized political and economic control. Palestinians in some Israeli-occupied territories are beginning to have some limited autonomy and self-rule, while need-based programs have been developed for Asian and Russian Jews to ease their adjustment to Israeli society. In

Muslims worship at a newly constructed mosque in the Tatar village of Yenganaevo in the former Soviet Union, 1990.

Sri Lanka, Sri Lankan Tamils lost many economic and educational rights and have been engaged in war for political autonomy with the majority Sinhalese who, following the end of British rule, instituted programs to benefit themselves and exclude the Tamils. Finally, in the Mauritius Islands, the four constituent ethnolinguistic groups share power through proportional political representation. One key issue about reforms designed to improve the status of minority groups is how effective they have been across nations. In nations that make a strong effort to aid at least some groups, it seems that some groups do enhance their economic posi-

tion, although the members of the groups benefiting most are those who are already fairly well off; it is not clear whether these gains are temporary or permanent. For example, groups such as Asian-Americans and ethnic Canadians have improved their economic position, while others such as African-Americans in the United States and the Maori in New Zealand have not.

Minority rights have been supported on an international level with the League of Nations since the early twentieth century, and in the post–World War II period, through the United Nations, although virtually all nations define minority rights matters as an internal affair not subject to intervention by other nations or international organizations. Thus, efforts by minorities to achieve self-determination through political separation are rarely effective, and more often are subject to harsh repressive actions by the national government; in fact, ethnic separatism is the most common form of violent ethnic conflict in the world today. Actions taken by governments to deny minority groups their rights include expulsion of the group, prohibitions on emigration, forced resettlement, denial of political representation, denial of linguistic freedom, restrictions on minority media, discrimination in economic and educational matters, denial of equal access to health care and equal protection under the law, and denial of their identity as a minority group. In the former Soviet Union, for example, various means were used to deny religious groups such as Jews, Muslims, Jehovah's Witnesses, Eastern-Rite Catholics, Pentecostal, and Old Believers the right to religious freedom. These included outlawing entire denominations; forcing denominations to merge; closing or restricting access to places of worship; killing, detaining, or imprisoning religious leaders; defaming groups in the press; banning traditional practices; and discriminating against members of the groups in housing, education, and employment. Among means used by groups and their supporters to gain rights are public opinion and education through international nongovernment organizations such as Amnesty International and the Minority Rights Group, legislation, lawsuits, and the preparation and ratification by various bodies of international documents supporting minority rights such as *The Covenant on Civil and Political Rights* and *The International Convention on the Elimination of All Forms of Racial Discrimination.* However, many of these documents, such as the Charter of the U.N., are often interpreted as pertaining to individual human rights, not to minority group rights, and thus have limited applicability in many minority rights situations. There is a major difference between minority rights and indigenous rights. Indigenous peoples often can claim special group rights based on their status as the first inhabitants of the region or, as in the United States, on the basis of treaties that acknowledge indigenous nations as politically autonomous nations.

Minority rights take two major forms: (1) negative or common or human rights, which generally involve freedom from discrimination and the same civil, cultural, political, and economic rights enjoyed by other citizens and (2) positive or identity rights, which have to do with the preservation or revitalization of the minority culture. Specific positive rights sought by minority peoples include the following.

1. Freedom to remain a member of the group or voluntarily leave it, perhaps through intermarriage or religious conversion

2. The right to be recognized as a distinct ethnic group within a nation

3. The right to political participation and representation

4. The right to use the group's own language in private and public, and to perpetuate its use through education

5. Freedom to pursue economic, political, and cultural development

6. Freedom from genocide, ethnocide, forced expulsion, or involuntary population transfers

7. The right to protection so as to maintain cultural, linguistic, political, and economic autonomy

8. The right to self-determination

See also CASTE; INDIGENOUS RIGHTS; MINORITY.

Bourdeaux, Michael, Kathleen Matchett, and Cornelia Gerstenmaier. (1970) *Religious Minorities of the Soviet Union.*

Fawcett, James. (1979) *The International Protection of Minorities.* Report No. 41.

Grove, D. John. (1993) "Have the Post-Reform Ethnic Gains Eroded? A Seven Nation Study." *Ethnic and Racial Studies* 16: 598–620.

Gurr, Ted R., and James R. Scarritt. (1989) "Minorities at Risk: A Global Survey." *Human Rights Quarterly* 11: 375–405.

Palley, Claire. (1978) *Constitutional Law and Minorities.* Report No. 36.

Sigler, Jay A. (1983) *Minority Rights: A Comparative Analysis.*

Van Dyke, Vernon. (1985) *Human Rights, Ethnicity, and Discrimination.*

Wirsing, Robert G., ed. (1981) *Protection of Ethnic Minorities: Comparative Perspectives.*

MISSIONS

As applied to religious activity, the term *mission* has a variety of meanings. As used in reference to Christianity, and in its most general sense, it refers to the goal of creating a world in which all people are Christian. In a more limited sense, it can also mean a specific missionary initiative (such as the mission to the Huron), a specific site of missionary activity (such as San Juan Mission), or a specific missionary organization (such as the New Tribes Mission). Christians today number about 1.8 billion out of a global population of about 5.4 billion. Muslims are the second largest group at about 970 million, followed by Hindus at 732 million.

Although often ignored and not perceived as a form of ethnic relation, missionary activity has been one of the major forms of ethnic relation for nearly 2,000 years. Almost by definition, because it requires contact between persons of different religions, and very often persons of different cultures, missionary activity is a form of ethnic relation. In addition, the Christian mission was a regular and major component of the Western colonization of much of the world. Since both settlement and exploitative colonialism always involved contact between Europeans and non-Western peoples, missionaries were also in contact—often for long periods of time—with peoples from other cultures. In the postcolonial world, missionary activity continues to be a major form of contact between people from the Western world and people in Latin America, Africa, and Asia.

Individuals who work toward converting adherents of a religion different from their own or nonbelievers are called missionaries or missioners. In some religions such as Islam or Pentecostal Christianity, all believers are also missionaries, as an expected activity of adherents of these religions is the conversion of nonbelievers. In most Christian denominations the missionary role is a special one occupied by religious specialists such as ministers, priests, brothers, sisters, and lay missionaries. All missionaries have a "calling" to do this work, and many receive special education and training. Within the general missionary role is further task specialization, with some missionaries performing ministerial work and others teaching, providing medical care, assisting with community and eco-

nomic development, and doing administrative work. In some locales today, and more so in the past, a missionary performs all or many of these tasks by him or herself. Some missionaries operate independently, although the majority are supported by a central church organization, a free-standing mission organization, or even a single congregation. The majority of missionaries come from cultures different from the one in which they work. However, in recent years there has been a trend toward using indigenous people as missionaries to their own society.

While all major religions seek converts to some extent, interest in missionary activity and its effects has been centered mostly on the Christian mission. This is mainly because the Christian mission has been closely tied to Western colonial expansion for over 500 years. Interest in the missionary aspect of the spread of other religions, such as Buddhism from south Asia to east Asia, and Islam from the Arabian Peninsula to North Africa, central Asia, and Southeast Asia, has been much less, although their spread certainly resulted in part from missionary activities.

Missionaries are often in competition with one another. It is not unusual for Catholic, various Protestant denominations, Mormon, and other missions represented by missionaries to work in the same region or with the same cultural group. For example, in northern Nigeria in the 1970s, Islamic, Catholic (Dominican), and Protestant (United Mission Society) missioners vied for converts among the local ethnic groups. The Muslims enjoyed a number of advantages including residence among the local population, a lifestyle more like that of the local population, support of the Nigerian government, and support of the Islamic Hausa, the dominant ethnic group in the region. Thus, conversion to Islam was more common, with entire villages most likely to convert to Islam, while only extended families converted to Protestantism, and only individuals to Catholicism. Similarly, in Alaska, the Russian Orthodox Church was the primary mission among the Tlingit until the sale of Alaska to the United States in 1867 and the arrival of American missionaries. When the Russian traders left the region, the Orthodox Church was the only Russian institution remaining. It gradually lost influence, concentrating its efforts on a few larger communities. It continues to exist, however, as a native Orthodox Church with Tlingit clergy, liturgy in the Tlingit language, and local parishes operating to meet the needs of the communities they serve. A similar situation pertains to Orthodox Eskimo and Aleut communities such as that of the Moravians, which have been more resistant to American missions than the Tlingit. As in the Tlingit situation, missionaries from different faiths or denominations not only work in one place at the same time, but often follow one another over time. For example, in colonial times, Latin American groups were heavily missionized by Roman Catholics. In recent decades, as Catholic missionary activity has decreased, many converts have converted again, this time often to Pentecostal Protestantism, whose expressive style, emphasis on miracles, and encouragement of lay ministers make it congruent with local cultural traditions.

As discussed below, while missions are found around the world, not all regions have been equally responsive to Christian missionary efforts or even to the presence of missionaries. The goal of missionary work is the conversion of the targets of the work to the religion of the missionary. Thus, as a form of ethnic relation, missionary work is characterized mainly by a desire of one group to change the culture of the other. Missionaries, of course, see this change as beneficial both to individual converts and to the culture as a whole, while critics of missionary activity regard such activity as mainly harmful or destructive of indigenous cultures.

The strategies and techniques used by missionaries vary widely over time and from situation to situation. Two strategies with major implications for ethnic relations are *indigenization* and *contextualization*. Indigenization refers to an approach in which the Gospel is presented in a way that can be best understood by indigenous peoples. One major aspect of indigenization is the translation of the Bible into indigenous languages, a task that dates to the beginnings of Christianity. Today, the Bible, the Gospels, and other religious documents have been translated into several thousand languages. Another form of indigenization is to present elements of Christianity in a way that fits with existing beliefs and symbols in the indigenous culture. For example, in the 1660s Catholic missionaries to the Tupi-Guarani in Paraguay and Brazil called the Christian God Tupa, after the local supernatural responsible for thunder, lightning, and rain; and called the Devil Yurupari or Giropari, after the names of harmful local forest spirits. Similarly, a common missionary practice is to incorporate indigenous dance and music into Christian ceremonies. Contextualization is a rather new development, and is seen by missionaries as moving beyond indigenization. Contextualization requires a consideration of the Bible, the indigenous religion, the indigenous culture, and then a fitting of elements of the religious message to elements of the indigenous culture. It also takes into consideration the reality that cultures vary both internally and over time, and that much of the stimulus for cultural change is external to the culture. Thus, a contextual approach might involve the building of an impressive church for use by a wealthy, powerful elite alongside the use of biblical passages by other members of the same community in indigenous healing ceremonies.

Missions and Colonialism

The worldwide nature of the Christian mission is a product of colonialism. Missionary activity was an integral part of the colonizing efforts of every European colonial nation beginning in the

1400s and extending throughout the colonial era. The predominance of missionaries today (see below) in regions of the most intense settlement colonization (North and South America) and exploitative colonization (Oceania, Africa, and Southeast Asia) is a direct result of the colonial experience. In colonial settings, missionaries played a major role in politics, religion, health, and education. They were often among the first reporters on indigenous cultures; and, therefore, some of the earliest, most complete, and perhaps most reliable descriptions of non-Western cultures in the New World before extensive European contact are those written by missionaries. The *Jesuit Relations,* for example, contains 73 volumes of letters, reports, and other documents relevant to the Jesuit mission in the northeastern United States and southeastern Canada, including much information on over a dozen indigenous peoples in the region.

As with the missionary endeavor in general, no all-encompassing generalizations can be made about the relationship between mission activity and colonialism, save for two. First, in addition to converting or saving souls, missionaries were interested in "civilizing" indigenous peoples. Second, whether they meant to or not (and the evidence is that most meant to), missionaries aided directly and indirectly the efforts of colonial officials, the military, land developers, traders, and others to either take indigenous land and resources and/or exploit the labor of indigenous peoples. The variation among missionaries was in the actual impact they had and how they pursued their goals. In South America, missionaries were an integral component of many pacification efforts, the first step in what became the wide-scale exploitation of indigenous peoples, the conquest of their territory, and the displacement and disappearance of many. In Africa, where resource exploitation, not European settlement, was the goal, missionaries were participants in the indirect-rule strategy as recruiters and educators of indigenous peoples who

performed administrative and clerical work in the colonial regimes. In North America, as elsewhere, the role of missionaries was determined to a large extent by the goals and colonization methods of the nations that supported or allowed for their work. Thus, there was considerable variation in these matters. For example, Catholic missionaries from Spain in the Southwest were part of the Spanish conquest in the region; they allowed and were themselves the victims of torture and killing in the name of conquest and conversion. In southern California, many indigenous peoples were forced to live at the local missions, forced to wear European-style clothing, forbidden to speak their native languages, and forced to perform labor. In New Mexico, the Spanish presence led to the establishment of a Catholic church at nearly all pueblo communities, but conquest and conversion were often incomplete, and today many Pueblo groups, such as the Taos, are both Catholics and adherents of their traditional kiva-based religion. In the Northeast, early missionaries often seemed as interested in civilizing the indigenous peoples as in converting them, and many encouraged permanent settlement, intensive agriculture, formal education, and trade with white settlers. Some missionaries, such as the Congregationalist Samuel Kirkland at Oneida, sided with the Colonists in the American Revolution, and encouraged their parishioners to do so as well.

Mission Activity in the 1990s

Contemporary Christian missions fall into five major categories. Evangelical missions cross-cut denominational differences and institutional structures and include a wide range of missionaries who all believe in the following: (1) acceptance of the Scripture as the word of God; (2) belief in the atonement of Jesus Christ; (3) a saving experience with the Holy Spirit; (4) proper use of the sacraments, and (5) a calling to convert non-Christians. Conciliar missions are missionaries sent out by churches who are members of church councils such as the World Council of Churches. Missionaries working in this tradition stress an ecumenical perspective with an emphasis on building unity among the churches, missions to the poor and people in Western cultures, contact with non-Christians, and applying the Gospel to everyday life. The Roman Catholic mission, as defined since the Second Vatican Council (1962–1965), emphasizes salvation in the context of human history and local culture, with an emphasis on work with the poor, the building of local communities, and an increased role for lay missionaries. Pentecostal and charismatic missions are perhaps more personal than the others in that adherents are empowered and guided directly by the Holy Spirit as evidenced by speaking in tongues or the receiving of gifts. Spirit baptism enables each believer to act as a witness, minister, and missionary, and thus is one major factor in the widespread appeal of Pentecostalism. Finally, there are missionaries from religions considered to be non-Christian (at least by mainstream Christian missionaries), such as the Church of the Latter-Day Saints (Mormons), Jehovah's Witnesses, the Unification Church, and New Age churches, who also seek adherents (often on a large scale) throughout the world.

In terms of current goals, Christian missionaries divide the world into three major regions: (1) "Those Who Call Themselves Christians" (the New World, western Europe, southwestern Africa, and Australia and most of Oceania); (2) "Have Heard, Limited Response" (the former USSR, China, east Asia, central and east Africa, and parts of south Asia); and (3) "Least-Evangelized World" (North Africa, Middle East, central Asia, south Asia, and China). Thus, those parts of the world with the fewest Christians and a history of resistance to missionary work are those where other religions such as Islam, Hinduism, or Buddhism are sufficiently established to combat missionary activity, or where the national governments, such as those

in China and the former Soviet Union, banned or restricted missionary activity. For this reason, the largest concentrations of missionaries today are found in nations considered to be in the Christian world—Brazil, Colombia, Ecuador, France, Germany, Kenya, Mexico, and the Philippines. At the same time, some nations in the unconverted world also have sizable missionary activity, including Japan, Indonesia, and Papua New Guinea.

The total number of missionaries in the world is unknown, and because of the proliferation of missionaries operating on their own or with the support of a single congregation or educational institution, they cannot be counted accurately. A recent count of what may be called mainstream Protestant missionaries found that there were 41,142 institutionally supported missionaries from the United States in 1992, down from 50,500 in 1988. In addition, there were 5,210 Catholic missioners from the United States, including priests, brothers, sisters, and lay missioners. When we add to these figures the sizable numbers of Mormon, Jehovah's Witness, Unification Church, and other missionaries overseas; missioners operating out of other nations such as Great Britain; and missionaries working in the United States, it becomes obvious why mission activity is a major form of ethnic relation around the world. The majority of missionaries are engaged in evangelism, but sizable numbers are also involved in health care, education, development projects, child care, and other activities.

One major issue facing missionaries today is their relationship to indigenous peoples, some of whom had been the objects of missionary activities during colonial times. Some missionaries take the position that economic development will inevitably impact these peoples, and will therefore change the lives of indigenous peoples around the world. They argue that allowing missionaries to arrive first and prepare the indigenous peoples for Western contact and the changes it will bring is more humanitarian than allowing the first Western contact to be with developers, land speculators, miners, farmers, ranchers, and other business concerns, whose interests are in either taking the land or exploiting the labor of indigenous peoples. These missionaries see themselves as cultural brokers who assist in planned change. This view contrasts with that of others, who either question whether large-scale change must always be the fate for indigenous peoples or see missionaries as participants in the development effort.

Other missionaries—seen as radical by many—who work with previously colonized peoples see their role as righting the wrongs of the past, and protecting and advocating for indigenous rights today. For example, in Brazil a new mass was celebrated in 1979 entitled "The Mass of the Land without Evil." The mass condemns colonialism, depicts the traditional South American Indian culture as damaged theologically by missionary work, and presents indigenous culture as a route to salvation and a better world. In some nations, not only missionaries but also community religious leaders such as priests and ministers are now among the leading advocates of indigenous rights. They often find themselves in conflict with the national government, who had supported missionary and religious activity in the past.

See also COLONIALISM; REVITALIZATION MOVEMENTS.

Barrett, David B. (1994) "Annual Statistical Table on Global Mission: 1994." *International Bulletin of Missionary Research* 18: 24–25.

Bowden, Henry W. (1981) *American Indians and Christian Missions: Studies in Cultural Conflict.*

Burridge, Kenelm. (1991) *In the Way: A Study of Christian Missionary Endeavours.*

Neill, Stephen. (1986) *A History of Christian Missions.* Revised for the second edition by Owen Chadwick.

Phillips, James M., and Robert T. Coote, eds. (1993) *Toward the 21st Century in Christian Missions.*

Rathburn, Robert R. (1976) *Processes of Russian-Tlingit Acculturation in Southeastern Alaska.*

Richardson, Don. (1988) "Do Missionaries Destroy Cultures?" In *Tribal Peoples and Development Issues: A Global Overview,* edited by John H. Bodley, 116–121.

Salamone, Frank A. (1974) *Gods and Goods in Africa.*

Shapiro, Judith. (1987) "From Tupa to the Land without Evil: The Christianization of Tupi-Guarani Cosmology." *American Ethnologist* 14: 126–139.

Siewert, John A., and John A. Kenyon, eds. (1993) *Mission Handbook: USA/Canada Christian Ministries Overseas.*

MIXED-ANCESTRY PEOPLES Mixed-ancestry or multiracial (racially mixed) peoples are socially recognized groups whose members trace their ancestry to men and women of what are considered to be different racial groups. Racial groups in this context means people who are defined and categorized by the society as being members of different ethnic groups because of differences in skin color and other physical characteristics. In most situations, the mixed-racial group is an artifact of European colonialism and began through relationships between male European colonizers and women who were either indigenous to the land being colonized or were slaves imported by the colonizers from Africa. Thus, in Louisiana,

Black Creoles are mainly descendants of slaves or freed slaves and French colonists. In Labrador, people called Settlers are descendants of native Inuit women and English settlers. In South Africa, Cape Coloureds are descendants of native peoples such as the Khoi and English and Dutch settlers.

One major exception to this general pattern is the 200 or so groups found since the early eighteenth century in some areas of the eastern and southern United States, lumped under such labels as American Isolates, Tri-Racial Isolates, Middle Peoples, and Quasi-Indians. These groups often formed through the offspring of male African slaves and white women and American Indians and African or freed slaves. Since they were considered nonwhite by whites, non-Indian by American Indians, and themselves chose to shun African identity, they were socially and residentially isolated and tended to form small, rural communities. Their isolation was also encouraged in some states by laws that forbade multiracial children to attend public schools, and stereotyping and discrimination that denied them legal and political rights and access to employment. Only in the last few decades have these groups been drawn into mainstream society and begun to disappear. However, some continue to exist as distinct communities, such as the Ramapo Mountain People (Jackson Whites) in New Jersey, who are of Dutch and African ancestry and who claim American Indian ancestry, and the Lumbee Indians in North Carolina and South Carolina (who deny African ancestry).

The defining characteristic of all multiracial people is that they are physically different from other groups in the population, as is the case with these isolated groups. The most obvious physical difference is skin color; these people are often lighter skinned than people of African ancestry and darker skinned than people of European ancestry. Additional physical features such as hair color and texture, size of the nose,

and body shape and size are also important markers of multiracial status. Because of their physical differences and lack of "racial purity," they were often excluded by all ancestry groups, discriminated against, and in some places have lived in relative isolation within their own communities, where they developed as distinct subcultures within the context of the dominant society. Thus, over time, some multiracial groups have come to be defined as distinct by themselves, not just on the basis of physical differences but also on cultural differences.

In general, relations between multiracial groups and other groups and society are determined by a number of considerations including the number of multiracial individuals, societal attitudes about "racial purity," and the extent and nature of political and economic dominance by the European colonizers. Cross-culturally, there has been much variation in the nature of relations between multiracial and other groups. Many of the groups classified as American Isolates represent one extreme in ethnic relations, in that for many generations they lived apart from mainstream American society with their participation limited mainly to employment in low-level service or manufacturing jobs. However, the American Isolate pattern was only one of a number in North America where contact among various European colonizers, American Indians, and African slaves produced a variety of multiracial groups.

One of these groups is the Settlers, who emerged through marriages between whites and Labrador Inuits in Canada in about 1763. Settlers were not considered to be Inuit by the provincial and national governments because of their partial white ancestry, and therefore suffered less discrimination than did the Inuit. In central Canada, and later in western Canada, a category of peoples known collectively as *metis* (from the French meaning mixed) developed from marriages between European (French-Canadian, Scots, English) traders and American Indian women. The marriages were advantageous to the traders as it gave them access to the American Indian groups who provided furs and other goods for trade. Metis later served the government as guides, interpreters, and American Indian agents. Under Canadian rule, Metis groups lost influence and political rights and were largely reduced to living in poverty on government land. In the twentieth century, the Metis have become increasingly politically active and have succeeded in establishing Metis colonies and associations to ensure their survival as a distinct cultural group.

The situation of the Black Creoles of Louisiana is considerably more complicated, because Black Creole identity is based on a combination of ancestry, language, and culture; an individual's ethnic identity might shift, based on the social situation and identity of the individuals involved in the social interaction. Black Creoles in Louisiana can be traced to relationships between French men and African slave or free women in the eighteenth century, with a strong Caribbean cultural influence added in the early nineteenth century by the arrival of African slaves and free persons from Haiti, and also by intermarriage with Spanish settlers. Today, Black Creole identity is based mainly on African and French or Spanish ancestry, with cultural uniqueness more important than physical features such as skin color.

In many nations of Latin America, multiracial groups do not take the form of relatively small, isolated groups as in North America, but instead form a significant percentage of the population. Throughout Middle and South America are millions of people labeled *mestizo*. Nine of the 17 nations of Latin America have populations that are more than 50 percent mestizo: Chile, 70 percent; Colombia, 50 percent; El Salvador, 89 percent; Honduras, 92 percent; Mexico, 75 percent; Nicaragua, 76 percent; Panama, 67 percent; Paraguay, 76 percent; and Venezuela, 70 percent.

In its broadest sense, *mestizo* refers to people with mixed American Indian and Spanish ancestry, although today in many contexts cultural features such as language, dress, food preferences, occupation, and house style, rather than ancestry, define a person or community as *mestizo*. Traditionally, mestizos occupied a middle place in the social stratification system—above the indigenous Indians and below the Europeans. Today, in nations with large mestizo populations, they are asserting considerable economic and political influence.

The social nature of mestizo identity is indicated by the definitional system the Yucatec Maya use in Mexico. The Maya refer to themselves as *indios*, and to whites as *dzul* (white man) and *xunan* (white woman). However, they also recognize that most people are of mixed Indian and white ancestry. Thus, those identified as *indios* are people who have a Mayan surname and live a Mayan lifestyle. Mayans who use a Spanish surname but live a Mayan lifestyle are called *kaz dzul* (mestizo), indicating that they are not truly Mayan. There is a third category of individuals who have Spanish surnames, live a white lifestyle, and have light skin who are called genuine *dzuls,* with the label *dzul* implying the higher status that accrues to those with a Spanish name, white lifestyle, and lighter skin color.

In northeastern Brazil there is a sizable mixed-ancestry population composed of people who trace their ancestry to African slaves and the Portuguese. Since colonial times, a variety of factors has encouraged African-European relationships and the resulting large population of people of mixed ancestry. These factors include: few white women in the early years of colonization, female slaves working as household help, conjugal unions outside marriage between white men and mixed-ancestry women, the desire in the past of African women to produce "lighter" children by marrying and reproducing with white men, and fewer legal and social restrictions on intermarriage. In Bahia Brazil these factors produced a population composed of three officially recognized groups—*pretos* (blacks), *pardos* (browns), and *brancos* (whites)—and four intermediate groups: *cabra* (lighter skin color and hair less kinky than *pretos*), *Cabo Verde* (very dark with white features and straight black hair), *sarará* (light skin color and red hair), and the *moreno* (tan skin color, white features, brown eyes, and dark hair). This complexity has yielded an equally complex social system, with "whiteness" preferred by some, the *morena* (female) considered ideal by others, and a link between social status and skin color, with higher status coupled with lighter color.

In South Africa the status of multiracial peoples, called *Cape Coloureds*, is less ambiguous. Cape Coloureds are South Africans of mixed ancestry usually including combinations of Europeans, indigenous peoples such as the Khoi, and Asian Indians. Within the apartheid system, Cape Coloureds were distinguished from the indigenous peoples such as the Khoi, Zulu, and !Xhosa, and the Europeans, who are mainly of English and Dutch descent. In addition to the Cape Coloureds, the system also placed Malays, Grigua, Chinese, Indians, and other Coloureds in the middle ground between Africans and Europeans. Under the apartheid system, Cape Coloureds were residentially segregated, had fewer legal and political rights than whites, and were mainly semiskilled and unskilled laborers. In the 1970s, the Cape Coloureds began to affiliate with the African national movements and, with the end of apartheid in 1994, have become a potent political force numbering about 3 million. Their support is sought by both the white National party and the African National Congress.

In India there are far fewer people of mixed European and indigenous ancestry, with the two most notable being the Anglo-Indians and the Goanese (Portuguese and Indian). Culturally, both groups have maintained a European identity and the English language. The Anglo-

This child of a black American father and Vietnamese mother was raised in a Vietnamese orphanage.

Indians have occupied a middleman minority position by taking administrative and service jobs requiring fluency in English.

See also APARTHEID; INDIGENOUS RIGHTS; RACE AND RACISM; SITUATIONAL ETHNICITY.

Berry, Brewton. (1963) *Almost White.*

Blu, Karen I. (1980) *The Lumbee Problem: The Making of an Indian People.*

Domínguez, Virginia R. (1986) *White by Definition: Social Classification in Creole Louisiana.*

Foster, John E., and Gerhard J. Ens. (1991) "Metis of Western Canada." In *Encyclopedia of World Cultures. Volume 1, North America,* edited by Timothy J. O'Leary and David Levinson, 226–229.

Greissman, B. Eugene, subed. (1972) "The American Isolates." *American Anthropologist* 74: 693–734.

Pierson, Donald. (1942) *Negroes in Brazil.*

Redfield, Robert, and Alfonso Villa Rojas. (1934) *Chan Kom: A Maya Village.*

Saladin, d'Anglure, Bernard. (1984) "Inuit of Quebec." In *Handbook of North American Indians. Volume 5, Arctic,* edited by David Damas, 508–521.

Schermerhorn, Richard A. (1978) *Ethnic Plurality in India.*

Van der Ross, R. E. (1979) *Myths and Attitudes: An Inside Look at the Coloured People.*

Williamson, Joel. (1984) *New People: Miscegenation and Mulattoes in the United States.*

MOLDOVA

The conflict involving Russians, Ukrainians, and Moldovans in the Republic of Moldova is an ethnic separatist movement in which the Russian and Ukrainian minorities in the Trans-Dniestr region seek to establish an independent Trans-Dniestr Republic. Called Moldavia during the Soviet era, Moldova is the smallest of the 15 constituent republics of the former USSR. After a long history of shifting borders and domination by outsiders such as Turks and Russians, what are now essentially Romania and Moldova were unified in 1918, although the Soviet Union kept a small strip that became the Moldavian Autonomous Republic. In 1940 the Soviet Union, with German support, obtained more territory from Romania and established the Moldavia Soviet Socialist Republic. In 1947 Moldavia was again divided; a segment was added to the Ukraine and another small strip went to what remained of the Moldavia SSR. With the demise of the USSR, beginning in 1989, Moldova became an independent republic, and then one of the 18 members of the Commonwealth of Independent States (CIS) of the former Soviet Union. Moldova has a population of about 4.3 million; 65 percent are Romanian, 35 percent Ukrainian, 13 percent Russian, and the remainder comprises smaller minorities of Gagauz Turks, Jews (Russian and Ukrainian), Armenians, Bulgarians, and Greeks, among others. Moldovan is a national, not ethnic, designation; persons identified as ethnically Moldovan are actually Romanian in culture. The percentages of Russians and Ukrainians may now be less than given above; numbers of both fled to Russia and the Ukraine to escape the fighting in Moldova in 1992.

One of the first and most significant acts of the Moldovan government to distance itself from Russia and the Soviet Union was the reestablishment of the Romanian language written in the Latin alphabet as the official language of the republic on 30 August 1989, a date now celebrated as a national holiday. Under Soviet rule, Russian, written in the Cyrillic alphabet, was the official language; many Russians and Ukrainians in Moldova have never learned to speak or write Romanian. Other steps were also taken to establish closer cultural and physical links to Romania, including switching to the Romanian time zone, regular air flights to and from Romania, the adoption of an upside-down version of the Romanian flag as the Moldovan flag, and the importation of books and textbooks from Romania. There were also discussions of unification with Romania, although political and economic difficulties in Romania left the majority of Moldovans opposed to immediate unification. The Moldovan government was attentive to some minority-group concerns, and moved to protect various rights, including the use of the Russian language for education in Russian schools and granting citizenship to Russian residents. From the viewpoint of the Romanian Moldovans, they were seeking to establish a multiethnic republic with rights and cultural freedoms guaranteed for all. Efforts toward Romanization were seen as reflecting the historical reality of ties to Romania and the Romanian culture of the Moldovan majority population.

Despite the Moldovans' intentions, these moves toward a Romanization of Moldova convinced members of other ethnic groups that they were in danger of becoming a discriminated-against minority. (The one exception was the small Jewish community, which began to experience far greater cultural and religious freedoms than it had under Communist rule.) A separatist movement by the Gagauz Turks in 1989 was resolved peacefully, but in the Trans-Dniestr region, where Ukrainians and Russians comprised 26 percent and 23 percent of the population, respectively, a full-scale separatist movement developed. The conflict also has irredentist overtones because the Trans-Dniestr region was historically part of the Ukraine, not Moldova, and therefore the indigenous population was Slavic and not Romanian. The region is of considerable economic importance. Although comprising only about 10 percent of the land mass of Moldova, 20 percent of Moldova's industrial output flows from the Trans-Dniestr region, and much of the energy for the republic is produced there as well.

In 1989 and early 1990, Moldovan Russians protested the change in language and other policies, and in September 1990 created the Trans-Dniestr Republic as an autonomous republic. In 1992, following continued unrest, mass protests, strikes, and full-scale violence broke out in the Trans-Dniestr region involving Russian separatist forces supported by Russian and Ukrainian Cossack mercenaries, some elements of the Russian Fourteenth Army stationed in the region, and the Moldovan police. Several hundred people were killed and thousands wounded; thousands of others fled to Russia and the Ukraine. The Russian Trans-Dniestr Republic is supported by Russia, which argues that it should be granted status as an independent republic (a move that some see as a preliminary step before annexation by Russia). Moldova is willing to give the republic considerable autonomy, but not the right to maintain its own police force and military, as requested by Russia. At this time, the Trans-Dniestr region functions as a semi-independent republic with a Soviet-style, Russian-dominated government that stresses centralized political and economic control and Russification, including restrictions on the use of the Romanian language.

Dimi, Nicholas. (1991) *From Moldavia to Moldova: The Soviet-Romanian Territorial Dispute.*

Dunlop, John B. (1993) "Will a Large-Scale Migration of Russians to the Russian Republic Take Place over the Next Decade?" *International Migration Review* 27: 605–629.

Gouboglu, Mikhail N. (1994) "Gaugaz." In *Encyclopedia of World Cultures. Volume 6, Russia/Eurasia and China,* edited by Paul Friedrich and Norma Diamond, 124–126.

MYANMAR (BURMA)

The Union of Myanmar, formerly known as Burma, has an area of 261,220 square miles and is located between south and southeast Asia on the Bay of Bengal. It is bordered by Bangladesh and India on the west, and China, Laos, and Thailand on the north and east. In

1993 the population of Myanmar was estimated to be 43.5 million, composed of the majority Burmans and several tribal groups including the Karen, Kachin, Shan, and Mon. Much of the Muslim population of several hundred thousand now lives as refugees, mainly in Bangladesh. Accurate demographic information on these groups is unavailable or badly out of date. Myanmar is currently ruled by a military government and is organized into seven states and seven divisions. The official language is Burmese, although the various minority groups speak their own languages.

Approximately 85 percent of the population is Buddhist. Under the government's *Burmese Way of Socialism* the economy has suffered enormously, because the price-control policy encourages citizens to sell their rice and other products in black markets along the border for higher prices than the government will pay, and to trade for foreign goods also available through the black market. The large number of Burmese ethnic-minority-group members living in neighboring countries as refugees contributes to the vitality of the black market.

The distinction between the designations *Burman* and *Burmese* is of significance. *Burman* refers to the specific ethnic group; *Burmese* refers to all the citizens of Myanmar, and to their language and culture. Burmese speakers make up about 70 percent of the population. More than 95 percent of Burmans are Buddhists, and have been since the eleventh century. The ancestors of modern Burmans probably migrated to present-day Myanmar from China about 3,000 years ago. From 1057 to the beginning of British rule in 1826, Burma was first a kingdom that, following incursions from the north, became a series of smaller principalities. After the arrival of the British, three Anglo-Burman wars from 1824–1884 eventually led to the subjugation of Burma by the British, who ruled the area as a province of India until nationalist fervor finally led to independence in 1948. Independence

was gained with the assistance of the Japanese, who occupied Burma during World War II and granted it independence from Britain. In fact, Burma saw Japanese, British, Chinese, and American troops during World War II. Some of the tension between the Burmans and other ethnic groups that has fueled internal strife for the past 45 years stemmed from the World War II experience. Ethnic Burmans tended to view the war as a national independence uprising, but many of the country's ethnic minorities fought with the British, and thus on the side opposite the Burmans. Ethnic Burmans fought with the Japanese and formed the Burman Independence Army (BIA). Leaders of this group trained in Japan and formed what became known as the Thirty Comrades, who eventually led the national liberation movement to independence in 1948. The ethnic minorities, on the other hand, fought on the Allied side. Many remained loyal to the British, with whom they shared religious and political interests.

The Karen (also called Kareang, Kariang, Kayin, Pwo, Sgaw, and Yang) mostly inhabit eastern Myanmar, though there are Karen in western Thailand as well, and are the largest ethnic minority in Myanmar. Accurate census figures are not available, but it is believed they number nearly 3 million, with an additional 185,000 in Thailand, of whom 10,000–20,000 live in refugee camps. The Karen group of languages is believed to be a subfamily of the Tibeto-Burman language family. Karen early history is poorly recorded, but certainly by the eighteenth century, Karen peoples had emigrated from central Asia to Southeast Asia, and were living in what is now Myanmar. They emerged as a significant group later in the eighteenth century when their increasing sense of oppression led to a series of unsuccessful attempts to gain autonomy. Many Karen converted to Christianity (or at least incorporated aspects of it into their own animistic religion) when British and American missionaries worked actively in the region in the eighteenth century. Prior to World War II, the Karen and the British had established an amicable relationship. The Karen desire for independence is partly a result of education provided by the British and the resulting major administrative role played by Karen in the British colonial government. Karen-Burman tensions intensified during World War II as they fought on opposite sides. The Karen National Union agitated for autonomy when national independence was on the horizon, and has fought for independence from Burmese rule since 1949.

The Kachin (also called Dashan, Jinghpaw, Khang, Singhpo, and Theinbaw) are primarily located in the Kachin state of Myanmar, as well as in China and India. They number about 1 million, although no accurate information is available. Their language is part of the Tibeto-Burman family, and almost all Kachin communities are Christian. Recorded history of the Kachin begins as early as the thirteenth century, but becomes much fuller toward the end of the eighteenth century. This more recent history is similar to that of the Shan (who will be discussed below), with whom the Kachin have close ties. During the Anglo-Burman wars, the Kachin attempted to capitalize on the collapse of royal Burma to gain autonomy, but were unsuccessful. Since Burmese independence in 1948, the Kachin state has been a constituent of the union, and the Kachin themselves have fought the Myanmar government for greater autonomy or independence.

The Shan (also called Burmese Shan, Chinese Shan, *Dai, Hkamti Shan, Ngiaw, Ngio, Pai-I, Tai Khe, Tai Khun, Tai Long, Tai Lu, Tai Mao, Tai Nu,* and *Thai Yai)* refer to themselves as *Tai.* They mainly inhabit the mountain valleys in eastern Myanmar. Shan may account for as much as 7 percent of Myanmar's population, although their actual number—which almost certainly exceeds 1 million—is not known. They speak Thai and identify themselves as Buddhists. Recorded history begins around A.D. 1000, when

they migrated to northern Burma from southern China. Their history since the eighteenth century has been largely linked to that of the Kachin in terms of autonomy movements. Divided into as many as 18 states before and during the British period, the region was consolidated into one Shan state following Burmese independence in 1948. Since the 1950s, and continuing to the present, the Shan have been part of the military struggle against the Burmese/Myanmar government to gain either independence or substantial autonomy.

There are approximately 1.3 million Mon (Mun, Peguan, Talaing, and Taleng) in Myanmar, according to recent projections. They are believed to have lived in what is now Myanmar for at least 1,000 years, and enjoyed political independence from the Burmese until 1757. Most live in southwestern Myanmar, and subsist by agriculture and fishing. Their economy has been hurt by the Burmese government allowing Thai commercial fishermen to exploit traditional Mon fishing grounds. Many Mon are now bilingual in Mon and Burmese, reflecting a general pattern of assimilation into Burman society. Many are also Buddhists, and are engaged in the independence struggle against the government.

Burmese Muslims, called *Rohingya* and who live mainly in Arakan state, date to the ninth century. Until Burmese independence, the Rohingya lived in relative harmony with their Buddhist neighbors. After independence, a Muslim *Mujahid* separatist movement gained control of part of Arakan state, leading to government reprisals and then a general harassment of Muslims elsewhere in Myanmar. In 1978 government violence led about 200,000 Muslims to flee to Bangladesh. Many eventually returned, but some still continue to leave in reaction to government repression, including efforts to deny them citizenship and economic rights, the renaming of Muslim historic sites, and referring to them as *Bengali* or *Kalas* instead of the preferred *Rohingya.* One motivation for government harassment is evidently to deter Muslims in exile from returning to Myanmar. The Muslim separatist movement has now been repressed, with Muslim resistance centered in the Rohingya Patriotic Front, the Rohingya Solidarity Organization, the Arakan Liberation Organization, and the umbrella Arakan Rohingya Islamic Front.

Together these groups have formed a multiethnic insurgency against the military government of Myanmar, with the latter officially called the State Law and Order Restoration Council (SLORC). In fact, the internal war currently being waged in Myanmar is now a combination of these groups, Burmese Communists, and prodemocracy Burman students. After nearly 30 years of military dictatorship, prodemocracy demonstrations erupted in 1988. Thousands of people were killed when troops fired into crowds of peaceful prodemocracy demonstrators. Mrs. Aung San Suu Kyi, who won the Nobel Peace Prize in 1991 and is the leader of the National League for Democracy, was placed under house arrest, where she remains. However, as a result of demonstrations and international pressures, the military government held the first free multiparty elections in May 1990, and the National League for Democracy prevailed overwhelmingly. The military government refused to hand over power and the international response was to withdraw aid programs. At the same time, the military has continued its battles against the multiethnic insurgency, which includes at least 7 million, throughout the country. As of 1993 the fighting in Myanmar has produced over 330,000 refugees: 245,000 Muslims in Bangladesh, 72,000 ethnic group members in Thailand and India, and 20,000 Kachin in China. The SLORC policy of destroying entire villages has also created tens of thousands of internally displaced peoples. SLORC has been much criticized by the international community for human rights violations, including confiscation of citizens' property, torture, mass rapes, forced relocations, and using ethnic minorities for forced labor. The city of Manerplaw, traditionally home to the Karen, has become a stronghold in the ongoing war in recent years, and opposition leaders of almost every major group have based their operations from there in their attempts to oust the military government. The fighting has become more intense in the past three years than for the past four decades. The minority groups are seeking independence or much greater autonomy within a federal democratic system.

"Burma in Search of Peace." *Cultural Survival Quarterly* 13(4): 1989.

Falla, Jonathan. (1991) *True Love and Bartholomew: Rebels on the Burmese Border.*

Lintner, Bertil. (1990) *Land of Jade: A Journey through Insurgent Burma.*

Steinberg, David. (1980) *Burma's Road toward Development, Growth, and Ideology under Military Rule.*

Yangwhe, Chao Tzang [Eugene Thaike]. (1987) *The Shan of Burma: Memoirs of a Shan Exile, Local History and Memoirs.*

version was successful, but traditional religious beliefs remain the primary practice of most tribes.

Although little is known for certain about the origin of the Naga peoples, it is known that they migrated south, most likely from northwestern China prior to the tenth century B.C. After the thirteenth century A.D. the various Naga tribes had extensive contact with the Ahoms, who ruled Assam from 1228 until 1826, when the British arrived. While the various tribes had different relationships with the Ahoms, including raiding, trade, and the payment of tribute, even the most restrictive relationships never resulted in total Assamese rule over the Naga region. The British took control of Nagaland after the annexation of both India and Assam, and only after significant guerrilla resistance, which lasted for much of the nineteenth century. Once under British rule, the Nagas were treated paternally by the British, who controlled the settlement of non-Nagas in the region and left local administration in British or Naga hands rather than use Indian officials as was the practice elsewhere. The British also encouraged Christian missionization. This differential treatment and a relatively high literacy rate, combined with the cultural differences and geographical isolation from India, enhanced the Nagas' sense of ethnic solidarity.

In the early twentieth century, nationalistic sentiment manifested itself in the Naga National Council (NNC), which demanded regional independence in 1947. After India emerged as an independent secular nation, the Naga region was granted statehood within India (the state of Nagaland, in 1963) in an effort to satisfy demands for political freedom. Despite this small concession, conflict continued until the declaration of a cease-fire in 1964 between the Nagaland Federal Government and the central government of India. Eight years later the cease-fire ended and the NNC was banned, followed by a three-year period of armed resistance by the

NAGAS IN INDIA The name *Naga* applies to more than 14 related tribal groups who inhabit the hill country along the border between India and Myanmar. The derivation of the name is unknown; it is used today as their official name by both the peoples themselves and outsiders. Its use by the Naga groups is motivated somewhat by political considerations, as it allows the culturally diverse groups to present a united front against the Indian government. Among major Naga groups are the Kacha, Angami, Rengma, Lhote, Sema, Ao, Konyak, Chang, Sangtam, Yachumi, and Tukomi. These and other Naga groups speak a total of 27 Naga dialects, with communication between groups possible via Naga Pidgin. In 1981 the population in the Indian state of Nagaland was estimated at 774,930, of which Nagas comprised approximately 75 percent, and does not include the many Nagas who live elsewhere in India and Myanmar. Religious practice differs among the various tribes, but generally centers around supernatural forces and spirits that deal with the cycle of life. In some Naga tribes the British attempt at Christian con-

NNC. In November 1975 the Shillong Accord between the Indian government and the Nagaland federal government was signed, which has effectively curbed violence since then. However, there are still sporadic outbreaks of violence, including a June 1993 Naga guerrilla attack on an Indian army convoy, leaving 32 dead. Naga resistance to Indian rule now centers around the National Socialist Council of Nagaland, which maintains an army of 2,000 guerrillas and seeks independence from India. It is one of a number of such groups operating in the relatively isolated region of northeastern India.

Anand, V. K. (1969) *Nagaland in Transition.*

Horam, M. (1977) *Social and Cultural Life of Nagas.*

Maxwell, Neville G. A. (1980) *India, the Nagas, and the North-East.*

NATIONAL MINORITY, CHINA

The government of the People's Republic of China recognizes 56 ethnic groups called *minzu*. About 96 percent of the Chinese population is Han Chinese, who are not considered minzu. The remaining 4 percent is classified into 55 national minority groups called *shaoshuminzu*. These range in size from 15 or more groups that number over 1 million people each, such as the Zhuang (14 million), Hui (8 million), and Koreans (2 million), to those numbering several hundred thousand, such as the Lisu (500,000), Naxi (250,000), and Tu (160,000), to smaller groups such as the Bulang (70,000), Jing (12,000), and Loba (2,500). Several hundred groups have asked the Chinese government for recognition as a national minority, but only 55 have received such recognition to date. The criteria used by the government to recognize groups are varied and often

Noted Muslim imans and mawla in a mosque in Xinjiang, China, 1985.

applied arbitrarily. Criteria include non-Han ancestry, religion (the Hui, for example are Muslim), language, common territory, economy, and common culture. In fact, intermmarriage, ethnic contact, contact with the majority Han population, and efforts in the past to eradicate ethnic variation have made these criteria less than completely appropriate as markers of unique ethnic identity. In many regions or political subdivisions, including those named after a national minority such as Ningxia Hui, ethnic variation is observable only in the rural villages, and even then there is considerable contact among different groups. Today, most groups are identified by names they have chosen or approved of, and recognition as a distinct group affords the groups equal rights with other groups within the Chinese political structure that controls the economy, population movements, family policy, and naming practices. At the same time, minorities are now permitted by the government to practice their traditional religions, use their native languages, and engage in cultural activities that do not counter government policies.

Chiao, Chien, and Nicolas Tapp. (1989) *Ethnicity and Ethnic Groups in China.*

Friedrich, Paul, and Norma Diamond, eds. (1993) *Encyclopedia of World Cultures. Volume 6, Russia/Eurasia and China.*

Ma Yin, ed. (1989) *China's Minority Nationalities.*

reside in another nation. Such groups in Europe today include Belarussians and Germans (Silesians) in Poland; Hungarians in the former Czechoslovakia; Romanians and Slovaks in Hungary; Hungarians in Romania; Albanians in Serbia (part of the former Yugoslavia); Slovenes, Albanians, and Austrians in Italy; Slovenes and Croats in Austria; and Turks in Bulgaria. Most of these national minorities are the result of shifting political boundaries in the past, which left a segment of one national population across the border in a neighboring nation.

The term is actually used with considerable imprecision. First, sometimes both Jews and Muslims are considered national minoritities, although Jews were never a nation in Europe and *Muslim* refers to followers of a religion and is not a political category. Second, the notion of *national minority* also excludes many regional or linguistic groups in western Europe, such as the Bretons in France or Catalans in Spain, and large non-European national populations, such as Turks in Germany and Algerians and Moroccans in France. The breakup of the Soviet Union, Yugoslavia, and Czechoslovakia; the reunification of Germany; efforts to establish a European Community; the fall of Communist rule in eastern Europe; massive population shifts; and an influx of guest workers from inside and outside Europe since World War II have made national minorities less of a concern in ethnic relations than in the past, with the exception of Albanians in Serbia and Hungarians in Romania.

See also ALBANIANS AND SERBS; HUNGARIANS IN ROMANIA (TRANSYLVANIA); MIGRANT WORKERS.

NATIONAL MINORITY, EUROPE

In the European context, national minority refers to a large population of people from one political nation who

Horak, Stephan M. (1985) *Eastern European National Minorities 1919–1980: A Handbook.*

Krejci, Jaroslav, and Vitezslav Velimsky. (1981) *Ethnic and Political Nations in Europe.*

NEPALESE IN BHUTAN

Bhutan is one of three Himalayan kingdoms, the others being Nepal and Sikkim. It covers an area of 47,182 square kilometers, is bordered on the north by Tibet, on the south and east by India, and on the west by Nepal. A monarchy, the Bhutan king has near absolute authority. Estimates of the Bhutan population vary from 600,000 to 1.5 million. Bhutan is a rural nation—there are no cities and the economy is based primarily on agriculture. Bhutanese are mainly Buddhists, with the Mahayana form dominant. Bhutanese is a national rather than an ethnic designation, and the dominant ethnic group are the Drupka. Bhutanese make up about 75 percent of the population, and speak Tibetan or Sangla, with Nepalese comprising the other 25 percent. The Nepalese population is composed of Rai, Gurung, and Limbu immigrants, and smaller numbers of high-caste Nepalese Brahmans and Chhetris, who moved to Bhutan in the 1960s and 1970s to work on infrastructure development projects such as road and dam building. Nepalese speak Nepali and are Hindu; they live in southern Bhutan, as they are prohibited from living in the northern half of the country.

In 1991 and 1992 about 95,000 Nepalese fled Bhutan and sought protection in Nepal (75,000) and India (20,000). The Nepalese claim to have been driven out by the Drupka-dominated military following the orders of King Jigme Singye Wangchuck. They see themselves as the victims of a forced assimilation and ethnic cleansing effort designed to destroy Nepalese culture in Bhutan and drive the Nepalese out, thereby reducing any threat to Drupka dominance. In the late 1980s, the government decreed that the Nepalese wear Bhutanese-style clothing, banned the use of Nepali in schools, and placed restrictions on Nepalese citizenship and property rights. In 1990 the Nepalese protested; the Bhutanese responded by burning Nepalese homes, closing schools, and arresting suspected protest leaders. Nepalese refugees also claim that the government engaged in a campaign of terrorism, including forced labor, rapes, beatings, forced relocation, and deportations. Evidently the terrorism campaign directly affected only a few individuals, but did achieve its purpose of forcing others to leave.

The Bhutanese government views the situation differently. To them the Nepalese are mainly illegal immigrants, and they cite census data that identified 113,000 illegal immigrants. In addition, they blame the protests and resulting government actions on Nepalese rebels, who are perceived as a threat to Bhutanese security. Underlying the Bhutanese position is their concern that the Nepalese will become numerically dominant and that Drupka control would be eroded, turning Bhutan into a Nepalese rather than Bhutanese nation. Their concern is motivated in part by the experience of Sikkim, where the indigenous population was outnumbered by Nepalese. It is also fueled by Bhutanese worries about the rapid growth rate of the Nepalese population, spurred, they believe, by Nepalese polygymous marriage and large families.

In Nepal, the refugees live in six camps with poor sanitation and housing facilities and a high rate of health problems. In India, they are not recognized as refugees but are allowed to live and work there, although there is some evidence that some have been forcibly returned to Bhutan. Either rebels or criminal gangs operating out of some refugee camps have been attacking Bhutanese officials and towns. Efforts by the Nepalese and Bhutanese governments to negotiate a settlement to the crisis have not yet proved fruitful.

Chakravvarti, Balaram. (1980) *A Cultural History of Bhutan.*

Jenkins, William M. (1963) *The Himalayan Kingdoms: Bhutan, Sikkim, and Nepal.*

U.S. Committe for Refugees. (1993) *World Refugee Survey.*

NIGERIA

The Federal Republic of Nigeria is located on the southern coast of West Africa, east of Benin, south of Niger, and west of Chad and Cameroon. Nigeria encompasses 356,667 square miles. As of 1991 the population was estimated at 88.5 million, making it Africa's most populous nation. Nigeria is home to more than 250 ethnolinguistic groups, with the major ones being the Hausa (21 percent of the population), Yoruba (20 percent), Igbo (17 percent), and Fulani (9 percent). The remainder includes groups such as the Kanuri, Nupe, and Tiv in the north. Islam is the dominant religion in most of northern Nigeria, but Christianity is dominant across much of the south. Nationwide, Muslims constitute 50 percent of the population and Christians make up 40 percent. The country is currently ruled by a military government led by General Ibrahim Babangida, and is divided into 21 states.

The Portuguese and the British began slave trading from Africa during the fifteenth and sixteenth centuries, and in 1861 the British annexed Lagos in southern Nigeria. At the Conference of Berlin in 1885, British supremacy over southern Nigeria was formally recognized, and in 1914 northern and southern Nigeria were combined into the British colony of Nigeria. Nigeria achieved independence on 1 October 1960 and was proclaimed the Federal Republic of Nigeria three years later. Although the British did take some measures to prepare the Nigerians for self-government, years of exploiting ethnic rivalries in order to rule through a divide-and-conquer strategy, and failure to consider how these patterns would affect efforts at forming a national government, hindered the possibility of a smooth transition to self-rule.

Yoruba is the named used by outsiders for a number of Yoruba-speaking groups who prior to British rule were never unified as a single people. Yoruba-speaking peoples prefer to refer to themselves by their subgroup names. There are about 20 million Yoruba in West Africa, mainly in southwestern Nigeria, Benin, and Togo, making them one of the largest groups in Africa. The Yoruba are mainly farmers, growing beans, maize, cassava, and yams for their own use, and kola nuts, cocoa, cotton, and tobacco for sale. The Yoruba include both Christians and Muslims, with elements of their indigenous beliefs intertwined with both. Under British rule the Yoruba were heavily missionized and involved in business and government, and controlled most of the key government positions in their region at the time of independence from Britain.

The Hausa-Fulani are often discussed as a single ethnic entity because of their interrelationship dating to the early 1800s. Prior to the nineteenth century the Hausa consisted of seven states, called the *Habe* states. The states were conquered by the Muslim Fulani in a *jihad* that placed Fulani rulers in control of each Hausa state. Over time, the ruling Fulani adopted the lifestyle, customs, and language of the Hausa, and the term *Hausa* now covers those people who were originally Hausa-speaking, assimilated Fulani, and other ethnic groups that have also been assimilated by the Hausa. There are 25 million Hausa in West Africa centered in northern Nigeria and adjacent Niger. The Hausa are 90 percent Muslim and played a central role in spreading Islam to other West African groups. Primarily rural agriculturalists, they grow millet, maize, and rice for home use, and cotton and peanuts for home use and sale. The cattle-herding Fulani provide a source of meat and its by-products. Hausa concepts of government rest on the notions of kinship, clientship, and titled offices.

The Igbo are found mainly in southeastern Nigeria and number about 9 million. Prior to British rule, the Igbo were not a unified people, and although the 200 or more Igbo communities were similar culturally, they conducted their affairs as autonomous political units. Traditionally, these units were lumped into five general categories: Northern, Western, Southern, Eastern, and Northeastern Igbo. The Igbo are mainly farmers who grow yams, cocoyams, and cassava for home use, and bananas, breadfruit, pears, kola nuts, and palm oil for trade. The Igbo are strong advocates of secular rule; their effort to secede, leading to civil war from 1967 to 1970, is an indicator of the importance they attach to this issue.

Ethnic, religious, and regional (north-south) rivalries have dominated Nigerian attempts since independence to develop a secular, democratic form of government. Federal elections were held in 1964, but proved unsuccessful in the face of assassinations, voter intimidation, and ballot-box stuffing. In the negotiations among regional leaders that followed, northern Muslims dominated, which served only to intensify traditional religious, regional, and ethnic rivalries. In addition, northern Nigeria has been the scene of frequent and deadly clashes between Muslims and Christians in the three decades since independence, fueled by conflicts over land ownership and political control. Many Christians in Nigeria regard the predominance of Islam in politics as a threat to secular government. In fact, for all but nine years since Nigeria gained independence from Britain in 1960, the country has been under military rule. Since that time there have been seven successful coups, and three of the nation's eight leaders have been assassinated. In 1967 the eastern region (populated mainly by Igbos) seceded, proclaiming itself the Republic of Biafra, which resulted in a three-year civil war that claimed nearly 1 million lives. In 1970 the secessionists admitted defeat, and have since been reintegrated into Nigerian society. In 1979 Nigeria returned to civilian government, but this lasted only four years, when a coup put the nation back under military rule. In 1985 General Ibrahim Babangida seized power. General Babangida has long claimed to be an advocate of return to civilian democratic rule, but has managed to postpone such a return by canceling elections four times since 1990.

Conflicts during the 1990s point to continued instability in Nigeria and the interplay of ethnicity, religion, and regionalism in Nigerian politics. In October 1991 Muslims and Christians clashed in the northern city of Kano, resulting in several hundred deaths. In January and August 1992 the old Tiv-Jakun (both groups are Christian) rivalry turned violent, with some 2,000–2,500 killed. The violence was precipitated by Jakun claims that the more numerous Tiv were intruding on their land. In May 1992 Christians in Kaluna Province, which is about half Christian and half Muslim, became concerned that the Muslims were attempting to undercut secular rule by restricting the building of churches and putting Christian schools under government control, yet allowing the building of mosques. Fighting between the Christian Kataf and Muslim Hausa-Fulani left 500–800 dead. In June 1993 free elections were held; three days afterward, a commission appointed by the military government ruled the election invalid due to alleged fraud and tampering, despite reports from outside observers that the elections appeared free and open. The winner was Moshood Abiola, a Muslim Yoruba from the south whose victory reversed a long pattern of rulers coming from the Muslim Hausa-Fulani group in the north. Supporters of Abiola charged that the results were voided to prevent Abiola from taking power and rioted in protest, as well as to demand an end to military rule. At this time, the question of when new elections will be held remains unresolved.

Adamu, Mahdi. (1978) *The Hausa Factor in West African History.*

Anam-Ndu, Ekeng A. (1990) *Consociational Democracy in Nigeria: Agenda for the 1990s and Beyond.*

Eades, J. S. (1980) *The Yoruba Today.*

Hill, Polly. (1972) *Rural Hausa: A Village and a Setting.*

Nwankwo, Arthur A. (1991) *Political Danger Signals: The Politics of Federalism, Census, Blanket Ban, and National Integration.*

Smith, R. S. (1988) *Kingdoms of the Yoruba.*

Uchendu, Victor C. (1965) *The Igbo of Southeast Nigeria.*

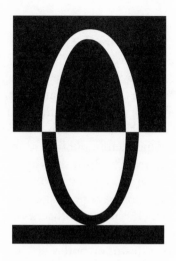

The Republic of Georgia encompasses 26,911 square miles and is bordered by the Black Sea on the west, Turkey and Armenia on the south, and Azerbaijan on the southeast. It is separated from Russia on the northeast by the main range of the Caucasus Mountains. In 1993 Georgia's population was estimated at 5.5 million, 70 percent of whom are ethnically Georgian. The remainder of the population is composed of small percentages of other ethnic groups, the largest being Armenian (7 percent) and Russian (6 percent); Ossetes account for approximately 3 percent. The official language is Georgian, and in 1989, 33 percent of the people considered Georgian their native language. Under the former Soviet Union, Russian was a mandatory school subject, and approximately 33 percent of Georgians, primarily those in cities, speak it fluently. Most Georgians belong to the Georgian Orthodox Church.

Georgia was annexed by Russia in 1801 and entered the USSR in 1922. It became a constituent republic in 1936. On 9 April 1991, following the collapse of communism and a 99 percent approval vote on a Georgian independence referendum, Georgia was declared a sovereign state.

Ossetes inhabit both sides of the central Caucasian mountain range that divides Russia and Georgia. The whole region of Ossetia is divided between the two federal republics; the North Ossetic Republic is part of the Russian Federation and the South Ossetic Autonomous Region belongs to the Republic of Georgia. The mountain range forms a natural border between the two, and has led to separate and independent development within each part. North Ossetia covers approximately 8,000 square kilometers; South Ossetia comprises approximately 3,800 square kilometers. As of 1970 there were approximately 430,000 people in the Soviet Union who considered themselves Ossetes. The Ossete population is not expanding, due to the prevalence of small families in the cities and the assimilation of Ossetes into both Russian and Georgian society. The Ossetic language is a member of the Iranian family of languages and has two distinct major dialects. In North Ossetia, Russian is the official language, and Georgian is the official language in the south. Most Ossetes are Christian, with a minority being Muslim, stemming from the seventeenth-century introduction of Islam to the area. Islam has never been a particularly widespread religion in the region, and the two religions have been able to coexist peacefully.

It is believed that the Ossetes are descendants of the Alanic tribes of southern Russia who migrated to the Ossetia region approximately 600 years ago, with Ossetes resident in Georgia longer than in Russia. Annexed by Russia in the late 1700s, the Ossetes never actually formed their own state until the beginning of the Soviet era, when the South and North Ossetia Autonomous Regions were formed in Georgia and

OSSETES AND GEORGIANS

Destruction to an Ossete residence by Georgian forces in November 1991. Civilians are often victims in ethnic conflict.

Russia (in 1922 and 1924, respectively). In 1936 North Ossetia gained greater autonomy as an autonomous republic within Russia.

In the late 1980s, the era of *glasnost* and decentralization, Ossetia, particularly South

Ossetia, began to push for greater independence, demanding greater freedom in politics, economics, and culture. Georgian resistance to these calls for autonomy have led to the ongoing conflict. Although Ossetian-Georgian relations have been difficult for centuries, fighting and tensions escalated in 1990, when South Ossetia declared itself an independent republic within the Soviet Union. Georgia responded by abolishing Ossetia's declaration and revoking its prior status as an autonomous region. The revocation was overturned by President Gorbachev, but that did not prevent violence from breaking out, with several dozen deaths on both sides, several thousand Georgians fleeing south into Georgia, and several thousand Ossetes fleeing north into North Ossetia. Georgia has accused Russia of arming the separatists as a means of incorporating all of Ossetia into Russia; Russia officially denies these allegations. These charges and countercharges by the Georgians and Russians have escalated the crisis and reduced the chance of a peaceful resolution.

Akiner, Shirin. (1986) *Islamic Peoples of the Soviet Union: An Historical and Statistical Handbook.*

Fritz, Sonja. (1994) "Ossetes." In *Encyclopedia of World Cultures. Volume 6, Russia/Eurasia and China,* edited by Paul Friedrich and Norma Diamond, 297–302.

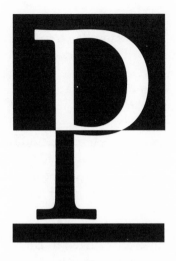

tive cultures to the dominant (usually national) society and are also part of a broader pattern of culture change that affects all aspects of native life. Pacification has been justified by colonists as a humane and morally correct strategy; in some situations, as in early efforts in Brazil and by some missionaries in Melanesia, this was a major motivation. However, economic and political domination was always the primary goal, if not for those carrying out the pacification, then for the government officials and developers interested in political and economic control of the region and its native peoples.

The term *pacification* is used somewhat inconsistently by social scientists and government officials, and is appropriate only in reference to those situations where the explicit government policy is to pacify indigenous cultures rather than to conquer or destroy them. Thus, the term is used primarily in reference to one aspect of native-colonial or government relations in Melanesia and South America, and not in reference to native-colonial or government relations in North America or Africa. In North America the native peoples were conquered and displaced onto reservations, while in Africa they were initially encouraged to raid for slaves, then colonized or exploited as a labor force, and eventually achieved political independence. Another confusion about the term is that warfare practices that are the target of pacification efforts may vary from one situation to another. Pacification efforts assume, of course, that the culture to be pacified is already warlike, an assumption that may not necessarily be true. Thus, one form of warfare to be controlled through pacification is indigenous peoples reacting in a warlike fashion to the encroaching dominant culture. For this reason, pacification always precedes intensive efforts to develop the resources in the territories of the pacified peoples. A second type of warfare to be controlled by pacification is warfare between indigenous peoples. When the culture or cultures to be pacified is known or strongly

PACIFICATION

Pacification refers both to the process and the end result of that process in which a culture is forced or chooses to "abandon warfare and cede control over the use of military force to a group perceived as more powerful...." (Rodman 1983, 1) Along with conquest, colonization, genocide, and ethnocide, pacification is a major strategy used by colonial powers and modern nations to subjugate indigenous peoples and acquire ownership or control of the natural resources in their traditional homelands. While the four other strategies involve cultural change or disruption in a general sense, pacification usually refers to government action designed specifically by the national government or a colonial power to end warfare waged by indigenous peoples. For example, pacification efforts in the twentieth century were undertaken on a broad scale by the British in Melanesia, Australians in New Guinea, and the Brazilian government in the Amazon region. However, pacification efforts are always only one component of a broader agenda ultimately designed to transfer control of local resources from the na-

suspected of being warlike (which is often the situation), the wars that are meant to be prevented are those between the culture and other native peoples—wars that do not directly threaten the colonists but are an impediment to their controlling the region and governing the native peoples.

The major arenas for pacification have been South America—especially Brazil—and New Guinea and the associated islands of Melanesia in the South Pacific. Comparison of pacification efforts in these two regions illustrates the major objectives, causes, techniques, and outcomes of pacification around the world.

Pacification in Brazil

Although localized efforts by traders, missionaries, land agents, and government officers had occurred previously, full-scale pacification began in Brazil in the early 1990s under the direction of the Indian Protection Service (IPS) for the express purpose of protecting the Indian cultures from traders, land developers, and others. The IPS strategy was to make contact with hostile tribes and convince them to end hostilities directed at outsiders, trusting the government to protect them and their interests. Beginning in the early 1900s, teams of unarmed IPS agents would approach an Indian village, leave gifts such as beads, mirrors, and steel machetes at the entrance, and then wait weeks or months for the Indians to accept the gifts. After again waiting some period of time, the agents would enter the village with an interpreter to convince the Indians to cease hostilities and trust the government agents to protect their interests. The agents were pacifist and patient, operating under the dictum: "Die if it be necessary, but never kill." (Davis 1977, 4) This approach to pacification is referred to as "classic pacification."

Such classic pacification was successful, and over 60 tribes were pacified, 67 Indian posts were established in the region, and no Indians and only a few agents were killed. However, the long-term effects of this pacification effort were devastating to the Indians. Between 1900 and 1957, more than 80 tribes were destroyed by disease, and others fled to the interior or were placed on small resource-poor reservations (called *parks*). The traditional territories of the pacified groups are now coffee plantations, rubber plantations, and the sites of towns, farms, factories, and mineral extraction operations. In addition, many of the surviving groups exist on the margins of Brazilian society and have lost their native languages, beliefs, and customs.

Beginning in about 1950, pacification efforts became overtly linked to Brazilian development and economic policy, with protection of Indians no longer a major consideration. Economic development of the Amazon Basin is the driving force, with the emphasis on building roads, mining, farming, establishment of towns and industry, and settlement by non-Indians. Indian policy stressed pacification, followed by relocation on small reservations isolated from areas of development. However, when existing reservations were in the way of development, they were further reduced in size or divided by roads. As with the more humanely motivated pacification of the early 1900s, the Indian tribes were devastated. For example, the highway program that began in 1970 has resulted in the disappearance, relocation, fleeing, or deculturation of all 29 tribes living in the vicinity of the proposed roads. The policy today is a combination of placement on reservations and integration into mainstream society through a combination of pacification, genocide, and ethnocide.

Pacification in Melanesia

Melanesia is in the South Pacific Ocean, and includes the large island of New Guinea and smaller, adjacent islands and archipelagos, such as the Solomon Islands. Pacification of insular Melanesia and the large island of New Guinea took different courses due to the nature of contact with European colonists. In the early 1800s, there was little interest in pacifying the local cultures. The islands were mainly a source of laborers, supplied to European recruiters by coastal peoples to work for three years on sugar plantations in Fiji and Queensland. Pacification began after 1850 when the British sought to colonize the islands, establish local plantations, and make the colonies self-sufficient. To do so, they attempted to end warfare among indigenous cultures and tried to prevent violent resistance to British settlement. With the aid of missionaries, who had previously been seeking pacification on their own, all native cultures were pacified either peacefully or through the use or show of force, and all came under British control. Unlike Brazil, pacification was encouraged and supported, but not directly managed, by the colonial government. Instead, it was managed by local colonial officials, who used small European police forces, sometimes supplemented by native police, missionaries, influential local leaders, and the imposition of taxes and other means to end indigenous warfare and limit resistance to European control.

On New Guinea, warfare was a ubiquitous feature of life among many of the distinct and numerous groups who lived in the highlands, although peaceful contact involving trade and marriage was also common. As with the islands, early European contact was confined to the coast; pacification of the interior highlands did not begin until after 1900, and was not achieved in most places until between 1930 and the 1960s. In the highlands, pacification meant the cessation of fighting among native cultures and the prevention of raids against the colonists, and was motivated by Australian interest in developing the interior. As on the islands, pacification was managed by local officials (although the process was strongly supported by the Australian government) who used military patrols and military posts in pacified regions to maintain peace.

The pacification process was accelerated and spread further to the interior during World War

Shavante tribesmen in Brazil's Matto Grosso aim arrows at a low-flying Brazilian plane carrying a pacification party.

II, motivated by the perceived need to secure the region and keep the local population under control. In all locales, successful pacification was followed by the establishment of plantations, military posts, towns, roads, airstrips, the introduction of a nationally administered legal system, and an economy based on wage labor. While most groups have remained pacified, beginning in about 1970 and continuing since New Guinea independence in 1975, some groups have resumed fighting with one another and have resisted government efforts to repacify them. It is unclear why fighting has resumed, but important causes include: (1) a weakening of peaceful trade and marriage relations among groups that may have controlled warfare in the past, (2) new political alliances among the groups, (3) the survival of traditional warfare patterns and associated beliefs such as political leadership based on the achievement of military glory, (4) a doubting of the ability of the national government to manage local conflicts, and (5) the failure of the government to replace warfare with other nonviolent conflict-resolution mechanisms.

Unlike pacification in Brazil, pacification in Melanesia did not destroy many of the native cultures, and also it has not been permanent in all regions. Of course, one of the major differences between the two regions is the political independence achieved by native peoples in Melanesia versus the political domination or destruction of Indians in Brazil.

The Melanesian experience also points to another important component of pacification—the need to replace indigenous warfare as a means of settling conflicts with nonviolent conflict-resolution mechanisms. In New Guinea and elsewhere, new nonviolent mechanisms include the use of village and regional courts; competing for property, as among the Goodenough Islanders in Melanesia or the Tlingit in North America; and the institutionalization of a legal system based on individual property rights.

See also COLONIALISM; ETHNOCIDE; GENOCIDE.

Brown, Paula. (1986) "Simbu Aggression and the Drive To Win." *Anthropological Quarterly* 59: 165–170.

Davis, Shelton H. (1977) *Victims of the Miracle: Development and the Indians of Brazil.*

Podolefsky, Aaron. (1984) "Contemporary Warfare in the New Guinea Highlands." *Ethnology* 23: 73–87.

Rodman, Margaret, and Matthew Cooper, eds. (1983) *The Pacification of Melanesia.*

PANETHNICITY

Panethnicity refers to the establishment of links between ethnic groups or subgroups and the founding of organizations that represent the collective or shared interests of these groups, who are seen as ethnically or racially homogenous by outsiders. Over the last two decades in virtually all nations with indigenous populations, ethnic groups have been forming political and economic panethnic links. The move toward panethnicity represents a new form of ethnic relation, in some nations supplanting ethnic separatism and assimilation as the primary form of ethnic relation. Panethnic movements around the world today are the result of a number of factors: (1) the social movements of the 1960s, especially those in the United States such as the Black Power and Women's movements, proved that coalitions representing large blocs of voters could have a political and economic impact on government policies and practices; (2) many nations are developing democratic forms of government, ending political repression, and holding open elections; (3) a general worldwide redefinition of the relationship between national governments and indigenous peoples is under way, with a slow but steady movement toward indigenous rights; and (4) the political reality that, by grouping together, otherwise small groups can form large voting blocs in regional and national elections.

Panethnic movements take many forms and have a variety of objectives. In Brazil, the Black Consciousness movement involves nearly 600 organizations, all working in various ways to teach younger generations the history of blacks in Brazil and to build a sense of black identity. These organizations include black Brazilians of different social classes, from all regions, and of different skin colors. They are composed of church-affiliated groups, such as the Pastoral of the Negro in the Rio de Janeiro suburb of Duque de Caxias; research organizations, such as Afro-

Brazilian Research Dance Company; state-sponsored agencies, such as the Center of Negro Culture and Art; special-interest groups, such as the Group of Black Women; and political organizations, such as the United Negro movement. In addition to these organizations, black panethnicity in Brazil is reinforced by various unique cultural features such as music (soul, imported from North America, and *samba)* and the black syncretic version of the *umbanda* religion. For example, the following *samba* song points to the black struggle for freedom in Brazil:

Can it be...
The dawn of liberty,
Or was it all just illusion?
Can it be...
The dreamed of Golden Law
Signed so long ago,
Was not the end of slavery?
        In the real world today,
Where is freedom?
Where see it? I don't see it.
        I dreamed...
The Zumbi of Palmares returned.
The blacks' misery ended;
        It was a new redemption.

In Ecuador, the Confederation of Indigenous Nationalities of Ecuador (CONAIE) unites American Indian groups (constituting 40 percent of the population) from the highlands, Amazon, and coast who traditionally, and under colonial rule, had existed separately. The Confederation has become a powerful force for social change and Indian rights, and works toward gaining 16 rights for all Indian groups, including the right to their traditional territory, water rights, and the right to cultural integrity. In Norway, Saami (Lapps) efforts to achieve a political voice were hampered by cultural differences between the more traditional inland groups and the more assimilated groups near the coast.

Outside interests were able to exploit this lack of cultural unity as well as the varying interests of the different regional groups to thwart Saami autonomy and rights. However, the formation of Saami panethnic organizations representing Saami groups across Scandinavia has resulted in an enhanced political voice for the Saami.

In the United States, panethnicity has involved both American Indians and immigrant groups. Major pan-Indian groups include the American Indian movement and the Indian Youth Council. Pan-Indian events include powwows, which are now organized in a formal year-round circuit. The powwows provide an arena for Indians from different groups to meet, and have become an important source of revenues. By showcasing modern forms of American Indian culture, powwows help to correct the stereotypical view of American Indians held by much of the non-Indian population. As with indigenous panethnic organizations elsewhere, those in North America cooperate with others in the region and around the world, creating a multilayered structure of indigenous panethnic associations (national, regional, and international), such as the World Council of Indigenous Peoples. In the United States, immigrant groups have also been involved in the panethnic movement. However, there is much variation from one ethnic collective to another in the degree of panethnic development. Asian-Americans, including Japanese-, Chinese-, and Korean-Americans, have a long history of efforts to develop pan-Asian organizations and institutions that represent all Asian-Americans. These include pan-Asian associations in all large cities, the *Amerasia Journal,* the *Asian Week* newspaper, and local uniethnic groups, who also address concerns of all Asian groups. In comparison, Latinos have formed relatively few panethnic links that join Puerto Ricans, Mexican-Americans, Cubans, and Hispanics in the Southwest. Evidently, despite homogeneity in language (Spanish) and religion (Roman

Catholicism), Latinos form relatively few links because of differences in social class and immigration history, different concerns, and the dispersed nature of the population. This suggests that cultural factors such as religion and language are perhaps less important than societal factors such as social class, geographical dispersion of the population, and the immigration history (much recent immigration tends to discourage panethnic links) in creating a climate that permits the creation of panethnic linkages.

In the world today, panethnic organizations, especially those representing indigenous peoples, play a central role in shaping government and United Nations policies. Some are directly recognized by the U.N., while others play a more informal role. The following list is a sampling of political panethnic organizations, and indicates the large number of indigenous peoples so represented.

American Indian Movement

Anti-Defamation League of the B'nai B'rith

Asian American Political Alliance

Confederation of Indigenous Nationalities of Ecuador

Consejo Indio de Sud America

Cordillera Peoples Alliance

East African Pastoralists

Federation of Alaskan Natives

Four Directions Council

Grand Council of the Crees

Indian Council of Indigenous Population

Indian Law Resource Center

Indigenous World Association

International Indian Treaty Council

International Organization of Indigenous Resources Development

Inuit Circumpolar Conference

Maori Unity Movement

National Aboriginal and Islander Legal Services Secretariat

National Association for the Advancement of Colored People (NAACP)

National Indian Youth Council

North American Indian Brotherhood

Saami Union

Unified Negro Movement

World Council of Indigenous Peoples

See also INDIGENOUS RIGHTS.

Brosted, Jens, et al., eds. (1985) *Native Power: The Quest for Autonomy and Nationhood of Indigenous Peoples.*

Espiritu, Yen Le. (1992) *Asian American Panethnicity: Bridging Institutions and Identities.*

Lopez, David, and Yen Espiritu. (1990) "Panethnicity in the United States: A Theoretical Framework." *Ethnic and Racial Studies* 13: 198–224.

NACLA. (1992) "The Black Americas, 1492–1992." In *Report on the Americas.* Volume 25, no. 4.

Nagel, Joane. (1982) "The Poltical Mobilization of Native Americans." *The Social Science Journal* 19: 37–45.

Padilla, Felix. (1985) *Latino Ethnic Consciousness.*

Wilmer, Franke. (1993) *The Indigenous Voice in World Politics: Since Time Immemorial.*

 **PEOPLES OF THE NORTH** The Peoples of the North, Small Peoples of the North, and Peoples of the Soviet North are all generic labels for the indigenous peoples of Siberia and the Russian North. Depending on

the criteria used to delineate these groups, there are from 26 to over 30 Peoples of the North who vary in size from over 1 million to only a few hundred, with 23 groups numbering less than 30,000 people each. Linguistically, the groups speak different languages or dialects that fall within the Uralic, Altaic, and Paleosiberian language families. The region today is dominated numerically, politically, and economically by Russians (known as Siberiaki) and other non-indigenous peoples such as Germans and Koreans.

Traditionally, the Peoples of the North, depending on their locale, subsisted by reindeer herding, trapping, hunting, and fishing. There was extensive contact between neighboring groups, and sometimes contact with very distant groups, in the form of trade, war, intermarriage, and ceremonies. Siberia was conquered by the Russians in the 1500s and colonization began, with many indigenous groups drawn into the fur trade and forced to pay tribute to the local and central authorities, often intermarrying with ethnic Russians and other Slavic settlers. During the Soviet Union era, many groups were forced to live in permanent villages, work in low-level industrial jobs, and were prevented from using their native languages, required to use Russian instead. The traditional shamanistic religion of many Siberian groups was also largely eradicated or forced underground as shamans were killed. The current status of many of these groups is now unknown, although the fall of communism in the former Soviet Union has led to efforts by many groups to revive the traditional culture and, combined with participation in local and national politics, to regain their rights.

Friedrich, Paul, and Norma Diamond, eds. (1993) *Encylopedia of World Cultures. Volume 6, Russia/Eurasia and China.*

Levin, M. G., and L. P. Potapov, eds. (1964) *The Peoples of Siberia.*

McDonald, R. St. J., ed. (1966) *The Arctic Frontier.*

PIDGINS AND CREOLES

Pidgin is a form of spoken and (less commonly) written communication between members of different cultures who speak mutually unintelligible languages. It is often the primary means of communication between the members of the two cultures (traditionally European colonizers and indigenous peoples), although pidgins have also been developed by indigenous peoples who, for example, need to interact in order to trade with one another. Compared to languages, pidgins have a smaller vocabulary, a simplified grammar, and are often used only for specific purposes. Most pidgins disappear rather quickly when there is no longer a reason for their use. Pidgins that survive and become the domestic language of a cultural community are called creoles. Creoles are used every day for many purposes, and thus are a more complex and developed form of language than pidgins.

Although many pidgins have disappeared, at least 100 pidgins and creoles are spoken around the world today, with those listed below having the most speakers:

Bahasa Indonesia

Bazaar Malay

Belize Creole English

Bislama (Vanuatu)

Cape Verde Creole

Caribbean Creole English

Congo Pidgins

Crioulo (Guinea)

French Guyana Creole

Gullah (Sea Islands)

Haitian French Creole

Hawaiian Pidgin/Creole

Krio (Sierra Leone)

Kru English (West Africa)

Lingua Geral (Brazil)

Louisiana Creole

Mauritian French Creole

Meskito Coast Creole (Middle America)

Papiamento (Dutch Antilles)

Réunionnais

Solomon Islands Pidgin

Sranan (Suriname)

Taal Dutch (South Africa)

Tok Pisin (Papua New Guinea)

An example of the key features of pidgins and creoles is provided by the Gullah creole language spoken by the Sea Islanders off the coast of Georgia. The Sea Islanders are African-American descendants of slaves brought to the islands to work the plantations. After the Civil War, the white plantation owners fled, leaving the Sea Islanders largely in control until the mid-twentieth century, when land development began putting pressure on Sea Islander culture. Gullah developed in this context of relative isolation from the mainland, and is based largely on English vocabulary and African grammatical forms, most likely from West African languages such as Fanti, Ewe, Yoruba, Igbo, Twi, and Kongo. It differs considerably from standard English, black English, and southern regional dialects of English.

As with many creoles, early observers often described it in ethnocentrically negative terms, and it was viewed as a sign of the inferior nature of Sea Islander culture. In 1922 a journalist wrote of the language: "Slovenly and careless of speech, these Gullahs seized upon the peasant English used by some of the early settlers and by the white servants of the wealthier colonists, wrapped their clumsy tongues around about it as well as they could, and enriched with certain expressive African words, it issued through their flat noses and thick lips." (Quoted in Jones-Jackson 1987, 135) Despite this description, Gullah is an established Creole language, although its use is declining. A number of inter-island variations in vocabulary, accent, stress, and intonation enable Gullah speakers to identify the home communities of other speakers.

Gullah has a mainly English vocabulary (most creoles are based on the vocabulary of colonial nations—Portuguese, Spanish, French, Dutch, and English), although with some structural differences and localized meanings. For example, "dark the light" in Gullah means "the sun was set" in English, "this side" means "this island," and "the sun de red for down" means "sunset" in English. In addition, there are marked grammatical differences between Gullah and English. First, in Gullah most verbs do not change form to indicate tense. Second, the word *for* has a greater variety of meanings, a common one being to indicate must or should, as in: "For see, she could see em plain," which means in English, "You (must) understand, she could see them plainly." Third, adjectives are repeated to indicate degree or quantity, as in "small small" for "very small" and "small small small" for "extremely small." Finally, in some forms of Gullah, pronouns do not indicate gender, and one pronoun is used for both the feminine and masculine. Today, as with many other creoles, Gullah is declining in use as the Sea Islanders are drawn into mainstream society through contact with whites on the islands and education.

Crystal, David. (1987) *The Cambridge Encyclopedia of Language.*

Hancock, Ian F. (1971) "A Survey of the Pidgins and Creoles of the World." In *Pidginization and Creolization of Languages,* edited by Dell Hymes, 509–523.

Jones-Jackson, Patricia. (1987) *When Roots Die: Endangered Traditions on the Sea Islands.*

Todd, L. (1974) *Pidgins and Creoles.*

PLURALISM

Pluralism is a form of ethnic relation within a nation in which groups differ from one another in important ways regarding values, social organization, customs, and behavior, but at the same time participate in and support societal institutions, and thus are all members of the same society. Pluralism comes in three primary forms. In *cultural pluralism*, each group has its own basic cultural features, such as its own religion, marriage customs, value orientation, and lifestyle, that tend to be perpetuated over time. At the same time, the groups are integrated into a national collective through participation in shared institutions such as the marketplace, government agencies, or the education system. A key feature of cultural pluralism is that the groups are not ranked hierarchically within the society, but are relatively equal in power, or at least no one group is so powerful that it can dominate the others. The second form of pluralism is *structural pluralism,* a situation in which contact between members of the groups is less frequent, less extensive, or more circumscribed than in culturally pluralistic societies. For example, the historical relations between African-Americans and Mexican-Americans vis-à-vis white Americans were characterized by both cultural distinctiveness and a lack of or restriction on the involvement of the former in the basic institutions of American society. A third form of pluralism is *political pluralism*, in which diverse groups form and interact in the context of competition for power or other societal resources.

These groups need not be ethnic; their existence is tied largely to narrow self-interest, and they are often impermanent.

Pluralism is sometimes used in a more limited sense in reference to some aspect of culture that varies among ethnic or regional groups that comprise a nation. For example, India can be described as a linguistically plural society because (1) a number of different languages are officially recognized in the constitution and (2) possible conflict over the use of Hindi as the national language has been controlled in a pluralistic manner. In addition to Hindi and English, which are the official national languages, regional or state languages are also officially recognized, widely spoken, and serve as the primary written language and language of instruction in many Indian states formed with linguistic criteria in mind. Among the major state or regional languages are Bengali, Gujarati, Kashmiri, Malayalam, Marathi, Oriya, Punjabi, Tamil, Telugu, Urdu, Kannada, Assamese, Sanskrit, and Sindhi. Despite the official recognition of these languages, since independence India has been plagued with a language controversy focused on the states' concern that Hindi would replace the state languages. This issue has been controlled, if not resolved, in a pluralistic manner. That is, by and large India has adopted a policy of bilingualism, with Hindi and English the official languages and also the languages of communication between the national government and the states. Either by design or preference, English is emerging as the major language of national communication, perhaps because, unlike Hindi or the state languages, it is not the native language of any indigenous peoples in India. At the same time, the use of state languages in education and government employment is protected by law.

Cultural pluralism is generally seen as characteristic of postcolonial multiethnic societies in Africa, south Asia, and the West Indies. It is also seen as a major underlying cause of ethnic and violent conflict in postcolonial Africa.

African nations are all multiethnic: In a sample of 27 nations, 8 had less than 10 ethnic groups, 6 had from 11–20, 9 had from 21–50, 3 had from 51–100, and 1 (Nigeria) had over 100. Of these 27 nations, 22 have experienced internal conflict since independence, usually ethnic or religious in nature. Additionally, the more ethnic groups in a nation, the more likely that violent conflict has occurred. While pluralism underlies ethnic conflict in many African nations, other factors are perhaps even more important than pluralism. These factors include preexisting ethnic rivalries, ethnic rivalries fermented by the colonial governments, political instability, unfamiliarity with democracy, scarce economic resources, and regionalism.

In the contemporary world the concept of pluralism is difficult to apply meaningfully because it assumes a horizontal ordering of groups and therefore ignores vertical or hierarchical orderings based on social class distinctions. Perhaps the best example of a contemporary pluralistic society is Mauritius. Mauritius is an island nation covering some 787 square miles in the Indian Ocean. In 1993 its population was an estimated 1.1 million. Mauritius is composed of four major ethnic categories: Hindus (52 percent), Muslims (16 percent), Chinese-Mauritians (3 percent), and the general population (29 percent). The general population category consists of a small number of Franco-Mauritians (2 percent), Christians, Coloureds, and Christian Tamils, and a larger number of Creoles who are Catholics of mixed African-European, Indian, or Chinese ancestry. While Hindus are the numerical majority, internal divisions such as the distinctive groups of Tamils (7 percent) and Telugu, as well as those based on caste, make them something less than a unified group. Similarly, the Muslims are internally differentiated on the basis of religious belief into Sunni, Shi'ite, and Ahmadis. Thus, Mauritius is both culturally and religiously pluralistic.

Mauritius pluralism is the product of both colonial policies that tended to encourage cultural autonomy, and conscious policies enacted since independence to encourage cultural diversity. For example, Mauritians explain the peaceful coexistence of four major religions with the expression *Each prays in his/her own way*. Similarly, parliamentary representation is ensured by awarding seats to eight losers in general elections. Symbolically, cultural diversity is expressed through multicultural events in which each group performs songs, dance, or poetry.

At the same time, as in any pluralistic society, there is the problem of building a sense of national identity and controlling conflicts between the ethnic groups. Linguistically, English is the official language of Mauritius; as in India, it is a compromise that prevents any native language from being dominant. Additionally, newspapers are written in French, and many Mauritians speak Kreol, which is becoming the de facto national language. In terms of the institutions of Mauritian life, all citizens are involved in the educational, political, legal, and economic institutions of society.

Alongside this national unity, members of each group feel a strong sense of ethnic identity. People tend to live near kin and interact socially either with kin or members of their ethnic group. Other groups are often described in ethnocentrically negative terms. Mauritians are also aware in everyday interaction that Mauritius is a multiethnic society, and the ethnic differences in belief, perception, and behavior can be a source of conflict. Still, Mauritius has been peaceful since 1968. This peace results from a mix of factors:

1. Mauritius is small and is isolated from the rest of the world

2. There is no one ethnic, political, or economic majority group

3. All groups are immigrants, and therefore

none make homeland claims to territory, the cause of much ethnic conflict elsewhere

4. Involvement and power in the economic and political arenas are shared

5. A shared language—Kreol—allows interaction and communication among the groups

6. All minorities have guaranteed constitutional rights

7. Virtually all Mauritians are participants in the institutions of society

8. Performance and qualifications, rather than ethnicity, are prerequisites for career advancement

9. Conflict among members of different groups is often, though not always, characterized by an avoidance of controversial topics, restraint, and a focus on tasks or events rather than social interaction

See also ASSIMILATION; CONSOCIATIONAL DEMOCRACY.

Brass, Paul R. (1991) *Ethnicity and Nationalism.*

Eriksen, Thomas H. (1992) "Containing Conflict and Transcending Ethnicity in Mauritius." In *Internal Conflict and Governance,* edited by Kumar Rupesinghe, 103–129.

Furnivall, J. S. (1948) *Colonial Policy and Practice.*

Smith, M. G. (1965) *The Plural Society of the British West Indies.*

———. (1986) "Pluralism, Race, and Ethnicity in Selected African Countries." In *Theories of Race and Ethnic Relations,* edited by John Rex and David Mason, 187–225.

Wai, Dunstan M. (1978) "Sources of Communal Conflicts and Secessionist Politics in Africa." *Ethnic and Racial Studies* 1: 286–305.

of genotypical traits such as blood type and the geographical and adaptive patterns of these traits rather than in racial classification. The general public uses race in two ways—as a label for *Homo sapiens*, as in *the human race*, and as a label for various types of cultural groups, such as nationalities *(the British race)*, religious groups *(the Jewish race)*, language groups *(the Slavic race)*, or distinct cultural groupings *(the Gypsy race)*. None of these uses conforms to the scientific use of the term, and all confuse cultural factors with physical characteristics. A third use of *race* is as a label for a type of social group that defines itself and/or is defined by other groups as different because of innate and unchangeable physical differences.

The second and third uses of the term *race* point to the problem involved in using the term, and the reason why many biological and social scientists believe that it should no longer be used. In both of these uses, real or imagined physical differences between groups are linked to real or imagined cultural and behavioral differences between groups, with the physical differences seen as the cause or, at a minimum, related to the behavioral differences. Thus, biology is merged with culture, often in a cause-effect relationship, ignoring the fact that much of human culture and behavior is wholly or partly learned, not inherited. Many early descriptions of non-Western cultures reflect this thinking. For example, in what is now Malaysia, indigenous peoples were described as follows:

> The Kelantan man is taller, better built, and stronger than the true Malay. He is probably also of a temperament more easy-going, more open and less excitable than his cousins to the south. (Graham 1908, 18)

Similarly, biological mixing through intermarriage and reproduction was seen as influencing personality traits in Africa:

> In spite of a very considerable mixture with Wadschagga from nearby Kilimandscharo, they [the Wakuafi] have completely kept their

RACE AND RACISM

The universal fascination with physical differences between groups, and the use of those differences to differentiate between *us* and *them*, is a result of the polytypic nature of *Homo sapiens*. That is, the human species contains a number of physical types as a result of common biological descent and adaptation to the same environment. Despite the routine use of the term *race*, and the frequent characterization of particular groups as races and individuals as members of specific races, experts do not agree on what the concept means, nor are there any generally agreed upon criteria that allow us to decide what groups constitute a distinct race. Instead, race means different things to different people. Human biologists and biological anthropologists sometimes use race or, in its place, subspecies to mean a subgroup of human beings characterized by certain phenotypical (observable) and genotypical (genetic) traits. However, even this scientific use of the term is falling into disuse because it is too imprecise and because human biologists are now mainly interested in the study

original character traits. Their imperiousness, rapacity, and cunning equal that of the Masai; in courage, on the other hand, they even surpass them. (Merker 1910, 9)

Again, racial features are linked to behavior:

The people of Gilgat, Astor and some of the countries beyond are a race with features of the Aryan type, and they claim to be of that stock....They are an independent and bold race, more straightforward than the Kashmiris and less bloodthirsty than the Pathan. (Gervis 1954, 230)

This last example also mentions one of the most misunderstood racial stereotypes—the so-called Aryan race. In fact, there is no such thing as an Aryan race. Aryan refers to speakers of Vedic Sanskrit, an Indo-European language, who settled in what is now India about 3,500 years ago. Their descendants now inhabit various parts of south Asia, but do not call themselves Aryans. In recent times, the label *Aryan* has been used by linguists in reference to a subfamily of Indo-European languages and was never meant as a racial or ethnic label. Its adoption by the Nazis as a racial term for northern and central Europeans who were considered the purest of the Aryan race was a politically motivated misuse of both the concept of *race* and the term *Aryan*.

In addition to confusing biology and culture, the concept of race has fallen into disuse because so-called physical indicators of racial differences such as skin color, stature, head size and shape, and hair texture vary more within any so-called race than between races. For most traits, there is more variation between males and females than between different races. This problem has not, however, slowed attempts at racial classification.

Scientific Racial Classifications

The word *race* was first used in reference to the classification of human beings by the French physician Francois Bernier, who in 1684 divided humans into four racial categories: Europeans (including western and southern Europeans), Asians, Africans, and Lapps. This first effort has been followed by dozens of other schemes published over the next three centuries that counted from 3 to 37 different races. As with Bernier's, all were based on observable physical characteristics such as skin color, size of the skull, and hair texture. Other influential classifications include those of Carrolus Linneaus, who listed the American, European, Asiatic, and Negro races; Johann Blumenbach, who counted five races—Caucasoid, Mongoloid, Ethiopian, American, and Malayan; and biological anthropologists Carleton Coon and Edward Hunt, who named seven—Caucasoid, Mongolion, full-sized Australoid, dwarf Australoid, full-sized Congoloid, dwarf Congoloid, and Capoids.

Blumenbach's scheme has been especially influential, as it is the basis of the still-popular model of white, yellow, red, and black races. In addition to these classifications that claim to account for all human forms, others have been suggested for specific regions, for example, the still-common one for Europe that divides the population on a north-south gradient into Nordic, Alpine, and Mediterranean types.

All of these classification schemes are now considered obsolete and of little use by students of human biological and cultural variation for the same reasons that the concept of race is considered of limited value.

National and Folk Classifications

In addition to these specieswide and now-little-used scientific schemes, some societies classify their inhabitants on the basis of race. In the United States, a clear distinction is made by many Americans between whites and nonwhites; any individual with observable features that suggest wholly or partially nonwhite ancestry is considered to be nonwhite. This practice of classifying all members of a society into one of two racial categories is known as *hypodescent*. Additionally, the U.S. government formally considers race in its census-taking activities, although the government makes no attempt to define the concept. Instead, a self-identification approach is used, with members of the population asked to classify themselves into one of the following categories:

White

Black

American Indian

Eskimo

Aleut

Asian or Pacific Islander

    Chinese

    Filipino

    Japanese

    Asian Indian

    Korean

    Vietnamese

    Hawaiian

    Samoan

    Guamanian

    Other Asian or Pacific Islander

Other Race

In addition, the Census Bureau also identifies people of Hispanic origin—Mexican, Puerto Rican, Cuban, Spanish, and from elsewhere in Latin America—although the Census Bureau acknowledges that Hispanic origin and race are distinct entities, and people of Hispanic origin can be of any race.

The South African apartheid system was also based on the principle of hypodescent, with all South Africans classified as either white or nonwhite. The white category comprises primarily people of Dutch and British ancestry, while all others are classified as nonwhite, including indigenous Africans such as the Khoi (Hotten-tot), Zulu, and !Xhosa; people of mixed ancestry such as Cape Coloureds and Bastars; Asian Indians; Chinese; and Malays.

In addition to scientific and government classifications, in many nations and societies the people themselves develop and interact with one another on the basis of folk-classification schemes. In the Bahia province of Brazil, for example, there are three officially recognized groups—*pretos* (blacks), *pardos* (browns), and *brancos* (whites) plus four intermediate types—*cabra* (lighter skin color and hair less kinky than *pretos*), *Cabo Verde* (very dark with white features and straight black hair), *sarará* (light skin color and red hair) and the *moreno* (tan skin color, white features, brown eyes, and dark hair). This complexity has yielded an equally complex social system with "whiteness" preferred by some, the *morena* (female) considered ideal by others, and a link between social status and skin color (lighter color coupled with higher status).

Racial Purity

The notion of racial purity, and efforts by one group to maintain its purity by not intermarrying and reproducing with other groups, is an important consideration in ethnic relations. In the contemporary world, Germany and Japan both define citizenship along biological lines, and allow relatively few non-Germans and non-Japanese to gain citizenship. Thus, some 400,000 Koreans resident in Japan—most of them born there—are not citizens, while in Germany only about 17,000 of 1.5 million Turkish residents are citizens. An ideology of racial purity and efforts to maintain purity concern some indigenous peoples as well. In North America, for example, the concept of being pure-blooded is tied to cultural traditionalism, with those who are of full American Indian descent considered more American Indian by themselves and others than those of mixed ancestry. For example, among the Piegan Blackfoot of Montana, the full-bloods see themselves as the descendants of the leaders and warriors of the prereservation times, and thus the carriers of true Blackfoot culture. One key marker of full-blood status is the absence of an

English, French, or American surname (its presence would indicate marriage between a Blackfoot woman and white man). The importance of full-bloodedness in maintaining traditional beliefs and customs is suggested by the Taos of New Mexico who, with an average of 95 percent American Indian ancestry, are both one of the most biologically pure American Indian groups and culturally one of the most traditional groups in North America. Taos opposition to intermarriage with other American Indians and non-Indians and rules that prohibit non-Taos from residing in the traditional pueblo have been major mechanisms for maintaining both biological and cultural integrity.

In the United States there is often discussion of the percentage of American Indian ancestry an individual can claim, for both legal reasons (in order to gain access to government services) and because in some circles it is considered prestigious to have some American Indian ancestry. Among the Blackfoot, for example, one community was described as populated by 53 percent full-bloods, 18 percent half-bloods, and 13 percent whites, with the other 16 percent being those who were one-fourth, one-eighth, five-eighths, three-eighths, and fifteen-sixteenths American Indian. Such figuring is notably imprecise because it assumes so-called racial purity for ancestors.

Racism

Racism is the belief that one race (usually one's own) is inherently superior to all other races. Also implicit in racism is the attribution of achievements of one race to its genetic superiority. Racism is a belief system that exists at the societal level and is passed on from one generation to the next through the socialization and educational institutions of the society. Racial prejudice and discrimination are attitudinal and behavioral manifestations of racism. Racism occurs in situations of cultural contact where cultural groups who differ in status and power also differ from one another in physical appearance. Forms of culture contact that involve this situation are military conquest, as in Africa in the late 1800s; settlement colonization, as in the New World and Australia; involuntary migration, as in the importation of slaves from Africa to the New World; and voluntary migration, as in the settlement of Latinos in the United States and Turks in Germany.

Racism is generally believed to be a product of Western civilization, and specifically of the settlement and exploitation of non-European lands and peoples. However, the seeds of racism were clearly in place before colonization and European control of the New World, much of Africa, and Oceania. The association of the color black with evil predates Christianity, and thus may have helped create a worldview that encouraged the negative evaluation of darker skinned African and American Indian peoples. In the sixteenth century, a line of thought emerged among scholars that *Homo sapiens* was actually a number of species, with the different races belonging to different species. Additionally, the reports of early explorers, government agents, and missionaries were filled with false or half-true accounts of the indigenous cultures that portrayed these peoples as less civilized than Europeans, and even less than human; that is, to list a few stereotypes, as cannibals, ritual sacrificers, and pagans.

Full-blown racism appeared in the colonial period, accompanying all forms of colonialism—slavery, serfdom, forced migrant labor, contract labor, and middle minorities. Racism emerged as an ideology to justify the exploitation of non-Western peoples used in these capitalistic ventures. Racism as an ideology fit closely with other ideologies popular in Europe in the middle to late 1880s. The most important among these ideologies were the Darwinian evolutionary theory and the notion of survival of the fittest, but also included were permanent racial types and stages of human evolution, with non-

Western peoples considered survivors from earlier, less civilized periods.

Racism has also been frequently associated with immigration, and especially with the voluntary immigration of people to a nation already occupied by others who are culturally different. In Australia, for example, there was a restriction on settlement by Asians for many years. In the United States, Italian immigrants of the early 1900s also experienced discrimination, and a disproportionate number were deported. One justification for discrimination against Italians was the belief that southern Italians were part African (their ancestors having bred with Africans) and therefore inferior to Americans of central and northern European ancestry. Similarly, the so-called Yellow Peril of immigrant Japanese and Chinese workers was met by restrictive immigration laws in 1921 and 1924 requiring that 80 percent of immigrants be from northern Europe. These laws were not repealed until 1965.

The vehemence with which racism is expressed and the degree of suffering by the victims of racism vary from society to society and can fluctuate in degree over time. In South Africa, apartheid created a caste system with complete separation of whites and nonwhites, with all power and most wealth controlled by the minority white population. In Nicaragua, the racism of the mestizos, who constitute 90 percent of the population, against Indians and blacks is more subtle. It manifests itself in a variety of ways, including a belief that the color black is evil, use of the word *negro* (meaning a person with black or very brown skin) as an insult, expressing racist beliefs only to close friends and relatives, and parents favoring their lightest-skinned child.

Race Relations

Anthropologist Pierre van den Berghe suggests that race relations throughout human history and around the world can be characterized as either paternalistic or competitive. The slave societies in the New World and the hacienda system of serfdom in parts of South America were paternalistic systems; the ruling group was a small minority of Europeans, and the slaves and serfs were imported slaves or indigenous peoples. These societies were stratified along racial lines, with nonwhites locked into the lowest strata and kept socially, economically, and politically separate from whites. However, they often lived with (as servants) or near whites and interacted openly, and sexual relations between white men and black or Indian women were permitted. There were often close emotional attachments between slave owners and some slaves, particularly household help and the women who raised the white children. In the paternalistic situation, whites saw themselves as benevolent rulers and their slaves or serfs as relatively harmless, childlike inferiors. Underlying most paternalistic systems was an economic symbiosis in which the whites were dependent on the work of slaves to produce raw materials such as sugar and cotton, and the slaves were kept dependent on the whites for basic necessities such as housing, food, and clothing.

Competitive race relations are typical of modern, industrialized societies where different race or ethnic groups are not kept separate nor in fixed superior-inferior statuses by law. While skin color or ethnic identity is still often a barrier to equal status and upward social mobility, it is not an absolute barrier, and upward social mobility is possible for members of all groups. In these societies, skills and knowledge are the key requirements in a highly competitive employment market, and groups are in competition for valued educational opportunities and jobs. This competition often takes an openly racist form with hatred and suspicion between groups, residential and social segregation, violence directed at smaller or weaker groups, and efforts by groups with control of the labor market to keep the other groups in their place.

Examples of competitive situations include anti–African-American, Italian, Jewish, and Latino attitudes and policies at various times in the twentieth century in the United States, anti-Chinese attitudes in Fiji, and anti-Turk attitudes in Germany. In general, the degree of racism exhibited in competitive situations tends to increase in difficult economic times when the groups in control see their security threatened by others who are physically or culturally different.

See also ANTI-SEMITISM; APARTHEID; COLONIALISM; ETHNOCENTRISM; ETHNOCIDE; GENOCIDE; MIXED-ANCESTRY PEOPLES; SLAVERY.

Banton, Michael, and Jonathan Harwood. (1975) *The Race Concept.*

Bodine, John J. (1991) "Taos." In *Encyclopedia of World Cultures. Volume 1, North America,* edited by Timothy J. O'Leary and David Levinson, 340–343.

Gervis, Pearce. (1954) *This Is Kashmir.*

Graham, Walter Armstrong. (1908) *Kelantan: A State of the Malay Peninsula: A Handbook of Information.*

Hacker, Andrew. (1992) *Two Nations: Black and White, Separate, Hostile, Unequal.*

Hockings, Paul. (1992) "Aryan." In *Encyclopedia of World Cultures. Volume 3, South Asia,* edited by Paul Hockings, 12–13.

Lancaster, Roger N. (1991) "Skin Color, Race, and Racism in Nicaragua." *Ethnology* 30: 339–353.

McFee, Malcolm. (1963) *Modern Blackfeet: Continuing Patterns of Differential Acculturation.*

Memmi, Albert. (1967) *The Colonizer and the Colonized.*

Merker, Meritz. (1910) *The Masai: Ethnographic Monograph of an East African Semite People.* Translated from the German for the Human Relations Area Files.

Molnar, Stephen. (1983) *Human Variation: Races, Types, and Ethnic Groups.* 2d ed.

Montagu, Ashley, ed. (1964) *The Concept of Race.*

Pierson, Donald. (1942) *Negroes in Brazil.*

Pozzetta, George, Jr. (1972) *The Italians of New York City, 1890–1914.*

Robbins, Lynn A. (1972) *Blackfoot Families and Households.*

Terkel, Studs. (1992) *Race: How Blacks and Whites Think and Feel about the American Obsession.*

van den Berghe, Pierre L. (1978) *Race and Racism: A Comparative Perspective.* 2d ed.

REFUGEES

According to the United Nations High Commissioner for Refugees, there were 18,998,700 refugees in the world in 1992. The table below lists the number of refugees by region, with the U.N. figures in the second column, and figures compiled by the U.S. Committee for Refugees in the third column. The discrepancy in the totals is due to the different definitions of refugee used in the two surveys. The U.N. uses the definition accepted under international law and set forth in the 1951 Convention and 1967 Protocol relating to the Status of Refugees:

[Any person who]...owing to well-founded fear of being persecuted for reasons of race, religion, nationality, membership of particular social group or political opinion, is outside the country of his nationality and is unable to or, owing to such fear, is unwilling to avail himself of the protection of that country; or who, not having a nationality and being outside the country of his former habitual residence...is unable or, owing to such fear, is unwilling to return to it.

Muslim evacuees from Srebrenica ride truck to Tuzla under U.N. protection.

The U.S. Committee for Refugees count does not include refugees permanently settled in some nations, so its count is lower than the U.N. count. Neither count includes internal refugees or internally displaced peoples—those forced to flee to another region in their home nation. Major ethnic conflicts that have produced significant numbers of internal refugees are those in South Africa, the former Yugoslavia, Sri Lanka, Myanmar (Burma), Tajikistan, Rwanda, India, Cyprus, Azerbaijan, Kenya, Turkey, Moldova, and Georgia.

Refugee Populations by Region of Asylum (1992)

Region	UNHCR	USCR
Africa	5,393,200	5,698,450
Asia	7,240,100	8,299,350
Europe	4,379,100	3,282,200
Latin America	885,500	107,700
North America	1,041,200	141,400
Oceania	59,600	27,800
Total	18,998,700	17,556,900

Refugees and Ethnic Relations

From the perspective of ethnic relations, ethnic conflict is both a cause and a consequence of refugee flows. The following table lists some major refugee flows resulting from recent or ongoing ethnic conflicts. The two sets of ethnic conflicts that have produced the greatest numbers of refugees are those following the breakups of the former Yugoslavia and the former Soviet Union. The conflicts in the former Yugoslavia region have produced over 2 million refugees—1.8 million who fled from one former republic to another, and at least 400,000 who fled to other nations in Europe. Probably the single largest ethnic refugee group is the Palestinians, who are usually not enumerated in refugee counts, but who now total some 2.7 million individuals worldwide.

Ethnic conflict can produce refugees in a number of ways. First, in difficult economic or political times, politicians often scapegoat ethnic minority groups, who are then forced to flee. Middleman minorities, such as Jews in various places throughout history and Asian Indians in Uganda in the 1970s, are examples of this pattern. Second, one group may be forced to flee when a more powerful group takes control of the national government and enacts oppressive policies against the smaller, weaker groups, such as with the Iraqi government and the Marsh Arabs in southern Iraq, many of whom fled to

Iran. Third, a powerful group in a multiethnic nation may seek to expel minority groups in order to achieve ethnic purity, as is perhaps the case with Greek Albanians, who are fleeing to Greece. Fourth, irredentist movements that involve the consolidation of all territories claimed by an ethnic group often include the displacement of other groups, as with the Bosnians or

Ethnic Refugees Resulting from Conflicts

Ethnic Group	Source Nation	Asylum Nation	Number
Tuareg	Mali, Niger	Algeria	40,000–50,000
Hutu	Burundi	Tanzania, Zaire, Rwanda	143,000
Tutsi	Rwanda	Uganda, Burundi, Zaire, Tanzania	83,000
Burmese Muslims	Myanmar	Bangladesh, Malaysia	245,000
Kachin	Myanmar	China	10,000
Mon, Karen	Myanmar	Thailand	70,000
Tibetans	China	India, Nepal	128,000
Atoni	Indonesia	Portugal	unknown
Acehnese	Indonesia	Malaysia	200
Bihari	India	Bangladesh	238,000
Chakma	Bangladesh	India	50,000
Nepalese	Bhutan	Nepal, India	95,000
Sri Lankan Tamils	Sri Lanka	India	181,000
Nagas	Myanmar	India	1,400
Tajiks	Tajikistan	Afghanistan	52,000
Russians	Tajikistan, Uzbekistan	Russia	300,000
Jews	Tajikistan, Uzbekistan	Israel	4,000
Uzbeks	Tajikistan	Uzbekistan	unknown
Kurds	Iraq	Iran, Turkey	72,000
Shi'ites (Marsh Arabs)	Iraq	Iran	30,000
Beta Israel	Ethiopia	Israel	50,000
Armenians	Azerbaijan	Armenia, Russia	300,000
Azerbaijani	Armenia	Azerbaijan	195,000
Bosnians	Bosnia/Herzegovina	Former Yugoslavia	1,045,000
		Western Europe	unknown
Croats	Croatia	Former Yugoslavia	350,000
		Europe	106,000
Ossetes	Georgia	Russia	100,000
Georgians	Georgia (Ossetia)	Georgia	15,000
Armenians	Georgia	Russia	30,000
Russians, Ukrainians	Moldova	Russia, Ukraine	100,000
Meskhetian Turks	Uzbekistan, Kyrgyzstan	Russia	50,000

Croats in areas claimed by Serbia. Fifth, ethnic separatist movements often lead to both internal and external population relocations as civilians on both sides flee the fighting and involved groups seek shelter elsewhere. For example, in Sri Lanka, the fighting between the Sinhalese and Sri Lankan Tamils has produced refugees in both groups as well as among the uninvolved Catholic population.

Refugee flows can also lead to ethnic tension and conflict in the nations in which the refugees seek asylum. Much of the antiforeigner sentiment in Europe in the 1990s can be traced to the arrival of ethnically different refugees and the pressure their presence places on already weak economies. Many nations have reacted to the influx of refugees by enacting more restrictive policies and practices because of perceived threats to their economic well-being, internal peace, and—in some nations—ethnic or cultural purity. One approach has been to make it difficult for asylum-seekers to reach the nation's borders. For example, the United States accepts more refugees than any other nation, but with opinion polls showing an increase in hostility to foreigners, from 1992 on, the government has turned Haitians back at sea to prevent them from reaching the Florida coast. Or, for another example, Italy first admitted several thousand Albanian refugees, then rounded them up and returned them to Albania. Other nations have also become more restrictive in accepting refugees. Hungary readily accepts European refugees, such as those from Bosnia, but now detains and often denies entry to refugees from Asia and Africa. The Greeks have resisted attempts by some 6,000 ethnically Greek Albanians to settle in Greece. The Greek government claims that Albania is forcing the Greek minority to leave in order to free itself from a non-Albanian ethnic minority. A second approach to controlling the refugee flow is what is called *humane deterrence*, which means less-than-adequate treatment for refugees. The United States has detained

Haitians in camps, Vietnamese boat people have been detained under inadequate living conditions for long periods of time in Hong Kong, Beta Israel (Falasha) religious practices have not been fully accepted in Israel, and identity checks on foreigners have been initiated in France. A third approach has been to enact more restrictive definitions of refugee status, which places the burden on the asylum-seeker to prove persecution in their homeland, and to prove why he or she cannot seek asylum in another country. Germany, for example, has amended its constitution to make its once very liberal immigration policy more restrictive by allowing authorities to send asylum-seekers to other nations that are considered safe havens.

At the same time, some nations have taken steps to ease the arrival and acceptance of refugees. In the United States, an initiative is under way to grant citizenship to many resident foreigners—that is, to make them Americans—as a way of reducing antiforeigner sentiment. In other nations, new administrative procedures are being developed to make it easier to distinguish political from economic refugees, and to process the former more quickly.

Once refugees are allowed to settle in a nation, there is the question of their adjustment to life in the host nation, the degree to which they assimilate, and whether they exist peacefully alongside resident citizens or only as a discriminated-against minority. There is some indication that the experience of immigrants in the past is not predictive of the current situation regarding refugees in Western nations like the United States; there is often considerable variation in the nature of refugee communities. Lao communities in the United States, for example, take a variety of forms: One is centered on a Buddhist temple in Virginia, another in Houston lacks any central organization, and a third in Louisiana closely resembles a traditional village in Laos. A second feature of refugee communities is a lack of ethnic cohesion and

Refugee from eastern Europe sleeps in an East Berlin railway station, 1990.

integration beyond the local level—that is, at least in the early years of settlement, there are relatively few organizations and mechanisms that unite the entire refugee community. A third feature is an often large and bureaucratic resettlement system that develops in the host nation to assist refugees. Over time, however, refugee communities are similar to immigrant communities in that the second and third generation rapidly assimilate and identity themselves as members of the host culture rather than the refugee culture.

See also ETHNIC CONFLICT; MIGRANT WORKERS; XENOPHOBIA.

DeVoe, Pamela A., ed. (1992) *Selected Papers on Refugee Issues.*

Gold, Steven J. (1992) *Refugee Communities.*

Muntarbhorn, Vitit. (1992) *The Status of Refugees in Asia.*

United Nations High Commissioner for Refugees. (1993) *The State of the World's Refugees: The Challenge of Protection.*

U.S. Committee for Refugees. (1993) *World Refugee Survey.*

RELIGIOUS CONFLICT

See ETHNIC CONFLICT.

REVITALIZATION MOVEMENTS.

The appearance of religious cults or movements is a common and recurring phenomena associated with contact between Western societies and indigenous non-Western cultures. Although such movements occurred in medieval Europe, and were perhaps the way the world religions of Christianity, Buddhism, and Islam began, they have been especially frequent over the last few centuries in regions of Western colonization. *Revitalization movements* is the term introduced by anthropologist Anthony Wallace in 1956 as a generic label for a number of different, though similar, types of social movements. Wallace defines a revitalization movement as "the deliberate, conscious, organized efforts by members of a society to create a new and more satisfying culture." (Wallace 1956, 279) While not all experts agree with this definition, it is the one most commonly followed today. A plausible alternate term is *justicating movement*, which suggests that the common feature of these social movements is that the people seek a more satisfying life, to which they feel entitled. The term *millenarian movement* is also used frequently as well.

Under the label *revitalization movement* fall four types of movements:

1. Crisis cults are group responses to a crisis involving activities of a cult

2. Nativistic movements involve efforts to revive elements of the indigenous culture

3. Messianic or prophet cults feature a messiah ushering in a new golden age

4. Millennial or chiliastic (Latin and Greek, respectively, meaning 1,000 years) movements, which foretell a period of social and spiritual bliss, not necessarily lasting 1,000 years

As noted above, revitalization movements have been especially common in regions of Western colonization where native peoples were subjugated and their traditional way of life repressed. This has been the case in Melanesia since World War I. Melanesia is a region of the South Pacific that includes the cultures of the large is-

land of New Guinea, the Bismark Archipelago, the Solomon Islands, Vanuatu, and New Caledonia. Revitalization movements in Melanesia are conventionally called *cargo cults* in reference to the prominent theme in many that Western goods will arrive for local consumption via Western ships and planes. This theme reflects the personal and cultural disorientation that often resulted from colonial contact with the indigenous cultures of the region. Among Melanesian movements are the Milne Bay Prophet Cult, the German Wislin movement, the Vailala Madness, the Taro Cult, the Naked Cult, the Chair-and-Rule and Marching Rule (Masinga) movements, the Tuka Cult, the Baigona Cult, the Lontis Cult, the Markham Cargo Cult, and the John Frum movement. Cargo cults were so common in New Guinea that they were reported to occur in remote areas where the people had never even met Westerners. These people evidently learned of Westerners and their material goods and the cults through contact with people closer to the coast, who were in turn in contact with Westerners. Although many of these movements were quickly suppressed by the colonial governments (mainly English, French, German, and Japanese), some had broader impact. Most notable is the John Frum movement, which began on the island of Tanna in Vanuatu in the 1930s and is still a powerful political force there, as well as on other islands.

Revitalization movements have also occurred elsewhere, though not with the same frequency. In Africa, the Congolese Kinbangu Cult has been described, although a more common religious response of African peoples to colonial domination was the formation of separatist Christian churches that accommodated traditional beliefs and customs. In the Caribbean, the Rastafarian movement has spread far beyond Jamaica where it originated. In the Amazon region of South America, the Tupi-Guarani Free Land movement has been described, as well as the nineteenth-century movements associated with Venancio Kamiko (Christu), a Baniwa Indian. In North America, the American Indian Ghost Dance, the Peyote Cult (incorporated in 1918 as the Native American Church), and the Handsome Lake Religion of the Iroquois are well documented. Revitalization movements are no longer so common, probably because indigenous peoples now more often seek to achieve control over their futures through political action.

The three descriptions that follow are of types of revitalization movements among cultures in different geographical regions. They illustrate the similarities as well as the variations among the movements.

The Rastafari Movement

The Rastafari is a black Jamaican religious movement that began in the early 1930s. Followers, called Rastafarians, Rastas, or Dreadlocks, now number over 100,000 in Jamaica and include an unknown number of others in the United States, Canada, most other Caribbean islands, many African nations, and Europe. Among the major features of Rastafari are the beliefs that Haile Selassie, the late emperor of Ethiopia, is the returned Jesus Christ; that God is black; that all Americans of African ancestry must return to Africa; that life in Jamaica is a life in exile; and that marijuana (*ganja*) is a gift from a god and is to be smoked as part of religious rituals. Rastafari also includes a strong condemnation of white oppression in the New World, referred to as Babylon. For nonbelievers, Rastafari is most often associated with the dreadlock hairstyle and reggae music. Rastafari began in Jamaica shortly after the coronation of Haile Selassie as the emperor of Ethiopia in 1930. The local conditions setting the stage for the movement were white oppression, poverty, and the philosophy of Marcus Garvey, stressing black pride. Despite government efforts to control the movement, including the imprisonment of some leaders, it

grew and expanded, and is now a firmly established global religion and political movement.

The Ghost Dance

The Ghost Dance is a well-described American Indian revitalization movement that promised the revival of the traditional culture, the expulsion of Europeans, and the return of deceased ancestors. The Ghost Dance actually occurred twice. It began about 1870 in present-day Nevada when a Northern Paiute man, Wodziwob, reported, through visions and dreams, that the Great Spirit and the spirits of deceased ancestors would return, that whites would vanish, and that earth would become paradise. The major manifestation of the movement was the dance itself, which would cause the visions to come true. The dance was conducted in a circle with an opening left through which the returning spirits could enter; the participants sang, painted their bodies and faces, and wore white clothing. The movement spread west and led to other movements such as the Earth Lodge Cult, Warm House Cult, and Bole-Maru Cult among groups in Oregon and northern California. In about 1886 the movement reappeared among the Paiute, this time through visions of a man named Wovoka. The message and dance were similar to the 1870 version, but this time it spread east and was adopted by a number of Plains groups before largely disappearing. Although the movement was clearly in response to encroachments by white missionaries, settlers, traders, and soldiers, subsequent research has shown that many of the beliefs and the dance itself reflected traditional practices, with the visions about disappearing whites and some Christian elements such as a belief in salvation added later.

The Vailala Madness

This movement is one of the first well-described revitalization movements, and is also a good example of a cargo cult. The Vailala Madness began among the Orokolo people (a number of related groups) living on Orokolo Bay on the southern coast of New Guinea. The cult takes its name from the mass hysteria that began in about 1919 and manifested itself in people acting giddy, reeling about, and losing control over their limbs. The origins of the cult are traced to an Orokolo man, Evara, who went into trance, experienced convulsions, and prophesied the arrival of a steamship carrying the bodies of deceased Orokolo ancestors along with Western goods such as rifles, flour, and tobacco. Followers also experienced trances and had visions of a new world and a new supernatural order, integrating traditional Orokolo spirits and Christian figures such as Mary, Noah, Adam, and Eve (the Orokolo had been in contact with missionaries for several generations). Tall poles were erected as radio towers to communicate with the supernatural world, Western-style furniture was set up in the villages, and traditional religious objects such as bull-roarers and masks were burned. When the prophecies and various sightings of arriving ships failed to prove true, the movement waned, and within a few years traditional practices largely resumed. While the movement itself disappeared, it did have the long-term effect of integrating traditional religious beliefs such as ancestor worship with Christianity, and served as a means for legitimizing the arrival and continued influence of Western culture.

The Causes of Revitalization Movements

Social scientists have set forth at least 15 explanations for revitalization movements, both in general and for specific types of movements; these explanations share a belief that revitalization movements occur in response to severe stress experienced by members of a society. Among the possible causes of this stress are colonial oppression, the collapse of traditional values, natural disasters such as famine or floods, warfare, and a discrepancy between what people desire and what they can actually achieve. Revitalization

movements, in whatever form they take, do occur following events likely to cause stress. Colonial oppression, wars, and famine, however, have been experienced in many cultures, yet only some develop revitalization movements. It seems clear that stress alone does not cause revitalization movements; other factors must already be present that encourage or allow their development. In her research using a worldwide sample of 60 societies, Judith Justinger sorted through a variety of these "predisposing" factors and examined their relationship to the appearance of revitalization movements. She found that revitalization movements are more likely to occur in societies where people believe that life can change for the better, that they can improve their own life situation, and that the existing pattern of distribution of wealth and power can be altered, as well as where the role for the prophet already exists in the belief system. Thus, contrary to what might be expected, revitalization movements tend to occur more often in cultures with a secular rather than a religious orientation. This, of course, raises the intriguing though yet unanswered question of why people with a secular orientation seek a religious solution to their problems.

Barrett, Leonard. (1977) *The Rastafarians: The Dreadlocks of Jamaica.*

Carroll, Michael P. (1975) "Revitalization Movements and Social Structure: Some Quantitative Tests." *American Sociological Review* 40: 389–401.

Justinger, Judith M. (1979) *Reaction to Change: A Holocultural Test of Some Theories of Religious Movements.*

Lessa, William A., and Evon Z. Vogt. (1965) *Reader in Comparative Religion: An Anthropological Approach.* 2d ed.

Mooney, James. (1965) *The Ghost-Dance Religion and the Sioux Outbreak of 1890.* Edited and abridged by Anthony F. C. Wallace. First published, 1896.

Suttles, Wayne. (1957) "The Plateau Prophet Dance among the Coast Salish." *Southwestern Journal of Anthropology* 13: 352–396.

Wallace, Anthony F. C. (1956) "Revitalization Movements." *American Anthropologist* 58: 264–281.

Williams, Francis E. (1923) *The Vailala Madness and the Destruction of Native Ceremonies in the Gulf Division.*

Worsley, Peter. (1957) *The Trumpet Shall Sound.*

Wright, Robin M., and Jonathan D. Hill. (1986) "History, Ritual, and Myth: Nineteenth Century Millenarian Movements in the Northwest Amazon." *Ethnohistory* 33: 31–54.

RUSSIANS IN THE FORMER SOVIET UNION

In 1989 there were 3,305,000 ethnic Russians living in the 15 non-Russian republics of the Soviet Union. In many of these republics, relations between ethnic Russian residents and the indigenous population have become hostile and conflictual since the breakup of the Soviet Union beginning in 1989. The majority of Russians or their ancestors had settled in the other republics either during the colonization that began in the 1600s and accelerated during the era of the Russian Empire, or as part of the Russification process of the Communist era. During colonization, large numbers of Russians settled in other republics, often displacing indigenous peoples and taking the best land for themselves. For example, the over 6 million Russians in Kazakhstan live in the fertile northern region, while the Kazakh live mainly in the south. Russification was the attempt by the Soviet government to make the Russian culture dominant in the Soviet Union. It included the relocation of ethnic Russians to other republics; the placement of Russians in key Communist party and government positions; restrictions on the use of non-Russian, particularly non-Slavic, languages; using the Russian language for instruction in schools; bans on the public expression of religion; and the stationing of Russian troops in the other republics.

With the breakup of the Soviet Union and the reorganization of the constituent republics, a central issue that has emerged is the status of ethnic Russians in the other republics and various forms of ethnic conflict involving Russians in other republics, the indigenous cultures, and sometimes the Russian government as well. The table below lists the number of Russians in each republic in 1989 and their percentage of the republic population. (Since then, at least 1 million have migrated to Russia, primarily from the central Asian republics.)

Number of Russians and Their Percentage of the Population in Former Soviet Republics in 1989

Republic	Russian Population	Percent of Population
Armenia	51,600	1.6
Azerbaijan	392,300	5.6
Belarus	1,342,100	13.2
Estonia	474,800	30.3
Georgia	341,200	6.3
Kazakhstan	6,227,500	37.8
Kyrgyzstan	916,600	21.5
Latvia	905,500	34.0
Lithuania	344,500	9.4
Moldova	562,100	13.0
Russia	119,865,900	81.5
Tajikistan	395,100	7.6
Turkmenistan	333,900	9.5
Ukraine	11,355,600	22.1
Uzbekistan	1,653,500	8.4

The nature of the relationship between Russians and the peoples of the non-Russian republics is diverse and includes efforts toward peaceful integration of the Russian minority, repression of Russian culture, mass emigration by Russians, and ethnic separatist movements. In general, relations tend to be most peaceful in those republics where Russians form only a small percentage of the population and where they are already somewhat integrated into republic life, as indicated by their ability to speak the indigenous language. Peaceful relations are the norm in Lithuania, where all Russians who so desired were granted citizenship in 1989; in Belarus, where the two groups are culturally similar (both are classified as Eastern Slavs), 25 percent of Russians speak Belarussian and strong political ties remain between Russia and Belarus; and in the northern region of Kazakhstan, which is heavily populated by Russians.

In other regions, relations are less peaceful and, in general, seem to be the result of two factors. First, the history of Russian dominance in most regions and indigenous resentment of that dominance and second, independence since 1989 has led to political, social, and economic instability and uncertainty across the former Soviet Union, and increased ethnic conflict often involving competition for land and political power. Although specific to the Kazakh in some ways, the history of Kazakh-Russian relations points to some common features of Russian dominance that have created resentment in indigenous (now, national) groups and underlie contentious ethnic relations today. The Kazakh are a central Asian people whose ancestors lived in the region for several thousand years and who emerged as a distinct ethnic group in the fourteenth and fifteenth centuries, with the cultural configuration traditionally identified as Kazakh in place by the end of the seventeenth century. Key overarching elements of traditional Kazakh culture included a seminomadic lifestyle based on herding and adherence to Islam, combined with elements of their traditional religion. The Kazakh have always so referred to themselves, but the Russians refused to do so until the early twentieth century, choosing instead to call them *Kyrgyz*, or variations thereof, to distinguish them from Russian Cossacks living in Siberia and northern Kazakhstan. (The Kyrgyz are a distinct, neighboring people.) Russian dominance began in the early 1700s when the Kazakh turned to Russia for protection from invaders from the east. By the 1730s some Kazakh had become Russian citizens, and by 1860 Russian control was solidified, with Russian Cossacks occupying the northern Kazakh region to protect the Russian Empire; the tsar became the supreme authority in place of Kazakh khans; the Kazakh economy was shifted from herding to a combination of herding, agriculture, trade, and industry; and Russian and other Slavic farmers settled the rich farmlands. During this period, the Russians consciously encouraged the practice of Islam as a way of gaining Kazakh allegiance. In 1916 a revolt against Russian colonialism led to the migration of several thousand Kazakh to China and Mongolia. Following the Bolshevik Revolution, the Kazakh were incorporated into the Soviet state as an autonomous republic. Collectivization of the economy, famine, and forced relocations took millions of lives, and again, many left to seek refuge in other regions of central Asia, and most never returned. In the 1930s the Kazakh, like other non-Russians, lost many people through the purges, including their *mullahs,* leaving many communities without Islamic religious leaders to this day. Both during and following World War II, millions of Russians and other Eastern Slavic peoples settled in the northern region of Kazakhstan, where today they form the majority population, with less than 2 percent speaking Kazakh. With this history of Russian dominance, typical of much of the former Soviet Union, hostile ethnic relations between indigenous peoples and Russians have become the norm following the breakup of the Soviet Union.

Mass outmigration of Russians has taken place in Kyrgyzstan, where Russians are blamed for the republic's economic problems; in Azerbaijan because of the Azerbaijani-Armenian conflict; and in the Chechen-Ingush region because of the desire by these peoples for separatism from Russia. Russians have experienced increased hostility and sometimes restrictions in Georgia, where Russia is resented for supporting the Abkhazian separatists; in Estonia and Latvia, where Russian troops are an irritant to the indigenous population; in Kyrgyzstan, as noted above; and in western Ukraine, where the Russian minority is being actively repressed through controls on the teaching of Russian and access to Russian-language radio and television programs. Elsewhere in the Ukraine, however, peaceful coexistence is more the norm, and in the south, the influx of Russians continues. In southern Kazakhstan, the Kazakh are displacing the Russians from political office, and have reintroduced Kazakh as the official language of the republic (although Russian has been retained for external relations). The concern about continued Russian control in republics with a large Russian population became apparent in Estonia in late 1993, when Russians captured 27 of 64 seats in the Tallin city council. An Estonian law, supported by Russia, allowed Russians to vote in local, though not national, elections and was partly responsible for the success of Russians in local elections. While causing concern among Estonians in Tallin, the election has lessened international criticism of alleged Estonian anti-Russian activities.

The former Soviet Union is the scene of a number of ethnic separatist movements, and Russians are involved in four of them. In Georgia, the Russians have been accused by the Georgians of supporting the Abkhazian separatists, presumably because Russia would like Abkhazia

to join Russia. In western Moldova, where Russians and Ukrainians form the majority of the population, Russian troops have supported the formation of the Trans-Dniestr Republic, a conflict that has caused thousands of deaths. In South Ossetia, the Russians have supported the Ossetes in their efforts to secede from Georgia and affiliate with the North Ossetes and Russia. In the Chechen-Ingush region of the northern Caucasus, the Russians have reacted to Chechen-Ingush wishes for political autonomy by militarily suppressing them.

While accepting at least 1 million migrants from other republics in the last few years, most of whom are housed in southern Russia, the Russian government of Boris Yeltsin is opposed to mass immigration on the grounds that it will cause further economic, political, and social problems. While accepting the reality that there will be sizable migration from some republics in the next few years, the Russian government is actively negotiating with some republics, such as Latvia and Estonia, to allow Russian residents to become citizens. In general, Russia favors republic policies that allow Russian resident in those republics to become citizens and remain there.

See also ABKHAZIANS IN GEORGIA; CHECHEN-INGUSH IN RUSSIA; MOLDOVA; OSSETES AND GEORGIANS.

Dunlop, John B. (1993) "Will a Large-Scale Migration of Russians to the Russian Republic Take Place over the Current Decade?" *International Migration Review* 27: 605–629.

Friedrich, Paul, and Norma Diamond, eds. (1993) *Encyclopedia of World Cultures. Volume 6, Russia/Eurasia and China.*

Murdock, George P. (1934) "The Kazakhs of Central Asia." In *Our Primitive Contemporaries,* 135–153.

were actually a numerical minority) encouraged attacks on the Hutu to deflect attention from widespread corruption, unpopular policies, and a weak economy. In Ghana in 1969 and 1970, African migrants from other West African nations were blamed by the government for urban crime, unemployment, and other social ills, and were beaten, driven from the country, and their businesses looted. In Uganda in 1972, all Asians (many of them born in Uganda) were forced to leave. In the 1990s, the policy has been reversed, and Asians are allowed to return to Uganda and reclaim their property. Asians in Uganda were a middleman minority—an ethnic minority that occupies a specialized economic niche, usually involving a middleman role between the producers and consumers of goods and services. Because they are socially isolated from mainstream society, middleman minorities are often the victims of scapegoating, with the two groups most frequently scapegoated—Jews and Gypsies—often serving a middleman role.

In other situations, scapegoating may develop among the members of the society, often among those most threatened by societal problems, and then be supported or allowed by the government. For example, violence directed against Turkish migrant workers in Germany in 1992 and 1993, while not instigated by the government, was followed by a change in laws to restrict immigrants entering Germany.

A key component of scapegoating is stereotyping: The ethnic minority is blamed as a group for the problems of the society with no consideration of individual differences within the group or the forces actually producing the problems. In fact, the scapegoated group often suffers most from the social ills for which it is blamed, and punishing or expelling the group rarely solves the problem. In fact, in some cases such as Uganda, the expulsion empties the nation of a valuable economic resource such as small businesses or government workers, leading to further political unrest.

SCAPEGOAT

A scapegoat is someone who bears the blame for another. The term is derived from a Hebrew ritual sacrifice associated with the Day of Atonement. As described in the Book of Leviticus, chapter 16, the ritual required the High Priest to designate one he-goat for God and one for Azazel, with Azazel meaning the act of sending away, the place sent away to, a scapegoat, or the rugged mountain. The purpose of the ritual was to transfer the sins of the Israelites to the goat and then remove the sins by sacrificing the goat.

From the perspective of ethnic relations, scapegoated groups are often small, relatively defenseless ethnic minorities who are singled out and blamed by the government or other members of society for economic, social, and political problems. Often it is the government that directly blames an ethnic minority for national problems as a way of shifting blame from itself. For example, following the end of colonial rule in a number of African nations, the government has blamed minorities for various national problems. In Rwanda in 1973, the ruling Tutsi (who

Anti-Semitic signs in Behringersdorf, Germany, 1935.

See also MIDDLEMAN MINORITIES; RACE AND RACISM; STEREOTYPES.

Allport, Gordon W. (1954) *The Nature of Prejudice.*

Weinstein, Warren. (1981) "Africa." In *Protection of Ethnic Minorities: Comparative Perspectives,* edited by Robert G. Wirsing, 208–244.

Werblowsky, R. J. Zwi, and Geoffrey Wigoder, eds. (1965) *The Encyclopedia of the Jewish Religion.*

SIKHS IN INDIA Sikhism is India's youngest monotheistic religion, centered around a devotion to the Ten Gurus and their scripture. The founder and first guru was Guru Nanak, who lived from 1469 until 1539; the last of the gurus died early in the eighteenth century. Orthodox Sikhs observe a code of conduct and discipline, including rules governing appearance and diet. The Orthodox Sikhs have become more visible and vocal, tending to dominate the public life of the community, but other Sikhs who are not orthodox in appearance or other facets of the code of conduct are accepted for their reverence of the Ten Gurus and their attendance at *gurdwara,* the Sikh places of worship. Since the late 1880s, Sikhs have stressed their religious, cultural, and social differences from the Hindu majority in India and have sought to maintain adiminstrative and political control over Punjab State, where they are the majority population. While Sikh communities exist in Southeast Asia, Africa, Europe, Great Britain, and North America, the Sikh homeland is Punjab, a northwest Indian state bordering on Pakistan. Punjab is the site of most of the Sikh holy places and shrines, including the Golden Temple in Armritsar.

With a population estimated at 897 million in 1993, India comprises mainly Hindus (83 percent), Muslims (11 percent), Christians (3 percent), and Sikhs (2 percent). Although the Sikhs constitute only a small percentage of the overall population of India, the nearly 18 million Sikhs reside almost exclusively in the state of Punjab, where they make up approximately 60 percent of the population, with Hindus comprising 36 percent. Sikh identity and unity have been strong in the region even before the British partitioning of its Indian colony into present-day India and Pakistan. In 1925 the Sikh Gurdwara Protection Committee was formed to maintain control over the sacred shrines, and has since been instrumental in Sikh politics. Although India is a federal republic that guarantees the rights of the different ethnic groups under the constitution, Sikhs and other minority groups maintain that they have been discriminated against by the central government. They also fear assimilation into the Hindu majority. Being deprived of equal opportunity in jobs and development and having inadequate representation in legislation are claims made not only by Sikhs, but by other minority groups throughout India as well.

Increased violence and a strengthened call for separatism have resulted in demands for the creation of a separate Sikh nation called *Khalistan*. The current conflict dates to 1978, with Sikh concerns about autonomy and Indian efforts to develop and extract resources from the region. The desire for Khalistan was strengthened in 1984 when Indian prime minister Indira Gandhi, in an effort to dislodge an armed extremist Sikh uprising, gave orders for an attack on the Sikhs' holiest shrine, the Golden Temple. In response to this attack, Prime Minister Gandhi was assassinated by her Sikh bodyguards in October 1984. The assassination led to massive riots against Sikhs by Hindus, resulting in the violent deaths of thousands of Sikhs, and tens of thousands left homeless. Since 1984 the number of deaths related to this separatist conflict has been in the thousands every year. Finally, in 1987, in response to the increasing violence in the Punjab State, the central government suspended the locally elected government and has kept the state under police rule. Even under the guard of Indian paramilitary troops, thousands of Punjabis have been killed—the vast majority of them Sikhs.

Many Sikhs realize that the creation of a separate Sikh nation—Khalistan—is not a politically or economically viable option, and that in all likelihood the Sikh community will remain a part of India. While the Sikh extremists continue to demand independence, the more mainstream goal among Sikhs is to achieve the status of an autonomous state within India. The political standoff now is one of strategy—neither the Sikh nor the Indian central government is willing to make the first move. The presence of the Indian army has done little to weaken the determination of those fighting for relief of the frustrations of their minority status, but the government is unwilling to address political issues until violent opposition has been controlled. In the past few years the Indian government has attempted to hold elections for parliament and the local legislature, but extremist groups have managed to thwart these efforts with threats of violence to those who participate. They claim that the government is staging rigged elections and, in general, even those Sikhs willing to participate have been dissuaded. In 1992 the Indian government initated a more aggressive policy of military control of the region, making the police a visible force in Sikh communities and driving militant Sikh separatists underground. Sikhs see themselves as the victims of state terorism, claiming that the police routinely harass women and children, rape women, murder innocent citizens, and imprison Sikhs without due process. The Indian government has effectively restricted investigations by human rights organizations, thus making it hard to judge the situation, but also providing indirect support for Sikh claims of human rights violations.

Brass, Paul. (1988) "The Punjab Crisis and the Unity of India." In *India's Democracy: An Analysis of Changing State-Society Relations,* edited by Atul Kohli, 169–213.

McLeod, W. H. (1990) *The Sikhs.*

O'Connell, Joseph, et al., eds. (1988) *Sikh History and Religion in the Twentieth Century.*

SINHALESE AND SRI LANKAN TAMILS

Sri Lanka (formerly called Ceylon) is an island nation located off the southeast coast of India. In 1993 the population was estimated to be 17.8 million. The capital is Colombo, with a population of 1.2 million; Jaffna, in the north, has a population of 270,000. The majority of the population is rural, living in thousands of small villages across the island and along the coasts. Formerly a British colony, Sri Lanka became independent through a peaceful transition in 1948.

The population is composed of four major ethnic groups: Sinhalese, Sri Lankan Tamils, Indian Tamils, and Sri Lankan Moors or Muslims. A fifth group, the Vedda, numbering several thousand, are descendants of the original inhabitants of the island. Their traditional culture has largely disappeared through contact with the Sinhalese and Tamil.

The Sinhalese constitute 75 percent of the population and speak the Sinhala language; about 70 percent are Theravada Buddhist, and the remainder are mostly Roman Catholic. They live primarily in the western, central, and southern provinces, where they are politically and economically dominant. The Sinhalese evidently emigrated to Sri Lanka from nothern India and were settled on the island by the third century B.C. By the first century B.C., a Buddhist Sinhalese civilization was established in Sri Lanka, lasting until the thirteenth century A.D. In 1505 the island came under European colonial control (Portuguese, 1505–1658; Dutch, 1658–1796; British, 1796–1948). The colonists introduced Roman Catholicism and Protestantism and a plantation economy centered on coffee, tea, cotton, and tobacco. Today, the Sinhalese are composed of two major subgroups, the Kandayan Sinhalese in the central highlands and the Low Country Sinhalese on the coasts. The Sinhalese today are mainly small farmers, service-industry workers, and civil servants.

The Sri Lankan Tamils comprise 11 percent of the population, and speak a dialect of the Tamil language spoken by Tamils in southeastern India. The majority are Hindu, although there are sizable minorities of Protestants and Roman Catholics. Sri Lankan Tamils are primarily located in the eastern and northern provinces, with cultural and political activity centered on the Jaffna Peninsula. The exact date of Tamil settlement on Sri Lanka is unknown, although Tamils from south India were certainly present during the period of Sinhalese civilization from the third to the thirteenth centuries. Following the collapse of the Sinhalese civilization in the thirteenth century, a Sri Lankan Tamil kingdom developed on the Jaffna Peninsula, with all of Sri Lanka coming under colonial control from 1505 to 1948. Modern Sri Lankan Tamil culture is a synthesis of Indian Tamil and Sinhalese culture, with additional borrowing from other south Indian cultures such as those of peoples in Kerala. Thus, Sri Lankan Tamils are culturally distinct from Indian Tamils and from the Sinhalese. Today, Sri Lankan Tamils subsist primarily as small farmers or wage laborers. Remittances from relatives living overseas are an important source of income.

Indian Tamils are descendants of Indian Tamils brought to Sri Lanka by the British in the 1800s as laborers on tea plantations, and constitute 8.5 percent of the current population. They also speak the Tamil language, although they are culturally distinct from Sri Lankan Tamils. Sri Lankan Moors or Muslims comprise 7 percent of the population, and live in the southern and western provinces; most speak Tamil, although an increasing number speak Sinhala as well.

The current ethnic strife in Sri Lanka is a violent ethnic separatist conflict that mainly involves the Sri Lankan Tamils and the Sinhalese. The Tamils seek political autonomy of some type for the eastern and northern provinces as a Tamil homeland, a desire opposed by the numerically and politically dominant Sinhalese. Under colonial domination, relations between the Tamil and Sinhalese were relatively peaceful, and for the first eight years of independence, Sri Lanka was ruled by a multiethnic coalition government. In 1956 Sinhalese politician S. W. R. D. Bandaranaike was elected prime minister, running on a platform that promised the designation of Sinhala as the official language. His election and populist appeal reflected widespread Sinhalese resentment of the number of Tamils holding government, professional, and business positions, and was an effort to shift power to the numerically dominant Sinhalese. In 1958 Sinhalese resentment turned bloody as some Sinhalese rioted against Sri Lankan Tamils in the south. Throughout the 1960s and into the 1970s, the Sri Lankan economy deteriorated and unemployment rates soared. The political unrest within the Sinhalese community that followed culminated in the emergence of a leftist youth movement, the Janatha Vimukthi Peramuna (JVP) or People's Liberation Army, as a powerful political force.

In the early 1970s the Sinhalese-dominated government set quotas on the number of Sri Lankan Tamils who could be admitted to universities or hold government jobs. In 1974, in response to Tamil exclusion from Sinhalese-dominated society, the Tamils asked that a Sri Lankan Tamil state be created in the northern and eastern provinces through peaceful negotiation. In 1978 Tamil was designated a national language, but when the Sinhalese were slow to respond to the Tamil request for autonomy, Tamil youths became violent and assassinated a number of Tamil leaders accused of being sympathetic to the Sinhalese. In 1981 Sinhalese security forces burned the central library in Jaffna and terrorized the population, who turned to the youths for protection. In 1987 Sinhalese rioted in Colombo and elsewhere in the south, destroying Tamil businesses and homes, and forcing many Tamils to flee north and east to safety.

The conflict has been violent since the early 1980s, with occasional periods of short-lived peace. The Tamil effort now rests on the activities of the Liberation Tigers of Tamil Eelam (LTTE), the major Tamil guerrilla army, with the Jaffna Peninsula their primary area of activity. In the 1990s they have faced internal criticism and opposition, primarily from the University Teachers of Human Rights, a Sri Lankan organization. Much criticism centers on their practice of demanding support payments of two gold sovereigns (about $260) from each Tamil family, and forcibly inducting boys into their units.

At various times, India has tried to broker a settlement, and in 1987, 60,000 Indian troops were placed in Tamil regions to control the violence. Before withdrawing in 1990 at the request of the Sinhalese government, the Indian army helped to control the violence, but Indian soldiers were also accused of killing thousands of Tamil civilians and destroying much property. The Indian army presence also led to political unrest in the south, where resentment led to JVP violence against Sinhalese officials, resulting in several thousand Sinhalese deaths. In 1987 former Indian prime minister Rajiv Gandhi was assassinated, and in March 1993 bombings in Bombay killed more than 250 people. The Tamils have been accused of both crimes, but deny responsibility. In 1990 the Muslims were drawn into the conflict when the Tamil Tigers destroyed mosques and villages and killed hundreds of people in Muslim communities in the east. Hundreds of thousands of Muslims subsequently fled to safety in the western province.

Ethnic conflict in Sri Lanka in the form of terrorism, riots, government-sanctioned attacks on civilians, destruction of property, and assassinations has caused at least 20,000 deaths since the early 1980s, the forced relocation of hundreds of thousands of Tamils and Muslims (many of whom have left Sri Lanka altogether), and bitterness among all involved. So far, the conflict has also failed to yield a political or military solution to the issue of Sri Lankan Tamil autonomy. As of late 1993, the Sinhalese army was largely in control of the situation, with Tamil separatists mainly confined to the northern Jaffna Peninsula, and the Sinhalese army a major presence in the region.

O'Ballance, Edgar. (1989) *The Cyanide War: Tamil Insurrection in Sri Lanka.*

Schwarz, Walter. (1988) *The Tamils of Sri Lanka.*

Tambiah, Stanley J. (1986) *Sri Lanka—Ethnic Fratricide and the Dismantling of Democracy.*

———. (1992) *Buddhism Betrayed? Religion, Politics and Violence in Sri Lanka.*

SITUATIONAL ETHNICITY

Situational ethnicity refers to the common practice in multicultural societies of ethnic groups or individuals shifting, hiding, or asserting their ethnic identity as a strategy for achieving some goal. Both groups and individuals are motivated to alter their identity when they believe that the new identity is to their political or financial advantage. Situational ethnicity can take the form of short-term shifts in identity to achieve limited goals. For example, people in Malaysia of various ethnic backgrounds all identified themselves as Malay when such solidarity was needed to resist incursions by developers. Or, situational ethnicity can take the form of permanent change designed to conceal one's identity, as among the Karaite Jews in Russia in the 1800s and Crimean Jews (Krymchaks) in the Soviet Union in the 1950s, both of whom rewrote their histories to prove that they were not Jews so as to escape discrimination and persecution. Situational ethnicity can also take the form of a redefinition of the basis of one's ethnicity. For example, the shift in the generic label from black to African-American is in part an attempt to create cultural and group identity based on a shared history, and discard an identity based on a European model of identity by skin color and biological descent. Finally, situational ethnicity can involve the revival or construction of a new identity. For example, beginning in the late 1960s, the opportunity for political influence in local development decisions and financial rewards for being a Chumash in California led a number of individuals (some who could prove Chumash descent and others who could not) and groups to identity themselves and receive official recognition as Chumash, despite the fact that Chumash culture and language were extinct.

For situational ethnicity to be successful, the new identity of the group must be accepted by the dominant group. Factors that influence dominant-group acceptance include the relative political and socioeconomic statuses of the groups, the distribution of resources among the groups, group size, immediate prospects for change, and perceived availability of limited resources. The Chumash, Karaites, and Krymchaks mentioned above were successful because local business and political interests accepted the Chumash claims, and the Russians allowed the Jewish groups to redefine themselves as non-Jews, exempting them from restrictive laws applied selectively to Jews. In the case of the Chumash, the local political and economic interests benefited by having access to legally required involvement by Chumash in development projects on ancestral Chumash land.

However, sometimes the dominant groups will resist ethnic identity changes, especially when such changes are not in their interest or conflict with their interests. For example, the Lumbee (a mixed-ancestry group in North and South Carolina) sought to improve their economic and political status by first defining themselves as white, an effort that failed, and then defining themselves as Indian, which proved more successful. Their former identity as black, of course, was not to their advantage in the segregated South.

An example of strong resistance by the dominant group is the ongoing case of the Golden Hill Paugussett Indians in Connecticut. In 1992 and 1993, the Paugussett filed lawsuits claiming several thousand acres of residential land in the city of Bridgeport and surrounding suburban towns. Their primary goal was to secure enough land in Bridgeport to build and operate a gambling casino. It was widely believed by the affected people and towns that the land claims were nothing more than an effort to scare government officials so that the Paugussett would be granted some land, awarded federal status as an American Indian tribe (a requirement for opening a casino), and licensed by the state to operate a casino. The Paugussett were motivated by the experience of the Mashantucket Pequots in eastern Connecticut who, a few years earlier, had opened what became an extremely successful casino. The Paugussett claims have been resisted by the in-

dividuals and towns affected, by state officials, and by the two state senators. In addition, in 1993 the state took action to halt the Paugussett practice of selling cigarettes at a large discount to the public on their small reservation, rejecting the Paugussett claim that as a state-recognized American Indian tribe they had no obligation to collect sales tax. What explains the successful use of their American Indian identity by the Pequots in eastern Connecticut to gain the right to develop and operate a casino (Connecticut law does not allow casinos) and the so-far troubled and failed attempt by the Paugussett? The major factor has been the willingness of the dominant white population to allow the Pequot casino, and its resistance to the Paugussett casino. Whites in eastern Connecticut either supported the Pequot right to build the casino or did not strongly resist for a number of reasons: (1) The Pequot already were recognized as an American Indian tribe and were known in the region as a distinct group with their own reservation, although they were culturally and physically indistinguishable from the local population. Thus, they needed only to assert their ethnicity to achieve their goals. (2) The casino was built on reservation land the Pequots already owned, so non-Indians were not threatened with a loss of land. (3) Eastern Connecticut was an economically unstable region, and the casino provided thousands of new jobs and a boost to the local economy, thus benefiting all residents of the region.

For the Paugussett, the situation is the opposite: (1) They are not well known as a distinct ethnic group; (2) physically, they are defined by outsiders as African-American rather than as American Indian or white; (3) they are not recognized by the federal government; and (4) their reservation is too small for a viable casino operation. Thus, from the perspective of most area residents, they are not a distinct ethnic group and have no ethnicity to assert; their need and demand for additional land threatens the security of local property owners; and Fairfield County in western Connecticut is one of the five wealthiest counties in the nation, with little incentive to support economic development via a gambling casino.

In addition to acquiescence by the dominant group, other physical, social, and psychological factors also operate to constrain the use and effectiveness of situational ethnicity. These include skin color, the place of the group in the ethnic stratification system, the fluidity of ethnic identity in multiethnic societies and the amount of information one has about the new identity, and the psychological capacity of members of the group to act differently.

Related to situational ethnicity is *ethnic impression management,* in which an individual or group selectively displays symbols of a specific ethnic identity in order to influence members of other ethnic groups. One form of such impression management is the public display of nonthreatening aspects of one's culture such as food, dress, jewelry, music, and dance, which can be appreciated by outsiders at an aesthetic level and thus require no knowledge of or involvement in the culture. A special form of impression management that generally occurs at the level of individual behavior is called *passing*—that is, behaving in such a way that an individual will be considered a member of a higher status or situationally more beneficial ethnic group. In Latin American nations with white, American Indian, and mixed-ancestry populations, defining oneself as white often provides enhanced access to wealth and influence.

See also ETHNIC IDENTITY AND SOLIDARITY; ETHNOCENTRISM.

Blu, Karen I. (1980) *The Lumbee Problem: The Making of an American Indian People.*

Keefe, Susan E., ed. (1989) *Negotiating Ethnicity: The Impact of Anthropological Theory and Practice.* NAPA Bulletin No. 8.

Lyman, Stanford M., and William A. Douglass. (1973) "Ethnicity: Strategies of Collective and Individual Impression Management." *Social Research* 40: 344–365.

Nagata, Judith A. (1974) "What Is a Malay? Situational Selection of Ethnic Identity in a Plural Society." *American Ethnologist* 1: 1215–1230.

Okamura, Jonathan Y. (1981) "Situational Ethnicity." *Ethnic and Racial Studies* 4: 452–463.

Royce, Anya Peterson. (1982) *Ethnic Identity: Strategies of Diversity.*

SLAVERY Practices and institutions labeled as forms of slavery have varied widely in form, content, and purpose throughout human history and across cultures. While it is impossible to provide a single definition that fits all situations, slavery in its most general sense is characterized by (1) a denial of rights or excessive restrictions or limitations on rights enjoyed by free persons, (2) forced labor without compensation, and (3) status as an ethnic outsider in the society where one is enslaved and complete separation from one's own ethnic group. Thus, throughout human history, slavery has been a major form of ethnic relations, with one group dominant over and exploiting the labor of members of another group who live in their midst. Although some individuals in some cultures might place themselves into slavery in their own society to pay a debt or as punishment for a crime, this form of internal slavery is rare in comparison to other types where slaves are ethnic outsiders.

Slavery has a long history in the human experience and was important in the development of both the Islamic and Western (Greek and Roman) civilizations and the European settlement of the New World. Slavery, primarily in the forms of both domestic and productive slavery, was also not uncommon in non-Western, nonindustrialized societies.

Slavery or related institutions are still common around the world, and the long-term effects of productive slavery are still being experienced by the descendants of slaves. The descendants of slaves are still a discriminated-against minority in the United States; in many South and Middle American nations, dark skin color is an obstacle to increasing one's socioeconomic status; and, among the Ashanti of West Africa, those with a slave ancestry are considered socially inferior. In a recent development that could have major economic implications, the Organization of African Unity is pursuing the possibility of asking the United Nations and other organizations to require European, New World, and Middle Eastern nations who allowed slavery in the past to pay reparations to African nations that were the source of slaves for these nations.

The above definition distinguishes slavery in its various forms from related institutions such as serfdom, peonage, compulsory military service, pawning, and imprisonment, all of which are forms of involuntary servitude.

From a historical and cross-cultural perspective, slavery comes in two primary forms—domestic and productive.

Domestic Slavery

Domestic slavery (also known as household and patriarchal slavery) was a form of slavery found in small-scale, nonindustrial societies whose economies were based on horticulture or simple agriculture. According to two worldwide surveys of slavery, with samples of 186 and 60 nonindustrial societies respectively, domestic slavery occurred in 35 percent of societies. The label "domestic" indicates that slaves in these societies performed mostly household work, including gardening, child care, wood and water fetching, and concubinage. In many societies they also performed other chores outside the household, such as accompanying their owners on travels, soldiering, trading, and serving as sacrificial victims. It is generally assumed by social scientists that one key feature of domestic slavery is that the slaves or their offspring were integrated into the families who owned them and eventually into the society. Most domestic slaves were women or girls who were either purchased from other societies, were born into slavery, or were taken in slave raids. Women were preferred over men for a number of reasons: (1) Most of the work performed by domestic slaves is work traditionally performed by women in horticultural societies; (2) women were more easily integrated into these societies because all women were exploited to some degree, and, through polygamous marriage or concubinage, female slaves could produce offspring for their masters; and (3) women were more easily controlled than male slaves, who might revolt or who provided sexual competition for their owners.

Although domestic slavery is distinguished from productive slavery, in any given society the distinction is often less than clear. Slaves might be used for a variety of purposes, their treatment varied widely, and the possibility of integration into society was not always certain. Perhaps the key distinction between domestic and productive slavery was that in the former, slaves played only a limited economic role, while in the latter they were a major source of labor in the economic system.

A few examples from around the world indicate the variations found in domestic slavery.

The Tlingit of the northwest coast of North America enslaved both Tlingit from other Tlingit subgroups and neighboring peoples such as the Flathead of Oregon. Only wealthy Tlingit owned slaves, who evidently performed domestic chores and perhaps helped hunt and fish, freeing their wealthy owners to engage in ceremonial and social activities. Slaves were also sacrificed by the wealthy as a sign of their wealth. Tlingit slaves were ethnic outsiders who were not integrated into Tlingit clans, and while living in the same houses as their owners were poorly treated; upon death, they were simply thrown into the ocean without ceremony. Tlingit slavery was ended by the Russians in the nineteenth century.

In pre-Communist China, the Black Lolo enslaved Han Chinese, who occupied the lowest status in Lolo society, beneath both the upper-class Black Lolo and lower-class White Lolo. Han slaves worked in the fields and in the households; they might also be enslaved by the White Lolo, but this was less common. Slaves were acquired by kidnapping Han travelers, raiding Han villages, or stealing slaves from other Black Lolo villages. While children of Han slaves were also slaves, over three or four generations they might establish their own households, disavow their Han ancestry, and assimilate into Lolo society as White Lolo, in which status they too could own Han slaves.

The Somali engaged in the slave trade as traders, but also used domestic slaves who existed as a social category beneath the outcaste *sab*, who performed most of the menial economic labor as part of a patron-client relationship with the Somali. Slaves, on the other hand, were owned by their masters, although they might be paid for their work, as those who traveled as traders certainly were. Somali domestic slaves could be integrated into society through marriage or sexual relations. A slave woman who married a *sab* remained a slave, but her children were *sab;* children of a slave woman and her master were free and looked after by the master. Slaves could

also win their freedom through manumission, although as freemen they did not enjoy the same status as Somali and had no clan affiliation. Since slaves were often treated as members of the family, free status provided little benefit.

Productive Slavery

Productive slavery (also called chattel or economic slavery) is the most significant form of slavery in terms of ethnic relations in the contemporary world. Although productive slavery has essentially disappeared, its effects are still felt and influence ethnic relations in much of the New World. Productive slavery was an economic arrangement in which slave owners, driven by the profit motive, used slaves as their labor force to produce raw materials for processing. Slaves were the property of their owners, who could buy, sell, trade, and use them in any way they chose and which market conditions permitted. However, in no slave society were slave owners given total control of all aspects of the lives of their slaves.

Productive slavery was justified by a European racist ideology that characterized Africans and other non-Europeans as nonhuman or inferior to Europeans. Productive slavery usually developed in advanced, nonindustrialized, agricultural societies where other sources of labor, such as hired free labor, were not available. While slavery was usually an economic arrangement in which slave owners sought to make a profit, the enterprise could be quite costly, given the expense of acquiring, transporting, and maintaining slaves. Another cost was frequent slave revolts, although only one (in Haiti) actually led to the overthrow of the government and the establishment of a free nation.

From the viewpoint of ethnic relations, slave owners had no interest in aiding slaves in maintaining their traditional cultures. Thus, slaves imported to the New World from various West African cultures were simply lumped as culturally the same, despite the fact that they spoke different languages and had many other cultural differences. In New World slavery, much of the traditional cultures was lost, although in some situations syncretic cultures developed, based on a mix of African, American Indian, and European cultural traits. Only recently, the Afrocentric movement has stressed the African origins of African-American culture in the Americas.

Slavery in the New World is the major example of productive slavery in human history. Between 1500 and 1850, approximately 12 to 15 million African slaves were imported to the New World by the Dutch, Spanish, Portuguese, English, and French. An undetermined number of American Indians were also enslaved, mainly by the Spanish and Portuguese in South America. The trans-Atlantic slave trade and New World plantation economy were a highly profitable economic arrangement for the European colonists—slaves from West Africa were captured mainly by other Africans from different ethnic groups. This activity represented a European-instigated expansion of traditional domestic slavery, and made raiding for slaves a major economic activity. Attention also shifted from taking women to taking men, who were more desirable for New World slavery. West Africa was, and remains today, a heavily populated region—even centuries of slave trade has had little effect on the overall population or on the ability of West African societies to sustain themselves. In the New World, the majority of slaves went to large plantations in Brazil, northern South America, and the Caribbean, with sugarcane plantations taking the majority of the slaves. In North America there were relatively few large plantations, and most slaves worked on family farms, where cotton and tobacco were the major crops. The slave trade and slavery ended in the 1800s. Britain outlawed slavery in 1808 and freed slaves in its colonies in 1838; by the 1870s nearly all slave societies had outlawed slavery. Brazil was the last New World society to do so, in 1888. Under pressure from European nations, slavery was also banned in the Islamic world and Africa by the twentieth century, although the practice persisted in some places until the middle of the century.

A variety of explanations has been offered for productive slavery. One suggests that slavery is a step in the evolution of human society, an

A copper engraving portrays a slave dealer auctioning slaves on the coast of Africa.

idea now dismissed, given that the majority of human societies never had slavery. Another explanation stresses the economic rationality of slavery, and suggests that slavery occurs when the costs of keeping slaves are less than the economic benefits reaped from their work. This explanation also suggests that slavery ends when the costs exceed the benefits. The weakness of this explanation is that it ignores the social and political costs and benefits of slavery that were often beyond the control of the slave owner. The most compelling explanation for productive slavery is the idea that, as in New World societies, when land is free or easily available and can be worked by the landowners, free labor will be difficult to acquire for large agricultural enterprises; therefore, the only way help can be obtained is through subjugation, with slavery being one alternative. This explanation also assumes that a strong centralized government will enact and enforce laws that support slavery, and that the economic system is sufficiently developed to support large-scale slave trading. All of these conditions were present in the New World during the slave era.

Islamic Slavery

Distinguished from both domestic and productive slavery is Islamic slavery, occurring throughout the Islamic world from A.D. 650 well into the twentieth century in some nations (slavery was not banned in Saudi Arabia until 1962 and Oman until 1970). The rules governing slavery were carefully spelled out in the Quran (Koran) and subsequent interpretations. As in all forms of slavery, enslavement of members of one's own ethnic group (in this case, Muslims) was forbidden. Slavery was of crucial importance in the Ottoman Empire, with Slavic slaves imported from the Balkans and others imported from Africa. Numbering perhaps 20 percent of the population in Istanbul, slaves performed much of the physical labor required to maintain the empire, serving as domestic help and as concubines un-

til the decline of slavery in the late 1800s. Islamic slavery, particularly in the Middle East, was both domestic and productive in purpose. About 18 million slaves were taken by Islamic nations in the 13 centuries from 650 to 1900. Many were used as household help, servants, and concubines, and some were used as soldiers. Female slaves, because of their worth as domestics and concubines, were especially valued, as were eunuchs for household service, and many boys were castrated for this purpose. Slaves taken or purchased in Africa were widely traded across the Middle East and Southeast Asia, and in some places, such as East Africa, slaves worked in productive roles on plantations in addition to their domestic duties. In Islamic slavery, there was a deep tradition of manumission, and allowing one's slaves to buy their freedom brought honor to the masters. Not all children of slaves became slaves; for example, children of concubines were considered free.

Contemporary Forms of Slavery

Both domestic and productive slavery are now mainly institutions of the past. Mauritania, the last nation to practice productive slavery, has essentially ended the institution, although former slaves continue to live in poverty. However, slavery or slaverylike practices in different forms is still common around the world, and some experts believe that there are now more individuals living in slavelike circumstances than at any point in human history.

The three major forms of slavery today are child labor, debt bondage, and forced labor. Other forms include servile marriage, in which women have no choice in getting married; prostitution; and the sale of human organs.

Perhaps as many as 100 million children worldwide are exploited for their labor. That is, they are forced to work, work long hours in unhealthy conditions, and are paid little or nothing for their labor. Some children are local or from the same nation as the exploiters, while in other cases they may be taken, with or without parental permission, and shipped elsewhere. Children so exploited may be as young as 5 years of age, and most are under 12. Forms of child labor include child carpet weavers in India, Pakistan, Nepal, and Morocco; child domestic servants in many West African nations, Bangladesh, and elsewhere; street beggars in many Third World nations, especially in cities that draw many Western tourists; prostitutes for the tourist trade in the Philippines and Thailand; and camel jockeys in the Middle East. The sale of children—by their parents and middlemen, often with government sanction—from poor families in Third World nations to wealthier people in developed nations is also considered a form of child labor, particularly since it is not always clear how much freedom the parents had in choosing to sell their child. Until the end of Communist rule, Romania was a major source of adoptive children for the United States, with Peru now filling that role. Child labor is considered desirable by employers because it is cheap, children are easy to control and replace, they can perform some tasks that require small fingers and more dexterity better than adults, and they are less likely to revolt.

Debt bondage is an economic arrangement in which an individual pledges his labor against debts. Ideally, he will work off the debt and will then be economically free. However, it rarely works this way, and most individuals and their families in debt bondage remain so for life. In some nations, that obligation is passed on to their children. In India alone there are an estimated 6.5 million people living in debt bondage. This situation was created in part by the absence of bankruptcy laws, which made it necessary for a person to place himself in debt bondage in order to repay his debts. Although debt bondage was banned by law in 1976, the practice continues in many rural regions. Debt bondage is common throughout all of South Asia, and is found in Pakistan, Nepal, and Bangladesh as well as India. Most of those in debt bondage perform agricultural work.

Forced labor refers to a situation where individuals are coerced into working in conditions that are often unsafe and usually for low wages. Recent examples of forced labor include the use of Brazilian Indians in forestry, mining, rubber tapping, and prostitution; forced prostitution in Turkey; Haitian sugarcane workers in the Dominican Republic; and Peruvian and Salvadorian domestic laborers in the United States. The latter are individuals who are in the country illegally, and thus are sometimes exploited by their employers. Knowing that they have less recourse to the judicial and administrative protection than would legal immigrants or citizens, their employers may pay them low wages and make them work long hours.

Perhaps the primary cause of modern forms of slavery is the vast differences in wealth between Western and some other nations and Third World nations, which leaves the residents of the latter vulnerable as a source of cheap labor for products and services to be sold to wealthy nations or their citizens. In addition, high levels of unemployment and poverty in many nations leave many people no choice but to allow themselves to be exploited in slavelike situations. A third factor is that in many nations, citizens are afforded more rights and protection than are noncitizens, making the latter vulnerable to exploitation. A final factor is ethnic and religious discrimination in some nations, which means that some groups will have less economic opportunity than others and are less likely to be protected from discrimination by the government.

See also COLONIALISM; RACE AND RACISM; SYNCRETIC CULTURES.

Centre for Human Rights. (1991) *Contemporary Forms of Slavery.* Fact Sheet No. 14.

Christensen, James. (1954) *Double Descent among the Fanti.*

Gordon, Murray. (1989) *Slavery in the Arab World.*

Jordan, Winthrop. (1974) *The White Man's Burden.*

Klein, Laura F. (1975) *Tlingit Women and Town Politics.*

Lewis, I. M. (1955) *Peoples of the Horn of Africa.*

Lin, Yueh-hwa. (1947) *The Lolo of Liang-Shan.* Translated from the Chinese by Ju Shu Pan.

Miers, Suzanne, and Igor Kopytoff, eds. (1977) *Slavery in Africa: Historical and Anthropological Perspectives.*

Nieboer, Herman J. (1900) *Slavery as an Industrial System.*

Patterson, Orlando. (1982) *Slavery and Social Death: A Comparative Study.*

Pryor, Frederic L. (1977) *The Origins of the Economy.*

Rubin, Vera, and Arthur Tuden, eds. (1977) *Comparative Perspectives on Slavery in New World Plantation Societies.*

Sawyer, Roger. (1986) *Slavery in the Twentieth Century.*

van den Berghe, Pierre L. (1981) *The Ethnic Phenomenon.*

STEREOTYPES

A stereotype is a belief or image in which a few attributes of a group are exaggerated or simplified, and the group is described or evaluated in terms of these attributes. Stereotypes can be negative or positive, and are commonly applied by members of an ethnic group to their own as well as to other ethnic groups. Most stereotypes of other groups are negative, while stereotypes of one's own group are usually positive (although they may be seen as negative by outsiders). Stereotypes often have some basis in reality, although they are oversimplifications and ignore the complexity of the behaviors described in stereotypical ways. For example, Jews in medieval Europe were widely believed to be dishonest and greedy because they were moneylenders, and cowardly because they were the frequent targets of physical abuse. The complexity ignored by these stereotypes is that Jews were forced to be moneylenders by religious laws of the time, which barred Christians from such activity, and that Jews were forbidden to own or carry weapons, thereby rendering them defenseless. Similarly, in the United States in the early twentieth century, Italian immigrants from southern Italy were seen as able to perform only hard, manual labor. While Italian men often did take such work, it was because they were prevented from finding work in the trades and industries that were open to other immigrants from central and northern Europe.

Stereotyping apparently occurs in all multicultural societies and evidently serves to simplify and help order a complex social world. This simplification becomes a cognitive model of the world and thus enables individuals to interact with others from different groups. Over time, the model is reinforced through the observation of behaviors that support the stereotype and the failure to observe behaviors that contradict it. Stereotyping is a key component of ethnocentrism, racism, and derogatory ethnic humor, as it provides the image of other groups that is the basis of these practices. In situations of open and prolonged ethnic conflict, what has been called a "mirror image" form of stereotyping might occur, in which each group holds a similar view of themselves that is the near opposite of the view they have of the other group. For example, in the 1970s both Indians and Pakistanis saw themselves as peaceful, religious, kind, democratic, and friendly, while they saw the other group as cruel, selfish, warlike, and dishonest.

See also ETHNIC HUMOR; ETHNOCENTRISM; RACE AND RACISM.

Allport, Gordon W. (1954) *The Nature of Prejudice.*

Royce, Anya Peterson. (1982) *Ethnic Identity: Strategies of Diversity.*

Segall, Marshall H., et al. (1990) *Human Behavior in Global Perspective.*

SYNCRETIC CULTURES

Whenever two or more cultures come into contact, there is a mixing of some elements from each. Syncretism is one specific type of cultural blending that, in its most extreme form, results in the development of a new culture or ethnic group characterized by numerous cultural traits and institutions that are an amalgam of traits drawn from different cultures. A less extreme example of syncretism involves the development of new forms of cultural institutions through a blending of traits but not a transformation of the entire culture. Syncretism is most evident among the African-ancestry cultures of the Caribbean region, including those in Brazil, along the northern coast of South America, in eastern Middle America, and on the Caribbean islands. The various blendings involve the West African cultures brought from Africa by slaves, American Indian cultures (especially Carib culture), and the cultures of the European settlers—Spanish, Portuguese, English, French, and Dutch.

African Brazilian Candomble, Cuban Santería, and Haitian Voudun (Voodoo) are all syncretic religions formed through a combination of theology and practices from African religions brought by slaves and the Roman Catholicism of the European colonizers. Voudun, for example, is based on African elements, primarily from the Fon of Benin, the Yoruba of Nigeria, and the Kongo of Zaire and Angola, coupled with the form of Roman Catholicism imposed by the French colonists. From African religions come various spirits, although they are often redefined to fit the Haitian situation, such as the Yoruba iron smithing spirit, Ogou, called Ogan in rural Haiti and seen as the spirit of military power; the image of Africa itself as the homeland and the home of the spirits; and African rites for serving the spirits. Added to this African base and merged with it are elements taken from Roman Catholicism, including specific rites such as baptism, Mass, and confession; Catholic prayers; the names of saints; and the role of the "bush priest," whose status is based on his ability to conduct Catholic rites in the original Latin. In Haitian Voudun and other syncretic religions, the elements do not simply exist side by side, but are often merged in various ways. For example, the African god Bondye, the "Good God," is linked with the Christian God while the Snake deity, Danbala, is linked to St. Patrick, who is depicted with snakes around his neck. Earlier in the twentieth century, social scientists viewed syncretic elements of a culture such the Voudun religion as an adaptive response to the colonial situation that enabled oppressed peoples to live in both their own and the world of the colonists. More recently, syncretism has become a mechanism of resistance and revolt, through which African-ancestry communities in Brazil, Suriname, Haiti, and elsewhere developed their own sense of a unique ethnic consciousness and used that consciousness to seek recognition and political power. In Brazil, syncretic religions are an important element in the black consciousness movement. In Haiti, Voudun played a role in the overthrow of the Duvalier government in 1986, as it had in the slave revolt of 1789–1804 that ended French rule, the only such revolt that has been successful in human history.

The label *syncretic cultures* is used for some peoples of Middle America known as Black Caribs or Garifuna; they are descended from African slaves and American Indians, and their modern culture is a mix of African, American Indian, and European elements. The Black Caribs of Honduras are descendants of escaped slaves who settled on the island of St. Vincent beginning in 1635 and the Carib Indians then resident there. After 1796, when the British took the island from the French, these Black Caribs fled west, ultimately settling in Honduras. As elsewhere, syncretism in Black Carib culture is most noticeable in the religion, which combines the Catholic liturgy, saints, and the afterworld with African ritual, theology, and spirits. Syncretism is also found in the economic system, in the diet, in kinship, and in politics. The Black Carib diet, for example, includes cassava bread and chili peppers (Carib Indian), fish stews and cooking in oil (African), and the growing of crops for sale (European) as well as for their own consumption.

Syncretism is a poorly understood phenomenon, and little is known about how cultural elements become integrated or why some elements of culture, such as religion, are more open to syncretization than are other elements, such as the kinship system, which is more likely to simply change, with the traditional replaced by the new. Additionally, the study of the development of syncretic cultures or cultural institutions is one of historical and ethnohistorical reconstruction, the findings of which are open to various interpretations. To some extent, interest in New World syncretism has waned in recent years; interest has shifted to the unique features—both past and present—of indigenous and diaspora cultures in the New World.

One factor that does seem to affect syncretism is the extent to which new elements fit with the old. An ongoing worldwide syncretic phenomenon is the attraction of many Gypsy peoples (most of whom are Roman Catholic) to Pentecostalism (both religions merged with some uniquely Gypsy beliefs and practices) due to the fit between aspects of Pentecostalism and the Gypsy ethos. For example, the Piemontese Sinti of northern Italy have been drawn to Pentecostalism by its use of miracle cures and divine revelation, which fit Sinti interests; the ease of becoming a minister (celibacy is not required); the ease of ministering (which is allowed in the Sinti language); and the communal nature of the rites, which bring different communities together.

See also ASSIMILATION; MIXED-ANCESTRY PEOPLES.

Apter, Andrew. (1991) "Herskovits's Heritage: Rethinking Syncretism in the African Diaspora." *Diaspora* 1: 235–260.

Bastide, Roger. (1960) *The African Religions of Brazil: Toward a Sociology of Interpretation of Civilizations.* Translated by H. Sebba.

Coelho, Ruy G. (1955) *The Black Carib of Honduras: A Study in Acculturation.*

Courlander, H., and Rémy Bastien, eds. (1966) *Religion and Politics in Haiti.*

Formoso, Bernard. (1992) "Piemontese Sinti." In *Encyclopedia of World Cultures. Volume 4, Europe,* edited by Linda A. Bennett, 199–201.

Herskovits, Melville J. (1966) *The New World Negro: Selected Papers in Afroamerican Studies.*

Murphy, Joseph M. (1988) *Santería: An African Religion in America.*

currently living in exile in India). The Dalai Lama is a Buddhist monk believed upon death to reincarnate as a small child who resumes leadership. Although accurate numbers are difficult to find, as many as one-fifth of the male population of Tibet have traditionally been Lamas, or monks. Tibetans are highly devoted to Buddhism and the Dalai Lama himself, and have remained devout in their adherence despite 43 years of Communist rule. The Tibetan language belongs to the Tibeto-Burma group, and is widely spoken, although Chinese is encouraged and taught in schools.

Tibetan Himalayan kingdoms may have appeared as early as the fourth century A.D. Recorded history indicates their presence by the seventh century, about the time when Buddhism became established. Tibetan Buddhism is based on a combination of beliefs and practices from Indian Buddhism, Tantrism, and indigenous religions. From A.D. 632 to 842, the Tibetan Empire ruled much of central Asia; it was during this period that Buddhism became a central feature of Tibetan culture and identity as a distinct ethnic group in the region. From the 1300s to the middle 1600s, a series of secular and theocratic dynasties ruled, with the Yellow Hat sect of Tibetan Buddhism and the Dalai Lama gaining control in about 1642 and ruling for 300 years. China claims that its sovereignty over the region goes back 1,300 years. China controlled all of Tibet from at least the 1700s, although for a period of 38 years in the early twentieth century, Tibet essentially ruled itself and had little administrative contact with the rest of China. During this period, from 1912 to 1950, China's central government was weak and engaged in civil war for some time. As a result, the remote and self-contained region of Tibet enjoyed de facto independence and self-rule. Several nations dealt with Tibet as if it were independent, but this was largely because of convenience and ease. It is important to note that no nation has ever formally recognized Tibet as an independent

TIBETANS IN CHINA

An autonomous region within the People's Republic of China, Tibet covers 470,000 square miles. Tibet's average elevation above sea level is approximately 12,000 feet; the region is bordered by the Himalayas on the south and the Kunluns on the north. Tibetans refer to themselves with names indicating geographical location or tribal group names. The Tibet Autonomous Region (its official name in China) borders India and Nepal; roads connect the region to the rest of China. It is a vast area, though thinly populated. The 1990 Chinese census lists 4.5 million Tibetans in China, about 2.25 million in Tibet, and the others in Qinghai, Gansu, Sichuan, and Yunnan provinces, where a number of autonomous districts have been designated for them. More than 100,000 refugees live in India and about 14,000 in Nepal. It is likely that more Han Chinese than Tibetans now live in Tibet, and in the plateau region they clearly outnumber the Tibetans. Tibetans are Buddhists, and for over 300 years they have been ruled by the Dalai Lama (the fourteenth Dalai Lama is

nation, and international law has no clear precedents that allow independence on the basis of historical occupancy. For their part, Tibetans see their nation as illegally occupied by the Chinese; the Chinese, of course, consider it as part of China.

In October 1950 the Chinese People's Liberation Army began to move into Tibet. It was not technically an invasion, because Tibet was officially a part of China. The self-rule of the previous 38 years, however, and the Tibetans' definition of themselves as ethnically distinct and politically separate from the Han Chinese led the Tibetans to feel that their nation had been invaded by an external force. In October of that year, Tibetan and Chinese forces faced each other at Chamdo, and Tibet was crushed. In the years since the so-called peaceful liberation of Tibet, a series of uprisings against Chinese control has been put down. The largest uprising occurred in 1959 in Lhasa, the capital of Tibet, in which at least 600 people were killed, according to Chinese sources. Tibetans estimated the death toll as much higher. The Dalai Lama fled to India, and nearly 100,000 Tibetans followed him. This exile community, centered in Dharamsala, has been the source of much information regarding the Tibetan point of view of the situation in Tibet. Although many consider Tibetan reports to be exaggerated, they are used to balance Chinese government reports, which are also viewed with some skepticism.

The Chinese Cultural Revolution, which took place from 1966 to 1979, was effective in damaging Tibetan culture. During the revolution, nearly all Tibetan monasteries, scriptures, and other historical and cultural material were systematically destroyed, and the practice of Buddhism was widely suppressed. The policy of the Cultural Revolution was the destruction of the four "Olds:" old thought, old culture, old traditions, old customs. In a land that was once home to between 3,000 and 4,000 monasteries and religious monuments, only 13 survived the

revolution, and perhaps as few as 200 have been rebuilt since then. The Chinese government claimed that Tibetans themselves were active participants in the destruction.

In April 1980 the Central Committee of the Chinese Communist party held special meetings to determine new policies for Tibet. As a result of the subsequent investigative visits to the region, a series of six new policies were instituted to develop a more prosperous and educated Tibet Autonomous Region, including the lifting of taxes, a substantial loosening of the restrictions on religion, granting greater economic support to the region, allowing freer expression of Tibetan culture, and giving greater responsibility to Tibetan administrators.

Today, the Chinese government claims to have helped spur the economic development of the region. On a broad scale, much greater religious freedom is allowed than ever before within Communist China, although in some regions pictures of the Dalai Lama are still forbidden in public places and many Han Chinese continue to regard Tibetan beliefs as primitive. The Tibetans, for their part, tend to view the Chinese as overly materialistic, a perception supported by Chinese control of industry and businesses in Tibet. Although Tibetans may enjoy a more modern and prosperous existence, many still feel that they are a separate culture and nation from the Chinese and should be independent. Public displays of these sentiments have been swiftly repressed by the Chinese, who in 1989 imposed martial law for 14 months in response to anti-Chinese protests by monks and nuns. The lifting of the martial law in 1990 was followed by an increase in the flow of Tibetan refugees to Nepal and India. In May 1993 what began as a relatively small (125 people) protest against inflation quickly grew in size and intensity, and shifted to a much more political agenda. Tibetans in exile are particularly critical of the Chinese practice of *thamzing*. Thamzing is a form of torture, confession, and public punishment in which a wrongdoer is confronted by family and community members, who participate out of fear of enduring thamzing themselves. It is unclear what possible solution may be reached, as China is unlikely to relinquish control of Tibet, which it has officially controlled since the eighteenth century.

More than 100,000 Tibetans live in India, a community established more than 30 years ago. Since 1986 some 14,000 refugees have made their way to India via Nepal. The Indian government allows them free entry and residence. Tibetan refugees in Nepal number 14,000, again dating to the 1959 exile. Many are permanently settled there and involved in the prosperous carpet-weaving industry. Most refugees who enter Nepal now only pass through on their way to India. Discussions between the Tibetans and the Chinese have not led to the Dalai Lama's return, even as a strictly religious leader, and the Chinese are adamant in their refusal to discuss the possibility of Tibetan independence or autonomy.

French, Rebecca. (1993) *The Golden Yoke: The Legal System of Buddhist Tibet.*

Mullin, Chris, and Phuntsog Wangyal. (1983) *The Tibetans: Two Perspectives on Tibetan-Chinese Relations.*

Snellgrove, David, and Hugh Richardson. (1980) *A Cultural History of Tibet.*

TIMORESE IN INDONESIA

The Atoni are the original inhabitants of the island of Timor, part of the Lesser Sundas archipelago that runs east of Java. The population of the entire island of Timor is approximately 1.51 million. Timor has been settled for thousands of years, not falling under European colonization until around 1520, when the Portuguese arrived on a search for sandalwood. By the end of the sixteenth century, Timor was Portuguese territory, the sandalwood export industry was established, and Christianity was gaining an increased number of converts.

Beginning in 1613 the Dutch waged a campaign to gain control of Timor and the surrounding islands. This came to fruition in 1849, when they finally gained control of West Timor. In 1949 West Timor was granted freedom from the Netherlands, with the exception of the small enclave called Oecusse Ambeno, which remained under Portuguese rule. Approximately 900,000 people now live in West Timor, and 550,900 in East Timor, the majority of whom are Roman Catholic. However, accurate demographic information has not been available for some time.

Despite continued rebellions, East Timor remained under Portuguese control until 1974. At that time Portugal determined that maintaining its colonies was no longer in its best interest, the main consideration being the rising cost of keeping control over various principalities that were actively resisting Portuguese rule. Taking its cue from revolutionary African leaders, East Timor formed FRETILIN *(Frente Revolucionaria do Timor Leste Independente,* or the Revolutionary Front of East Timor). On 28 November 1975 FRETILIN declared the colony to be independent and renamed it the Democratic Republic of East Timor. Though the Portuguese government and the government of East Timor had undergone negotiations that would have allowed for complete independence in 1978, civil war prevailed and FRETILIN became the de facto government. Portugal never formally recognized this early independence even though it was preparing to grant independence.

Independence did not last long. An Indonesian invasion of East Timor came almost immediately after the declaration of the Democratic

Republic of East Timor. Indonesia was motivated by a number of considerations, the two key ones being the difficulty it would face in invading East Timor later after it was accepted as an independent nation by the international community, and Indonesia's desire to discourage other peoples from seeking independence. The nations of the world did nothing to stop this invasion, perhaps because Western nations were most interested in supporting the development of a stable, non-Communist government in Indonesia. In any case, there was no attempt to stop or punish Indonesia's blatant disregard for international law, although Indonesian rule of East Timor is not recognized by any of the members of the United Nations (U.N.). Despite persistent reports of human rights violations including torture, execution, and religious persecution of the Atoni, who continue to resist Indonesian control even 18 years later, little international action has been taken to reverse the situation. Indonesians are predominantly Muslim, while Timorese are mainly Roman Catholic. Immediately prior to the invasion, population estimates for East Timor averaged around 650,000. In 1980 that number had been reduced to about 550,000 (according to Indonesian officials), nearly 15 percent less. Other sources claim the population has been reduced by as much as 50 percent. These deaths are a result of fighting, executions, and famine: The Indonesian government has taken to the destruction of crops in an effort to starve the people into submission.

Until recently, efforts to pass a U.N. resolution criticizing Indonesia for its blatant and extreme violation of human rights had been blocked by Australia and Japan, as well as the United States, all of whom have strong economic interests in Indonesia. With a new administration, the United States shifted its support to the European Community's effort to pass such a resolution, and in March 1993 the first such resolution passed. International attention was drawn to the issue in November 1993, when Indone-

sian security forces opened fire on a crowd of Timorese who had gathered at the funeral of a supporter of East Timorese independence. At least 50 people were killed, but death reports ranged up to 200. Also in 1993, Indonesia and Portugal agreed to hold talks to find a solution acceptable to both countries. Having never formally relinquished control over East Timor, Portugal is now advocating self-determination, but Indonesia claims that the East Timorese have chosen to be part of Indonesia. Most observers believe it unlikely that the East Timorese would choose to remain a part of a nation that has carried out a policy of intimidation, torture, and persecution for the entire duration of its presence.

Ormeling, F. J. (1956) *The Timor Problem: A Geographical Interpretation of an Underdeveloped Island.*

Sherlock, Kevin. (1980) *A Bibliography of Timor.*

Suter, Keith. (1982) *East Timor and West Irian.*

TOURISM

More people travel to other nations and encounter people from other ethnic groups through tourism than by any other means. Tourism is now the world's largest economic enterprise, generating some $400 billion each year. While the largest number of tourists today come from the major industrialized nations of the world—the United States, Canada, Great Britain, Germany, France, Scandinavia, Japan, Switzerland, and Italy—no nation is untouched by the effects of tourism. A tourist "is a temporarily leisured person who voluntarily visits a place away from home for the purpose of experiencing a change." (Smith 1989, 1) Tourists and mass tourism are essentially twentieth-century phenomena, and tourism has become a major source of revenue in many nations since the end of World War II. Prior to the twentieth century, tourism was mainly an activity of the wealthy, who spent portions of the year at second residences located in a more desirable climate. The recent growth of tourism, and especially travel to other regions of one's own nation or other nations, is a product of industrial and postindustrial society. Among specific factors that have facilitated tourism are the shorter work week, longer and paid vacation periods each year, two-income families, consumer credit to finance vacations, early retirement, increased longevity, and a decrease in the desire to save money. Rapid and relatively low cost air travel and the internationalization of the hotel industry, which allows the provision of homelike accommodations virtually anywhere in the world, have facilitated the rapid growth of tourism.

Types of Tourism

Anthropologist Valene Smith notes that tourism comes in five major forms: ethnic, cultural, historical, environmental, and recreational. All forms bring members of different ethnic groups into contact and therefore all have potential implications for ethnic relations.

Ethnic tourism generally takes the form of organized tours, often with a professional guide such as an anthropologist or a member of the host group, that place the members of the tourist group in direct contact with members of the host ethnic group. The purpose of ethnic tourism is to allow the tourists to experience a culture that is markedly different from their own. The experience can take the form of observing ceremonies and dances within their cultural context, visits to homes, shopping in stores owned by members of the host group that sell art or handcrafts manufactured by host artisans, and tours of the community. Ethnic tours may focus on one culture or cover a number of different cultures; for example, some tours to the Ameri-

can Southwest include visits to both Apachean and Pueblo communities. Depending on the languages spoken and the inclinations and personalities of the tourists and hosts, ethnic tourism may provide the opportunity for informal face-to-face interaction between tourists and hosts. Ethnic tourism might involve the observation of many features of a culture, as in visits to Pueblo communities in the southwestern United States where tourists can observe the daily public life of the community, or it may only involve the observation of certain cultural features, such as the architecture and funeral ceremonies of the Toradja in Indonesia or initiation ceremonies of the Chambri in Papua New Guinea. Ethnic tourists are a self-selected group, often with an interest in learning about and understanding the culture they are visiting. However, as they often have stereotypical (positive and negative) images of the culture and spend little time visiting, ethnic tourism rarely produces any real long-term change in knowledge or attitudes about other cultures.

Cultural tourism is similar to ethnic tourism, although the focus is on an often idealized or reconstructed representation of a culture or cultural tradition. In both types of tourism, a primary motivation for the tourist is a "search for authenticity," which, it has been suggested, is lacking in the industrialized and post-industrialized societies that produce most tourists. Cultural tourism has many different examples: powwows marketed to the general public, American Indian fairs, and rodeos; living recreations of maritime, farming, rural communities, and such diverse communities as the Cajuns and Shakers; cultural centers, such as Rotorua in New Zealand, the Polynesian Cultural Center in Hawaii, and the Indian Pueblo Cultural Center in New Mexico; as well as dance, music, and theater performances and art and handcrafts produced for tourists. Depending on the situation, contact between tourists and members of the host community may by limited or frequent. However, since the representation of the host culture is meant to attract and entertain the tourists, cultural tourism usually results in an oversimplification and standardization of the host culture. What is displayed of the culture is mostly the material aspects, in the form of tools, weapons, clothing, boats, and houses, and expressive culture in the form of dance, music, and theater, which can be appreciated at an aesthetic level by tourists who may have no knowledge of the culture. Cultural tourism is extremely popular with tourists and often financially beneficial to the host community.

Historical tourism is the veneration of the past, largely through visits to important sites in Western and other civilizations such as Rome, Athens, Jerusalem, the Yucatan Peninsula, and Angor Wat in Cambodia. Historical tourism is nearly always linked to a highly developed tourist industry in both the tourist and host nations. Interest in the host culture is usually incidental or secondary, and contact between tourists and local people is mostly economic, with the former purchasing and the latter providing products and services.

Environmental tourism, or ecotourism, is travel to usually distant and often remote places to see and experience a different environment. For Western and East Asian tourists, these include tropical rainforests in Southeast Asia and South America, savannah lands in Africa, and the mountains of northern south Asia. When the regions are also the home of non-Western cultures, ethnic tourism is often combined with environmental tourism, and the indigenous peoples are then brought into the tourist industry both as attractions and as providers of goods and services.

Recreational tourism offers relaxation in an environment or enjoyment of activities that are not available at home. Recreational tourism often centers around warm, sunny locales with water at hand for such activities as swimming and boating, and also often involves the pursuit of enjoyment through sports. Recreational tourism is seasonal, with the summer months and long vacation periods drawing most tourists. The effect of recreational tourism on non-Western cultures is unclear, and different observers often arrive at different conclusions regarding the positive versus negative effects on the local community.

Effects of Tourism

All forms of tourism began expanding rapidly in the non-Western world in the 1960s as political leaders, developers, and the tourist industry reacted to and helped to create a demand for international tourism. Initially, tourism was thought to be a relatively inexpensive form of economic development in Third World nations and economically struggling regions situated in warm, sunny climates with interesting sites and indigenous peoples. Thus, various tourism development plans were enacted in New Zealand; many smaller Pacific islands such as Fiji and Tonga; Indonesian islands such as Java, Bali, and Sulawesi; Spain; the southwestern United States; both the Pacific and Caribbean coasts of Mexico and Central America; and various locales in South America. While the effects of tourism are widely discussed by experts, it is important to remember that tourism is usually but one component of a broader pattern of socioeconomic development, and as such may not be the cause, or perhaps may be only a partial cause, of effects attributed to it.

In general, the economic effects of tourism have not been as beneficial as originally believed. One major problem is that tourism is not as cheap or as reliable an income generator as originally predicted. Seasonal fluctuations, natural disasters such as hurricanes, shifts in tourist interests, and the effects of recessions in tourist-providing nations all make tourism an unpredictable and uncontrollable economic investment for the host nation. Additionally, developing a tourist industry and keeping it competitive with other nations requires considerable expense to construct and expand airports, enlarge ports, and build and maintain roads, all of which are paid for by the host nation or with money borrowed from Western nations or international organizations, which must be repaid with interest. Other tourist facilities such as hotels, casinos, and restaurants are often financed and owned by outsiders, who remove the profits from the local economy. Some estimates suggest that 80 percent of tourist dollars spent in Third World nations are returned to the Western world.

For the people themselves, reliance on tourism often brings either a decline in, or an end to, the traditional economic system based on agriculture and the domestic production of food, and involves the people in the international money economy. This involvement often takes the form of the sale of land to developers, employment in low-wage service jobs (porters, waiters, and maids), and the commercialization of aspects of the traditional culture; that is, the sale of dances, art, music, and religious practices to tourists.

These economic changes are sometimes accompanied by social changes, including an increase in prostitution, drug use, and crime; conflicts over political power; factionalism between traditionalists and those who prefer to participate in the tourism; and the destruction of the traditional culture.

At the same time, it is obvious that the effects of tourism are not always negative. Among the benefits are the retention of traditional customs that might have otherwise disappeared if not for the tourist market, the re-creation of pride in one's cultural heritage among indigenous peoples who have suffered under colonialism, the calling of attention to fragile or disappearing cultures or environments, and the creation of employment, particularly for younger members of the community.

As regards the effect of tourism on ethnic relations, the effect on individual tourists depends on the type of tourists they are. Those who seek only diversion or adventure may be little influenced by contact with another culture, while those seeking authenticity, a learning experience, or a new sense of their place in the world may be profoundly affected by their cross-cultural encounter. In general, however, it appears that no form of tourism seems to enhance relations between Westerners and indigenous peoples. Rather, because of the preconceived ideas with which tourists arrive, the performance nature of much ethnic and cultural tourism, and the limited contact between the tourists and hosts, tourism has little direct effect on ethnic relations. It is possible that in some cases the effect is to increase hostility, especially in postcolonial situations where the hosts see government-imposed tourism as the continuation of colonial domination.

Experiences with tourism in three different cultures point to the variety of effects it can have on non-Western cultures. Tourism has been a mostly positive experience for the Mashantucket Pequot of eastern Connecticut, who in 1991 opened what has become an extraordinarily profitable gambling casino on their reservation. The casino has made the Pequot rich, provided thousands of jobs for their white neighbors in an economically depressed region, and has become a model for other American Indian nations seeking to open or expand gambling operations.

For the Basques in a seacoast community in northern Spain, the effects of tourism have been mixed. Because of its location, the community is an ideal tourist destination, offering an airport, fishing, sailing, beaches, golf, restaurants, and quaint shops that attract over 40,000 people each year to a village of 10,000. Tourism has raised the value of local land, increased the standard of living, created economic security, made families into independent economic units, and increased the size and upward mobility of the middle class. But it has also produced family battles over the inheritance of family property, made the townsfolk dependent on tourism, isolated families and made them vulnerable to outside developers, and left the aged without a social-support network.

The experience of the African-American Sea Islanders of the Georgia and South Carolina coastal islands has been largely negative. Development of the islands for tourism began in the early 1950s; developers bought up much of the Sea Islanders' land on some islands such as Hilton Head, and built hotels, condominiums, shopping centers, restaurants, golf courses, and other facilities for year-round retirees and seasonal tourists. As Sea Islanders say, "everything change up now," meaning that they own less land, are a minority population on many major islands, pay higher taxes, face high unemployment, work mainly as low-paid service workers, send their children to schools dominated by white values, are ridiculed for speaking their traditional Gullah language, and see the wildlife and marshlands threatened by pollution and overdevelopment.

Tourism and Indigenous Arts

Art, produced and sold by host peoples, is often a key component of ethnic, cultural, and environmental tourism. As with tourism in general, interest in indigenous art as an art form rather than as a cultural curiosity is a twentieth-century development. The demand for indigenous art by outsiders, and outsiders' taste in art and ability to pay, has led to major changes in indigenous art forms. Anthropologist Nelson Graburn places these changes into seven broad categories. First is the disappearance of a traditional art form, an event that is actually quite rare. Second is the appearance of contact-influenced art, in which the basic form and cultural role of the art remains the same, although new tools may be used or there may be small changes in technique. Third is the appearance

of commercial fine arts that are produced in the same way as traditional art, but for sale to outsiders rather than for indigenous use. Fourth is the appearance of souvenir art—items mass-produced cheaply with little or no concern for traditional style or technique, and meant for sale to tourists. Fifth is a shift in art style to reintegrated art forms that combine traditional styles with introduced techniques or materials. Sixth is the development of assimilated fine arts when an artist adapts the art form of outsiders. Seventh is the development of popular arts when an artist uses outside forms to express traditional themes.

Brameld, T., and M. Matsuyama. (1977) *Tourism as Cultural Learning: Two Controversial Case Studies in Educational Anthropology*.

Cohen, Erik. (1979) "A Phenomenology of Tourist Experiences." *Sociology* 13: 179–201.

Crick, Malcolm. (1989) "Representations of International Tourism in the Social Sciences: Sun, Sex, Sights, Savings, and Servility." In *Annual Review of Anthropology*, edited by Bernard J. Siegel, 307–344.

Gewertz, Deborah, and Frederick Errington. (1991) *Twisted Histories, Altered Contexts: Representing the Chambri in a World System*.

Graburn, Nelson H. H., ed. (1976) *Ethnic and Tourist Arts: Cultural Expression from the Third World*.

Graburn, Nelson H. H., and J. Jafari, eds. (1991) "Tourism Social Sciences." Special Issue of *Annals of Tourism Research* 18.

Greenwood, Davydd J. (1972) "Tourism as an Agent of Change: A Spanish Basque Case." *Ethnology* 11: 80–91.

Harrison, David, ed. (1992) *Tourism and the Less Developed Countries*.

Jones-Jackson, Patricia. (1987) *When Roots Die: Endangered Traditions on the Sea Islands*.

MacCannell, Dean. (1992) *Empty Meeting Grounds: The Tourist Papers.*

Smith, Valene L., ed. (1989) *Hosts and Guests: The Anthropology of Tourism.* 2d ed.

Turner, L., and J. Ash. (1975) *The Golden Hordes: International Tourism and the Pleasure Periphery.*

TRANSNATIONAL MIGRATION

Transnational migration refers to the process through which migrants maintain ties to their homeland, therefore implying that migrants live in a world in which they routinely cross national and cultural boundaries. Much of the boundary crossing takes place through various ties with one's family, household, wider kinship network, and local community in one's nation of origin. Thus, from the transnational perspective, a migrant is not simply an isolated individual who lives and works in a new and distant land, but someone who remains intimately and regularly linked to others in his or her homeland; in fact, it may be these ties that motivate or enable him or her to migrate. Transnational ties take a wide variety of forms, including the sending of remittances to family members; return to the nation of origin; regular contact through mail and phone calls; chain migration, in which individuals from the same region, local community, or family follow earlier migrants; political ties through political organizations in the host nation; economic support of political movements in the homeland; the sending of clothes and food from the homeland to immigrants; temporary residence with and other types of support from earlier immigrants upon arrival in the host nation; the provision of child care in the homeland; and reverse remittances, among others. While the exact types of ties tend to vary from situation to situation, in most situations they tend to form the basis for ongoing networks of social interaction.

Transnational migration is but one of a wide range of transnational flows in the modern world. Major types of flows include:

1. The flow of people through economic migration, tourism, asylum, exile, etc.

2. The flow of technology and information to support the technology and its use, primarily through multinational corporations and international development projects

3. The flow of money, investments, and capital investment

4. The flow of information, images, and symbols through magazines, newspapers, television, and film

5. The flow of ideas and values

A major and ongoing debate among social scientists about these flows is whether they are leading to a world community or whether they are producing cultural variation around the world.

Although transnational ties have characterized virtually all immigrant situations throughout human history, they now appear to be a more central and ongoing feature of immigration than in the past. To some extent this is due to the relative ease with which migrants today can communicate with the homeland and travel back and forth via airplane. When we contrast the ease of modern communication and transportation with that available to nineteenth- and early twentieth-century immigrants to the United States and Canada, it is understandable why transmigration is a more common feature of immigration today than in the past, and why it is easier for migrants to maintain a bicultural lifestyle and, over time, develop a bicultural identity that enables them to function effectively and alternatively in two cultures. At the same time, homeland ties were strong for earlier generations of migrants, and remain so for many today, as evidenced by political and economic support for independence movements in the homeland, the maintenance of ethnic associations in the host nation, and tourism to explore one's roots.

In a broader sense, assuming that transmigration represents a new type of migration pattern, it may also be due to changes in the world economic system, the movement toward a world order, and the involvement of far more workers at all levels of national economies in an expanding world system that crosses national boundaries.

Traditional social-science explanations for the flow of migrant workers generally emphasized the push-pull, supply-demand, and assimilation aspects of the situation in which immigrants cross national boundaries. Push-pull suggests that higher wages in some nations attract workers who make lower wages or live in poverty in other nations. Supply-demand suggests that a demand for workers or certain types of workers, such as domestics or low-skilled workers, in one nation is matched by a surplus of qualified workers in another nation. Following the European experience in the United States, it is assumed that many of these workers and their families will assimilate to the dominant culture in the host nation, and ties to the homeland will weaken markedly. The transnational approach provides a different interpretation in that it stresses the soft or fluid nature of many national boundaries and the economic and political linkages among nations and institutions within them; while not ignoring the push-pull and supply-demand elements, this approach also emphasizes the cross-cultural nature of immigration in the modern world.

One exceedingly common form of transnationalism is the flow of money from the immigrant community to the homeland. This often takes the form of remittances, in which a portion of what is earned in the host nation is sent to family in the homeland. In many oceanic societies with large overseas populations, such as Tonga and Samoa, remittances are now a major element of the local economy. Formerly subsistence economies have turned into consumer economies, in which remittances returned from relatives in the West (Australia, New Zealand, the United States) allow those in the homeland to purchase goods produced in the West. Remittances are extremely common elsewhere as well, and are a worldwide phenomenon.

Wealth flows from immigrant communities back to the homeland in other ways as well. One pattern is for those who have lived and worked overseas to return to the homeland, using money saved to purchase property or invest in a business in the homeland. For example, returnees to southern Italy from the United States often purchase small farms, while Yemenis who work in Saudi Arabia, upon their return to Yemen, often invest in small shops and services, most of which supply or service consumer goods purchased with remittances sent by migrants still outside Yemen. Thus, remittances and wealth brought back upon return to the home community tend to involve the community in the international marketplace as consumers of products produced elsewhere. This demand for consumer goods creates a demand for more money, which in turn requires continued migration in search of wage labor when such labor is unavailable or poorly paid in the homeland. The return of Yemeni workers to the homeland also has a cultural dimension in that they must show that they are loyal to the community and still adhere to local customs before they are completely reintegrated into community life.

For Dominican immigrants to the United States, the accumulation of wealth is important as a way of achieving middle-class social status in the homeland. Upon return, their status is demonstrated by the conspicuous consumption of Western-produced consumer goods. Again, as in Yemen and elsewhere, a circular pattern is created at the local level in which family, kinship, and community ties mesh with patterns of wealth distribution in the overarching context of international business and the international division of labor.

Another form of economic tie to the homeland is capital investment in economic institutions in the homeland. Such investment, of course, only takes place when the overseas community amasses significant wealth. This pattern prevails among post-1965 Indian immigrants to the United States who, arriving as professionals, have amassed much wealth (through work, two-income families, and frugality), which some have invested in India. Some investments have gone to support the development of new businesses, banks, and industries, while others have taken the form of bonds or savings accounts. The experience of these immigrants, called Non-Resident Indians (NRIs) points to many of the international and human issues involved in transnational migration. The NRIs are torn between their satisfactory life in the United States and loyalty to India, and maintain regular contact with friends and relatives, read the Indian popular press, and inculcate their children with Indian beliefs and customs. The Indian government and business community use this loyalty to India to encourage investment, although there is also resentment that the nonresident community plays such an active role in Indian politics and its economy. From the viewpoint of ethnic relations, the role and status of the NRI community raise basic questions about what it means to be Indian and the ability of an individual to have two cultural identities.

Beyond its economic effects listed above, transnational migration has major repercussions on the structure and processes of gender relations, child rearing, the family, and the community, both in the homeland and overseas. However, these repercussions are dependent on a variety of factors beyond the immigrant experience, including the nature of the family or relationships before immigration, the type of immigration, and generational changes in patterns of immigration, therefore showing no clear pattern across cultures.

See also ASSIMILATION; DIASPORA; ETHNIC IDENTITY AND SOLIDARITY; ETHNIC MEDIA; MIGRANT WORKERS; REFUGEES; TOURISM.

Appadurai, Arjun. (1990) "Disjuncture and Difference in the Global Cultural Economy." In *Global Culture: Nationalism, Globalization and Modernity*, edited by Michael Featherstone, 295–310.

Colton, Nora A. (1993) "Homeward Bound: Yemeni Return Migration." *International Migration Review* 27: 870–882.

Grasmuck, Sherri, and Patricia R. Pessar. (1991) *Between Two Islands: Dominican International Migration.*

Lessinger, Johanna. (1992) "Investing or Going Home? A Transnational Strategy among Indian Immigrants in the United States." In *Towards a Transnational Perspective on Migration: Race, Class, Ethnicity, and Nationalism Reconsidered*, edited by Nina G. Schiller, Linda Basch, and Cristina Blanc-Szanton. Annals of the New York Academy of Sciences 645: 53–80.

Portes, Alejandro, and József Borocz. (1993) "Contemporary Immigration: Theoretical Perspectives on Its Determinants and Modes of Incorporation." *International Immigration Review* 23: 606–630.

Schiller, Nina G., Linda Basch, and Cristina Blanc-Szanton, eds. (1992) *Towards a Transnational Perspective on Migration: Race, Class, Ethnicity, and Nationalism Reconsidered.* Annals of the New York Academy of Sciences 645.

TRIBE

Tribe and *tribalism* are two terms used frequently and inconsistently in reference to ethnic groups around the world. The term *tribe* is used in four basic ways.

First, it has been used in cultural anthropology for about 100 years to refer to a specific category of society that displays a particular type of sociopolitical organization. In this typology, the non-Western, nonindustrialized societies of the world are classified as either bands, tribes, chiefdoms, or states. Tribal societies, who prior to dramatic cultural change resulting from contact with industrialized societies numbered several thousand, are characterized by an economy based on horticulture and/or pastoralism, social organization centered on village communities or kinship groups such as lineages or clans, an absence of social classes, little or only weak centralized political leadership, and relatively frequent warfare among villages. Thus, from this perspective, only some of the world's societies are tribes, and it is incorrect to refer to a group as a tribe unless it is of this sociopolitical type. Anthropologists have attempted to categorize all societies of the world (or at least all known, well-described societies—about 1,500 in all) using this band-tribe-chiefdom-state typology. However, in reference to societies today, the typology is difficult to apply because most cultures have changed markedly in the last 50 years. This typology also suggests an evolutionary progression throughout human history, for as one moves along the scale, each type of society is larger, is more complex, and exerts more control over its natural and social environment than the previous type.

The second usage of *tribe* also involves efforts to produce a typology of cultural types. However, here the attempt is less fine and subject to easier misinterpretation. In this sense, *tribe* refers to all so-called primitive cultures of the world, in contrast to all so-called civilized cultures. When used objectively, the term primitive cultures (small-scale, preliterate, nonliterate, nonindustrialized) refers to those at the low end of the scale of social, political, technological, and economic complexity, while civilized cultures are at the high end. For example, among the cultures of the indigenous New World at the time of first contact with Europeans, most of the hundreds of American Indian cultures would be considered tribal or primitive, while the Inca, Aztec, and Maya would be considered civilized. When used objectively in this way, such use of the concept of *tribe* is legitimate, although perhaps not very enlightening. However, the use of *tribe* or *tribal* as an equivalent for primitive, and in opposition to civilized, often opens the door for ethnocentric, simplistic, and sometimes racist interpretations. These interpretations have appeared recently in the use of the concept of *tribe* in discussions about the role and status of indigenous peoples around the world and multicultural education in the United States. At one extreme are those who take an ethnocentric, judgmental view of tribal culture. An example is the view expressed by historian Arthur Schlesinger, Jr., in his *The Disuniting of America.* Early on, he quotes the *Economist:* "The virus of tribalism," says the *Economist,* "...risks becoming the AIDS of international politics—lying dormant for years, then flaring up to destroy countries." (Schlesinger 1992, 11) His definition of tribalism becomes clear later: "As for tribalism, the word *tribe* hardly occurs in Afrocentric lexicon; but who can hope to understand African history without understanding the practices, loyalties, rituals, and blood-feuds of tribalism." (Schlesinger 1992, 78) This same view of tribalism as basically divisive also appears regularly in news reports of ethnic conflict in southeastern Europe in the early 1990s, despite the reality that none of the participants—Croats, Bosnian Muslims, Serbs, and Albanians— are tribes, following the definition discussed above.

At the other extreme are those who ignore some of the realities of tribal-level societal organization, and romanticize tribal life. For example, the July-August 1992 issue of the *Utne Reader* devotes nearly 40 pages to so-called "tribal cultures" and how the tribal way of life can serve as a model for a better world. The first paragraph of the article sums up this viewpoint:

> The majority of humans have lived tribally for about 495 of the last 500 generations, which encompasses the roughly 10,000 years of recorded history. Our ancestors lived in roving bands, small villages, and extended families, developing and refining the social graces necessary to keep their communities viable. But many of us in the West have wandered away from the community in search of some personal vision, perhaps the Holy Grail or the American Dream....Some of us still know how to live with one another and the environment—the last remaining tribal peoples.

This view also has little to do with the concept of *tribe* as it has been traditionally used by social scientists.

Third, *tribe* has been used as a concept to mark cultures as distinct social entities. Thus, in this usage, we refer to the Badaga tribe, the Kota tribe, the Kurumba tribe, and the Toda tribe, four neighboring groups of the Nilgiri Hills of south India. The use of the word *tribe* indicates that each is a separate social entity, distinct from other social entities. Thus, *tribe* is in some sense an equivalent concept to ethnic group, with *tribe* used more commonly for small non-Western cultures, and *ethnic group* for the present-day descendants of immigrants in new lands. Various attempts have been made to define the basic features of a tribe as it is used in this way, focusing on factors such as common territory, name, language, sense of common identity, religion, and technology. In general, however, when *tribe* has been used in this way, a group is usually identified as a distinct group because it speaks a language different from its neighbors, occupies a defined territory, and has a distinct name (although the name may be given by outsiders

rather than by the group itself). In the 1960s and 1970s there was rigorous debate among some anthropologists about how to objectively define and use *tribe* in this way. This issue was never resolved, and soon gave way to more immediate issues such as culture contact and culture change. Today, most anthropologists and other social scientists are usually willing to consider a group a distinct group (whether or not it is labeled a tribe) if the people themselves believe that they are a distinct group.

The fourth and final major usage of the term *tribe* involves specific legal and political arrangements that accrue to groups and the members of those groups in specific nations. In the United States, the designation of over 300 American Indian groups as *tribes* (or some related term such as *communities, towns, nations, bands, reservations, rancherias, colonies,* or *pueblos*) defines the legal and political relationships between the group and federal and state governments. Similarly, the designation of a group in India as a Scheduled Tribe indicates that the government considers it to be "backward," and that its members are eligble for special benefits not available to others. Thus, the label *tribe* takes on a clearly defined legal meaning that may have major political and economic consequences for the tribe, its members, and other members of the nation.

See also INDIGENOUS PEOPLES.

Ghurye, G. S. (1963) *The Scheduled Tribes.* 3d ed.

Native American Directory. (1982).

Sahlins, Marshall. (1968) *Tribesman.*

Schlesinger, Arthur M., Jr. (1992) *The Disuniting of America.*

Service, Elman R. (1962) *Primitive Social Organization.*

Winthrop, Robert H. (1991) *Dictionary of Concepts in Cultural Anthropology.*

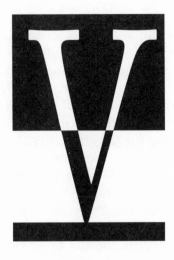

Vietnamese population is heavily concentrated in the plains and along the coast, and efforts to settle Vietnamese in the highlands have not been successful. Vietnam is officially an atheistic nation, although actual religious belief reflects a mixture of Buddhism, Confucianism, Taoism, ancestor worship, and animism.

The number of ethnic Vietnamese in Cambodia today is unknown, although in the early 1970s they numbered several hundred thousand. Mass executions, deportations, and fleeing reduced the population markedly in the late 1970s. The status of ethnic Vietnamese in Cambodia and their relationship with the Khmer and the national government need to be understood in the context of European colonization and involvement in the region dating to the nineteenth century.

The Khmer kingdom existed from A.D. 802–1432; after a period of decline and Thai and Vietnamese rule, it became a French colony (1864) and then, along with Laos and Vietnam, the Union of French Indochina (1884). Anti-Vietnamese sentiment among the Khmer dates to nineteenth-century Vietnamese efforts to take Cambodian territory and Cambodian perceptions that the Vietnamese sought to "civilize" them. Such a notion is insulting to the Cambodian elite, who consider themselves culturally superior to the Vietnamese. The French administration in Cambodia preferred to employ the Vietnamese in low-level administrative positions and also to import Vietnamese to work in craft industries and on plantations. By the early twentieth century, Cambodian nationalists began to use anti-Vietnamese rhetoric as one means of building a national consciousness, although only the urban elite, and not the rural peasants, were overtly anti-Vietnamese. Independence from France was achieved in 1953, and from then until 1970 Cambodia was ruled as a constitutional monarchy by Norodom Sihanouk. By the 1960s, if not earlier, an official policy had emerged in which Cambodian nationhood was linked to

VIETNAMESE IN CAMBODIA

Cambodia and Vietnam are neighboring nations in Southeast Asia, sharing a common border along the west of Vietnam and the east of Cambodia. From 1975 to 1989 Cambodia was officially called Kampuchea. The primary ethnic group in Cambodia is the Khmer, while the Vietnamese predominate in Vietnam. The Khmer (who called themselves Khmae) constituted about 90 percent of the estimated 9 million people in Cambodia in 1993. The remainder of the population is composed of Vietnamese, Chinese, Muslim Cham (also called Khmer Islam), and tribal peoples in the hill country of the north. The Khmer are mainly Theravada Buddhists, although the incorporation of local traditions places their religion outside mainstream Buddhism. The ethnic Vietnamese are the majority population in Vietnam, with an estimated national population of 71.8 million in 1993. Vietnam is also the home of numerous other ethnic groups, including Chinese, Hmong, Khmer, and numerous tribal groups in the highlands of both the north and south. The ethnic

Khmer ethnicity, the Khmer language, and Theravada Buddhism. Obviously, such a policy excluded the ethnic Vietnamese.

In 1970 Sihanouk was overthrown in a military coup, and Cambodia, now called the Khmer Republic, was ruled by Lon Nol until 1975 when the Communists, known as the Khmer Rouge, triumphed in a civil war. During the Vietnam War in the 1960s, the Vietnamese ran a portion of the Ho Chi Minh trail through Cambodia, and the United States secretly bombed Cambodia, creating tensions between Vietnam and Cambodia and, at least from the viewpoint of the Cambodian government, producing more evidence that the Vietnamese were to blame for the political and economic turmoil in Cambodia. Anti-Vietnamese sentiment continued as a government policy under Lon Nol, reaching new

extremes under the Khmer Rouge and their leader Pol Pot, whose agenda was a massive restructuring of Cambodian (called Kampuchea) society. This restructuring included relocating people from cities to rural areas, forming collectivized work organizations, banning Buddhism, mass executions, and restricting the flow of food, clothing, and shelter, which led to hundreds of thousands of deaths. As for the Vietnamese in Cambodia, the Khmer Rouge expelled many in the east near the Vietnamese border, killed thousands of others, and through harsh treatment forced still others to flee to Vietnam. In addition, Cambodians thought to be friendly with Vietnamese were routinely killed as enemies of the state. In response to Cambodian raids into Vietnam, the Vietnamese invaded Cambodia in 1978; within a year they had driven out the Khmer

Mass execution site in Cambodia near Phnom Penh, 1981, showing remains of victims of the Pol Pot regime.

Rouge and installed a new Khmer government supported by Vietnamese officials and troops. Under the new government, anti-Vietnamese sentiment declined, although they (along with the Chinese) were still considered by some as ethnic foreigners. Critics of the new government charged that it was a puppet regime of Vietnam and that the Vietnamese were interested in destroying Cambodian culture.

By 1989 Vietnamese influence had waned, a new government was established, and Cambodia was renamed the state of Cambodia. However, Sihanouk supporters, the Khmer Rouge, and other factions refused to cooperate, and in 1991 a new coalition government was formed with U.N. supervision. Today, Cambodia is again governed by Sihanouk in a coalition with the victors of the 1993 election. The position of the Vietnamese in Cambodia—now diminished in number and influence—is still unsettled. Open discrimination has mostly disappeared, although not all Vietnamese have been granted Cambodian citizenship, and the Vietnamese fear that future political stability might lead to new attacks on their community.

Ablin, David, and Marlowe Hood, eds. (1984) *Cambodian Agony.*

Tarr, Chou Meng. (1992) "The Vietnamese Minority in Cambodia." *Race & Class* 34: 33–47.

Vickery, Michael. (1986) *Kampuchea: Politics, Economics, and Society.*

The world system, as an entity different from a world economy or world empire, is the single, capitalist world economy that has been evolving in Europe since the late fifteenth century. During that time Europe experienced considerable unrest from peasant revolts and wars, famine, depopulation, plagues, and a decline in economic productivity that threatened the control and security of the ruling feudal lords. The feudal lords turned to the then relatively weak nations for protection, which tended to strengthen the nations and open national boundaries for trade, which was controlled by the merchant class. Colonization, settlement, slavery, expanded trade, and other manifestations of European expansion continued the evolution of the world system over the centuries.

The world system consists of three elements or sets of components in continual relation with one another—core, periphery, and semiperiphery—which are economically linked to form the world system. The core consists of militarily strong, stable, bureaucratic nations with large professional and skilled labor forces and high productivity. Ethnic relations in the economic sphere of core nations are characterized by a professional class dominated by members of the major ethnic group, a class of workers representing a mix of groups, and a class of low-skilled workers consisting mainly of members of ethnic minority groups. The core corresponds to what is called the First World, and includes nations such as the United States, Germany, Sweden, and Japan. The periphery consists of weak, politically unstable nations, many of which have come into existence following the end of colonialism with inefficient, repressive governments. Ethnic relations in these nations are characterized by a ruling and professional class dominated by ethnic groups favored by the European colonists, a working class of indigenous peoples who have migrated from the rural regions to urban centers, and a subsistence- or semisubsistence-level sector composed of rural, indigenous peoples. Sometimes these small, indigenous cultures are thought to be outside the world system; however, they are not, and one survey of 87 cultures shows that all were negatively influenced by the world system, with the basic subsistence patterns changed or destroyed in 84 percent. The semi-periphery corresponds to what is called the Third and Fourth worlds (although some cultures in the Fourth World are also found in the periphery), and includes nations such as Bolivia, Zaire, and Cambodia. The semiperiphery occupies an intermediary position between the core and periphery, and in fact many of the nations here were formerly in the core or in the periphery. Semiperipheral nations are national middlemen, importing and exporting products from each of the other two sectors. Both the ruling and professional classes are dominated by the major ethnic group, while indigenous peoples or ethnic minorities form somewhat separate communities. China,

Canada, and Egypt are examples of semiperipheral nations. In addition to these spheres (which are better seen as relations, as they are in constant interaction with one another), the key features of the world system are the component nations and capitalism.

A consideration of the world as a world system joined together through ongoing economic relations (and also, to a lesser extent, political relations) has implications for the nature and patterning of ethnic relations around the world. In this view, ethnic relations are mainly the result of the relative position of an ethnic group in the world division of labor. Specific considerations that influence the status of any group and ethnic relations are the nation's place in the world system, its ethnic composition, the relationship between social classes, and ethnic distinctions. Ethnic conflict is explained as beneficial to the world system because ethnic groups in peripheral nations provide an exploitable labor pool, and because ethnic conflict inhibits the development of a broader class-based consciousness that would be a greater threat to the world system.

See also COLONIALISM; DIASPORA; MIGRANT WORKERS; REFUGEES; TRANSNATIONAL MIGRATION.

Bradley, Candace, et al. (1990) "A Cross-Cultural Historical Study of Subsistence Change." *American Anthropologist* 92: 447–457.

Thompson, Richard H. (1989) *Theories of Ethnicity: A Critical Appraisal.*

Wallerstein, Imanuel. (1974) *The Modern World-System, I: Capitalist Agriculture and the Origins of the European World-Economy in the Sixteenth Century.*

———. (1979) *The Capitalist World-Economy.*

Wolf, Eric. (1984) *Europe and the People without a History.*

Nazis on Turks and other foreigners in Germany as *xenophobic.*

Little is known cross-culturally about which emotions and behaviors are in fact xenophobic, whether or not xenophobia occurs in all individuals and all cultures, whether it is rational or irrational, and its origins. Xenophobia is linked to ethnocentrism, although not all forms of ethnocentrism involve the extreme hatred and fear that define xenophobia.

See also ETHNOCENTRISM.

Allport, Gordon W. (1954) *The Nature of Prejudice.*

Shaw, Paul R., and Yuwa Wong. (1989) *Genetic Seeds of Warfare: Evolution, Nationalism, and Patriotism.*

Sluckin, M. (1979) *Fear in Animals and Man.*

XENOPHOBIA Xenophobia is an emotional state characterized by a fear, hatred, or aversion to outsiders or foreigners. Xenophobia also refers to behaviors meant to harm or exclude outsiders that presumably result from these feelings of hate and fear. In the context of ethnic relations, foreigners or outsiders are members of other ethnic, religious, racial, or national groups. Xenophobia is an individual psychological state in that it is individuals, rather than groups, who experience it. However, the concept is sometimes used in reference to alleged group sentiments and behavior, such as descriptions of German or French efforts to restrict settlement by people from other nations and attacks by German neo-

German Skinhead rally, 1992.

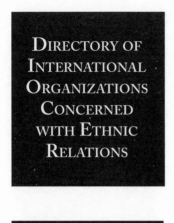

DIRECTORY OF INTERNATIONAL ORGANIZATIONS CONCERNED WITH ETHNIC RELATIONS

This section lists and describes some organizations whose mission is relevant to ethnic relations around the world today. Listed are only organizations whose focus is worldwide. Organizations whose focus is a particular ethnic group, nation, or region are not listed here. Many of these can be found listed in *Human Rights: A Reference Handbook* (ABC-CLIO, 1989) as well as various directories of organizations. Organizations whose names are followed by an asterisk (*) submitted the descriptions provided here or their descriptions are based mainly on information supplied by the organization for use in this volume.

AMNESTY INTERNATIONAL*
International Secretariat
1 Easton Street
London WC1X 8DJ
England

Amnesty International (AI) is a worldwide movement independent of any government, political grouping, ideology, economic interest, or religious creed. It plays a specific role within the overall spectrum of human rights work. The activities of the organization focus strictly on prisoners. It seeks the release of men and women detained anywhere for their beliefs, color, sex, ethnic origin, language, or religion, provided they have not used or advocated violence. These are termed *prisoners of conscience.* It advocates fair and early trials for all political prisoners and works on behalf of such persons detained without charge or without trial. It opposes the death penalty and torture or other cruel, inhuman, or degrading treatment or punishment of all prisoners, without reservation. Amnesty International also opposes abuses by opposition groups: hostage taking, torture and killings of prisoners, and other arbitrary killings. Amnesty International, recognizing that human rights are indivisible and interdependent, works to promote all the human rights enshrined in the Universal Declaration of Human Rights and other international standards, through human rights education programs and campaigning for ratification of human rights treaties.

Amnesty International is impartial. It is independent of any government, political persuasion or religious creed. It does not support or oppose any government or political system, nor does it support or oppose the views of the victims whose rights it seeks to protect. It is concerned solely with the protection of the human rights involved in each case, regardless of the ideology of the government, opposition forces, or the beliefs of the individual.

Amnesty International does not grade countries according to their record on human rights; instead of attempting comparisons it concentrates on trying to end the specific violations of human rights in each case.

The organization visits countries to meet prisoners, interview government officials, investigate allegations, and observe trials; it carries out detailed research on violations of human rights worldwide; and initiates national and international campaigns to publicize patterns of human rights abuses. It has declared an annual Amnesty International Week. Cases of prisoners and other victims are printed in its International Newsletter each month so that concerned individuals may organize appeals on their behalf and publicize each prisoner's situation. The *Amnesty International Report*, published annually, covers Amnesty International's concerns about human rights violations in over 160 countries. (Each year numerous specific reports on human rights violations are published in Arabic, English, French, and Spanish.)

Amnesty International has over 8,000 volunteer groups in over 70 countries, organized sections in 51 countries, and individual members, subscribers, and supporters in over 150 countries and territories. Each group works on behalf of at least two prisoners of conscience in countries other than its own and participates in the organization's global campaigns. The current Secretary General is Pierre Sané.

Amnesty International is governed by a nine-member International Executive Committee (IEC). It includes eight volunteer members, elected every two years by an International Council comprising representatives of the worldwide movement, and an elected member of the International Secretariat.

Amnesty International's funding reflects the movement's independence and its reliance on broad public support. No money is sought or received from governments. The hundreds of thousands of donations that sustain the organization's work come from the pockets of its members and the public. Amnesty International is financed by subscriptions and donations from its worldwide membership. To safeguard the independence of the organization, all contributions are strictly controlled by guidelines laid down by the International Council.

Amnesty International has formal relations with the United Nations Economic and Social Council (ECOSOC); the United Nations Educational, Scientific and Cultural Organization (UNESCO); the Council of Europe; the Organization of American States; the Organization of African Unity; and the Inter-Parliamentary Union.

ANTI-SLAVERY INTERNATIONAL
180 Brixton Road
London SW9 6AT
England

Anti-Slavery International (ASI) is the world's oldest international human rights organization. It was founded in 1839 as the British and Foreign Anti-Slavery Society, five years after the emancipation of slaves in British colonies. In 1909 it merged with the Aborigines Protection Society, which was campaigning for the rights of indigenous peoples.

The purposes of ASI, as stated in the Constitution, are the elimination of slave owning and slave trading, the abolition of all forms of forced labor approximating slavery, the protection and advancement of peoples and groups who are not strong enough to protect themselves, and the defense of human rights in accordance with the principles of the Universal Declaration of Human Rights of 1948.

ASI has an international membership and is supported by subscriptions and donations from the general public and by grants from various organizations such as trusts, foundations, and aid agencies for specific research projects. It has consultative status with the United Nations Economic and Social Council; it is also a nongovernmental organization in consultative status (Category C—mutual information) with the United Nations Educational, Scientific and Cultural Organization (UNESCO); ASI is also on the International Labour Organization's (ILO) special list.

ASI was instrumental in setting up the United Nations Working Groups on Slavery

(1957) and on Indigenous Peoples (1982), as well as the United Nations Voluntary Fund for Indigenous Peoples (1985), and the United Nations Voluntary Trust Fund on Contemporary Forms of Slavery (1991). It has initiated research in many countries on violations of human rights and published the findings in its annual journal, *The Anti-Slavery Reporter,* or in separate reports. ASI is a major source of information on slavery and indigenous peoples through its library and documentation.

To reach its objectives, ASI uses various approaches:

1. Research that establishes first the existence of significant slavery-like conditions and identifies specific cases to indicate degrees of severity and second the existence of threatened tribal groups, the impact of current development policies, and the possibility of alternative development strategies. In particular, emphasis is on research to identify factors in the systems of exploitation that can be changed in the short and medium terms and how present development strategies help or hinder the elimination of exploitative conditions.

2. Enhancing and facilitating the work of concerned individuals and organizations in the countries mainly affected.

3. Recommendations to governments in particular, but also to organizations within affected countries such as labor unions and international organizations such as United Nations Economic and Social Council. Recommendations can take the form of suggesting new legislation, amendments to existing legislation, better enforcement procedures, changes in the education system, and so on.

4. Publicity, through the *Anti-Slavery Reporter* and *Anti-Slavery Newsletter,* special reports, bulletins, submissions to international monitoring organizations, and facilitating media coverage.

5. Campaigning to encourage people to take action in the form of lobbying, letter-writing, mounting exhibitions, and talks to other organizations.

CULTURAL SURVIVAL*
215 First Street
Cambridge, MA 02142

Founded in 1972, Cultural Survival helps indigenous peoples and ethnic minorities survive, both physically and culturally, the rapid changes that contact with expanding industrial society has brought. By supporting projects designed by tribal and ethnic peoples, Cultural Survival assists these groups to come to terms with national and international socioeconomic systems. Basic to Cultural Survival's work is the belief that cultural differences are inherent in humanity; protecting this human diversity enriches our common earth. The work of the organization traditionally focused on rainforest peoples of South America but in recent years has expanded to assist peoples in Africa, Asia, and North America, including Afghan refugees in Pakistan, refugees of the Balkan wars, and Solomon Islanders in Melanesia. It has also been active in disseminating the results of scholarly research on indigenous peoples.

Cultural Survival Enterprises (CSE) is the not-for-profit trading division of the organization that helps native societies to market natural products while preserving the natural ecosystem. CSE assists indigenous peoples living in fragile ecosystems by helping them modify traditional resource-management schemes and generate income through processing and marketing products in the international market. CSE sells raw materials to manufacturers at 5 percent above the U.S. wholesale price and negotiates profit-sharing agreements with companies purchasing raw materials. All the funds generated by these agreements are returned to forest groups and support organizations. These funds promote the development and growth of new and existing organizations, help fund additional projects, and help to build the infrastructures necessary to support production within rainforest communities.

Cultural Survival also provides educational resources for learning about the connections between people and the environment. Cultural Survival publishes the *Cultural Survival Quarterly* and Cultural Survival Reports, a series of books on indigenous and ethnic groups. Cultural survival is supported by individual membership dues, sales of its products, fundraising events, and donations.

HUMAN RIGHTS ADVOCATES*
P.O. Box 5675
Berkeley, CA 94705

Humans Rights Advocates (HRA) promotes and protects fundamental human rights in California, the United States, and worldwide, through the use of international human rights and humanitarian law. Since 1978, HRA has been helping to protect the fundamental human rights of individuals and groups such as Tibetans, the peoples of the Caucasus, and gays and lesbians.

HRA has assisted migrant workers and asylum seekers in California, administrative detainees in Asia, and people without food in Ethiopia. HRA's innovative work in the law of armed conflicts is instrumental in directing needed emphasis to rights frequently neglected: the rights of civilian war victims and prisoners of war, and the interrelationship between armed conflict and human rights violations. HRA has helped draw attention to the issue of population transfer as a violation of human rights. It has examined nationalities conflicts as a source of human rights abuses and has coordinated exploration of bilateral and multilateral responses to that problem. It has also sought to bring international atten-

tion to the growing problem of environmental refugees, persons displaced by widespread pollution of streams and lands, and by development projects.

HRA focuses on three types of assistance: advocacy at the United Nations, Litigation, and Education.

Advocacy at the United Nations
As a fully accredited Non-Governmental Organization, HRA participates actively in the work of the United Nations Commission on Human Rights and its Sub-Commission on Prevention of Discrimination and Protection of Minorities. HRA testifies at the annual sessions of those bodies.

Litigation
HRA provides its expertise and assistance to lawyers involved in lawsuits in which international human rights law can be used effectively. In the past, work has entailed filing amicus curiae briefs, providing expert witness on international law questions, giving strategic advice at the trial and appellate levels, and making its resource materials available to other lawyers. HRA members have testified before Congress and the California Legislature on issues involving international human rights law.

Education
HRA organizes conferences and seminars to educate lawyers, judges, and activists about how international human rights and humanitarian law can be used in U.S. courts and international fora to stop, protest, or seek relief from practices that violate fundamental rights. HRA members also speak to community groups, law classes, and U.N. affiliated organizations.

HRA publishes a newsletter twice a year; maintains a resource library including U.N. documents, legal briefs, and other materials; prints and distributes articles and papers; and supplements the U.N./Human Rights Collection of the Law Library of the University of California at Berkeley (Boalt Hall).

HRA is run by a board of directors, with the assistance of a national advisory board.

HUMAN RIGHTS FUND FOR INDIGENOUS PEOPLES*
c/o International Work Group for Indigenous Affairs
Fiolstraede 10
DK 1171 Copenhagen K.
Denmark

Established in 1984, the Human Rights Fund for Indigenous Peoples is a federated organization consisting of four human rights organizations working on indigenous affairs:

Anti-Slavery International (ASI)
180 Brixton Road, London SW9 6AT, England

Co-Ordinating Group on Indigenous Affairs (KWIA)
Breugelstraat 31- 33, B-2018 Antwerp, Belgium

International Work Group for Indigenous Affairs (IWGIA)
Fiolstraede 10, DK 1171 Copenhagen, Denmark

Working Group for Indigenous Peoples (WIP)
PB 4098 Minahassastraat 1, 1009 AB Amsterdam, The Netherlands

The main purpose of the fund is to promote indigenous interests in an international context and to enable indigenous people and their representatives to gain an expertise with international treaty bodies. The primary activity of the fund is supporting indigenous peoples' participation at forums of the United Nations in Geneva, particularly at the Working Group on Indigenous Populations (UNWGIP). A meeting of the fund takes place each year (April/May) to assess applications for assistance, taking into account the list already approved by the United Nations Voluntary Fund.

The UNWGIP was established in 1984 under the Human Rights Commission in order to draw up international standards for the rights of indigenous peoples. It consists of five experts who listen to the statements of indigenous representatives over a period of two weeks. In these statements indigenous peoples have an opportunity to express their concerns, describe the problems facing their communities, and influence the creation of human rights standards. The meeting is unique as it is the only international gathering of indigenous peoples on a regular basis. It provides indigenous representatives with the means to address governments, to meet each other, talk to international lawyers, and establish contacts. All of these activities are important for informing the international community of violations of human rights.

In recent years the fund has also supported participation at higher bodies of the United Nations, such as the Human Rights Commission and the Sub-Commission on the Prevention of Discrimination and Protection of Minorities.

The fund receives its money from nongovernmental organizations in Scandinavia, the United Kingdom, and the Netherlands. In 1992 its budget was about $50,000. The grants to participants cover all or part of travel, accommodation, and food. In 1992, 22 participants from 19 countries received assistance. The fund does not provide any predetermined criteria of the nature of participation. Some participants deliver statements, some participate in the drafting process, some primarily observe the sessions. Several members of the HRFIP are usually present to provide informal assistance. The fund publishes an annual report.

HUMAN RIGHTS WATCH
485 Fifth Avenue
New York, NY 10017

Human Rights Watch is a nonpartisan, U.S.-based organization that monitors the human rights practices of governments throughout the world. Five regional organizations make up the Human Rights Organization: Africa Watch, Americas Watch, Asia Watch, Helsinki Watch, and Middle East Watch, in addition to the Fund For Free Expression. Human Rights Watch became the umbrella organization for these regional divisions in 1987.

The largest such organization in the United States, Human Rights Watch investigates murders, kidnapping, torture, psychiatric abuse, censorship, deprivation of political freedom, and destruction of ethnic identity. Human Rights Watch attempts to end these abuses by applying pressure to monitored governments, most commonly in the form of public exposure and embarrassment. Specifically, the organization documents and publicizes these abusive practices. In the same fashion it also monitors violations of laws of war and applies pressure on governments to force them to end such actions. Human Rights Watch maintains close contact with Amnesty International, with which the organization shares the same basic principals and goals.

Human Rights Watch accomplishes its goals through a staff of lawyers, journalists, and regional experts that compiles information about human rights practices and infringements thereupon. In the United States, Human Rights Watch has devoted itself to shaping U.S. foreign policy. A chief goal is to harness the economic and moral power of the U.S. government and to use that power to promote human rights.

The organization is funded by private foundations and individuals; it does not accept government funding. Human Rights Watch is governed by an executive committee, with separate committees also governing the constituent organizations. The organization publishes the *Human Rights Watch Newsletter,* the *Human Rights Watch World Report, Human Rights Watch in the News,* and occasional special reports. In the United States, its offices are located in New York City and Washington, D.C.

THE INTERNATIONAL LEAGUE FOR HUMAN RIGHTS
432 Park Avenue, South
New York, NY 10016

The International League for Human Rights traces its origins to a French citizens' rights group started in the early 1900s. It was officially founded in the United States by Americans and Europeans in 1941 under the leadership of Roger Nash Baldwin. It was incorporated in New York State in 1942. The league's mission is to fight for the promotion and protection of human rights around the world, particularly those guarantees contained in the United Nations Universal Declaration of Human Rights adopted in 1948. The work of the league is supported by members' dues and donations and is carried out by a Board of Directors, a paid staff, and volunteers. The league has consultative status with the ECOSOC, ILO, and UNESCO, and ties to other nongovernmental organizations. Before his death in 1989, the league had close ties with Andrei Sakharov, the exiled Soviet human rights advocate who served as Honorary President of the league.

To achieve it mission, the league helps frame international human rights documents, develop mechanisms of enforcement, develops programs to end human rights abuses, marshalls public opinion, lodges protests with governments, negotiates on behalf of victims, protects human rights advocates, and assists other human rights organizations. Among recent activities were the documentation of human rights abuses by both Armenians and Azerbaijani Turks in their ethnic conflict, protesting attacks on Turkish human rights advocates, and a special project focusing on violence against women and gender discrimination.

The league publishes the *Human Rights Bulletin*, the *In Brief* series, and the *ILHR Annual Review*, as well as special reports.

INTERNATIONAL RESCUE COMMITTEE, INC.
386 Park Avenue South
New York, NY 10016

The International Rescue Committee, Inc. (IRC) is a nonsectarian voluntary agency that helps refugees who escape from political, religious, and racial persecution, as well as uprooted victims of war, civil strife, and famine. The IRC was founded in 1933, at the request of Albert Einstein, to assist anti-Nazis trapped in Hitler's Germany. Today, IRC facilities in refugee camps and resettlement offices, staffed by IRC workers and volunteers, are located in Africa, Asia, the Middle East, Central America, Europe, and the United States. The IRC's first concern is relief and medical aid to enable sick, hungry, and wounded refugees to survive. The IRC also provides special feeding programs for malnourished children, schooling, self-help and training programs; it also reunites families, resettles refugees in new countries, and helps facilitate their economic and social adjustment to their new home. Among refugees helped recently are Kurds in Turkey, Liberians in Guinea, Cambodians and Burmese in Thailand, Vietnamese boat people, and Nicaraguans in Costa Rica. The IRC publishes an annual report and a newsletter, *IRC Field Reports*. It is headquartered in New York City, with other offices around the United States and in 16 other countries.

LAWYERS COMMITTEE FOR HUMAN RIGHTS
330 Seventh Ave.
New York, NY 10001

The mission of the Lawyers Committee for Human Rights is to protect and promote fundamental human rights. To achieve this mission, the Lawyers Committee focuses its efforts on:

1. Working with and supporting the work of in-country indigenous and nongovernmental organizations

2. Documenting human rights violations and confronting the violating nations

3. Pressing for a consistent and principled approach in U.S. foreign policy as regards human rights

4. Pressing for stronger human rights policies at the UN and other international organizations

The Lawyers Committee also has a complimentary but distinct Refugee Project that serves an advocacy role in ensuring that refugees receive humane and dignified treatment and legal protection.

The Lawyers Committee was founded in 1978 and is headquartered in New York City with another office in Washington, D.C. It has a staff of about 38 whose work is supplemented by the pro bono activities of volunteer lawyers. The Lawyers Committee is supported by a combination of grants, contributions from law firms and individuals, and revenues from the sale of publications. Publications include the Reports and Briefing Papers series.

MINORITY RIGHTS GROUP*
379 Brixton Road
London, SW9 7DE
England

Minority Rights Group (MRG) is an international nongovernmental organization working to secure justice for minorities suffering discrimination and prejudice, and the peaceful coexistence of majority and minority communities. It emphasizes ethnic, religious, and linguistic minorities and, particularly, communities who are without power in both the northern and southern hemispheres.

Founded in the 1960s, MRG informs and warns governments, the international community, nongovernmental organizations, and the wider public about the situation of minorities worldwide. This work is based in three main areas: research and analysis of minority groups and issues, activism at the local level, and advocacy in the international arena.

Research and Analysis of Minority Groups and Issues

During the last two decades MRG has published over 100 reports and in recent years has extended its range to include a book series, conference reports, and occasional papers. The reports are translated into many languages. To date 20 titles have been published in 12 different languages, while the affiliate in France (GDM) has a list of titles published in French. MRG has a policy of seeking the highest caliber authors with minority rights experience from the region in which the research is being carried out.

Activism at the Local Level

Working with local partners to try to achieve a better understanding of minority issues, MRG acts locally by challenging prejudice and promoting public understanding through information and education activities. MRG has the policy of championing minority rights rather than campaigning for any specific minorities, since it is for minorities representing themselves. It works towards empowering minority communities by informing them of international standards and other models of practice.

Advocacy in the International Arena

MRG's main objective here is to inform and educate policy makers and the wider public on minority issues. It promotes and distributes its research reports and papers to a wide audience, from UN officials in Geneva and New York to minority organizations. In collaboration with local partners and local communities it also makes direct representations to decision makers. This can achieve particular results for minorities in specific countries or lead to the improvement and implementation of international standards on minorities.

MRG also has an Education Department that provides not only information on minorities for young people, educators, and associated professionals, but also materials that address the issues of discrimination and prejudice in Britain's multicultural society. It pursues this work by means of its publications and through its information service to students and teachers. One example of the department's publications is *Voices from Eritrea, Somalia and Kurdistan*, a three volume dual-language collection of autobiographical writings by refugee children at school in London. The series raises the issues of human rights and being a refugee.

MRG believes that the best hope for a peaceful world lies in identifying and monitoring potential conflict between communities, advocating preventive measures to avoid the escalation of conflict, and encouraging positive action to build trust between majority and minority communities; it is developing an international network of affiliates, like-minded organizations, and contacts within local communities to cooperate on these issues.

MRG has consultative status with the United Nations Economic and Social Council, and its international secretariat is in London. Legally it is registered both as a charity and as a limited company under United Kingdom law, with an international governing council.

OXFAM*
274 Banbury Road
Oxford OX2 7DZ
England

Oxfam began life in 1942 as the Oxford Committee for Famine Relief. Along with similar groups of volunteers across the United Kingdom, its concern was for the women, men, and children starving in Nazi-occupied Greece, where famine had killed 400,000 people during the Allied blockade. The groups protested against the British commitment to total blockade of Europe, wanting to send "controlled relief" to Greece and Belgium. In early 1943, the Oxford Committee registered as a charity, and fundraising began in earnest. Food and clothing were sent to Europe and distributed by church and voluntary groups. Shortages and the destruction caused by the war continued to inflict suffering throughout Europe for several years after the end of the war. However, by the late 1940s, the pressing need for post-war relief aid for Europe had declined, and many of the relief committees closed down. The Oxford Committee decided to extend its operations to include the "relief of suffering arising as a result of wars or of any other causes in any part of the world."

Today Oxfam has an annual income of around £80,00,000 raised in the United Kingdom and Ireland for relief and development programs in 71 countries around the world and is run by paid, professional staff and a network of volunteers. Compared with the need, Oxfam has only small amounts of money to spend, so the funding must be effective and, where possible, encourage processes of change on a wider scale.

Oxfam's programs throughout the developing world are managed by staff teams operating from some 40 centers and overseeing programs of emergency relief and development assistance. The teams base their work on an analysis of the causes of poverty. They identify the poorest and most marginal groups and draw up plans that focus on priority problems, addressing them in ways that can be shared and repeated with a minimum of outside help.

In 1992–1993, Oxfam allocated £45.8 million to 2,900 projects in over 70 countries; 32 percent was allocated for emergency relief.

The allocation of money was: Africa (south of the Sahara), 51 percent; Asia, 16 percent; Latin America and the Caribbean, 19 percent; Middle East, 9 percent; world general, UK, and eastern Europe, 5 percent.

Oxfam's work can be divided into three types—emergency relief, sustainable development, and advocacy and influencing.

Emergency Relief
Oxfam is geared to react quickly in times of crisis. Whether dealing with the results of natural disasters, like floods and earthquakes, or of conflict and war, Oxfam helps people meet their basic needs for food, water, shelter, and clothing. Emergency relief has to be provided quickly, after careful on-the-spot assessment: listening to what people say, and then supporting their efforts. Oxfam staff coordinate their work with local government officials and other organizations. The determination of people to do what they can for themselves is often best supported by the provision of seeds and tools to enable them to grow their own food. Disaster preparedness is another important area of work: if people can be helped to plan strategies for coping with possible calamities, they will be in a stronger position to tackle them if and when they occur.

Sustainable Development
Oxfam supports small-scale development for people in villages, towns, and cities, to help them develop their potential and improve their living standards. For example, Oxfam may fund a grain bank organized by a village cooperative. The bank buys surplus grain at fair prices from

villagers after harvest when prices are low and resells it to them at times of shortage at equally fair prices, to avoid the huge price swings in the markets. The bank supplies seed at a reasonable cost for the next season, and some banks sell fertilizers and pesticides, also at fair prices. Grain banks are just one example of sustainable development that makes the most of people's own hard work by enabling them to become more self-sufficient.

Advocacy and Influencing

Oxfam helps local organizations working for change in their own countries, at community or national levels. This might involve them in urging their own governments to look at ways of changing their own society. It could also mean communicating in the northern hemisphere, to try to influence policies and behavior. Whether in meetings with government, United Nations, and European Community officials, briefing journalists, or taking part in conferences such as the United Nations Earth Summit, Oxfam staff speak from their experience of relief and development work.

The common element in all aspects of Oxfam's work is supporting poor people in their efforts to gain more control over their lives and to achieve peaceful change. The most successful development and relief programs are those in which people have been really involved.

Oxfam produces a range of materials about its work, both free and for sale, covering a range of countries and issues, for adults, children, and young people. Oxfam's Young People's Team produces materials for teachers and youth workers, designed to explore the issues raised by teaching and learning about world development.

Oxfam also publishes books, including short, illustrated "Country Profiles," setting its work in context; briefing papers for researchers and journalists; practical and technical manuals for development workers; and research reports as a basis for advocacy on behalf of the poor.

REFUGEE POLICY GROUP*
1424 16th Street, N.W.
Suite No. 401
Washington, DC 20036

The Refugee Policy Group (RPG) is an independent policy research organization that focuses on the interconnections between refugee and related humanitarian problems, and the issues of peace and security, development, and human rights.

RPG uses impartial research and evaluation approaches. Having no operational or institutional stake in the outcome of policy decisions, it seeks advice from individuals with differing perspectives and incorporates these views into its analyses. It spends considerable time in the field acquiring first-hand information from refugees, those directly concerned with their assistance and protection, and local inhabitants who are affected by their presence. Policy findings are tested against the realities of program implementation to ensure that they will have the maximum impact on actual practice.

The RPG brings together representatives of varying responsible perspectives to increase understanding of issues, and where possible, to promote greater agreement on policies and encourage those who make policy and develop programs to use available research. It supports the research of others by providing advice on priorities and by reviewing and commenting on papers and maintains a repository of significant documents on refugee issues for their own and others' use. Publications include the periodic *RPG Review,* an annual report, and books and pamphlets.

RPG work is supported by an advisory council of leading refugee program experts and a board of trustees drawn from corporations, international organizations, government, academia, and private agencies.

RPG's recent priorities are to promote:

1. Greater awareness that international migration will be an issue of paramount impor-

tance in the 1990s. Major political and economic changes bring with them the prospects for dramatically increased movements of people. How the challenges presented by these movements of people are addressed will have a powerful effect upon the direction of further political and economic change.

2. Recognition that civil conflicts displace millions of people internally as well as externally. The inadequacy of current legal, institutional, and program arrangements to address the situations of internally displaced persons leaves these millions of people exposed to the dangers of war, famine, and human rights abuse.

3. The development of effective plans and programs for the repatriation of refugees and displaced persons in the wake of the potential settlement of longstanding conflicts such as in the Horn of Africa, Cambodia, Afghanistan, Central America and Mozambique. How these repatriations are conducted will have an enormous affect upon the prospects for rehabilitation, development, and sustained peace in these areas.

4. The incorporation of development concepts and organizations into the handling of mass movements of people. Dependency is too often a consequence of being a refugee. Mass movements of people typically continue to be addressed as emergencies long after the emergency conditions have subsided and there are opportunities for reconstruction and development to begin.

5. Understanding of the intimate connections between peace, development, human rights, and the resolution of refugee and displaced persons problems. Refugee movements are caused by persecution, human rights abuses, wars, and civil strife. These situations are often compounded by poverty, famine, and environmental degradation. Refugees and displaced persons are not merely the consequences of these problems, however. They are also active parties in determining whether peace and stability will come to their homelands.

6. Greater attention to the assistance and protection needs of special refugee populations, such as women, children and the elderly. The majority of the world's refugees and displaced persons are women and children. The systems in place for providing assistance and protection to refugees are often not sufficiently attuned to the special needs and resources of these groups. As a result, major issues such as the sexual assault of refugee women, their health needs, and education for refugee children go unaddressed.

REFUGEES INTERNATIONAL*
21 DuPont Circle, N.W.
Washington, DC 20036

Refugees International (RI) is a private, independent, nonprofit organization dedicated to defending and promoting the human rights of people who have been forced to flee their homeland. RI provides an international voice that speaks on behalf of refugees for protection, care, and the opportunity to build productive lives.

RI was formed in 1979 by 30 individuals from eight countries as a response to the forced repatriation of Cambodian refugees from Thailand. Pushed back at gunpoint into the country they had risked their lives to flee, thousands of innocent men, women, and children who had survived four years of genocide, died from landmines, starvation and reprisals. Determined to fight such injustice and tragedy, RI was founded to provide a voice for refugees that would focus the world's attention on their plight and prevent needless loss of life.

With a wide network of international partners, RI monitors and analyzes refugee crises.

259

RI then prepares issue briefs, with recommendations, for policy makers to enable them to pursue fair and compassionate refugee policy. Using a combination of quiet diplomacy and the power of public opinion, RI presses governments and international organizations to improve protection for refugees. RI works in coalition with other advocates to develop and promote effective strategies and lasting solutions to address the needs of refugees.

RI has conducted fact-finding missions to Asia, Africa, Central America, and the former Yugoslavia to survey refugee situations. Trip reports outlining objective policy recommendations are widely disseminated within the international community. Many of RI's policy proposals have been implemented by government agencies. RI intervenes on behalf of individuals and groups of refugees who have not been adequately cared for by the international system. As a result of RI's work, lives have been saved and families have been reunited.

RI is based in Washington, DC, and historically has concentrated on the refugee situation in Southeast Asia. RI is now broadening its work in Central America, Africa, and the former Yugoslavia.

RI is supported by the contributions of individuals, private foundations, and private corporations. In order to maintain independence and objectivity, however, RI neither solicits nor accepts government funding.

THE SAVE THE CHILDREN FUND*
17 Grove Lane
Camberwell
London SE5 8RD
England

Save the Children (SCF) works to achieve lasting benefits for children within the communities in which they live by influencing policy and practice based on its experience and study in different parts of the world. In all of its work Save the Children endeavors to make a reality of children's rights.

Ultimate responsibility for Save the Children is vested in the Council, the trustees of the organization. HRH The Princess Royal has been the president of Save the Children since 1970 and plays an active role in SCF affairs.

Save the Children's headquarters is based in London. There are six departments at SCF's headquarters: Overseas, UK and European programs, Public Affairs, Personnel and Administration, Fundraising, and Finance. Each department is headed by a director who reports to the director general. Directors are responsible for the day to day management of SCF.

In most overseas countries there is a field director who is responsible for the administration of SCF's work in that country. In the UK projects are managed through a structure of divisional management teams. There is a network of approximately 800 fundraising branches throughout the UK. Branches are run by volunteer members.

Save the Children works in partnership with governments, local communities, and other organizations with the aim of providing lasting benefits for children. Save the Children supports projects in some 50 countries worldwide: in Africa, Asia, the Middle East, Latin America, the Caribbean, eastern Europe, and throughout the UK.

Projects aim to provide health, education, and welfare opportunities that are appropriate, affordable, accessible, and sustainable. Overseas Save the Children works in areas including food security, sustainability in the health sector, refugees, alternatives to institutional care, AIDS, and disability. Save the Children also provides emergency relief during major disasters and supports people's efforts to rebuild their lives. In the UK work is based in the community and includes family centers, schemes to support children and young people, and work with the criminal justice system, disabled children, prisoners' families, and Travellers.

Major publications are *World's Children* (quarterly), *Annual Report, Annual Review,* and a range of other publications, including educational materials.

SURVIVAL INTERNATIONAL
310 Edgeware Road
London W2 1YD
England

Survival International is an international organization whose major purpose is to assist indigenous peoples in safeguarding their rights. The organization provides financial assistance to indigenous peoples urgently in need of such assistance, seeks to inform the general public of the value of indigenous cultures, and strongly speaks out against and supports action designed to stop the ethnocide or genocide of indigenous peoples. Survival International is supported by donations and grants from non-governmental organizations. It has consultative status with the United Nations Education, Scientific, and Cultural Organization (UNESCO) and the United Nations Economic and Social Council (ECOSOC) and maintains relations with other organizations involved in indigenous rights issues. The headquarters is in London, with other offices in France, Italy, and Spain and local organizations in over 60 other nations. Publications include the *Urgent Action Bulletin, Survival International News,* and *Survival International Annual Review.*

THE UNITED NATIONS HIGH COMMISSIONER FOR REFUGEES*
P.O. Box 2500
1211 Geneva 2 Depot
Switzerland

The mission of the United Nations High Commissioner for Refugees (UNHCR) is to provide assistance and protection to the world's nearly 19 million refugees.

Based in Geneva, Switzerland, UNHCR was created by the United Nations General Assembly and began work in 1951 aiding millions of European refugees in the aftermath of World War II. Its founding mandate defines refugees as those who have fled their countries because of a well-founded fear of persecution for reasons of their race, religion, nationality, political opinion, or membership in a particular social group and who cannot or do not want to return.

Since its creation more than 40 years ago, UNHCR has helped more than 30 million refugees, earning two Nobel Peace Prizes in the process—but the refugee problem continues to grow, more than doubling over the past decade. Each day in 1992, an average of 5,000 people fled their homes because of war, human rights abuses, and persecution.

By mid-1993, there were 18.9 million refugees around the world and another 20 million men, women and children were displaced in their own lands. One in every 134 people on Earth has been forced into flight.

Protecting the right of these people to seek and enjoy asylum from persecution is not easy. Countries of first asylum, often poor themselves, sometimes grow weary of the needs of those being given sanctuary. Occasionally, they try to push refugees back across the border; and people in rich countries, fearing that the influx of asylum-seekers is becoming unmanageable, sometimes slam doors in their faces. UNHCR strives to reopen those doors and to keep them open.

UNHCR's most important function is known as *international protection*—trying to ensure that no refugee is returned involuntarily to a country where he or she has reason to fear persecution.

UNHCR also promotes adherence to international agreements on refugees and monitors the behavior of individual states to ensure that they respect those agreements. When refugees are mistreated or forcibly repatriated, UNHCR protests to governments at the highest level.

UNHCR traditionally helps those who have fled their homelands because of threats to their lives or liberty. Sometimes these include mass movements of people fleeing civil conflict and other man-made disasters. Over the years, UNHCR also has been asked by the U.N. Secretary-General to assist people internally displaced in their own lands.

In addition to providing protection to refugees, UNHCR also provides food, water, shelter, medical care, and other emergency aid to those fleeing.

In the longer term, UNHCR seeks durable solutions for the plight of refugees. These possible solutions for refugees are of three categories:

1. Voluntary repatriation back to their original homes

2. Integration in the countries where they first sought asylum

3. Resettlement to a third country.

The current High Commissioner for Refugees is Sadako Ogata, a former Japanese diplomat and academic who assumed her post in February 1991. She reports annually to the U.N. General Assembly through the Economic and Social Council. The High Commissioner's material assistance programs are approved and supervised by the UNHCR Executive Committee, composed of 46 member countries. The Executive Committee also advises the High Commissioner at her request on the exercise of her functions.

UNHCR's expenditures are financed by a very limited subsidy from the regular budget of the United Nations (to be used exclusively for administrative costs), as well as by voluntary contributions from governments, nongovernmental organizations and individuals. UNHCR's total expenditures for 1993 are estimated at $1.37 billion, up from $1.07 billion in 1992.

UNHCR currently has 2,445 staff members working in 176 offices in 110 countries. Among the major refugee assistance programs being carried out by UNHCR in early 1993 were Afghanistan, Armenia/Azerbaijan, Benin and Ghana (refugees from Togo), the Cambodia repatriation, the Comprehensive Plan of Action for Indo-Chinese refugees, Georgia, the Guatemala repatriation, several programs in the Horn of Africa, the Mozambique repatriation, the Sri Lanka repatriation, Tajikistan, and the former Yugoslavia.

UNHCR is the lead U.N. agency for humanitarian operations in former Yugoslavia, where it is providing assistance to nearly 3.5 million people. At an estimated cost of $420 million for 1993, the emergency humanitarian operation in the former Yugoslavia is by far the largest of UNHCR's worldwide programs.

Publications produced by UNHCR's Public Information Office include the quarterly *Refugees* magazine, with a circulation of 200,000, in English, French, German, Italian, Japanese, and Spanish. The office also issues numerous press releases, regular information bulletins giving an in-depth look at ongoing emergency operations, brochures, posters, and calendars. The Public Information Office also has its own video unit, which provides footage of global refugee operations to television stations and networks around the world. The video unit also produces numerous films on a variety of UNHCR-related subjects, ranging from children to specific operations.

THE U.S. COMMITTEE FOR REFUGEES
1025 Vermont Ave., N.W., Suite 920
Washington, DC 20005

The U.S. Committee for Refugees, (USCR) is a public information program of the American Council for Nationalities Service dedicated to providing clear, objective information to the public and policy makers to assist and protect refugees and internally displaced persons around the world. Through its publications, videos, the media, and expert testimony, USCR seeks to mobilize the public and official awareness into a more humanitarian response to the uprooted victims of persecution and war.

For over 30 years, the USCR's mission has been to:

1. Defend the basic human rights of refugees, most fundamentally, the principle of *nonrefoulement:* no forced return of a person with a well-founded fear of persecution to his or her homeland

2. To defend the rights of asylum seekers to a fair and impartial determination of their status;

3. To defend the right to decent and humanitarian treatment for all internally displaced persons.

The USCR meets this mission by observing and documenting refugee emergencies; offering clear, objective information about the these situations to the public and policy makers; and publishing and distributing information to a variety of audiences through the annual *World Refugee Survey,* the monthly *Refugee Reports,* and videos.

The USCR is a private, not-for-profit organization and is supported by contributions, income from the sale of publications, and support from private foundations in the United States.

WORLD COUNCIL OF INDIGENOUS PEOPLES
100 Argyle Avenue
Ottawa, Ontario
Canada K2P 1B6

The World Council of Indigenous Peoples (WCIP) was founded in 1975 following the First International Conference of Indigenous Peoples in Port Alberni, British Colombia. The genesis of the WCIP dates to the early 1960s and the efforts of George Manuel, then President of the Indian Brotherhood of Canada. The objectives of the WCIP are to (1) promote unity among indigenous peoples of the world; (2) strengthen their organizations; (3) encourage the abolition of any possibility of genocide or ethnocide; (4) combat racism; and (5) ensure political, economic, social, and cultural justice for indigenous peoples based on the principle of equality among them and with the people of the countries which surround them. The WCIP acts to achieve these goals by generating a collective and unified response for indigenous peoples, and consolidating their local, regional, and national organizations.

WCIP programs and activities include:

Economic and Social Development. The promotion of social and economic improvement and development with indigenous participation toward self-determination through training programs, research, scholarships, exchange programs, and social programs.

Inter-Institutional Forums and Relations. The promotion and consolidation of efforts toward the recognition of indigenous rights through the formulation of legislation, policies, and instruments especially regarding human rights, indigenous rights, the strengthening of indigenous organizations, and research.

Information and Documentation. To make known the situation of indigenous peoples through documentaries, radio programs, and the periodical *WCIP Newsletter.*

Special Programs. Initiatives toward special issues such as the 500-Years-Beyond 1492 project, peace and development, and resistance to the Human Genome Project.

The WCIP is governed by a general assembly composed of delegates from local organizations in each of the member nations, an executive council of one president, two vice-presidents, and representatives from each member region. The activities of the organization are carried out by the general director and his or her staff in the central office in Ottawa and in regional offices. The WCIP has consultative status with the Economic and Social Council of the UN, UNESCO, and the International Labor Organization as well as cooperative relationships with other nongovernmental organizations and governments. It is funded by grants from governmental organizations and private organizations.

BIBLIOGRAPHY

Ablin, David, and Marlowe Hood, eds. (1984) *Cambodian Agony.*

Adamu, Mahdi. (1978) *The Hausa Factor in West African History.*

Ahmad, Imtiaz, ed. (1981) *Ritual and Religion among Muslims in India.*

Ahmed, Akbar S. (1980) *Pukhtun Economy and Society: Traditional Structure and Economic Development in a Tribal Society.*

Akiner, Shirin. (1986) *Islamic Peoples of the Soviet Union: An Historical and Statistical Handbook.*

Allport, Gordon W. (1954) *The Nature of Prejudice.*

Altstadt, Audrey L. (1992) *The Azerbaijani Turks: Power and Identity under Russian Rule.*

Anam-Ndu, Ekeng A. (1990) *Consociational Democracy in Nigeria: Agenda for the 1990s and Beyond.*

Anand, V. K. (1969) *Nagaland in Transition.*

Anderson, Benedict. (1991) *Imagined Community: Reflections on the Origin and Spread of Nationalism.* Rev. ed.

Anderson, Robert T. (1975) *Denmark: Success of a Developing Nation.*

An-Na'im, Abdullahi A., ed. (1992) *Human Rights in Cross-Cultural Perspective: A Quest for Consensus.*

Anti-Semitism World Report (1992).

Appadurai, Arjun. (1990) "Disjuncture and Difference in the Global Cultural Economy." In *Global Culture: Nationalism, Globalization and Modernity,* edited by Michael Featherstone, 295–310.

Apte, Mahadev L. (1985) *Humor and Laughter: An Anthropological Approach.*

Apter, Andrew. (1991) "Herskovits's Heritage: Rethinking Syncretism in the African Diaspora." *Diaspora* 1: 235–260.

Ardagh, John. (1987) *Germany and the Germans: An Anatomy of a Society Today.*

Balandier, Georges. (1970) *The Sociology of Black Africa.*

Balkan War Report. (1992–) Bulletin of the Institute for War & Peace Reporting.

Bamzai, P. N. K. (1962) *A History of Kashmir.*

Banton, Michael, and Jonathan Harwood. (1975) *The Race Concept.*

Barrett, David B. (1994) "Annual Statistical Table on Global Mission: 1994." *International Bulletin of Missionary Research* 18: 24–25.

Barrett, Leonard. (1977) *The Rastafarians: The Dreadlocks of Jamaica.*

Barry, Brian. (1975) "Review Article: Political Accommodation and Consociational Democracy." *British Journal of Political Science* 5: 477–505.

Barth, Frederick, ed. (1969) *Ethnic Groups and Boundaries: The Social Organization of Cultural Difference.*

Basso, Keith H. (1979) *Portraits of "the Whiteman": Linguistic Play and Cultural Symbols among the Western Apache.*

Bastide, Roger. (1960) *The African Religions of Brazil: Toward a Sociology of Interpretation of Civilizations.* Translated by H. Sebba.

Belote, Linda S. (1983) *Prejudice and Pride: Indian-White Relations in Saraguro, Ecuador.*

Bendix, Regina. (1992) "National Sentiment in the Enactment and Discourse of Swiss Political Ritual." *American Ethnologist* 19: 768–779.

Benedict, Ruth. (1934) *Patterns of Culture.*

Benet, Sula. (1974) *Abkhasians—The Long-Living People of the Caucasus.*

Berger, John, and Jean Mohr. (1975) *A Seventh Man.*

Berndt, Ronald M., and Catherine H. Berndt, eds. (1984–1985) *Collection of Essays on Aboriginal Land Rights for the Guidance of the Government of Western Australia Aboriginal Land Inquiry 1983–1984. Anthropological Forum* 5(3).

Berreman, Gerald D. (1979) *Caste and Other Inequities: Essays on Inequality.*

Berry, Brewton. (1963) *Almost White.* New York: Macmillan.

Berry, John W., et al. (1992) *Cross-Cultural Psychology: Research and Applications.*

Bessaigner, Pierre. (1958) *Tribesmen of the Chittagong Hill Tracts.*

Binder, David, and Barbara Crossette. (1992) "As Ethnic Wars Multiply, U.S. Strives for a Policy." *New York Times* 7 February: 1, 14.

Binur, Yoram. (1990) *My Enemy, My Self.*

Black, Eric. (1992) *Parallel Realities: A Jewish/Arab History of Israel/Palestine.*

Blauner, Robert. (1972) *Racial Oppression in America.*

Blu, Karen I. (1980) *The Lumbee Problem: The Making of an Indian People.*

Boahen, A. Adu. (1987) *African Perspectives on Colonialism.*

Bodine, John J. (1991) "Taos." In *Encyclopedia of World Cultures. Volume 1, North America,* edited by Timothy J. O'Leary and David Levinson, 340–343.

Bodley, John. (1982) *Victims of Progress.*

Bonacich, Edna. (1973) "Theory of Middleman Minorities." *American Sociological Review* 38: 583–594.

Bourdeaux, Michael, Kathleen Matchett, and Cornelia Gerstenmaier. (1970) *Religious Minorities of the Soviet Union.*

Bowden, Henry W. (1981) *American Indians and Christian Missions: Studies in Cultural Conflict.*

Bradley, Candace et al. (1990) "A Cross-Cultural Historical Study of Subsistence Change." *American Anthropologist* 92: 447–457.

Brameld, T., and M. Matsuyama. (1977) *Tourism as Cultural Learning: Two Controversial Case Studies in Educational Anthropology.*

Brass, Paul R. (1983) *Caste, Faction and Party in Indian Politics: Faction and Party.* Volume 1.

———. (1985) *Caste, Faction and Party in Indian Politics: Election Studies.* Volume 2.

———. (1988) "The Punjab Crisis and the Unity of India." In *India's Democracy: An Analysis of Changing State-Society Relations,* edited by Atul Kohli, 169–213.

———. (1991) *Ethnicity and Nationalism.*

Brewer, Marilynn B., and Donald T. Campbell. (1976) *Ethnocentrism and Intergroup Attitudes.*

Brosted, Jens, et al., eds. (1985) *Native Power: The Quest for Autonomy and Nationhood of Indigenous Peoples.*

Brown, Donald E. (1991) *Human Universals.*

Brown, Paula. (1986) "Simbu Aggression and the Drive To Win." *Anthropological Quarterly* 59: 165–170.

Brownlie, Ian. (1992) *Basic Documents on Human Rights.*

Bun, Chan Kwok. (1993) "Rethinking Assimilation and Ethnicity: The Chinese in Thailand." *International Migration Review* 27: 140–168.

Burger, Julian. (1987) *Report from the Frontier: The State of the World's Indigenous Peoples.*

"Burma in Search of Peace." (1989) *Cultural Survival Quarterly* 13(4).

Burnet, Jean R., and Howard Palmer. (1989) *Coming Canadians: An Introduction to a History of Canada's Peoples.*

Burridge, Kenelm. (1991) *In the Way: A Study of Christian Missionary Endeavours.*

Cantlie, Audrey. (1984) *The Assamese.*

Carroll, Michael P. (1975) "Revitalization Movements and Social Structure: Some Quantitative Tests." *American Sociological Review* 40: 389–401.

Castles, Stephen, H. Booth, and T. Wallace. (1984) *Here for Good.*

Centre for Human Rights. (1991) *Contemporary Forms of Slavery.* Fact Sheet No. 14.

Chakravarty, S. R., and V. Narain, eds. (1986) *Bangladesh: History and Culture.*

Chakravvarti, Balaram. (1980) *A Cultural History of Bhutan.*

Chaliand, Gerard. (1980) *People without a Country: The Kurds and Kurdistan.*

Chaudhuri, Buddhadeb. (1991) "Ethnic Conflict in the Chittagong Hill Tracts of Bangladesh." In *Economic Dimensions of Ethnic Conflict,* edited by S. W. R. de A. Samarasighe and Reed Coughlan.

Chaudhuri, Nirad C. (1979) *Hinduism: A Religion To Live By.*

Chiao, Chien, and Nicolas Tapp. (1989) *Ethnicity and Ethnic Groups in China.*

Christensen, James. (1954) *Double Descent among the Fanti.*

Coelho, Ruy G. (1955) *The Black Carib of Honduras: A Study in Acculturation.*

Cohen, Erik. (1979) "A Phenomenology of Tourist Experiences." *Sociology* 13: 179–201.

Cohen, Steven. (1983) *American Modernity and Jewish Identity.*

Colton, Nora A. (1993) "Homeward Bound: Yemeni Return Migration." *International Migration Review* 27: 970–882.

Condominas, Georges. (1965) *L'Exotique Est Quotidien.*

Conner, Walker. (1994) *Ethnonationalism: The Quest for Understanding.*

Cooper, Roger. (1982) *The Baha'is of Iran.*

Corbridge, Stuart. (1987) "Ousting Singbonga: The Struggle for India's Jharkhand." In *Colonialism and Development in the Contemporary World,* edited by Chris Dixon and Michael Heffernan, 153–182.

Cottaar, Annemarie, Leo Lucassen, and Wim Willems. (1992) "Justice or Injustice? A Survey of Government Policy towards Gypsies and Caravan Dwellers in Western Europe in the Nineteenth and Twentieth Centuries." *Immigrants and Minorities* 11: 42–66.

Courlander, H., and Rémy Bastien, eds. (1966) *Religion and Politics in Haiti.*

Craig, Gordon. (1982) *The Germans.*

Crick, Malcolm. (1989) "Representations of International Tourism in the Social Sciences: Sun, Sex, Sights, Savings, and Servility." In *Annual Review of Anthropology,* edited by Bernard J. Siegel, 307–344.

Crocchiola, Stanley F. L. (1967) *The Jicarilla Apaches of New Mexico, 1540–1967.*

Cross, Malcolm, ed. (1992) *Ethnic Minorities and Industrial Change in Europe and North America.*

Crystal, David. (1987) *The Cambridge Encyclopedia of Language.*

Curtis, Michael, ed. (1986) *Antisemitism in the Contemporary World.*

Danda, Dipali G., and Sanchita Ghatak. (1985) *The Semsa and Their Habitat.* Anthropological Survey of India, Memoir No. 64. Calcutta.

Darby, John, ed. (1985) *Northern Ireland: The Background to the Conflict.*

Davis, Shelton H. (1977) *Victims of the Miracle: Development and the Indians of Brazil.*

de Reuck, Anthony, and Julie Knight, eds. (1967) *Caste and Race.*

de Silva, K. M., and S. W. R. de A. Samarasinghe. (1993) *Peace Accords and Ethnic Conflict.*

De Vos, George, and Hiroshi Wagatsuma, eds. (1966) *Japan's Invisible Race.*

Del Mundo, Fernando. (1993) "Vietnamese Returnees Find New Hope in the Future." *Refugees* 92: 34–36.

DeVoe, Pamela A., ed. (1992) *Selected Papers on Refugee Issues.*

Di Leonardo, Micaela. (1984) *The Varieties of Ethnic Experience: Kinship, Class, and Gender among California Italian-Americans.*

Dimi, Nicholas. (1991) *From Moldavia to Moldova: The Soviet-Romanian Territorial Dispute.*

Dirks, Nicholas B., ed. (1992) *Colonialism and Culture.*

Dobyns, Henry F. (1966) "Estimating Aboriginal American Population: An Appraisal of Techniques with a New Hemispheric Estimate." *Current Anthropology* 7: 395–416.

Domínguez, Virginia R. (1986) *White by Definition: Social Classification in Creole Louisiana.*

Donnelly, Nancy D. (1992) "The Impossible Situation of Vietnamese in Hong Kong's Detention Centers." In *Selected Papers on Refugee Issues,* edited by Pamela A. DeVoe, 120–132.

Douglass, William A. (1975) *Echalar and Murelaga: Opportunity and Rural Exodus in Two Spanish Basque Villages.*

Dow, James. (1995) *The Encyclopedia of World Cultures. Volume 8, Middle America and the Caribbean.*

Dumont, Louis. (1970) *Homo Hierarchicus.*

Dundes, Alan. (1987) *Cracking Jokes: Studies of Sick Humor Cycles and Stereotypes.*

Dunlop, John B. (1993) "Will a Large-Scale Migration of Russians to the Russian Republic Take Place over the Next Decade?" *International Migration Review* 27: 605–629.

Eades, J. S. (1980) *The Yoruba Today.*

Eban, Abba. (1984) *Heritage: Civilization and the Jews.*

Edgerton, Robert B. (1992) *Sick Societies: Challenging the Myth of Primitive Harmony.*

Elmer, Glaister A., and Evelyn A. Elmer. (1988) *Ethnic Conflicts Abroad: Clues to America's Future?* AICF Monograph Series, no. 8.

Enloe, Cynthia. (1980) *Ethnic Soldiers: State Security in Divided Societies.*

Eriksen, Thomas H. (1992) "Containing Conflict and Transcending Ethnicity in Mauritius." In *Internal Conflict and Governance,* edited by Kumar Rupesinghe, 103–129.

———. (1993) *Ethnicity and Nationalism: Anthropological Perspectives.*

Erlich, Vera S. (1966) *Family in Transition.*

Ertekun, N. M. (1984) *The Cyprus Dispute and the Birth of the Turkish Republic of Northern Cyprus.*

Espiritu, Yen Le. (1992) *Asian American Panethnicity: Bridging Institutions and Identities.*

Esposito, John L. (1984) *The Islamic Threat: Myth or Reality.*

Esslemont, J. E. (1980) *Baha'u'llah and the New Era.* First published 1923.

Extra, G., and L. Verhoeven, eds. (1993) *Immigrant Languages in Europe.*

Falla, Jonathan. (1991) *True Love and Bartholomew: Rebels on the Burmese Border.*

Fawcett, James. (1979) *The International Protection of Minorities.* Report No. 41.

Fein, Helen, ed. (1992) *Genocide Watch.*

Felice, William. (1992) *The Emergence of Peoples' Rights in International Relations.*

Fenton, William N. (1957) *Factionalism at Taos Pueblo, New Mexico.*

Fleras, Augies, and Jean Leonard Elliott. (1992) *The "Nations Within": Aboriginal-State Relations in Canada, the United States, and New Zealand.*

Formoso, Bernard. (1992) "Piemontese Sinti." In *Encyclopedia of World Cultures. Volume 4, Europe,* edited by Linda A. Bennett, 199–201.

Foster, John E., and Gerhard J. Ens. (1991) "Metis of Western Canada." In *Encyclopedia of World Cultures. Volume 1, North America,* edited by Timothy J. O'Leary and David Levinson, 226–229.

Foster, Robert J. (1991) "Making National Cultures in the Global Ecumene." *Annual Review of Anthropology* 20: 235–260.

French, Rebecca. (1993) *The Golden Yoke: The Legal System of Buddhist Tibet.*

Friedrich, Paul, and Norma Diamond, eds. (1993) *Encyclopedia of World Cultures. Volume 6, Russia/Eurasia and China.*

Fritz, Sonja, and David Testen. (1994) "Ossetes." In *Encyclopedia of World Cultures. Volume 6, Russia/Eurasia and China,* edited by Paul Friedrich and Norma Diamond.

Fuller, Graham E. (1989) *The West Bank of Israel: Point of No Return.*

Furnivall, J. S. (1948) *Colonial Policy and Practice.*

Geertz, Clifford. (1963) *The Interpretation of Culture: Selected Essays by Clifford Geertz.*

Gellner, Ernest. (1983) *Nations and Nationalism.*

Gerner, Deborah. (1991) *One Land, Two Peoples: The Conflict over Palestine.*

Gervis, Pearce. (1954) *This Is Kashmir.*

Gewertz, Deborah, and Frederick Errington. (1991) *Twisted Histories, Altered Contexts: Representing the Chambri in a World System.*

Ghurye, G. S. (1963) *The Scheduled Tribes.* 3d ed.

Gmelch, Sharon B. (1986) "Groups that Don't Want In: Gypsies and Other Artisan, Trader, and Entertainer Minorities." *Annual Review of Anthropology* 15: 307–330.

Gold, Stephen J. (1992) *Refugee Communities.*

Goldschmidt, Arthur, Jr. (1991) *A Concise History of the Middle East.* 4th ed.

Gordon, Milton. (1964) *Assimilation in American Life: The Role of Race, Religion, and National Origins.*

Gordon, Murray. (1989) *Slavery in the Arab World.*

Gouboglu, Mikhail N. (1994) "Gaugauz." In *Encyclopedia of World Cultures. Volume 6, Russia/Eurasia and China,* edited by Paul Friedrich and Norma Diamond, 124–126.

Graburn, Nelson H. H. (1981) "1, 2, 3, 4...Anthropology and the Fourth World." *Culture* 1: 66–70.

———, ed. (1976) *Ethnic and Tourist Arts: Cultural Expression from the Third World.*

Graburn, Nelson H. H., and J. Jafari, eds. (1991) "Tourism Social Sciences." Special issue of *Annals of Tourism Research* 18.

Graham, Walter Armstrong. (1908) *Kelantan: A State of the Malay Peninsula; A Handbook of Information.*

Granqvist, Raoul. (1984) *Stereotypes in Western Fiction on Africa: A Study of Joseph Conrad, Joyce Cary, Ernest Hemingway, Karen Blixen, Graham Greene, and Alan Paton.* Umea, Sweden: Umea Papers in English, no. 7.

Grasmuck, Sherri, and Patricia R. Pessar. (1991) *Between Two Islands: Dominican International Migration.*

Greenwood, Davydd J. (1972) "Tourism as an Agent of Change: A Spanish Basque Case." *Ethnology* 11: 80–91.

Greissman, B. Eugene, subed. (1972) "The American Isolates." *American Anthropologist* 74: 693–734.

Grimes, Seamus. (1993) "Residential Segregation in Australian Cities: A Literature Review." *International Migration Review* 27: 103–120.

Grove, D. John. (1993) "Have the Post-Reform Ethnic Gains Eroded? A Seven Nation Study." *Ethnic and Racial Studies* 16: 598–620.

Gurr, Ted R. (1993) *Minorities at Risk: A Global View of Ethnopolitical Conflicts.*

Gurr, Ted R., and James R. Scarritt. (1989) "Minorities at Risk: A Global Survey." *Human Rights Quarterly* 11: 375–405.

Gutman, Israel, ed. (1990) *The Encyclopedia of the Holocaust.* 4 vols.

Hacker, Andrew. (1992) *Two Nations: Black and White, Separate, Hostile, Unequal.*

Halpern, Joel M., and Barbara Kerewsky-Halpern. (1986) *A Serbian Village in Historical Perspective.*

Hamilton, Roberta. (1988) *Feudal Society and Colonization: The Historiography of New France.*

Hammel, Eugene A. (1993) "Demography and the Origins of the Yugoslav Civil War." *Anthropology Today* 9: 4–9.

Hancock, Ian F. (1971) "A Survey of the Pidgins and Creoles of the World." In *Pidginization and Creolization of Languages,* edited by Dell Hymes, 509–523.

———. (1992) "The Roots of Inequality: Romani Cultural Rights in Their Historical and Social Context." *Immigrants and Minorities* 11: 3–30.

Handler, Richard. (1988) *Nationalism and the Politics of Culture in Quebec.*

Hannerz, Ulf. (1969) *Soulside: Inquiries into Ghetto Culture and Community.*

Hansen, Edward. (1977) *Rural Catalonia under the Franco Regime: The Fate of Rural Culture since the Spanish Civil War.*

Hanson, F. Allan. (1975) *Meaning in Culture.*

Harris, Joseph E., ed. (1982) *Global Dimensions of the African Diaspora.*

Harris, Rosemary. (1972) *Prejudice and Tolerance in Ulster: A Study of Neighbours and "Strangers" in a Border Community.*

Harrison, David, ed. (1992) *Tourism and the Less Developed Countries.*

Hasluck, Margaret. (1954) *The Unwritten Law in Albania.*

Hauff, Edvard, and Per Vaglum (1993) "Integration of Vietnamese Refugees into the Norwegian Labor Market: The Impact of War Trauma." *International Migration Review* 27: 388–405.

Hays, Terence, ed. (1992) *Encyclopedia of World Cultures. Volume 2, Oceania.* (See articles on Bau, Lau, and Rotuma).

Hechter, Michael. (1975) *Internal Colonialism: The Celtic Fringe in British National Development, 1536–1966.*

———. (1986) "Rational Choice Theory and the Study of Race and Ethnic Relations." In *Theories of Race and Ethnic Relations,* edited by John Rex and David Mason, 264–279.

Heiberg, Marianne. (1989) *The Making of the Basque Nation.*

Heinz, Wolfgang S. (1991) *Indigenous Populations, Ethnic Minorities and Human Rights.*

Herskovits, Melville J. (1966) *The New World Negro: Selected Papers in Afroamerican Studies.*

Hertzberg, Arthur, ed. (1960) *The Zionist Idea.*

Hewitt, B. George, and Elisa Watson. (1994) "Abkhazians." In *Encyclopedia of World Cultures. Volume 6, Russia/Eurasia and China,* edited by Paul Friedrich and Norma Diamond, 5–10.

Hicks, George L. (1976) *Appalachian Valley.*

Hill, Polly. (1972) *Rural Hausa: A Village and a Setting.*

Hobsbawm, Eric, and Terrence Ranger, eds. (1983) *The Invention of Tradition.*

Hockings, Paul. (1980) *Ancient Hindu Refugees: Badaga Social History, 1550–1975.*

———, ed. (1992) *The Encyclopedia of World Cultures. Volume 3, South Asia.*

———. (1992) "Aryan." In *Encyclopedia of World Cultures. Volume 3, South Asia,* edited by Paul Hockings, 12–13.

Horak, Stephan M. (1985) *Eastern European National Minorities 1919–1980: A Handbook.*

Horam, M. (1977) *Social and Cultural Life of Nagas.*

Horowitz, Donald L. (1985) *Ethnic Groups in Conflict.*

Howard, Michael C. (1991) *Fiji: Race and Politics in an Island State.*

Hurtsfield, Jennifer. (1978) "'Internal' Colonialism: White, Black and Chicano Self-Conceptions." In *Ethnic and Racial Studies* 1: 60–79.

Izady, Mehrdad R. (1992) *The Kurds: Concise Handbook.*

Jaimes, M. Annette, ed. (1992) *The State of Native America: Genocide, Colonization, and Resistance.*

Jebsen, Harry, Jr. (1976) "Assimilation in a Working Class Suburb: The Italians of Blue Island, Illinois." In *The Urban Experience of Italian-Americans,* edited by Pat Gallo, 64–84.

Jenkins, William M. (1963) *The Himalayan Kingdoms: Bhutan, Sikkim, and Nepal.*

Jokes for All Occasions (1921).

Jonassohn, Kurt, and Frank Chalk. (1987) "A Typology of Genocide and Some Implications for the Human Rights Agenda." In *Genocide and the Modern Age,* edited by Isidor Wallimann and Michael N. Dobkowski, 3–20.

Jones-Jackson, Patricia. (1987) *When Roots Die: Endangered Traditions on the Sea Islands.*

Jordan, Winthrop. (1974) *The White Man's Burden.*

Justinger, Judith M. (1979) *Reaction to Change: A Holocultural Test of Some Theories of Religious Movements.*

Kalley, Jacqueline A. (1989) *South Africa under Apartheid.*

Lambley, Peter. (1980) *The Psychology of Apartheid.*

Keefe, Susan E., ed. (1989) *Negotiating Ethnicity: The Impact of Anthropological Theory and Practice.* NAPA Bulletin No. 8.

Khazanov, Anatoly. (1989) *The Krymchaks: A Vanishing Group in the Soviet Union.* Research Paper No. 71.

Kilson, Martin, and Robert Rotberg, eds. (1976) *African Diasporas: Interpretive Essays.*

Klein, Laura F. (1975) *Tlingit Women and Town Politics.*

Kligman, Gail. (1988) *Wedding of the Dead: Ritual, Poetics, and Popular Culture in Transylvania.*

Kluckhohn, Clyde, and Dorothea Leighton. (1946) *The Navaho.*

Knudsen, John Chr. (1992) "'To Destroy You Is No Loss.'" In *Selected Papers on Refugee Issues,* edited by Pamela A. DeVoe, 133–144.

Kolenda, Pauline. (1978) *Caste in Contemporary India: Beyond Organic Solidarity.*

Kramer, Jane. (1993) "Neo-Nazis: A Chaos in the Head." *The New Yorker,* 14 June 1993: 52–70.

Krejci, Jaroslav, and Vitezslav Velimsky. (1981) *Ethnic and Political Nations in Europe.*

Kuper, Leo. (1985) *The Prevention of Genocide.*

Kyle, Keith. (1984) *Cyprus.*

Lagacé, Robert O., ed. (1977) *Sixty Cultures.*

Lancaster, Roger N. (1991) "Skin Color, Race, and Racism in Nicaragua." *Ethnology* 30: 339–353.

Landau, Jacob. (1990) "Irredentism and Minorities in the Middle East." *Immigrants and Minorities* 9: 242–248.

Lang, David M. (1966) *The Georgians.*

Lawson, Edward, ed. (1991) *Encyclopedia of Human Rights.*

Lawson, Stephanie. (1991) *The Failure of Democratic Politics in Fiji.*

Layton-Henry, Zig, ed. (1990) *The Rights of Migrant Workers in Western Europe.*

Lebow, Richard N. (1976) "Vigilantism in Northern Ireland." In *Vigilante Politics,* edited by H. Jon Rosenbaum and Peter C. Sederberg, 234–258.

Legendre, Camille. (1982) *French Canada in Crisis: A New Society in the Making?*

Lemarchand, René. (1970) *Rwanda and Burundi.*

———. (1974) *Selective Genocide in Burundi.*

Lemkin, Raphael. (1944) *Axis Rule in Occupied Europe.*

Lessa, William A., and Evon Z. Vogt. (1965) *Reader in Comparative Religion: An Anthropological Approach.* 2d ed.

Lessinger, Johanna. (1992) "Investing or Going Home? A Transnational Strategy among Indian Immigrants in the United States." In *Towards a Transnational Perspective on Migration: Race, Class, Ethnicity, and Nationalism Reconsidered,* edited by Nina G. Schiller, Linda Basch, and Cristina Blanc-Szanton. *Annals of the New York Academy of Sciences* 645: 53–80.

Levin, M. G., and Potapov, L. P., eds. (1964) *The Peoples of Siberia.*

LeVine, Robert A., and Donald T. Campbell. (1972) *Ethnocentrism: Theories of Conflict, Ethnic Attitudes, and Group Behavior.*

Levinson, David, ed. (1991–1994) *Encyclopedia of World Cultures.* 10 vols.

Lewis, Bernard. (1990) "The Roots of Muslim Rage." *Atlantic Monthly.* September: 47–60.

Lewis, Herbert S. (1993) Jewish Ethnicity in Israel: Ideologies, Policies and Outcomes." In *Ethnicity and the State,* edited by Judith D. Toland, 201–230.

Lewis, I. M. (1955) *Peoples of the Horn of Africa.*

Lewis, Oscar. (1965) *Village Life in Northern India.*

Liégeois, Jean-Pierre. (1986) *Gypsies and Travellers.*

Lijphart, Arend. (1977) *Democracy in Plural Societies.*

Lim, Linda Y. C., and L. A. Peter Gosling. (1983) *The Chinese in Southeast Asia. Volume 1, Ethnicity and Economic Activity. Volume 2, Identity, Culture, and Politics.*

Lin, Yueh-hwa. (1947) *The Lolo of Liang-Shan.* Translated from the Chinese by Ju Shu Pan.

Lincoln, W. Bruce. (1993) *The Conquest of a Continent: Siberia and the Russians.*

Lintner, Bertil. (1990) *Land of Jade: A Journey through Insurgent Burma.*

Lipstadt, Deborah. (1993) *Denying the Holocaust: The Growing Assault on Truth and Memory.*

Lizarralde, Manuel. (1992) *Index and Map of the Contemporary South American Indigenous Peoples.* Unpublished manuscript, University of California at Berkeley.

Lockwood, William G. (1975) *European Moslems: Economy and Ethnicity in Western Bosnia.*

Loizos, Peter. (1981) *The Heart Grown Bitter: A Chronicle of Cypriot War Refugees.*

Longworth, Philip. (1969) *The Cossacks.*

Lopez, David, and Yen Espiritu. (1990) "Panethnicity in the United States: A Theoretical Framework." *Ethnic and Racial Studies* 13: 198–224.

Lyman, Stanford M., and William A Douglass. (1973) "Ethnicity: Strategies of Collective and Individual Impression Management." *Social Research* 40: 344–365.

Ma Yin, ed. (1989) *China's Minority Nationalities.*

MacCannell, Dean. (1992) *Empty Meeting Grounds: The Tourist Papers.*

McDonald, Maryon. (1989) *"We Are Not French!" Language, Culture and Identity in Brittany.*

McDonald, R. St. J., ed. (1966) *The Arctic Frontier.*

McDonogh, Gary. (1986) *Good Families of Barcelona: A Social History of Power in the Colonial Era.*

McDowall, David. (1992) *The Kurds: A Nation Denied.*

McFee, Malcolm. (1963) *Modern Blackfeet: Continuing Patterns of Differential Acculturation.*

McLeod, W. H. (1990) *The Sikhs.*

Magas, Branka. (1993) *The Destruction of Yugoslavia: Tracking Yugoslavia's Break-up 1980–1992.*

Mandelbaum, David G. (1970) *Society in India.* 2 vols.

Mann, E. A. (1992) *Boundaries and Identities: Muslims, Work and Status in Aligarh.*

Marquard, Leo. (1962) *The Peoples and Policies of South Africa.*

Masri, Iris Habib el. (1978) *The Story of the Copts.*

Matossian, Mark K. (1962) *The Impact of Soviet Policies in Armenia.*

Maxwell, Neville G. A. (1980) *India, the Nagas, and the North-east.*

Medhurst, Kenneth. (1982) *The Basques and Catalans.*

Memmi, Albert. (1967) *The Colonizer and the Colonized.*

Merker, Meritz. (1910) *The Masai: Ethnographic Monograph of an East African Semite People.* Translated from the German for the Human Relations Area Files.

Merrill, William L., Edmund J. Ladd, and T. J. Ferguson. (1993) "The Return of the *Ahayu:da.*" *Current Anthropology* 34: 523–567.

Messina, Anthony M., et al., eds. (1992) *Ethnic and Racial Minorities in Advanced Industrial Democracies.*

Miers, Suzanne, and Igor Kopytoff, eds. (1977) *Slavery in Africa: Historical and Anthropological Perspectives.*

Miller, Judith. (1991) "Strangers at the Gate: Europe's Immigration Crisis." *The New York Times Magazine.* 15 September 1991: 32–37, 49, 80–81.

———. (1992) "The Islamic Wave." *New York Times Magazine.* 31 May 1992: 22–26, 38, 40, 42.

Minority Rights Group. (1990) *World Directory of Minorities.*

Mock, Stephan, and Guide Meyer. (1993) "Breaking the Cycle of Violence." *Refugees* 93: 22–23.

Molnar, Stephen. (1983) *Human Variation: Races, Types, and Ethnic Groups.* 2d ed.

Montagu, Ashley, ed. (1964) *The Concept of Race.*

Mooney, James. (1965) *The Ghost-Dance Religion and the Sioux Outbreak of 1890.* Edited and abridged by Anthony F. C. Wallace. First published, 1896.

Moore, Jack B. (1993) *Skinheads, Shaved for Battle: A Cultural History of American Skinheads.*

Moxon-Browne, Edward. (1983) *Nation, Class, and Creed in Northern Ireland.*

Mullin, Chris, and Phuntsog Wangyal. (1983) *The Tibetans: Two Perspectives on Tibetan-Chinese Relations.*

Muntarbhorn, Vitit. (1992) *The Status of Refugees in Asia.*

Murdock, George P. (1934) "The Kazakhs of Central Asia." In *Our Primitive Contemporaries,* 135–153.

Murphy, Dervla. (1987) *Tales from Two Cities: Travel of Another Sort.*

Murphy, Joseph M. (1988) *Santería: An African Religion in America.*

———. (1993) *Working the Spirit: Ceremonies of the African Diaspora.*

Muslih, Muhammad Y. (1988) *The Origins of Palestinian Nationalism.*

Myrdal, Gunnar. (1944) *An American Dilemma.*

NACLA. (1992) "The Black Americas, 1492–1992." In *Report on the Americas.* Volume 25, no. 4.

Nagata, Judith A. (1974) "What Is a Malay? Situational Selection of Ethnic Identity in a Plural Society." *American Ethnologist* 1: 1,215–1,230.

Nagata, Shuichi. (1960) *Modern Transformations of Moenkopi Pueblo.*

Nagel, Joane. (1982) "The Political Mobilization of Native Americans." *The Social Science Journal* 19: 37–45.

———. (1993) "Ethnic Nationalism: Politics, Ideology, and the World Order." *International Journal of Comparative Sociology* 34: 103–112.

Naidu, Vijay. (1992) "Fiji: Ethnicity and the Post-Colonial State." In *Internal Conflict and Governance,* edited by Kumar Rupesinghe, 81–102.

Naroll, Raoul. (1983) *The Moral Order: An Introduction to the Human Situation.*

Nayacakalou, R. R. (1975) *Leadership in Fiji.*

Neill, Stephen. (1986) *A History of Christian Missions.* Revised for the second edition by Owen Chadwick.

"The New Face of America: How Immigrants Are Shaping the World's First Multicultural Society." Special Issue of *Time.* Fall 1993.

Nichols, Johanna. (1994) "Chechen-Ingush." In *Encyclopedia of World Cultures. Volume 6, Russia/Eurasia and China,* edited by Paul Friedrich and Norma Diamond, 71–76.

Nieboer, Herman J. (1900) *Slavery as an Industrial System.*

Nietschmann, Bernard. (1988) "Third World Colonial Expansion: Indonesia, Disguised Invasion of Indigenous Nations." In *Tribal Peoples and Development Issues: A Global Overview,* edited by John H. Bodley, 191–207.

Nwankwo, Arthur A. (1991) *Political Danger Signals: The Politics of Federalism, Census, Blanket Ban, and National Integration.*

O'Ballance, Edgar. (1989) *The Cyanide War: Tamil Insurrection in Sri Lanka.*

O'Connell, Joseph, et al., eds. (1988) *Sikh History and Religion in the Twentieth Century.*

O'Laughlin, J., and G. Glebe. (1984) "Residential Segregation of Foreigners in German Cities." *Tijdschrift voor Economische en Sociale Geografie* 74: 373–384.

O'Leary, Timothy J., and David Levinson, eds. (1990) *Encyclopedia of World Cultures. Volume 1, North America.*

Okamura, Jonathan Y. (1981) "Situational Ethnicity." *Ethnic and Racial Studies* 4: 452–463.

Olson, James S. (1979) *The Ethnic Dimension in American History.*

Olson, Paul A. (1989) *The Struggle for the Land: Indigenous Insight and Industrial Empire in the Semiarid World.*

Ormeling, F. J. (1956) *The Timor Problem: A Geographical Interpretation of an Underdeveloped Island.*

Ortiz, Alfonso, ed. (1983) *Handbook of North American Indians. Volume 10, Southwest.*

Ott, Sandra. (1981) *The Circle of Mountains: A Basque Shepherding Community.*

Padilla, Felix. (1985) *Latino Ethnic Consciousness.*

Paine, Robert. (1985) "The Claim of the Fourth World." In *Native Power,* edited by Jens Brostad, et al., 49–66.

Palley, Claire. (1978) *Constitutional Law and Minorities.* Report No. 36.

Patterson, Orlando. (1982) *Slavery and Social Death: A Comparative Study.*

Peach, Ceri, Vaughan Robinson, and Susan Smith, eds. (1983) *Ethnic Segregation in Cities.*

Peretz, Don. (1990) *Intifada: The Palestinian Uprising.*

Pettigrew, Thomas F. (1964) *A Profile of the Negro American.*

Peukert, Detlev. (1987) *Inside Nazi Germany: Conformity, Opposition and Racism in Everyday Life.*

Phillips, James M., and Robert T. Coote, eds. (1993) *Toward the 21st Century in Christian Mission.*

Piasere, Leonardo. (1992) "Peripatetics." In *Encyclopedia of World Cultures. Volume 4, Europe,* edited by Linda A. Bennett, 195–197.

Pierson, Donald. (1942) *Negroes in Brazil.*

Pilon, Lise. (1990) "French Canadians." In *Encyclopedia of World Cultures. Volume 1, North America,* edited by Timothy J. O'Leary and David Levinson, 130–133.

Plant, R. (1986) *The Pink Triangle: The Nazi War against Homosexuals.*

Podolefsky, Aaron. (1984) "Contemporary Warfare in the New Guinea Highlands." *Ethnology* 23: 73–87.

Portes, Alejandro, and József Borocz. (1993) "Contemporary Immigration: Theoretical Perspectives on Its Determinants and Modes of Incorporation." *International Immigration Review* 23: 606–630.

Pozzetta, George, Jr. (1972) *The Italians of New York City, 1890–1914.*

Prill-Brett, June. (1988) *Preliminary Perspectives on Local Territorial Boundaries and Resource Control.* Cordillera Studies Center Working Paper 6.

Pryor, Frederic L. (1977) *The Origins of the Economy.*

Ramaga, Philip V. (1993) "The Group Concept in Minority Protection." *Human Rights Quarterly* 15: 575–588.

Rathburn, Robert R. (1976) *Processes of Russian-Tlingit Acculturation in Southeastern Alaska.*

Redfield, Robert, and Alfonso Villa Rojas. (1934) *Chan Kom: A Maya Village.*

Rex, John, D. Joly, and C. Wilpert, eds. (1988) *Immigrant Associations in Europe.*

Reynolds, Henry. (1981) *The Other Side of the Frontier.*

Reynolds, Vernon, Vincent Falger, and Ian Vine. (1987) *The Sociobiology of Ethnocentrism.*

Richardson, Don. (1988) "Do Missionaries Destroy Cultures?" In *Tribal Peoples and Development Issues: A Global Overview,* edited by John H. Bodley, 116–121.

Riggins, Stephen H., ed. (1992) *Ethnic Minority Media: An International Perspective.*

Robbins, Lynn A. (1972) *Blackfoot Families and Households.*

Rodman, Margaret, and Matthew Cooper, eds. (1983) *The Pacification of Melanesia.*

Rogers, Rosemarie, ed. (1985) *Guests Come To Stay: The Effects of European Labor Migration on Sending and Receiving Nations.*

Royce, Anya Peterson. (1982) *Ethnic Identity: Strategies of Diversity.*

Rubin, Vera, and Arthur Tuden, eds. (1977) *Comparative Perspectives on Slavery in New World Plantation Societies.*

Rummel, R. J. (1991) *China's Bloody Century: Genocide and Mass Murder since 1900.*

Rupesinghe, Kumar. (1987) "Theories of Conflict Resolution and Their Applicability to Protracted Ethnic Conflicts." *Bulletin of Peace Proposals* 18: 527–539.

Ryan, Stephen. (1990) *Ethnic Conflict and International Relations.*

Safran, William. (1991) "Diasporas in Modern Societies: Myths of Homeland and Return." *Diaspora* 1: 83–99.

Sahlins, Marshall. (1968) *Tribesman.*

Sahliyeh, Emile. (1993) "Ethnicity and State-Building: The Case of the Palestinians in the Middle East." In *Ethnicity and the State,* edited by Judith D. Toland, 177–200.

Saladin d'Anglure, Bernard. (1984) "Inuit of Quebec." In *Handbook of North American Indians. Volume 5, Arctic,* edited by David Damas, 508–521.

Salamone, Frank A. (1974) *Gods and Goods in Africa.*

———. (1986) "Colonialism and the Emergence of Fulani Identity." In *Ethnic Identities and Prejudices: Perspectives from the Third World,* edited by Anand C. Paranjpe, 61–70.

Salo, Matt T. (1979) "Gypsy Ethnicity: Implications of Native Categories and Interaction for Ethnic Classification." In *Ethnicity* 6: 73–96.

Samarasinghe, S. W. R. de A., and Reed Coughlan, eds. (1991) *Economic Dimensions of Ethnic Conflict.*

Sawyer, Roger. (1986) *Slavery in the Twentieth Century.*

Schermerhorn, Richard A. (1978) *Ethnic Plurality in India.*

Schiller, Nina G., Linda Basch, and Cristina Blanc-Szanton, eds. (1992) *Towards a Transnational Perspective on Migration: Race, Class, Ethnicity, and Nationalism Reconsidered.* Annals of the New York Academy of Sciences, 645.

Schlesinger, Arthur M., Jr. (1992) *The Disuniting of America.*

Schwarz, Walter. (1988) *The Tamils of Sri Lanka.*

Scott, George M., Jr. (1990) "A Resynthesis of the Primordial and Circumstantial Approaches to Ethnic Group Solidarity: Towards an Explanatory Model." *Ethnic and Racial Studies* 13: 147–171.

Segal, Daniel A. (1988) "Nationalism, Comparatively Speaking." *Journal of Historical Sociology* 1: 301–321.

Segall, Marshall H., et al. (1990) *Human Behavior in Global Perspective.*

Sekelj, Laslo. (1993) *Yugoslavia: The Process of Disintegration.* Translated from Serbo-Croatian by Vera Vukelic.

Sender, Henry. (1988) *The Kashmiri Pandits: A Study of Cultural Choice in North India.*

Service, Elman R. (1962) *Primitive Social Organization.*

Shapiro, Judith. (1987) "From Tupa to the Land without Evil: The Christianization of Tupi-Guarani Cosmology." *American Ethnologist* 14: 126–139.

Shaw, Paul R., and Yuwa Wong. (1989) *Genetic Seeds of Warfare: Evolution, Nationalism, and Patriotism.*

Sheffer, Gabriel, ed. (1986) *Modern Diasporas in International Politics.*

Sherlock, Kevin. (1980) *A Bibliography of Timor.*

Shils, Edward. (1957) "Primordial, Personal, Sacred and Civil Ties." *British Journal of Sociology* 8: 130–145.

Siewert, John A., and John A. Kenyon, eds. (1993) *Mission Handbook: USA/Canada Christian Ministries Overseas.*

Sigler, Jay A. (1983) *Minority Rights: A Comparative Analysis.*

Simic, Andrei. (1973) *The Peasant Urbanites.*

Slowe, Peter M. (1991) "Colonialism and the African Nation: The Case of Guinea." In *Colonialism and Development in the Contemporary World,* edited by Chris Dixon and Michael Heffernans, 106–120.

Sluckin, M. (1979) *Fear in Animals and Man.*

Smith, David M. (1983) *Living under Apartheid.*

Smith, M. G. (1965) *The Plural Society of the British West Indies.*

———. (1986) "Pluralism, Race, and Ethnicity in Selected African Countries." In *Theories of Race and Ethnic Relations,* edited by John Rex and David Mason, 187–225.

Smith, R. S. (1988) *Kingdoms of the Yoruba.*

Smith, Valene L., ed. (1989) *Hosts and Guests: The Anthropology of Tourism.* 2d ed.

Smooha, Sammy. (1987) "Jewish and Arab Ethnocentrism in Israel." *Ethnic and Racial Studies* 10, no. 1.

Snellgrove, David, and Hugh Richardson. (1980) *A Cultural History of Tibet.*

Solomos, John, and John Wrench, eds. (1992) *Racism and Migration in Contemporary Europe.*

Spicer, Edward. (1971) "Persistent Identity Systems." *Science* 401: 795–800.

Stack, J. F., Jr., ed. (1986) *The Primordial Challenge: Ethnicity in the Contemporary World.*

Stannard, David E. (1992) *American Holocaust: Columbus and the Conquest of the New World.*

Stavenhagen, Rodolfo. (1987) "Ethnic Conflict and Human Rights: Their Interrelationship." *Bulletin of Peace Proposals* 18: 507–514.

Steinberg, David. (1980) *Burma's Road toward Development, Growth, and Ideology under Military Rule.*

Subervi-Vélez, F. A. (1986) "The Mass Media and Ethnic Assimilation and Pluralism: A Review and Research Proposal with Special Focus on Hispanics." *Communication Research* 13: 71–96.

Sumner, William Graham. (1979) *Folkways and Mores.*

Suny, Ronald G. (1983) *Armenia in the Twentieth Century.*

———. (1988) *The Making of the Georgian Nation.*

Suter, Keith. (1982) *East Timor and West Irian.*

Suttles, Wayne. (1957) "The Plateau Prophet Dance among the Coast Salish." *Southwestern Journal of Anthropology* 13: 352–396.

Szulc, Tad. (1993) "Cyprus: A Time of Reckoning." In *National Geographic* 184: 104–130.

Tambiah, Stanley J. (1986) *Sri Lanka—Ethnic Fratricide and the Dismantling of Democracy.*

———. (1992) *Buddhism Betrayed? Religion, Politics and Violence in Sri Lanka.*

Tarr, Chou Meng. (1992) "The Vietnamese Minority in Cambodia." *Race & Class* 34: 33–47.

Terkel, Studs. (1992) *Race: How Blacks and Whites Think and Feel about the American Obsession.*

Ternon, Yves. (1981) *The Armenians: History of a Genocide.*

Thernstrom, Stephan, ed. (1980) *Harvard Encylopedia of American Ethnic Groups.*

Thompson, Richard H. (1989) *Theories of Ethnicity: A Critical Appraisal.*

Titiev, Mischa. (1944) *Old Oraibi: A Study of the Hopi Indians of Third Mesa.* Papers of the Peabody Museum, Harvard University 22(1).

Todd, L. (1974) *Pidgins and Creoles.*

Trouwborst, Albert. (1965) "Kinship and Geographical Mobility in Burundi." *International Journal of Comparative Sociology* 4: 166–182.

Turner, L., and J. Ash. (1975) *The Golden Hordes: International Tourism and the Pleasure Periphery.*

Uchendu, Victor C. (1965) *The Igbo of Southeast Nigeria.*

United Nations. (1993) *Human Development Report.*

United Nations High Commissioner for Refugees. (1993) *The State of the World's Refugees: The Challenge of Protection.*

U.S. Committee for Refugees. (1993) *World Refugee Survey.*

van den Berghe, Pierre L. (1978) *Race and Racism: A Comparative Perspective.* 2d ed.

———. (1981) *The Ethnic Phenomenon.*

Van der Ross, R. E. (1979) *Myths and Attitudes: An Inside Look at the Coloured People.*

Van Dyke, Vernon. (1985) *Human Rights, Ethnicity, and Discrimination.*

Vansittart, Eden, and B. V. Nicolay. (1915) *Gurkas.*

Verdery, Katherine. (1983) *Transylvanian Villages: Three Centuries of Political, Economic, and Ethnic Change.*

Vickery, Michael. (1986) *Kampuchea: Politics, Economics, and Society.*

Viski, Károly. (1932) *Hungarian Peasant Customs.*

Wade, Mason. (1968) *The French Canadians, 1760–1967.* 2 vols.

Wade, Peter. (1993) *Blackness and Race Mixture: The Dynamics of Racial Identity in Colombia.*

Wai, Dunstan M. (1978) "Sources of Communal Conflicts and Secessionist Politics in Africa. " In *Ethnic and Racial Studies* 1: 286–305.

Wakin, Edward. (1963) *A Lonely Minority: The Modern History of Egypt's Copts; The Challenge of Survival for Four Million Christians.*

Wallace, Anthony F. C. (1956) "Revitalization Movements." *American Anthropologist* 58: 264–281.

Wallerstein, Imanuel. (1974) *The Modern World-System, I: Capitalist Agriculture and the Origins of the European World-Economy in the Sixteenth Century.*

———. (1979) *The Capitalist World-Economy.*

Walliman, Isidor, and Michael N. Dobkowski, eds. (1987) *Genocide and the Modern Age.*

Weiner, Myron. (1986) "Labor Migrations as Incipient Diasporas." In *Modern Diasporas in International Politics,* edited by Gabriel Sheffer, 47–74.

Weinstein, Warren. (1981) "Africa." In *Protection of Ethnic Minorities: Comparative Perspectives,* edited by Robert G. Wirsing, 208–244.

Werblowsky, R. J. Zwi, and Geoffrey Wigoder, eds. (1965) *The Encyclopedia of the Jewish Religion.*

West, Stanley A., and June Macklin, eds. (1979) *The Chicano Experience.*

Whalen, Lucille. (1989) *Human Rights: A Reference Handbook.*

Wiarda, Howard J. (1985) *Ethnocentrism in Foreign Policy: Can We Understand the Third World?*

Wieviorka, Michel. (1993) *The Making of Terrorism.* Translated by David G. White.

Williams, Francis E. (1923) *The Vailala Madness and the Destruction of Native Ceremonies in the Gulf Division.*

Williamson, Joel. (1984) *New People: Miscegenation and Mulattoes in the United States.*

Wilmer, Franke. (1993) *The Indigenous Voice in World Politics: Since Time Immemorial.*

Winthrop, Robert H. (1991) *Dictionary of Concepts in Cultural Anthropology.*

Wirsing, Robert G., ed. (1981) *Protection of Ethnic Minorities: Comparative Perspectives.*

Wirth, Louis. (1928) *The Ghetto.*

Wistrich, Robert S. (1991) *Antisemitism: The Longest Hatred.*

Wolf, Eric. (1959) *Sons of the Shaking Earth.*

———. (1984) *Europe and the People without a History.*

Woolard, Kathryn. (1989) *Double Talk: Bilingualism and the Politics of Ethnicity in Catalonia.*

World Bank. (1982) *Tribal Peoples and Economic Development: Human Ecological Considerations.*

Worsley, Peter. (1957) *The Trumpet Shall Sound.*

Wright, Robin M., and Jonathan D. Hill. (1986) "History, Ritual, and Myth: Nineteenth Century Millenarian Movements in the Northwest Amazon." *Ethnohistory* 33: 31–54.

Wyman, David S. (1984) *The Abandonment of the Jews: America and the Holocaust 1941–1945.*

Yangwhe, Chao Tzang [Eugene Thaike]. (1987) *The Shan of Burma: Memoirs of a Shan Exile, Local History and Memoirs.*

Zaehner, R. C. (1962) *Hinduism.*

Zenner, Walter. (1991) *Minorities in the Middle: A Cross-Cultural Analysis.*

Zulaika, Joseba (1988) *Basque Violence: Metaphor and Sacrament.*

ILLUSTRATION CREDITS

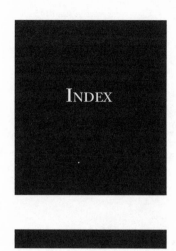

INDEX